# Locating Global Advantage

*Industry Dynamics in the*
*International Economy*

# Innovation and Technology in the World Economy

A SERIES EDITED BY

*Martin Kenney, University of California, Davis / Berkeley Round Table on the International Economy*

*Bruce Kogut, Wharton School, University of Pennsylvania*

# Locating Global Advantage

Industry Dynamics in the

International Economy

*Edited by*

Martin Kenney

*with*

Richard Florida

*Stanford University Press, Stanford, California, 2004*

Stanford University Press
Stanford, California
©2004 by the Board of Trustees of the Leland Stanford Junior University
Printed in the United States of America

Library of Congress Cataloging-in-Publication Data

Kenney, Martin
    Locating global advantage : industry dynamics in the international economy / edited
by Martin Kenney with Richard Florida.
        p.   cm. — (Innovation and technology in the world economy)
    Includes bibliographical references and index.
    ISBN 0-8047-4757-1 (alk. paper) — ISBN 0-8047-4758-x (pbk. : alk. paper)
        1. International economic integration.   2. International business enterprises.
3. Globalization.   4. Electronic industries—Location.   I. Kenney, Martin.
II. Florida, Richard L.   III. Series

HF1418.5 .L33      2004
338.8'8—dc21                                                        2003018429

This book is printed on acid-free, archival-quality paper.

Original printing 2004

Last figure below indicates year of this printing:
13  12  11  10  09  08  07  06  05  04

Typeset at Stanford University Press in 10/12.5 Minion

# Acknowledgments

The papers in this book are the result of four workshops funded by the Sloan Foundation. We also thank three graduate students, Jennifer Bair, Theresa Lynch, and Greg Linden, who helped organize parallel graduate student workshops. Our workshops were enriched by the participation of Avron Barr, Lee Branstetter, Tim Bresnahan, Steve Cohen, Rob Feenstra, Gary Gereffi, Gordon Hanson, Bruce Kogut, William Miller, Shirley Tessler, and John Zysman. The authors of all eight industry chapters and the editors acknowledge the Alfred P. Sloan Foundation for the research support that made these papers and this book possible. Special thanks go to Hirsh Cohen, Frank Mayadas, and Gail Pesyna, the project officers, who encouraged all of the contributors to pursue their interest in better understanding how industries globalize. Patient, understanding, and committed project officers are essential for this type of research.

We would like to thank Gary Fields, Nichola Lowe, and Tim Sturgeon for invaluable suggestions, and we gratefully acknowledge the efforts and suggestions of three reviewers. We also thank Sarah Brassmassery and Allison Gillespie for their assistance throughout this project. We both thank the authors for being so willing to help facilitate the process of putting this volume together. Patricia Katayama and Nathan McBrien of Stanford University Press helped mightily in making this book a reality.

M.K.
R.F.

# Contents

# Tables

# Figures

# Preface

## In Vino Veritas?

PAUL DUGUID

Is there truth in wine as Pliny said? Or is there just a brief flash of delusive (if delightful) insight that soon gives way to dullness? I shall leave that to readers of this preface to decide. But as I read the intriguing essays in this book I was frequently reminded of the eighteenth- and nineteenth-century wine trade. Before I try to show why, I must quickly acknowledge that, as Abernathy et al. wisely note in their chapter, there is undoubtedly something profoundly new about the new globalization. It is this new new thing that the different case studies and Kenney's and Kogut's broad overviews address so well. Nonetheless, historians of earlier global trade will find in these exemplary case studies much that is familiar. In the wine trade, for example, as in the modern economy, commodities came from numerous competing points of production, covered vast distances, and passed through multiple hands to reach the major international market. Before the twentieth century, that major market was Britain. Here production was negligible, but because consumption was prodigious, merchants could exert significant influence back along the whole chain. This collection makes a similar point about supply chains that lead from overseas production to consumers in the United States, where production dwindles as consumption grows, and with it control over the supply chain.[1]

But, critically, these essays are not simply about chains, industries, or markets. They are also about particular firms. Directly or indirectly, each essay records the ability of particular firms—specific links in these long supply chains—to achieve relative autonomy, and in the process assert control over the chain as a whole without, intriguingly, having to resort to formal integration. This "action at a distance"—both spatially and organizationally—is a distinctive feature of the new globalization, as firms disaggregate the old hierarchical forms. There are, in particular, several discussions here of "pressures" and "squeezes" exerted by dominant players over subordinate ones. While there are many clear examples, the most outstanding is surely McKendrick's stark account that 196 million disk drives are manufactured by eight firms but result in no significant profit. That is a squeeze indeed.

Such examples of supply chain subordination prompt me to wonder who gets to dominate, how, and how they manage to hold on, despite the dramatic pace of change that Kenney rightly emphasizes in his introduction. Clearly, many of the successful firms described here have risen to both prominence and relative dominance in their particular supply chain without having to assume formal upstream or downstream control through integration. Yet from what point they dominate seems highly variable. Sometimes it's retail (Wal-Mart in clothing and apparel markets), sometimes it's an OEM (Dell and Hewlett Packard, whose rise up Curry and Kenney's Table 5.2 is perhaps as remarkable as it is unremarked, in the PC market),[2] sometimes it's a major producer (Intel in the chip business), and sometimes (though not a central topic of discussion here) a software firm (such as Microsoft in the PC value chain). Undoubtedly, there are numerous contributing factors, many with a particularly modern character, and several that are quite industry specific. But this action at a distance, this struggle for dominance in global supply chains, was also, I shall try to show, a distinctive feature of the old globalization. So a look at the era when firms traded globally (admittedly in a smaller world) but before they were hierarchically integrated might still throw some light on the challenges facing globally active firms today now that many have disaggregated.[3]

A brief glance at a longish *durée* (some two hundred years) in the history of the port wine trade reveals power similarly accruing to particular points in the chain, allowing particular firms not only to compete effectively with rivals but also to dominate their suppliers and even their customers. For while they must cooperate, links in these chains inevitably live in tension with one another. And as the case studies here suggest, significant rents accrue to the dominant link while others both up and down the chain get squeezed. (We'd surely all rather be Intel than a beleaguered packaging and testing house in Southeast Asia.) "Winning" the game of "vertical competition," as Curry and Kenney suggest, can be as important (and rewarding) as beating your competitors in the marketplace.

## A Short History of the Port Trade

If, as several writers in this volume claim, history matters, then wine should certainly tell us something about international trade. It is one of the oldest international commodities. Heroditus speaks of boats carrying wine to Babylon in the sixth century B.C.E. A century later, Greek trade was sufficiently important (and lucrative) to be the subject of legislation. Pliny's *Natural History* includes some forty foreign wines among the ninety varieties available in Rome at the beginning of the Christian era. If the Dark Ages were not much kinder to wine than to learning (Goths, Vandals, and Huns, with their strong preference for beer and violence, seem to have been the linear ancestors of Britain's "lager louts"), the Middle Ages saw a resurgence in both, with monastic vineyards, as productive as their libraries, fostering trade from the vine-rich regions of the Mediterranean and southern Europe to the colder regions in the north. The wine trade grew with the European economy and wine merchants proved eager, restless entrepreneurs.

As often happens with transnational trade, England's thirst for foreign-produced commodities came into conflict with its foreign policy. France became as natural an enemy as it was a natural source for wine. With the English government repeatedly embargoing French wine, diplomacy as much as supply constrained demand. Portugal, eager for a Protestant ally to keep it free of the predatory Catholic power over its border, was an obvious alternative. For England, there were other wine-producing options. But Portugal had an Atlantic-facing coast: proximity to major markets, as so many authors here note, helps.

The year 1703 marked a significant point in this blend of trade and diplomacy. The queen of England and the king of Portugal signed the Methuen Treaty guaranteeing Portuguese wine lower duties than French wine in England. In return, it guaranteed to English woolens unfettered access to Portugal. Addressing central issues of international trade—comparative advantage and the international division of labor, in particular—the treaty is of interest to more than wine (or textile) historians. Adam Smith saw in the treaty an invidious tax on domestic consumers. The Methuen advantage, in his eyes, was all Portugal's. The Anglo-Portuguese economist Ricardo, however, saw things quite differently. Such trade, he thought, allowed the two countries with complementary assets to gain comparative advantage. More recent analysis of Anglo-Portuguese trade (Sideri 1970) tipped this balance once more, but in the opposite direction to Smith. In short-term annual budgetary balances, the two may have shown comparative advantage, but not in long-term development. The complementary assets represented, on England's side, the rising industrial economy, but on Portugal's side, the falling, agricultural economy. So England developed its "new economy," while Portugal, under physiocratic governments, was left with the old.

Several of the essays in this volume (in particular, Linden et al.) do show labor divided principally between high value-added work in one part of the world and low value-added "old economy" assembly work elsewhere. Much of Western Europe, Japan, and the United States works in the knowledge economy; the people of Southeast Asia, China, and Mexico are more likely to work for it. Consequently, modern debates over the benefits of this form of globalization sound strikingly similar to those initiated by Smith and Ricardo over the Methuen Treaty. Yet, as Leachman and Leachman show, Taiwan's semiconductor manufacturing is in the forefront of innovation and has proven sustainable and very profitable. Similarly, as McKendrick's study suggests, Singapore has benefited greatly by becoming the global manufacturing headquarters for hard disk drives. In other words, these papers do show that not all manufacturing regions can be assigned to the "old economy." The challenge raised by all these papers and faced by governments around the developing world, then, is to understand the different conditions and outcomes of comparative advantage in globalization.

The Methuen Treaty raises one more critical yet controversial topic that recurs throughout these essays: government intervention. The bilateral arrangements for textiles allowed under MFA (Abernathy et al.) has clear antecedents in the Methuen Treaty, as, in their way, do the local content (Sturgeon and Florida) and antidumping (Murtha et al.) laws: these serve, much as the discriminatory wine tax against the French, to keep undesired goods out of a particular market.

The early history of the port trade is rife with government intervention. Wine was not only much desired but also shipped in bulk containers. Consequently it was an easily taxed commodity. From the Methuen Treaty on, British governments continuously tinkered with the fiscal arrangements for its most popular wine until, with Gladstone's "single bottle" act of 1860, port finally lost its exceptional status. From their end, Portuguese governments sought to promote (and feed their treasury from) this important trade. Faced with increasing disarray in the 1750s, the Portuguese demarcated the port wine region—the Alto (or upper) Douro River valley where the port grapes are grown. (Port takes its name from the city of Oporto, the entrepôt at the mouth of the Douro River.) This demarcation survived until 1834, when a new, economically liberal Portuguese government removed all regulation. (Curiously, this deregulation occurred just as other countries started to adopt this innovative idea—one that is echoed not only in modern wine regions but also in maquiladoras, free ports, and other types of fiscally privileged zones.)

The end of regulation spurred a burst of globalization impressive even by today's standards. Before the lifting of restrictions, wine had flowed principally to Great Britain and Ireland, with lesser amounts trickling to northern Europe and to outposts of the Portuguese and British empires. Upon liberalization, these trickles swelled. The widely connected port merchants sent wine to Baltimore, Boston, New York, and Philadelphia; to Halifax, Newfoundland, Quebec, and Nova Scotia; to Archangel, Riga, and St. Petersburg; to Amsterdam, Bremen, Copenhagen, Genoa, Hamburg, Stettin, and Stockholm; to Tenerife, Madeira, and the Canaries; to the Cape of Good Hope, Jamaica, St. Johns, Barbados, and Demerara; to Pernambuco, Valparaiso, and Batavia; to Hobart, Sydney, Bombay, Calcutta, and Madras; and to Jersey and Guernsey. Only Asia and Antarctica are missing from this global sweep.

As this expansion indicates, as merchant accounts show, and as historians remind us, the merchants of the past were integrated into far-flung trading networks. Most merchants needed fewer than six degrees of separation to span the globe.[4] When opportunity arose, relatively passive links between merchants on opposite sides of the globe turned into active trading relations with extraordinary speed, allowing merchants to practice arbitrage in both goods and bills of exchange across space and time—a practice still vital, as I suggest below, to globalization today.

## Struggle in the Supply Chain

Unfortunately, for those who see in this dramatic expansion of the port trade a clear lesson about the benefits of trade liberalization, boom swiftly turned to bust. Low-cost imitations, potent substitutions, falling reputation, dwindling protection, and widespread falsification made the previously complacent port trade struggle to protect its appeal and reputation, in the short term, and its markets in the long. The highly disaggregated supply chain made such organization complicated. But the way in which the port trade took on this task is instructive.

This unruly chain began in the Alto Douro with the smallest farmers who sold grapes to big farmers. With these and their own larger crops, the big farmers made wine. To this they added brandy (one of the distinguishing features of port) to stabilize the wine, which they stored through winter. As stockholding is expensive and risky, all but the wealthiest farmers hoped to sell their wine in early spring to either brokers or exporters who then took the wine to Oporto. There more brandy was added, the wine was stored (young port is harsh and crude) before exporters blended it for export (using their own stocks and, if these fell short, those of brokers), and it was shipped to British ports in response to orders from importers. These sold the wine to hoteliers, innkeepers, wine merchants, and retailers, who in turn sold to consumers.

Most tensions in this chain revolve around stockholding. Wine was costly and volatile. When it moved, high duties had to be paid. When it sat, it tied up large amounts of capital. If it aged well, it could command high prices to justify the investment. But stocks could both deteriorate (aging a product that can literally go sour is always risky) or depreciate if the next year's wine was better. Furthermore, taste and fashion fluctuated rapidly and unpredictably. No one wanted to be caught holding depreciating stocks. Yet no one wanted to be out of wine when the market surged. (For this reason, the brokers, a little like Ingram's and other wholesalers today, played a critical role in the chain, providing just-in-time wine.)

So the port chain faced many of the stockholding issues discussed in this volume: from the textile industry, with its volatile fashions, to the auto industry, with its high-cost components, to the PC, chip, and hard-disk industry, with their rapidly depreciating components. Port, like the PC (Curry and Kenney) and its various components, especially semiconductors (Leachman and Leachman) and hard disk drives (McKendrick), and garments (Abernathy et al.), had some of the properties of Curry's and Kenney's "hot potato." Everyone wanted adequate supply, but not the stockholding risks. Each link sought to pass these to someone else up or down the chain. As Sturgeon and Florida suggest, this urge to transfer stockholding risks may even explain the way in which objects are designed. The modularity of the PC and the car allows not only for distributed production but also for the easy transfer of stockholding from more powerful to less powerful participants. Port, too, had "design features" that allowed such transfers. Standard explanations of the brandy it contains are enological. Some explanations, however, are more strategic, arguing that brandy was added because, though it did not affect the time needed for the wine to become drinkable, it decreased the time it needed to become transportable (Thudichum and Dupré, 1872). Thus brandy allowed the farmers to pass the cost of storage to exporters and exporters to pass it to importers. In response, the importers engaged in a "blend-to-order" policy, a little like Dell's "built-to-order" strategy. Blending to order, while allowing customers greater choice, allowed importers to pass such customized wine hurriedly to customers (in this case, merchants, inns, hotels, and retailers). If these could not as quickly persuade the end user either to "lay down" venerable wine or to drink cheap wine, they ended up as the most likely candidates to bear the cost in this supply-chain game of pass the parcel.[5] But retailers and wine-merchants (described by one port merchant as "the most rotten set in London") had a tendency to default on payments, causing tremors all down the chain. So a great deal of what Abernathy et al. call "short cycle" storage fell to the more solvent importers in Britain, while the "long cycle" storage fell to the exporters in Oporto. As these two were also often closely linked through interlocking shareholdings, inevitably it was these two that pushed to organize the supply chain in their particular interests.

They faced, of course, competition from others in the chain, each of whom no doubt realized that those who did not squeeze would instead be squeezed. So, farmers sought to put their stamp on the trade, appealing implicitly to the concept of *terroir* to turn the brand they burned on their barrels into recognizable signs of quality assurance in the retail marketplace. Here, in a nationally divided trade, they were probably undone as much by the historic Portuguese demarcation as by their British "vertical competitors." Whereas in France, in the absence of strict demarcation, the names of particular chateaux became a sign of reliability, in Portugal the demarcation and the tradition of blending wines from different estates at export tended to obscure the role and name of the originating farmers. Nonetheless, certain estates (such as Roriz) did acquire a reputation in Britain as, on the one hand, wine merchants used them as tokens of quality, and on the other, farmers tried to subordinate the supply line, diminish the role of middlemen, and establish their own outlets in Britain.

At the opposite end of the chain, wine merchants sought to overcome their bad collective name and establish individual good ones. They were aided by the fact that port in the nineteenth century was more or less anonymous. It was advertised as "good," "strong," "rich," "natural," "old," and the like, but just as the names of the originating chateaux (or *quintas,* as they are known in Portugal) were obscured, so were those of most of the middlemen. Instead, wine merchants in Britain offered their names as the distinguishing feature. The practice starts early. *The Daily Courant* of 1703 and after, for example, advertises many generic wines (port, lisbon, claret, burgundy, and the like). The only proprietary names that appear are those of wine merchants and innkeepers. Slowly wine merchants grasped the significance of this position. Advertisements for port and sherry for sale at H. B. Fearon's turn subtly into advertisements for "H. B. Fearon's port." By the mid–nineteenth century, the new names in wine marketing and retailing— Hedges & Butler, Gilbey's, Victoria Wines—required exporters in Portugal to bottle port in Oporto with proprietary labels and corks as if Hedges & Butler, Gilbey's, and Victoria Wines had their own Oporto operation. In the process, they increasingly standardized their product for multiple retail outlets so that, as one historian puts it, "a Gilbey claret bought at Reading, say, should have the same look and taste as a claret bought in Wolverhampton

. . . a consumer in other words, could learn to rely on a Gilbey's label. . . .
They marketed standard brands."[6]

In effect, the retailers were transforming their strategy from the equivalent
of the "build to order" (BTO) strategy, familiar in the modern PC market, to
the equivalent of "buyers' own brand" (BOB) retailing, familiar in the modern food and wine industry, whereby, once again, retailers get their name on
the label while their suppliers become anonymous and interchangeable.

## Standards and Brands

Two things relevant to both past and present are I hope evident by now.
First, as the quotation above indicates, the struggle ran along, not across,
supply chains. If retailers established the identity, standardization, and reliability of the wine this way, they effectively made all others in the chain
anonymous and put in their own hands effective control of the disaggregated
chain. (If one supplier caused problems, Gilbey's could—and did—switch to
another without customers being any the wiser.) Second, the key weapons in
this struggle are standards and brands. If you can establish a reliable standard
that is as predictable in Wolverhampton as Reading, if you can associate your
name with that standard, and if you can protect that name, then you can
grow from niche to mass markets and make others dance to your tune.
Hence the triumphantly (if, for some, only transitorily) significant names in-
voked in this volume—Nike, Wal-Mart, Dell, HP, Zenith, Sharp, Intel, Microsoft, Sony, AMD, Jeep, Volkswagen, Nokia, and Motorola.

So in the middle of the century the wine trade in general became a rather
familiar battle of standards and names. "Tawny" (once an insult) turned into
the term for one particular category of wine. "Vintage" port was transformed
from a general to a specific term to designate wine aged for the high-end
market. And "ruby" was introduced to characterize the wine for the cheap
market.[7] And firm names known today—not only Hedges & Butler, Gilbey's,
and Victoria but also Cockburn, Graham, Sandeman, Taylors, and Roriz—
became prominent and valuable trademarks. In homage to their value, these
names were rapidly flattered by imitators, appropriated by fraudsters, protected by courts, alienated in sales, and seriously cultivated by owners.

What is noticeable about this list, as well as its modern equivalent above,
is that neither represents only one particular point in the supply chain. Wal-
Mart and Victoria are retailers, HP and Sandeman are intermediators, Intel
and Roriz are producers. Although they occupy different points in the chain,
each manages to stake a claim for itself.

Of particular interest are the intermediators, who might seem to have no essential role to play. Indeed, one contemporary champion of the farmers insisted in 1883 that with "the compression of space and time," farmers should be able to sell to consumers without any rent-seekers intervening. The language remains fresh in debates about disintermediation today.

But while some were cut out and others subordinated, a few intermediators did manage to take charge of their own supply chain. Although wine merchants and retailers pushed to make themselves the ones whose name would become the brand, they suffered, as I noted, from their own notoriety and the regularity with which their names appeared in lists of bankrupts. The generally short lives of retailers made them a risky source for wines that the buyer might not get to drink for one, two, or more decades. To whom would you protest if the wine turned out bad, but the retailer went under twenty years ago? Better established merchants fought this by broadcasting their age ("Established Upwards of 45 Years," "Importers for 40 Years," "Established 1793," and so forth). But they also started to use the more enduring names of suppliers. Thus, while retailers like Gilbey's sought to make their suppliers anonymous, others boasted that their port was Sandeman's, Cockburn's, or Offley's "shipping." Such claims played the role that the label "Intel inside" plays for low-end PC assemblers or VARs, providing for purchasers a warranty of quality that the VAR itself lacks credentials to provide.

But unlike Intel's trademarked claim, exporters' names were not necessarily used with permission—nor even with the exporter's wine. Thus the exporters themselves moved to protect their own name, and in the process to promote their brand over that of the retailers and the farmers. They did this in a variety of ways. They participated in the standard setting for the main types of wine ("tawny," "vintage," and "ruby"), as described above. They increasingly took over bottling.[8] (Wine had previously been bottled at a variety of different points in the chain: exporter, importer, retailer, and even consumer.) And they began to promote their brands as available "at most respectable retail houses." In so doing, they suggested to consumers that, while the importer was essential, retailers played an inconsequential and substitutable role in supply.[9] And so, with standard and brand strategies of their own, they fought back against the retailers in the tussle to see who could both assert their own brand and blot out that of their vertical competitor.

Yet, as is usually the case with vertical competition, cooperation was also important. Exporters, importers, and retailers needed each other, and were often complicit in others' competitive strategies. As Acer both manufactures PCs under its own name and assembles computers for competitors, so port firms like Sandeman provided both Sandeman-branded port and retailer-branded port (for Gilbey's). Here the exporter wisely segmented the market, allowing the new retail chains to service the cheaper end of the market with "buyers' own brands," while promoting their own name on high-end and vintage wines.[10]

## Arbitrage in the Space of Flows

There are, then, intriguing parallels between nineteenth- and twenty-first-century global chains. But can it be said that the age of sail and steam can tell us truths about what has grandly been called the "space of flows" (Castells 1996)? I believe it can. In particular, the parallels help emphasize that it is not only the length of the globalized supply chain that is of interest. We need to note as well its particular shape and the topography of power that it instantiates. The parallels also suggest that, while many explanations of modern supply chain management have technological causes, these may be necessary but not sufficient. Business process innovation, in particular the skillful manipulation of brands, has proved an effective means to shape a supply chain.[11] And thus overheated rhetoric about a new economy built on new technology is likely to miss critical aspects of where value is added (and rents extracted) in the flow of goods and information.

Indeed, old and new juxtaposed particularly help understand the limits to claims about the "compression of space and time." A key word here, which I mentioned above, is *arbitrage*. Global businesses, both old and new, make their money through arbitrage between prices at the point of production and prices at the point of consumption.[12] For arbitrage to be possible, the flow between these two places has to be impeded, by government regulation and borders, by coordination and communication problems, by transportation costs, and so forth. While these remain, intermediaries, arbitraging across the barriers, will also remain. (Disintermediation, that is to say, is not the same thing as disaggregation.)

Much as histories of the port trade need to understand the impediments it faced, so the essays in this volume, then, are all in their way studies of modern impediments to flow and the resulting arbitrage. The flow of material goods is constrained by tariffs, embargoes, prejudice, but also, more simply, by transportation, its time and costs. The river and the estuary, so important to the growth of the port trade, have perhaps today been replaced by such things as the highway and the FedEx airport hub. More adaptable than rivers, these new interchanges nonetheless have a significant determining relationship on global flow and continue to ensure, in Kogut's words, that "we never escape the pull of geography." The magic of a communications infrastructure will not magically lift those without transportation infrastructure into the "new economy," in part because aspirants to the new usually have to prove their value by working on material goods, not informational ones.

Less discussed in these pages, but ever present, are the impediments to the flow of labor and their role in the ensuing global arbitrage of wages. The space of flows, an informational concept, does not readily allow for the flow of labor. Thus many people remain inescapably trapped in low-wage areas, making arbitrage by intermediaries easier. In several of the cases outlined here, arbitrageurs have to balance the price of goods and labor in the form of weight and wages. Goods that are cheap to transport, such as DRAM, can be sourced from the accessible lowest-wage areas. Those that are too heavy to transport either cheaply or quickly, such as car engines, come from points geographically closer to the market. So, because of impediments to the flow of goods and labor, countries can still gain disproportionately, rather as Portugal did, from the serendipity of proximity. The dramatic differences, despite other similarities, between FDI and GDP in Ireland and New Zealand would seem to bear this out. Distance is not dead.

Capital, of course, flows more readily than either goods or labor. It always did. (The original commercial meaning of *arbitrage* referred to the trade of bills of exchange between markets to take advantage of different currency rates.) Here too, however, the essays note that flow is not completely unimpeded. Modern global firms, these essays remind, have also to be skilled at arbitraging around currency fluctuation, as Oporto merchants were before them.[13] Today, instead of just moving cash to counter unfavorable shifts in exchange, supply chains move production itself to other regions. A weak but relatively stable exchange rate with the dollar can thus be a great asset, though investing arbitrageurs are in part investing in the stability of that weakness.

Finally and intriguingly, the essays remind us that knowledge does not, as many seem to feel it must, escape the pull of geography. There are impediments to the flow of knowledge. Yet, while we can understand that port merchants clustered in Oporto, because that's where the commodity comes from, it isn't as easy to see why knowledge also clusters. Gilder would have us believe that in the telecosm, "anyone can transmit any amount of information, any experience, any opportunity to anyone or everyone, anywhere, at any time, instantaneously, without barriers of convenience or cost, the resulting transformation becomes a transfiguration" (Gilder 2000: 263–64). But in reality the world still resembles the world of the port merchants, where dominant clusters in one place exert distal control over distributed supply chains. Today the critical clusters are, in fact, knowledge clusters. They are found in places like Silicon Valley, Route 128, Fairfax, Virginia, Detroit, and in similar spots around the United States and the developed world. In these places the design work, the high-value intellectual property, increasing returns, and even increasing control continue to reside, as most of these essays emphasize. Indeed, paradoxically it is knowledge workers, whose labor is in theory independent of location, who apparently need (and are allowed) to travel most. So Silicon Valley becomes increasingly polyglot, and the knowledge economy appears to concentrate in the United States. As the essays here indicate, the international division of labor is increasingly a division between knowledge work, which clusters in the metropoles (though the movement of the laborers is relatively unrestricted), and manual labor, which flows around the globe to fit with new supply chains (though the movements of the laborers are highly restricted as the global supply chain spreads and disaggregates to allow for arbitrage).

*Arbitrage*, it's worth noting, initially referred to a capacity for self-determination, which is the converse of subordination. And, as I have tried to show and the following essays wonderfully illustrate, in the new global supply chains as in the old, participants struggle to achieve self-determination. The stakes are high. The losers face subordination or even bankruptcy. And technological shifts alone are not enough to unpick the lock that location and brands can give the winners.

## Notes

1. I accept Kenney's reservation that a chain is not necessarily a good metaphor, but as it is the generally accepted one, I use it here.

2. Given its recent decision to purchase Compaq and the well known difficulty that technology firms have in integrating mergers, the meteoric rise of Hewlett Packard may presage a similarly dramatic fall.

3. These comments draw heavily on two important, recent, and historically informed treatises: one by Gary Fields (2003), which compares Dell's reorganization of the PC supply chain in the late twentieth century with the rise of the Net to Swift's reorganization of meat packing in the late nineteenth century with the rise of the railway; the other by Teresa da Silva Lopes (2002), which looks at both the integration and disintegration of supply chains in the alcoholic beverage industry at the end of the twentieth century. Where Fields stresses the significance of technological innovation, Silva Lopes stresses innovations in marketing, branding, and intellectual property.

4. See in particular Woolf (1982), Curtin (1984), and Hancock (1995).

5. As the century progressed, the novelist Anthony Trollope (1927) noted, consumers increasingly expected wine merchants to stock high-quality wine, allowing consumers to send "for a dozen at a time, and wisely impose upon [the merchant] the duty of keeping the wine,—and charging for the capital required" (p. 76).

6. Waugh (1957), pp. 18 and 19.

7. At about the same time, the French were classifying their grand cru.

8. In this they followed the lead of the Champagne houses, who had imposed their name on the trade by bottling in France rather than in Britain.

9. Here port exporters were following beer brands (particularly Bass and Guinness) that advertised their brands as available.

10. The port trade, this integration suggests, shows aspects of the modern chain as if in a film run backward. The modern global supply chain described in this book is the result of shift from large, hierarchically ordered supply to a disaggregated model. The port trade was actually moving in the other direction. It began disaggregated, but as different players came to dominate their particular supply chain, integration followed. The Oporto exporters, in particular, integrated backward into production and forward into imports, and for some, retail. Similarly, well-branded retailers integrated backward into both imports and production. And some producers even integrated forward.

11. The most powerful brand in the digital world, Microsoft, has almost always been a technological follower. It has, however, both managed its brand and squeezed its upstream and downstream supply chain with innovative ferocity.

12. Those who propound the annihilation of space and time (Gilder 2000; Cairncross 1997) need to explain how businesses will make money.

13. Several Oporto bill-brokering merchants crucially helped the Rothschild brothers service their continental loans during the Napoleonic and later wars.

# Contributors

FREDERICK H. ABERNATHY joined John T. Dunlop in a 1979 study of the tailored clothing industry, which led to the establishment of the Textile/Clothing Technology Corporation [TC2]. His continued involvement with the apparel industry led the Alfred P. Sloan Foundation to support research resulting in the book he coauthored, *A Stitch in Time* (Oxford, 2000). He is Abbott and James Lawrence Professor of Engineering, and Gordon McKay Professor of Mechanical Engineering at Harvard University.

MELISSA M. APPLEYARD is an Assistant Professor of Business Administration at the Darden Graduate School of Business Administration, University of Virginia. Her research examines the motivation behind and consequences of knowledge sharing in technology-intensive settings. Her research on knowledge diffusion both across and within company boundaries has been published in academic and practitioner journals, as well as books. Currently Appleyard is analyzing the role of knowledge accumulation in shaping buyer-supplier alliances and the global patterns of knowledge diffusion in the semiconductor industry.

CLAIR BROWN is Professor of Economics and the Director of the Center for Work, Technology, and Society at the University of California, Berkeley. Prof. Brown has published extensively on labor market issues. She heads the human resources group of the Sloan Competitive Semiconductor Manufacturing (CSM-HR) program at U.C. Berkeley. She coauthored *Work and Pay in the United States and Japan* (with Nakata, Reich, and Ulman; Oxford, 1997). Brown's work on the relationship between work roles, economic growth, and living standards and how the standard of living has changed during the twentieth century is examined in *American Standards of Living, 1918–1988* (Blackwell, 1994).

JAMES CURRY is Professor-Researcher in the Department of Social Studies at the Colegio de la Frontera Norte in Tijuana, Baja California, Mexico. He has recently published articles on manufacturing in the U.S.-Mexico border region and open source software. He is currently involved in research projects on the personal computer industry in North America and Mexico, and electronic commerce in the United States and Latin America.

PAUL DUGUID is an independent scholar. For the past ten years he has been a research associate at the University of California, Berkeley. From 1988 to 2001 he was a consultant at the Xerox Palo Alto Research Center. He is currently (2001–2002) a fellow of the Center for the Public Domain and a visiting professor at Copenhagen Business School. He is coauthor, with John Seely Brown, of *The Social Life of Information* (Harvard Business School Press, 2000) and numerous articles on topics from the design of interfaces to the design of organizations. His recent articles on the port trade have appeared in the *Scandinavian Economic History Review, The European Yearbook of Business History,* and the Portuguese journal *Douro.*

JOHN T. DUNLOP has had an extensive career in labor relations and government, including serving as U.S. Secretary of Labor from 1975 to 1976 and, more recently, as chair of President Clinton's Commission on Worker-Management Relations. He has also served as a mediator and arbitrator in a wide range of industries and is the author of more than ten books on labor relations and labor economics. He is the coauthor of *A Stitch in Time* (Oxford, 2000). He is Lamont University Professor, Emeritus at Harvard University.

RICHARD FLORIDA is the Heinz Professor of Regional Economic Development at Carnegie Mellon University and founder and codirector of the Sloan Software Industry Center there. He is author of several books, including most recently *The Rise of the Creative Class* (Basic Books, 2002) and also *Industrializing Knowledge* (with Lewis Branscomb and Fumio Kodama, MIT Press, 1999), *Beyond Mass Production* (Oxford University Press, 1993), and *The Breakthrough Illusion* (Basic Books, 1990) the latter two with Martin Kenney. He is a co-organizer of the Sloan Globalization Network and calibrated with Tim Sturgeon on the Globalization of the Automobile Industry project reported in this volume.

JANICE H. HAMMOND investigates how manufacturing and logistics systems develop the speed and flexibility to respond quickly and efficiently to changing customer demand—critical capabilities in the retail-apparel-textile channel. She is the UPS Foundation Professor of Business Logistics at the Harvard Business School. She is a coauthor of the book *A Stitch in Time* (Oxford, 2000).

JEFFREY A. HART is Professor and Department Chair of Political Science at Indiana University, Bloomington. His coauthored book, *Managing New Industry Creation: Global Knowledge Formation and Entrepreneurship in High Technology*, was published by Stanford University Press in 2001. In addition to publishing many books as well as articles in leading academic journals, he has worked at the Office of Technology Assessment of the United States Congress, helping to write *International Competition in Services* in 1987. Hart has been a visiting scholar at the Berkeley Roundtable on the International Economy.

MARTIN KENNEY is a Professor in the Department of Human and Community Development at the University of California, Davis, and a Senior Project Director at the Berkeley Roundtable on the International Economy at the University of California, Berkeley. Most recently, he edited the book *Understanding Silicon Valley* (Stanford 2000). He has studied the globalization of the electronics industry and is currently working on the evolution of venture capital in the United States and globally. He has authored or edited four books and more than a hundred articles and book chapters.

BRUCE KOGUT is the Dr. Felix Zandman Professor of International Management at the Wharton School of the University of Pennsylvania, and Co-Director of the Reginald H. Jones Center for Management Policy, Strategy and Organization. He has been a visiting scholar at the Humboldt University in Berlin, Stockholm School of Economics, Science Center Berlin, and the Ecole Polytechnique, Paris. His research has been on such topics as labor markets for ideas and the effects on organizations, the expansion of U.S. and Japanese firms internationally, alliances and networks, and the competitiveness of countries. His current research focuses on the virtual location of software and intellectual labor activities in the global economy. His research has been supported by the German Marshall Fund, Fulbright, International Research and Exchange Board, the French Ministry of Science and Technology, the National Institute of Standards and Technology, and Wissenschaftszentrum in Berlin.

CHIEN H. LEACHMAN is an Assistant Research Engineer in the Engineering Systems Research Center at the University of California, Berkeley. She has served on the staff of the Competitive Semiconductor Manufacturing Program at UC Berkeley since 1993. She was an Assistant Professor of Operations and Information Management at the University of Connecticut in 1995–96. She holds a Ph.D. in Management Systems from SUNY Buffalo, and an MBA and BA in Business Administration degrees from Chengchi University in Taiwan. She is the author of twelve publications concerning information systems, decision support, and semiconductor manufacturing.

ROBERT C. LEACHMAN is a Professor of Industrial Engineering and Operations Research at the University of California, Berkeley, where he serves as Director of the Competitive Semiconductor Manufacturing (CSM) Program. He is the author of more than 50 technical publications concerning production operations management and productivity improvement, and he has been a consultant in these areas to many corporations. He received his A.B. degree in Mathematics and Physics, an M.S. in Operations Research, and a Ph.D. in Operations Research, all from UC Berkeley, and has been a member of the UC Berkeley faculty since 1979. In 1995 he was the winner of the Franz Edelman Award Competition sponsored by the Institute for Operations Research and the Management Sciences (INFORMS), and in 2001 was the runner-up for the Franz Edelman Award.

STEFANIE ANN LENWAY is Professor, Department Chair, and Carlson Term Chair of Strategic Management and Organization at the University of Minnesota. Her coauthored book, *Managing New Industry Creation: Global Knowledge Formation and Entrepreneurship in High Technology*, was published by Stanford University Press in 2001. She has published numerous articles in leading academic journals on the role of managerial mindsets in global strategy implementation, business-government strategic interaction, and the politics of international trade. Lenway is a member of the Board of Governors of the Academy of Management.

GREG LINDEN is a Post-doctoral Fellow at the Center for Work, Technology and Society, a research unit at the University of California, Berkeley, where he earned a Ph.D. in Economics in 2000. He has published extensively on various aspects of the global electronics industry and consulted on projects in Asia dealing with industrial policy in high-technology industries. His current research interests include the competitive dynamics of the electronics industry, research consortia in the semiconductor industry, the emergence of global competitors from industrializing countries, and the effect of foreign direct investment on economic growth.

DAVID G. MCKENDRICK is Research Director of the Information Storage Industry Center at the University of California, San Diego, and coauthor of *From Silicon Valley to Singapore: Location and Competitive Advantage in the Disk Drive Industry* (Stanford University Press, 2000). Prior to joining UCSD, he taught in the business schools at the University of California, Berkeley, and the University of Texas at Dallas. He received his Ph.D. in business from the University of California, Berkeley.

THOMAS P. MURTHA is Associate Professor of Strategic Management and Organization at the University of Minnesota's Carlson School of Management. His coauthored book, *Managing New Industry Creation: Global Knowledge Formation and Entrepreneurship in High Technology*, was published by Stanford University Press in 2001. He has published articles in leading academic journals on the role of managerial mindsets in global strategy implementation, and on business-government strategic interaction. Tom Murtha has also written on the arts and consumer electronics for leading newspapers and magazines, including *Rolling Stone* and the *Minneapolis Star Tribune*.

TIMOTHY J. STURGEON is a Research Associate and Executive Director of the Industrial Performance Center's Globalization Study at the Massachusetts Institute of Technology (MIT). Prior to this, Mr. Sturgeon served as Globalization Research Director for the International Motor Vehicle Program at MIT. He received his Ph.D. in Economic Geography for a dissertation entitled *Turnkey Production Networks: Industrial Organization, Economic Development, and the Globalization of Electronics Contract Manufacturing*. His articles have appeared in a number of edited volumes, scholarly journals, and trade magazines. Prior to entering academe, he held a variety of industry and consulting positions.

DAVID WEIL has written widely on the impact of technology and human resource policy on business performance based in part on his studies of the retail-apparel-textile industries. His research spans the areas of labor market policy, industrial and labor relations, occupational safety and health, and regulatory policy. He is Associate Professor of Economics at Boston University School of Management and Research Fellow, John F. Kennedy School of Government, Harvard University.

# Locating Global Advantage

*Industry Dynamics in the
International Economy*

# CHAPTER ONE

# Introduction

MARTIN KENNEY

Globalization is much more than simply moving employment and activities from developed nations into nations with lower-cost labor forces. Such a simple conclusion obscures the complicated skein of cross-border relationships that have evolved out of firm strategies seeking to balance a kaleidoscope of variables including labor and inventory costs, transportation, quality, concentration of valuable knowledge in clusters, and temporal proximity to customers. Understanding firm strategies at a single moment in time is complicated enough, but unfortunately these variables also fluctuate. For example, Singapore—at one time a low-cost environment with a weak infrastructure for hard disk drive manufacturing—over two decades evolved into a high-cost environment with a very sophisticated infrastructure. Today Singapore is a manufacturing, R&D, and logistics center. For firms, the global map is a gigantic, evolving chessboard upon which boundedly rational corporate strategists operating in internal and external political environments must not only situate production but also decide to make or buy.[1] These decisions, though complicated, are not random; corporate managers are responding to real constraints and opportunities.

For most Americans, the closest interaction with the enormous number of nations in the United Nations occurs on visits to their local Wal-Mart, which, of course, means that the world is in our homes, a part of our everyday life. A stroll through Wal-Mart's aisles reveals national origin labeling on objects from Bangladesh, China, Haiti, Honduras, Indonesia, Korea, Mauritius, Mexico, Taiwan, and a myriad of other nations. But as the chapters in this book show, these labels are deceptive, because the product is an assemblage of physical and intellectual inputs from yet other nations. The goods we buy are the end result of an elaborately choreographed transnational odyssey. These objects are part of an economy whose tendrils reach ever further outward, linking, integrating, and transforming both far-flung and nearby places.

Firms and industries generate powerful economic forces shaping the lives of all human beings. Often industries are treated as black boxes, a perspective implying that economic shifts, technological change, and market dynamics will shape every industry similarly. Our chapters recognize that firms are remarkably different, and thus their repertoires for creating advantage are diverse. We are unified by an understanding that firms within industries are evolving, as are the locations in which they operate. Current configurations are responses to past conditions and prior firm strategies. History matters, insofar as previous decisions shape the contemporary landscape within which firms compete for future competitive advantage.

In the current conjuncture, firms scan the globe for favorable combinations of production factors and factor prices. And yet, as Paul Duguid in his foreword and Bruce Kogut in his concluding chapter remind us, cross-border trade has a long history. All of the parties to this trade have attempted to create power asymmetries to strengthen their bargaining positions versus those of their partners and rivals. The resulting configurations can lock in for extended periods. However, as Kogut points out in his chapter, multinational firms often also operate as highways for the diffusion of knowledge, thereby sowing the seeds of change. Firm strategies are important for creating regional economies and institutions.

## Locating Global Advantage

This book is the result of an ongoing commitment by the Alfred P. Sloan Foundation to study how U.S. firms are both actors in and subjects of globalization.[2] The foundation's tenet has been that the evolution of national economies and firm behavior can be understood only through intensive examination of firm actions within an industry context. All of the chapters focus on the organizational configuration and locational choices of U.S. firms. Although the decisions and actions of these firms can be critical to local economic development, the chapters were not meant to assess the economic development impacts of corporate actions. Nonetheless, this book will be useful for readers interested in international development, as the chapters elucidate the dynamics that frame corporate locational choices.

The contributors to this volume share certain common beliefs, both methodological and philosophical. Fieldwork (especially practitioners' interviews) is particularly important; it is only through factory visits and personal interviews that a researcher can grasp the dynamics within which corporate actors make decisions. We also are influenced by evolutionary economics (Nelson and Winter 1982) and share its perspective that firms and industries can be understood only in a historical context. Put succinctly, globalization is an evolutionary process.

*Locating Global Advantage* quite properly studies the spatial dimension. Each of the authors treats the spatial dimension as an organizational and operational outcome of an evolutionary set of decisions, and as such the meaning of various locations may not be so obvious. But, more important, our authors recognize the evolutionary and nonergodic character of spatial configurations (Arthur 1994; David 1986) and the evolution of places as knowledge-laden locations or learning regions (Florida 1995; Storper and Salais 1997). To rephrase Storper and Walker (1989), firms and industries build places, and this process is the source of clusters that benefit from both traded and untraded interdependencies.

To examine the globalization of industries, the authors recognize that often the production and marketing of a commodity are segmented into juridically separate organizations or, as Winter (1987) termed them, "units of accrual." While recognizing that the intellectual roots of the social division of labor (Sayer and Walker 1993) can be traced at least as far back as Adam Smith, we draw most directly upon Michael Porter's (1990, 1986) concept of value chains, Kogut's (1985) concept of value-added chains, and Hopkins's and Wallerstein's (1986) concept of commodity chains, which was further developed by Gereffi (1994, 1999). The chapter authors more frequently use the term *value chain* because it explicitly recognizes the significance of less commodified activities such as R&D and marketing.[3]

There are difficulties with the "chain" metaphor, which is probably more appropriate for thinking about the internal activities of the firm but can create a misleading image when considering the production of an assembled product. The other metaphor that has long been used to describe these interfirm ties is, of course, "networks" (Bartlett and Ghoshal 1989). More recently, the use of networks to describe social and economic relationships has become ubiquitous. Despite some felicitous aspects of networks as a metaphor for the way a production system might be modeled, there are also difficulties. For example, in the network conceptualization there is no sense of a relatively unidirectional motion of goods toward the consumer (though obviously information and money flow in the other direction). If a metaphor is necessary, then we believe a more appropriate metaphor would be the one used often in industry—namely, that of a dendritic river basin that drains into the sea, which is the final consumer. However, the authors in this book, for the sake of ease and uniformity, adopt the chain metaphor.

We are interested in how and why the various processes involved in value creation are distributed among different firms. For example, as Leachman and Leachman show, the producers of DRAMs (dynamic random access memories) and microprocessors for personal computers integrate a larger portion of the value chain than do firms involved in the custom logic chip chain. For custom chips an interorganizational division of labor between chip design firms and silicon foundries has evolved. Even within industries there is often an astonishing richness in the way interorganizational linkages are structured. This is very often overlooked by those who have not studied the firms and industries closely. Individual industries have their own logic, so globalization and vertical disintegration should be expressed differently in each industry (for an excellent overview, see Dicken 1998).

Our book complements research in international trade economics that recognizes that differing industries have distinct profiles in how they organize their praxis and create advantage (Feenstra 1998). Still, for methodological reasons, economists generally view globalization in terms of trade statistics disaggregated at the three- or four-digit Standard Industrial Category (SIC) code. While helpful, these studies sometimes suffer from a lack of specificity and thus ignore firm strategy. They also find it difficult to explain the reasons for changing patterns of trade. For example, SIC Code 3344 contains all semiconductors including DRAMs, microprocessors, and other logic chips, but the difficulty with this aggregation, as Leachman and Leachman indicate, is that corporate strategies, spatial and organizational configurations, and evolutionary dynamics in each category differ.[4] This is not easily captured in the statistics but can obscure some of the underlying firm choices shaping the global economy and America's place in that economy. For example, is a semiconductor designed and marketed by a Silicon Valley firm, but fabricated in Taiwan, a Taiwanese semiconductor, an American semiconductor, or what? The chapters provide the thick description that excavates below numbers and statistics to expose the difficult, complicated world of business in a global economy.

## Five Cross-cutting Dynamics

The richness of these industry studies provides insight into five dynamics that are propelling globalization and appear in different guises in nearly every chapter. The first dynamic concerns the technological and organizational advances in the fields of transportation and communication that operate in the background of each industry. The second dynamic is the multifaceted drive for greater speed, in terms of speed-to-market, more rapid product design, and more rapid inventory turnover—all meant to reduce various cycle times. Unrelenting cost pressure that continually commodifies existing products forcing businesses to lower costs is the third dynamic. In situ knowledge creation, whereby deep experience and capabilities are concentrated in certain locations or industries, is the fourth dynamic. Finally, the fifth dynamic concerns management's decisions regarding where to site the various corporate functions in relationship to their customers. These dynamics pressure firms to continually consider the location for various activities. Like a kaleidoscope for which each twist of the cylinder creates a different picture, in each industry and even industrial subsector, these dynamics create different patterns.

### Transportation, Communications, and Globalization

The decreasing cost and increasing speed and capabilities in transportation and communication networks are the foundations for the expanding reach of global value chains. Technical improvements allow firms to pursue innovative approaches to operating the value chain. Multimodal transportation systems based on standardized cargo containers for land-sea shipping and sophisticated air freight systems have shortened the elapsed time and increased reliability. These innovations and others are loosening some earlier locational constraints.[5] Transportation improvements lag compared with the even more dramatic decline of information transmission prices. The result has been an electronic data interchange web connecting an ever greater number of the nodes in the value chain, thereby increasing information sharing. Decreasing costs of communication are only one benefit, as significant as the far greater flexibility and transmission bandwidth created by developments such as the graphical nature and open protocols of the Internet (Cohen et al. 2001).

This is not the first time that new transportation and communication technologies have affected the organization of capitalism. Chandler (1977) credited the railroad and telegraph as critical technologies in enabling the creation of the multidivisional firm. In the last decade, there has been a metamorphosis of transportation providers into logistics firms capable of handling both the movements of bits of information and atoms of product. Increasingly, communications networks permitting the tracking of an artifact's progress from inception to the final consumer are interlinking a value chain's disparate activities. The impacts of these advances are stunning. By one account, in 1980 U.S. logistics spending was 17.2 percent of total GDP, and of that 9 percent of total GDP was inventory investment. By 1995 this had dropped to 10.8 percent and 4.3 percent, respectively (Lappin 1996). Today, transport costs constitute only approximately 1 percent of the final price of consumer goods (Taggart 1999). From the rapid replenishment system described by Abernathy et al. for garments to Dell's build-to-order PC production system described by Curry and

Kenney, the transportation and communications advances are providing firms with more efficient and transparent logistics systems.

Logistics specialists such as UPS or Federal Express not only handle deliveries on a global scale but are also capable of undertaking some measure of final assembly: packaging, inventory management, and distribution. Retailers, assemblers, suppliers, and logistics firms responsible for moving the physical goods are having their software systems woven into an integrated global web. What began as a just-in-time (JIT) system that required close proximity between assemblers and suppliers is evolving into a JIT system spanning national boundaries and oceans as firms strive to access widely dispersed production factors even while reducing inventory costs and depreciation risks by keeping goods continuously flowing downstream toward the final consumer. Logistics firms experience continuous pressure to further shorten transit times, improve delivery predictability, and lower costs. As the recent West Coast dock lockout showed, there is also heightened vulnerability caused by the constantly swelling tide of goods in motion. For example, the number of freight containers handled by the world's ports increased from 6.3 million in 1972 to 163.7 million in 1997, while prices on the Asia-U.S. route dropped by an inflation-adjusted 65 percent during the same time period (Taggart 1999).

Although shipping costs have dropped significantly, communication and data processing costs have fallen far more precipitously, while international (and national) bandwidth has grown dramatically. For example, the annual cost of leasing an E-1 telecommunications circuit from New York to London dropped from $125,000 in October 1998 to approximately $10,000 in February 2002, an annual decrease of 50 percent per year (Telegeography 2002). Put differently, the investment cost per minute decreased from $2.443 per minute in 1956 to $0.001 in 2001 (Blake and Lande 2001). The decreasing cost of communications permits the transmission of ever greater amounts of information in real time, thereby keeping upstream participants in the value chain better informed, allowing them to make more timely decisions, thus decreasing uncertainty. The Internet has created even more opportunities to use communications systems to rationalize the value chain (see, for example, Hammond and Kohler 2001; Kenney and Curry 2001; Fields 2003).

Users can take advantage of the availability of low-cost communications bandwidth to develop innovative solutions to production and distribution bottlenecks, thereby minimizing the impediments to the flow of goods. For example, new information systems make it possible to pack garments into shipping containers in Hong Kong properly ordered so that they can be unloaded directly into U.S. retail stores. This eliminates the need to unload the container en route, thereby saving time and money (Taggart 1999). As another example, Leachman and Leachman show that these communication networks permit real-time monitoring by Silicon Valley chip designers of the progress of their orders in Taiwanese fabrication facilities.

In the contemporary market, delivery times are often more important than prices; failure to get the right part or component or even the finished product to the right place at the right time may cause bottlenecks and adversely affect an entire value chain—or simply miss the market. We are witnessing the unfolding of a system capable of ever more closely synchronizing production with demand, thereby removing inventory that is not in motion. The continuing improvement in logistics of air, sea, and land freight continues to drive transportation costs down, while computational advances combined with less expensive communication technologies are increasing the predictability and transparency of the supply chain. But most powerfully, each advance creates the base for yet further experimentation.

*Time and Speed*

Clock time appears to be invariant. And yet, each industry operates on a different tempo. Transportation and communications are only one dimension of the time equation with which managers wrestle (Fine 1998; Kenney and Curry 1999). Businesses must constantly grapple with the relationship between space and time (Schoenberger 1997). One salient expression of this is just-in-time production, which was introduced to the U.S. automobile industry by Japanese manufacturers (Womack et al. 1990). On a more fundamental level, the history of capitalism indicates a secular trend toward an accelerating pace. With the exception of the television industry, accelerating the tempo of activity seems a central concern of managers. The character of globalization is shaped by the emphasis on time and speed.

The preoccupation with time management is not new to contemporary industry.[6] For example, the standardization of time into time zones was spearheaded by the railroad firms (O'Malley 1990). However, today's firms face more complex temporal dimensions than those contained in simple concepts such as transit times (Curry and Kenney 1999). For example, as Abernathy et al. indicate, location and distance affect the placement of activities, but that is only the most obvious dimension of temporality. More recently, other temporal dimensions such as speed to market and speed in terms of ramping up production have become considerations for globalization. In the case of hard disk drives (HDDs), McKendrick shows how important managing a rapid production ramp-up in Singapore is for corporate success. In the case of the semiconductor industry, Leachman and Leachman show how being late to the market can significantly depress profitability. Even the automobile industry has been pressing to shorten its three-year design cycles.

Technological time and its grim reaper, obsolescence, are central issues in a number of chapters.[7] Each of our chapters on HDDs, personal computers, flat panels, and semiconductors indicates that they are plagued by endemic and rapid technological change that inexorably devalues yesterday's products. As Abernathy et al. show, in "fashion-forward" garments, a similar dynamic is manifested because of the creativity of designers and the changing sensibilities of customers. For these items, the market value of products is transient and product life spans are truncated. A fashion-forward item or personal computer idling in a shipping container on the way from a distant low-cost production site could easily lose much of its value prior to being unpacked. This obsolescence threat affects an industry's spatial fix—that is, where various activities are undertaken (Harvey 1982).

Producers of assembled goods can have an even more difficult situation because components may "age" at different speeds. For example, as Curry and Kenney show, a personal computer contains components such as fans, the case, and floppy drives that age very slowly, and components such as semiconductors and HDDs that age very rapidly. Within a single box, the effect of time varies dramatically by component. The components that are most subject to aging should, of course, be purchased as close as possible to the time when the final consumer purchases the PC.

Temporal dynamics color the industrial organization and geography of each industry. In the emerging industrial environment characterized by rapid new product development and accelerated production and delivery times (D'Aveni 1994), slower-moving firms will find that moving production to lowest-cost foreign labor sites will not necessarily prevent them from being outflanked. As our chapters show, for some firms the temporal dynamics are forcing a relocation of certain functions closer to the final customer, while in other cases it has meant that there must be a closer integration between value chain nodes in different countries.

## Pricing Pressure and Overcapacity

Competition has always been fierce, but during the last decade it appears to have become more ferocious than ever. Japan is already grappling with deflation, which some believe is occurring in the United States. Every industry in this book suffers pricing pressure, which is manifested at the macroeconomic level by price declines, or, at least, near price stagnation, combined with strong productivity growth. In 2002, overcapacity plagued the auto, PC, television, HDD, and semiconductor industries, though in semiconductors this was previously a cyclical phenomenon. In industries such as garments and televisions, which are dependent on large retailers (or what Gereffi 1994 terms buyer-driven chains), profit margins are thin, even for Wal-Mart. In DRAMs, Flat Panel Displays (FPDs), and HDDs, profits are cyclical and only the leaders experience profits during the positive portions of their business cycles. With the exception of Dell, none of the major PC firms enjoy predictable profits—and Dell as the price leader continues to drive prices lower. For most firms the pressures appear only to be increasing.

The intense pricing pressure forces a continual reassessment not only of the proper spatial location of value-chain activities but also whether to perform them internally or to outsource them. As Sturgeon and Florida show in autos, outsourcing has resulted in an increase in jobs among the parts suppliers employing less expensive, usually nonunionized labor as opposed to the high-wage unionized assemblers. In addition, the importation of finished automobiles from lower-wage production facilities in Mexico continues to increase, though U.S. parts exports to Mexico increased apace. In the PC industry, Dell recently introduced a very low price machine (retail $499) assembled by the Taiwanese firm Mitac in China and shipped directly to the customer. Each ratcheting down of prices conditions consumers to expect still lower prices, thus placing pressure on rivals to match the reduction or face a market share loss.

For many of these industries, the endemic overcapacity has been insoluble. Sturgeon and Florida describe this problem for the auto industry: even while the industry suffers from global overcapacity, Japanese and European assemblers continue expanding factories and building new plants in North America. In 2001 semiconductor overcapacity was perhaps the worst it has ever been, as a result of a boom in plant construction during the late 1990s and a slump in consumer demand. With prices stagnant, the only way to increase profits is either to lower costs or to increase efficiency. Locating a plant or some of the processes in a lower factor cost environment can momentarily overcome the price pressure problem. And yet, paradoxically, this often increases global capacity.

With the high cost of labor in developed nations, there is a constant temptation to relocate not only routine production, but also engineering and other activities, to lower wage environments. Skilled personnel are not uniformly distributed, however, so relocation is constrained by the capabilities of the workforce. Because of the pricing pressure, China has become the destination of choice for relocated production activities, a shift that both solves and exacerbates overcapacity and the downward pressure on prices. However, even for developing nations such as Malaysia and Mexico, which are losing production to China, there is the possibility of upgrading. It should be possible to carve out production niches by further increasing the division of labor. And yet, despite all of this turbulence, design, R&D, and marketing have largely remained located in their traditional havens, where labor costs are high. In the meantime, manufacturing or certain manufacturing processes have been relocated, often repeatedly.[8] Most recently, firms have begun offshoring some of their business processes to nations like India (Dossani and Kenney 2003).

Overcapacity and downward pressure on prices appear to be inextricably linked with globalization. For routine assembly activities, the allure of low wages is powerful, but not overwhelming. The continuing brutal competition almost surely means that overcapacity will remain high, as firms continue to ramp up production in lower-cost environments. This could be further exacerbated if the deflationary environment continues.

## Knowledge, Capabilities, and Clusters

The relationship between specialized knowledge and clusters has been recognized since at least Alfred Marshall (1890). Outside of economic geography, this insight was largely ignored by the social sciences. Then in the early 1980s, clustering once again attracted scholarly attention from outside the geography community. The enormous interest in the book *The Second Industrial Divide* by Michael Piore and Charles Sabel (1984) heralded this reawakening.[9] In the early 1990s, economist Paul Krugman (1991) and business strategy professor Michael Porter (1990) highlighted the importance of clusters for business performance. These contributions and others sparked a line of research examining the linkages between firms and the external knowledge in their locational environment (see Almeida and Kogut 1997, 1999; Jaffe et al. 1993; Kogut 2000). Brown and Duguid (2000b) explained this by the participation of the denizens of these regions in networks of practice through which knowledge and information flow.[10] Murtha et al. persuasively illustrate the importance of active participation in the knowledge creation process by recounting how the U.S. firms that actively participated in creating the FPD cluster in Japan profited handsomely. Most significant, those U.S. firms choosing not to participate in that localized knowledge-creation process, which in this case was concentrated in Japan, were unable to enter the industry profitably. Paraphrasing the Peter Sellers movie, being there is important.

Industries are based on sets of knowledge bases and capabilities that are created, at least temporarily, spatially fixed, and exercised in specific social environments (Brown and Duguid 2000b; Kogut 2000; Kogut et al. 1993; Dunning 2000). Very broadly speaking, an industry can either cluster or not, and then a cluster can either consist of rivals (i.e., a horizontal cluster) or complementary firms (i.e., vertical clusters) such as suppliers and customers—or contain both.[11] The industries in this book exhibit a spectrum of clustering behaviors.[12] For example, the PC industry exhibits little clustering outside of Taiwan (and now China), where manufacturing is clustered, while in HDDs, as McKendrick shows, there is a dominant design cluster in Silicon Valley and a production cluster centered in Singapore.

As Kogut indicates in his concluding chapter, the relationships between multinational firms and regions are complex and contingent and should be understood in processual terms rather than as single events. Our chapters indicate a complicated skein within which there is an interaction between firm-based knowledge and region-based knowledge that is difficult to fully disentangle, quite specific, tacit, and even inimitable (Gertler 2001). The firm-based knowledge is, as Kogut argues in his conclusion, embedded in routines and may be transmitted transnationally, though not without friction, difficulty, and frequent failure. Regional knowledge is far more constrained to place and contexts. Brown and Duguid (2000b) perceptively note that Xerox Palo Alto Research Center had enormous difficulty transferring knowledge inside Xerox, but the knowledge transferred nearly effortlessly to the surrounding Silicon Valley community. Thus firms have internal knowledge that they can attempt to transmit internally, even while they absorb external knowledge and contribute to a knowledge commons (Kogut and Zander 1992).

*Proximity to the Customer*

From the Anglo-Portuguese wine industry to the PC industry, proximity to customers can make the difference. As shown in each of the chapters, firms must decide the relative importance of proximity to customers. Given the increasing efficiency of transportation and communications, it might be thought that low factor costs would become the dominant aspect of deciding where to locate. However, in a number of value chains, proximity to customers can modify and even in some cases overwhelm factor costs such as inexpensive labor. The importance of proximity to customers can be driven by very different reasons. For example, in the auto industry the importance of customer proximity at the international level is driven by a combination of trade barriers and an ability to better understand the market by immersion in it. At the macro-regional level, the strong supplier base in the U.S. Midwest helps offset the high costs of labor and thus continues to attract investment, if not directly in the Midwest, then in the Middle South. In personal computers, Dell has been remarkably successful by assembling computers in the market within which they will be sold (with the exception of the previously mentioned low-priced machine assembled in China). However, in the Dell case the location of the supplier's production is not as significant an issue as proximity to the final customer. The chapters carefully examine the role of proximity in determining location.

Each segment of the value chain has a downstream customer. Thus, there are a number of supplier-customer relations, each of which might require a different spatial configuration. In some cases, the market is another set of downstream corporations, while in other cases, it is the final consumer. In textiles, as Abernathy et al. demonstrate, it is the rapidity of change in the tastes of the final consumer in particular products that determines the most efficient production location. On the other hand, Murtha finds that in the case of FPDs, for U.S. equipment and materials makers, proximity to customers was critically important, while proximity to U.S. notebook computer vendors did not appear to be of great significance for the FPD producers. Most interestingly, it is also possible that the necessity of proximity may also shift over time as production cost factors, the role of tacit knowledge, and brand strength change.

The detailed research in these chapters highlights the fact that proximity to customers is often loosely used, and that it is more valuable to consider which corporate function(s) should be located in close proximity to the customer. For example, is proximity required for R&D, design, headquarters, and/or manufacturing, and why? In the auto industry, Sturgeon and Florida show that the new global suppliers have been pressured to locate their R&D facilities close to their auto assembler customers' R&D facilities. In garments and textiles, there seems to be little pressure to locate any functions close to each other. In the PC industry, Dell requires that suppliers except Intel place a warehouse within twenty minutes of its assembly facilities. In the television industry, there seem to be no immediate clustering requirements regarding R&D or television tube facilities, although over the longer run the tube facilities are attracted to large clusters of TV assembly plants, because of the costs and risks of transporting tubes long distances. Our chapters show that it is necessary to decompose the concept of proximity to customer and comprehend when and what makes proximity economically attractive.

## The Chapters

This book is divided into three parts. The first examines globalization in three mature industries in order of their chronological emergence: garments/textiles, automobiles/auto parts, and televisions. The garments industry pioneered the Industrial Revolution, and the auto industry pioneered mass production. The television industry built upon the pre–World War II radio industry and grew quickly in the postwar period, but by the early 1970s it had become a relatively mature industry. The end-users for the products of these three industries are household consumers, and brands are extremely important for their success. Given their long histories and the development of powerful interest groups, these industries also are far more subject to government intervention in the form of tariffs, duties, quotas, and various other trade restraints.

Globalization in the garment and textile industry is fascinating, because despite the fact that it is one of the oldest industries, success depends on closely tracking consumer preferences. Since it is a fashion industry and consumers are fickle, inventory risk is a pervasive problem. Garment production was one of the first industries to be moved offshore because of the relative lack of skills needed for assembly processes and the low-capital intensity. The casual observer accepts that it is natural for garment production to move to the lowest cost environment, particularly given the enormous pricing pressure on manufacturers. Drawing upon their book *A Stitch in Time*, in Chapter 2 Abernathy et al. show that for certain garments, a new locational logic has emerged motivated by what they term "lean retailing." In this system, retailers carry only minimal inventory, finding that it is more economical to rapidly replenish goods that have sold. Lean inventory decreases the risk of holding stocks that might become obsolete with a quick change in consumer preference. However, leanness implies that the danger of being out of stock increases. Rapid replenishment depends upon having factories close to the end market and linked to retailers by sophisticated communications systems. This desire for rapid replenishment has led to a production shift for many types of garments for the U.S. market from Asia to the Caribbean Basin and Mexico, while in Western Europe production is being relocated from Asia to North Africa and Eastern Europe. Firms must balance between production and transportation costs and speed, which, in rough measure, is a function of distance and transportation modality. They explore the trade-offs that garment firms must make when deciding where to source their production. This is illustrated by a provocative demonstration of how low labor costs can be offset by the inventory cost savings and risk reduction that can be achieved by producing in a higher cost environment in closer proximity to the customer.

The third chapter, on the automobile industry, provides insight into many facets of globalization. The automobile is a particularly interesting product, because it is the paragon of the mass production system, and with more than thirty thousand individual parts, it is the most complicated and bulky mass-assembled product. Because of the large number of parts and interdependence involved, Sturgeon and Florida study the globalization of both the auto assemblers and their major suppliers. Given its complexity and importance to national governments, globalization in the automotive industry has always had a political dimension.

They argue that there are four different forms of globalization underway in the industry. The first form of globalization is characterized by increasing imports and exports, though they predict that this trend will decline because of the second form, which consists of the establishment of assembly plants in closer proximity to the final consumer. The impact of this form of globalization will be moderated by a movement to establish new plants in low-wage nations, such as Mexico for the United States market and Spain and Eastern Europe for the Western European market. Because of this, they predict that the shipment of automobiles across oceans will decrease. However, the new plants being established by foreign competitors are exacerbating an already severe overcapacity problem that is driving prices down. The third form is the cross-national consolidation through merger and acquisition of the industry into an ever fewer number of major auto assemblers. The final form is the globalization of vehicle platforms and models as the same vehicle is introduced in a number of different markets. The evolution of these different forms not only affects the auto assemblers but also is propelling the establishment of global parts suppliers that can service their customers in every market. However, these new forms are not simply spreading automobile production uniformly over the landscape, since transplants tend to be sited relatively close to traditional automobile manufacturing regions, albeit with some shifts to proximate, lower-wage environments. More important, Sturgeon and Florida find that global design clusters are emerging, given the increasing need for interaction between auto assemblers and parts suppliers earlier in the vehicle design process. Their chapter richly illustrates the multiple dimensions of globalization, and how the interaction between assemblers and parts suppliers affects the dimensions of globalization.

In the fourth chapter by Martin Kenney, the long sweep of globalization in the television industry is examined using North America as a case study. The spatial configuration of the value chain for televisions, unlike that for automobiles, has shifted substantially during the last five decades as it has for a number of other industries in this book. And yet, transportation and communication, though significant, have not profoundly influenced the industry. What has been most important is finding relatively low cost labor pools in reasonably close proximity to the final consumer. In terms of speed of change and obsolescence, of course, shrinking inventory is important, but televisions do not experience the same loss of value dynamics as garments and PCs. However, since televisions are commodities, price pressures are ferocious.

Chapter 4 examines the shifting location of television production, and documents the reasons for the growth and decline of U.S. firms and domestic production. Fittingly, this globalization begins with RCA's transfer of technology to Japan and ends with the relocation of television production to northern Mexico. Segmenting the television value chain into components, color picture tubes (CPTs), and final assembly provides the reader with greater insight into the unfolding and constantly changing map of globalization, which in the case of North America ends with a production cluster created by Asian firms in northern Mexico to serve the U.S. market. This Mexican production cluster that began with simple assembly has deepened as it has attracted an increasing number of parts makers from Asia and CPT producers from the United States, drawn by Mexico's proximity to U.S. consumers.

Part II examines globalization in the new industries formed in the postwar period. In Chapter 5, James Curry and Martin Kenney examine the dynamics of globalization in the personal computer industry, which plays a major role as a consumer of the outputs of the component industries studied in the chapters that follow. Its juxtaposition with the television industry discussed in the previous chapter is also fascinating because the PC shares so many similarities with the television in terms of assembly process and components; in fact many believe these two products might converge.

As Linden et al. in their chapter and, to a lesser degree, Murtha et al. in their chapter argue, the centrality of the desktop PC may decline in the case of semiconductors and FPDs. This may also be true in the HDD industry with the advent of TiVo, which uses an HDD to record television programs. Thus the television might compete with the PC even if the proverbial convergence never occurs, and it will provide new outlets for the components discussed in Part II.

Another feature distinguishing the industries in Part II is that they experience value erosion based on the speed of technical change. They share this emphasis on speed with the oldest industry in Part I, garments, revealing that technical change and fashion experience similar loss-of-value dynamics.

The PC industry is characterized by extremely rapid change caused by the devaluation of its constituent semiconductors and the HDD. This rapid pace creates a business environment in which proximity to the final customer is especially important because long transit times for a finished PC can lead to significant losses of value.

This intense pace of depreciation creates an interesting anomaly. Taiwan is the only discernible PC cluster in the world, housing the headquarters for firms that in factories situated around the world assemble more than 50 percent of all PCs sold; yet the most important brand name firms are not located in this cluster. The reason is that the highly modular nature of the PC with its rigorously specified interfaces between components means that tacit knowledge about production is not especially important. Proximity to the market is more critical. Thus, while one might think that the ease of assembly and ready availability of all the constituent components of the PC would allow Asian firms to gain dominance, this is not the case. U.S. firms dominate the industry because they not only provide the components with the greatest value added but also are located in, and can learn from, the world's largest market and its highly sophisticated customers.

The next three chapters discuss industries that produce the three most valuable PC components, and the concluding industrial chapter argues that, at least in semiconductors, a "post-PC" world is dawning. In Chapter 6, McKendrick draws upon and extends his research, first presented in the book *From Silicon Valley to Singapore*, to elucidate how the dynamics of globalization affect the HDD industry. The HDD is the final major assembled component in the PC that continues to be dominated by U.S. producers. This chapter traces the historical evolution of the spatial configuration of the manufacturing, R&D, and headquarters functions. It finds that R&D and headquarters functions continue to be clustered in Silicon Valley, with a smaller cluster in Japan, even while manufacturing is concentrated in Asia, especially Southeast Asia and China. In fact, the HDD industry demonstrates that it is possible to internalize both R&D and manufacturing within the firm and manage both processes, though they occur on different continents. HDDs resemble semiconductors and FPDs in that they experience rapid change, short product cycles, and severe cost pressures. However, in contrast to semiconductors and FPDs, an HDD consists of a relatively large number of components that must be physically assembled to very tight tolerances. As in the case of DRAMs, the need for speed, cost, and quality have meant that the leading firms have integrated much of the value chain and conduct manufacturing in-house. In contrast to PCs, consumer proximity was not necessary for the HDD industry.

In Chapter 7, Murtha et al., drawing upon their book *Managing New Industry Creation*, examine the global dimensions of the establishment and growth of the flat panel display industry. They show how the initial research was undertaken in the United States, but the commercialization occurred in Japan, where an early cluster of FPD manufacturers and equipment makers ignited a knowledge-creation dynamic that soon outdistanced firms not located in the cluster. They differ from conventional accounts by showing how a number of U.S. firms that embedded themselves in and contributed to this knowledge-creation dynamic experienced great success. In FPDs, globalization was a process of participating in a very local knowledge-creation dynamic. For materials and equipment suppliers, proximity to lead customers was vital for success, because of the great amount of tacit information that was both exchanged and mutually created.

The semiconductor has probably been the most important artifact of the second half of the twentieth century. Semiconductors are the devices that process data; they are components that make computing and the Information Age possible. Semiconductors share a technical commonality with FPDs—namely, they are both based upon the substrate silicon. Unfortunately, the market for semiconductors is treacherous because of notoriously rapid improvement cycles, escalating capital expenditures, and brutal competition.

The final two industrial chapters comprising Part II examine the semiconductor industry from different perspectives. In Chapter 8, Leachman and Leachman examine the status and development of semiconductor production along two dimensions: spatial location and the organizational integration of the design and production functions. The pattern of globalization varies depending upon the type of semiconductor being produced. In the case of microprocessors and DRAMs, producers continue to integrate design and manufacturing, although for different reasons. In the case of logic chips, a surprising spatial and organizational division of labor has emerged. This chapter explains the reasons why Taiwan has developed a cadre of firms that specialize in logic chip fabrication for companies around the world. They show how these Taiwanese chip foundries provide a "market-based collective action" solution to problems that the design firms face.

Linden, Brown, and Appleyard complement the chapter by Leachman and Leachman by examining the relationship between designers of logic chips and their customers. They suggest that the locational patterns of the semiconductor industry may be transformed by a shift of revenues and profits away from the PC world epitomized by the U.S. firm Intel (by far the most profitable semiconductor firm in the world) toward telecommunications products. They argue that the proliferation of communication devices using a variety of competing standards combined with regional differences in communications infrastructure presents an opportunity for semiconductor firms that are rooted in Europe or Asia and have strong relationships with telecommunications providers. They feel that this will lead to a shift from the PC world in which U.S. semiconductor firms were dominant to a pattern in which dominance will accrue to the semiconductor firm best able to form alliances with network owners such as NTT DoCoMo, Deutsche Telekom, or SingTel, which will begin to drive the functionality designed into the semiconductor.

The concluding chapter by Bruce Kogut synthesizes and extends the findings of the industry chapters into a more comprehensive understanding of globalization. The central actor in his understanding is the multinational corporation (MNC), which is an agent in the diffusion of knowledge embedded in artifacts, industrial processes, and organizational routines through its cross-border activities. And yet he finds that, despite their global reach, the MNCs are unable to escape "the pull of geography." This pull is due to the knowledge and capabilities embedded in regions. Further, these regional qualities are not static but rather evolve and increase in tandem with economic action; learning-by-doing is a powerful force for localization. Through their purposive action and interaction with other local institutions, the MNCs modify the global geography of knowledge and capabilities. This contribution allows the reader to see the earlier chapters in new ways by interpreting and extending the chapter findings.

## Conclusion

Globalization will continue to be a topic of intense debate. These contributions will not end that debate; however it is our hope that they will contribute to a more nuanced understanding of the actual dimensions of globalization. Whereas the debate has treated globalization as a uniform phenomenon, our chapters show that it has proceeded differently in each industry. I have identified five dynamics that are present in all of these industries. The chapters will show that these dynamics are shaped by the contours of each industry.

Although the chapters are about firms, the reader will immediately notice the importance of places. Locating global advantage is about firms finding locations with favorable factor prices, but it is also, as Kogut asserts, about how firms interact with those places to evolve positive externalities such as improved skill levels in the workforce, the creation or attraction of suppliers, and an infrastructure of collective goods such as universities, research institutions, and transportation or communications facilities. Such developments can actually magnify the pull of geography over time and permit the activities undertaken in that location to climb the value-added ladder. Conversely, other developments can diminish the efficacy of one place and promote another—such as the movement of the locus of television production from the United States to Mexico. These chapters illustrate what Storper and Walker (1989) have referred to as the inconstant geography of capitalism.

These chapters will show policy-makers that the impacts of globalization differ by industry and the particular configuration of its value chain. For example, had the U.S. government intervened in the HDD industry to prevent manufacturing jobs from going offshore, it is likely that they would have destroyed the entire industry. In the case of the FPD industry, Murtha et al. show that U.S. government intervention led to catastrophic results for those firms obeying government dictums. The U.S. firms that plunged into the industry-creation process in Japan were amply rewarded. In the television industry, repeated government efforts to save U.S. firms failed. However, in response, Japanese television firms moved operations to the United States and, at least for two decades, ensured that U.S. workers were employed. All of these chapters demonstrate that policy must be shaped with the industry realities and dynamics in mind; otherwise it will fail either mildly or, in certain cases, catastrophically.

These chapters communicate the excitement and enjoyment we all have experienced during our studies. We believe that only through intensive study of specific industries and its firms can one understand the rhythm of business. This work is not easy, as firms and industries are among the most complicated social structures created by human beings. They are shaped by, and help to shape, not only physical space but also labor markets, communities, and even our cultural heritage. It is our hope that this book will inform policy-makers and encourage yet more scholars to study the microdynamics of globalization.

## Notes

1. We do not take a position in the debate on the nature of either the firm or the multinational corporation, and likely our authors would disagree among themselves—something that we editors appreciate, because we do not believe that these debates are closed. Ours is a more limited focus; we seek to provide solid empirical studies that those interested in these issues can use for their theory building. On the nature of the firm, there is almost an inexhaustible literature; some of the classics are Kogut and Zander (1992), Nelson and Winter (1982), Penrose (1959), and Williamson (1985). On the nature of the firm from the organizational capabilities perspective, an important recent edited contribution is Dosi et al. (2000). For the literature on the MNE, classic citations include Dunning (1980), Hamel and Prahalad (1994), Porter (1985), and Vernon (1971).

2. An excellent cross-national comparative perspective is Dunning (1997).

3. For an excellent further discussion of the relative merits of these two terms for chains and their intellectual merger, see Gereffi (2001).

4. In the import-export databases, this is reported as Harmonized Tariff Schedule number 85415000.

5. For discussions of containerization and air freight, see Taggart (1999) and Lappin (1996). The importance of transportation for the economic growth of capitalism has been recognized by economists at least as far back as Karl Marx. Marx paid special attention to improvements in terms of speed. In more recent times, economists, especially Douglass North (1958, 1968), have examined the impacts of ocean freight rates. They were less interested in measuring—or perhaps less able to measure—the importance of qualitative changes such as increased speed and reliability. For modern just-in-time production systems, reliability is as important as speed, and, in certain cases, as important as cost. Reliability has become a major criterion for judging supplier quality.

6. One of the first economists to consider the importance of time for capitalist businesses was Karl Marx (1981). Of particular interest here is the discussion of circulation time—that is, the time goods spend outside the production process. For businesses, the time a good spends idling is money lost. The time and motion studies of Fredrick Winslow Taylor focused largely on time when the worker was not in motion, but also displayed much interest in greater efficiency in goods handling. Given the significance of time, it is remarkable how little theoretical attention it has received.

7. For a discussion of the interaction between knowledge creation and obsolescence, see Kenney (2001).

8. Florida (2002) discusses the desire of the most creative individuals to live in pleasant environments. For tasks requiring these kinds of labor power, firms do not have unfettered locational flexibility.

9. Roughly contemporaneously, geographers including Michael Storper, Richard

Walker, and Allen Scott were undertaking research on business clusters, or what they termed "agglomeration economies." See, for example, Storper and Walker (1989) or Scott (1988); for a more recent discussion, see Sayer and Walker (1993).

10. The classic citation on embeddedness is Granovetter (1985).

11. The literature on clustering and the reasons for clustering is enormous. See, for example, Krugman (1991) and Harrison (1996).

12. There have been a large number of taxonomies of districts offered. See, for example, Krugman (1991) and Markusen (1999).

PART ONE

# CHAPTER TWO

# Globalization in the Apparel and Textile Industries

## What Is New and What Is Not?

FREDERICK H. ABERNATHY

JOHN T. DUNLOP

JANICE H. HAMMOND

DAVID WEIL

## Introduction

In the first half of the nineteenth century, American vessels carried Indian (and later American) cotton to Britain, and Lancashire goods to Asia. In the latter half of the nineteenth century, American cotton cloth competed actively in China, temporarily dominating the market in North China and Manchuria. As the quality of yarn and cloth manufactured in Japan and China rose during the first decades of the twentieth century, demand grew for American cotton, which displaced the shorter-staple Indian fiber. Particularly after World War I, when Japan developed techniques for blending American and coarser cottons, American cotton came to dominate the Asian cotton trade. The United States was also active in exporting textile machinery.[1]

It would be disingenuous to deem globalization of the textile and apparel industries a recent phenomenon. As the above quotation from Bruce Reynolds makes clear, the movement of textile and apparel products across international boundaries predates recent decades or even the twentieth century. Indeed, international trade in apparel and textiles goes back well before the periods described above and has been a favorite example of the gains from trade used by economists going back to David Ricardo. So what is all the fuss about the globalization of the textile and apparel industries?

The answer is that there is "old news" and "new news" in this story. The old news is that the movement of apparel and textile products between nations arises from the comparative factor costs and productivities for labor, capital and other inputs between nations and their impact on product costs, as modified by transportation, insurance, and related costs. Old news is that the flow of goods is mediated by changes in international exchange rates, as evidenced most recently during the Asian fiscal crisis. Finally, quotas and tariffs continue to affect global trade of apparel and textile products now, as they have for centuries, given the changing desire of countries to protect their nascent apparel and textile industries (often viewed as the foundation of industrialization policies) from foreign competition.[2]

So, is there anything "new" about the globalization of apparel and textiles? This question has particular policy salience given that the current system of bilateral agreements on quotas for apparel and textiles (the Multi-Fiber Arrangement) that has been in place for decades will come to an end in 2005 and that in the years following, China will also became a full player in a quota-free world of trade under the World Trade Organization (WTO). Many commentators surveying and forecasting the future scene rely on the "old news" factors described above and forecast rapid shifts in the sourcing of global textile and apparel, with most of those goods moving to low-wage nations in Asia, especially China. This view is evinced by many U.S. textile and apparel manufacturers, government agencies, labor union officials, and the governments of nations that, as we shall see, have been recent beneficiaries of globalization.

There is also "new news" to be told about globalization. That news challenges some of the notions about what will drive change in the flow of apparel and textile goods in the next decades. Although factor prices and comparative productivity, exchange rates, transportation costs, and tariffs will continue to affect patterns of sourcing, a new set of factors related to the distribution of products plays an increasingly important role.

Before looking at actual patterns of trade in the United States, we sketch out the important changes that have occurred in the distribution of products in the U.S. market. We then, through a brief presentation of a model of on-shore versus off-shore production, demonstrate why the calculus of sourcing decisions has changed. With this as grounding, we turn to the evidence on the national origins of apparel products sold in the U.S. market and describe major shifts in those sourcing patterns. We then analyze the role of "old" and "new" factors in explaining the shifts. Given the major changes in trade laws that will affect (some say transform) the global sourcing of apparel and textile trade, we assess the impact of projected changes in trade agreements in 2005 and beyond on patterns of apparel and textile sourcing in light of our findings. We conclude by relating our work on apparel and textiles to the general themes of this volume.

## New Factors in Global Sourcing: Lean Retailing and the Supplier Problem

### Lean Retailing and Product Proliferation

Two changes profoundly affect the problems faced by suppliers of consumer industries: the spread of a new form of retail distribution in the United States, "lean retailing," which now characterizes much of the retail sector; and increasing product proliferation of consumer goods. Lean retailing and product proliferation together change the basic production problem facing suppliers and supply chains. As we will develop below, this in turn changes one of the key drivers of international sourcing of apparel products.

In contrast to the infrequent, large bulk shipments between apparel manufacturers and retailers under the traditional retail model, lean retailers require frequent shipments made on the basis of ongoing replenishment orders placed by the retailer. These orders are made based on real-time sales information at the stock-keeping unit level (or SKU, the specification of the product at the most detailed level), which is collected at the retailer's registers via bar code scanning and aggregated centrally. Orders based on these data are sent to suppliers, often weekly for each store. With the advent of lean retailing, suppliers must replenish a higher percentage of their products within a selling season. Rather than specifying that manufacturers respond to a single, fixed order placed far in advance of required delivery time, leading lean retailers require that a replenishment order be filled in as little as three days (Abernathy et al. 1999, 2000a). The diffusion of lean retailing across different channels of retail distribution—mass merchants, department stores, specialty stores—means that apparel and textile suppliers now replenish a high percentage of their products within a selling season.[3]

Product proliferation compounds the problem posed by lean retailing because suppliers must provide a growing number of products on a replenishment basis. Even the apparent sameness of products like men's dress shirts masks a much larger set of offerings. A Lands' End pinpoint cotton oxford dress shirt, available only in white or blue, seems the most basic of apparel. Along with the usual choice of neck and sleeve length, the customer may choose from four collar types and three cuts (regular, trim, and tall). The total number of combinations available to consumers of this basic dress shirt adds up to 577.[4] Yet this represents only one line of men's pinpoint dress shirts offered by the company. Add to it other weights and types of fabric, solid colors, stripes, plaids, and styles, and the number of offerings quickly goes into the tens of thousands.

Product proliferation means that a quantity of demand that might have been spread across a hundred different products in 1980 might now be spread across a thousand. If those products are provided on a replenishment basis, each week the supplier awaits the electronic "call" of its retail customers to tell which one should be sent. For many products, the call may be an infrequent and unpredictable event—even for a large manufacturer.

Take the case of a major jeans manufacturer that sells about 100 million pairs of jeans per year. Since the manufacturer carries somewhere between 25,000 and 40,000 SKUs at one time, average annual sales per SKU equal between 2,500 and 4,000. That means it will sell on average only between forty-eight and seventy-seven units of a typical SKU per week. Although popular SKUs may sell ten or even a hundred times as many per week, less popular items may sell less than ten in any week *across all retail stores in the United States.*

The confluence of product proliferation and lean retailing profoundly changes the problem faced by a supplier. Supplier responsiveness to replenishment orders is central to lean retailing. Dealing with variability in demand has therefore become crucial to suppliers competing in a lean retailing world. Even for basic products, demand varies from day to day and from week to week. Thus, even if a retailer follows the simplest strategy of ordering at the beginning of each week exactly those items that sold during the previous week, manufacturers must be prepared to ship an unknown number of items each week. Since very few manufacturers can produce items in the limited lead time retailers allow for replenishment, they must fill such orders from their finished goods inventory. And, as one would expect, the higher the variation in week-to-week demand, the more inventory relative to average demand a manufacturer must hold to meet retailers' high service expectations.

### The Manufacturer's Problem and Its Impact on Global Sourcing

Most apparel producers search for ways to decrease their production costs. One of the most popular is to go to offshore producers or contractors that have lower labor costs, even though their transportation costs and lead times are higher than for local producers. A manufacturer providing goods to the U.S. market must balance the benefits of more proximate but costly sources that offer short-cycle local production against lower-cost offshore operations that require far longer lead times.

Lean retailing demands that an apparel manufacturer be able to fill retailers' orders on three to five days' notice; hence the requested items must be in finished goods, ready to pick and pack to meet the individual store's specific orders. The replenishment orders for any given SKU vary considerably from week to week, even when the orders from all retail outlets are aggregated. To meet this weekly variation in demand, the apparel manufacturer must carry significant levels of finished goods for each SKU; the amount varies from SKU to SKU depending on its demand variability.

A measure of the variability of demand for a given SKU is its coefficient of variation ($C_V$ is defined as the standard deviation of weekly demand divided by the average weekly demand). In modeling the sourcing decision, we use the $C_V$ of each SKU in a given style as one of the inputs to the production scheduling process. Other inputs are the factory cycle time (the time from placing an order until it is delivered to the manufacturer's Distribution Center [DC]), the cost of fabric and trim delivered to the factory, the labor cost of assembly and shipping to the DC, and the cost of capital to finance the work-in-process (WIP) and finished goods (FG) inventory.

Generally speaking, if you assemble products in locations distant from the retail market in order to take advantage of existing low labor costs, then transportation costs are higher and lead times longer than if you assembled the garments closer to the DC. If you assemble far away and use low-cost transportation, the cycle time is much longer than if you manufacture closer to the DC. If your distant factory's cycle time is much longer than the nearby plant's, then to provide the same level of service to retailers, the FG inventory levels must be higher than if you used a shorter cycle plant, because it would take a long time to correct the FG inventory when there are unexpectedly high sales of a given SKU. High $C_V$ SKUs might have a particular week's demand eight to ten times the average; therefore the FGs must be more than eight to ten weeks of average demand, because the week following the very high demand might also be higher than average.

Lean retailers wish to minimize their in-store inventory for each SKU, hence retailers' demand that their orders be fulfilled at a very high rate, typically 95 percent or higher. Such order fulfillment constraints imply higher FG inventories. Without retailers' constraints on order fulfillment or the penalties they assign to suppliers with low service levels, it might be more profitable for a manufacturer to miss an occasional sale to a retailer rather than carry the inventory to meet the demand. The importance of this constraint to the supplier depends on the profit margin of a sale and the cost of capital to finance the inventory.

The following simulation illustrates the trade-offs facing such a firm.[5] The simulation allows us to compare the profit and inventory levels from using different combinations of a short-cycle local plant and a much slower offshore plant. In this example, it is assumed that the production costs of the short-cycle plant are 20 percent higher than the offshore plant and the production cycle times are two weeks (short cycle) and eleven weeks (offshore). The scheduling algorithm employed in the simulation involves loading the short-cycle plant

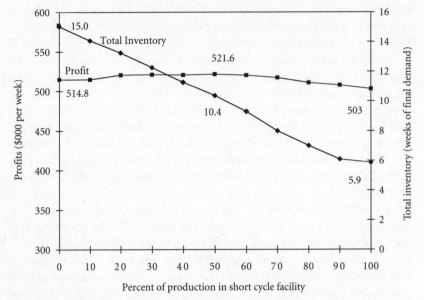

FIG. 2.1. Impact of Short Cycle Manufacturing on Profits and Inventory, Simulation Results. Cycle time of the short cycle plant = 2 weeks; cycle time of the off-shore plant = 11 weeks. Source: Abernathy, Dunlop, Hammond, Weil 2000b.

with the highest $C_V$ products and then working down until the plant capacity limit is reached. This means that the short-cycle plant capacity is used for products that are expected to incur large weekly variations in demand. Figure 2.1 presents the resulting profit and total inventory levels for different capacity mixes of the two plants.

The relationship between profit and inventory depicted in Figure 2.1 has important implications for sourcing decision-making. First, the maximum profit does not occur with all manufacturing done offshore, but at nearly half-local and half-offshore. In this example, half of the weekly demand has relatively large week-to-week variation in demand. At the most profitable mix of the two sources, the local short-cycle plant is producing on average all of the high-variation SKUs. Perhaps even more important than the profit results from the model is the inventory story. Total inventory drops from fifteen weeks of demand with all production offshore to a little less that ten and a half weeks at the 50 percent production ratio. If all production is local (short cycle), the required inventory drops just below six weeks.

One repercussion of lean retailing is that more of the risk from holding the wrong product at the wrong time is shifted backward onto the supply chain. This problem is compounded by product proliferation, since a given level of demand will be spread across a larger number of SKUs with lower average demand and higher levels of variability—that is, higher $C_v$s. As a result, there is significant financial risk associated with a manufacturer carrying fifteen weeks of inventory of any consumer product, especially a perishable commodity like apparel. A sudden drop in the demand for a line of goods means that a supplier faces liquidating fifteen or more weeks of product, simply because it cannot "turn off the tap" of supply instantaneously.[6]

The example presented above represents only one set of simulation results.[7] In terms of profitability, the optimal allocation of production capacity to a local plant and an offshore plant involves the cost of carrying the higher inventory of the offshore plant versus lower inventory costs though higher production cost at the local plant. If the cost of capital rises, inventory becomes more expensive and the most profitable position shifts toward local production. If the cycle time difference between the plants in the two locations decreases, then the most profitable allocation shifts toward the offshore plant.

The specific allocation results and their effects on profitability and risk vary according to the mix of products being produced by the manufacturer. Figure 2.1 illustrates, however, the fact that manufacturers increasingly need to incorporate lead time and demand variance considerations in their sourcing decisions given lean retailing and product proliferation. The resulting sourcing patterns may look very different as a consequence.

## Impacts of Old and New Factors on Apparel Globalization

The insights from the above model can be linked to sourcing decisions. One of the advantages offered by Mexico, Latin America, and the Caribbean apparel suppliers to U.S. retailers is their proximity to the U.S. market (Gereffi 1994, 1999). Proximity means less time elapses from the time orders are placed to when they are delivered for shipment to retail purchasers. Indicative of this are lead times between the two regions. Case evidence collected by the authors suggests that lead times for U.S. suppliers with operations or contractors in Mexico may range from four to as much as nine weeks. For retailers sourcing out of China, typical lead times may range from seven to sixteen or more weeks.

In addition, the ability to ship via land (Mexico) or only short distances by sea potentially implies more direct (and simpler) infrastructure connections relative to sourcing in more distant countries in Asia. The more variability added to the shipment process through underdeveloped or constrained transportation networks, fragmented administrative processes for trade, concerns about terrorism, political instability, or weather-related problems, the more risk facing the supplier and consequent need to hold larger buffer inventories. As a result, a company providing ongoing replenishment to retail customers could reduce the amount of goods in its replenishment pipeline (and therefore the total amount of inventory it held) by sourcing products closer to the United States. With these broad predictions as a background, we turn to an examination of actual sourcing patterns over the last decade in order to see if they provide evidence of supplier responses along the lines suggested.

*Apparel Sourcing Patterns, 1984–2000*

U.S. consumers commonly perceive China as the largest source of imported apparel products. Although that perception was accurate in the early 1980s, it no longer holds today. Figure 2.2 compares the sources of imports into the U.S. market (measured in square meters) in 1984 versus 2000. The figure shows that the volume of apparel imported into the United States from the share of total imports arising from the combined output of China, Hong Kong, Taiwan, and Korea—often referred to as the Asian Big Four—fell from 63 percent in 1984 to 19 percent in 2000.[8] At the same time, the combined output from Mexico and a group of Caribbean countries proximate to the United States rose from 7 per-

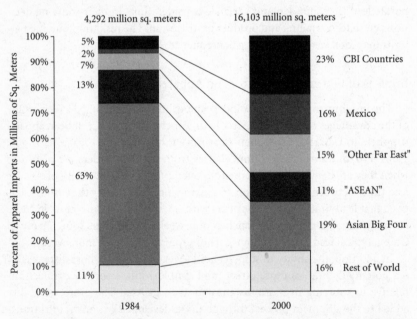

FIG. 2.2. Changes in the Sources of U.S. Apparel Imports, 1984 and 2000. ASEAN countries include Philippines, Indonesia, Thailand, Malaysia, and Singapore. Source: U.S. Department of Commerce. Conversion to physical units by the Office of Textiles and Apparel, U.S. Department of Commerce.

cent of total imports in 1984 (measured in square meters) to 39 percent in 2000.[9]

Figures 2.3 and 2.4 provide more detailed evidence of this dramatic shift. Figure 2.3 shows that Mexico and the CBI countries surpassed the Asian Big Four in physical volume in 1995. Figure 2.4 shows that the Mexico/CBI block surpassed the Asian Big Four in value of shipments in 1998. By 2000, the Mexico/CBI block accounted for $17.9 billion of imports into the U.S. market, versus $17.7 billion for the Asian Big Four.[10]

The shift in sourcing can be attributed to a constellation of traditional factors including comparative labor and factor costs and productivities, transportation costs, exchange rates, tariff structures, and quotas. To these traditional factors, we would add the growing importance of proximity to market for apparel suppliers given lean retailing and its attendant effects, discussed above. In order to ascertain whether part of the shift can be attributed to the impact of retail restructuring, we look more deeply at the underlying data on patterns of shifts between the markets, beginning with the effects of quota restrictions.[11]

*The Impact of Quotas*

A first explanation for the dramatic shifts in sourcing portrayed in Figures 2.2 through 2.4 is that they arise from the effects of quotas and tariffs. Several major changes in the system of trade agreements pertaining to apparel have occurred during the period that potentially impact the sourcing of goods. Since the late 1950s, the growth of textile and apparel imports into the United States has been limited through a series of bilateral agreements with other governments that specify limitations on product categories and annual increases in the growth of those quotas over the prior period. In 1974 a more comprehensive system of "managed" trade agreements was ratified in the so-called Multi-Fiber Arrangement (MFA). The system of managed trade under the MFA allowed signatory countries to negotiate bilateral agreements on quotas and tariffs throughout the 1980s and 1990s.[12]

In 1995, arising from the Uruguay Round of multilateral negotiations under the General Agreement on Trade and Tariffs (GATT), the system of trade restraint created by the MFA was replaced by the Agreement on Textiles and Clothing (ATC) and became part of the broader World Trade Organization agreements. Central to this transition was agreement by all WTO members to eliminate all quotas on textiles and apparel over a ten-year period, culminating on January 1, 2005.

Yet despite the major changes signaled by these international agreements, it should be noted that both quotas and tariffs remained in place for a significant

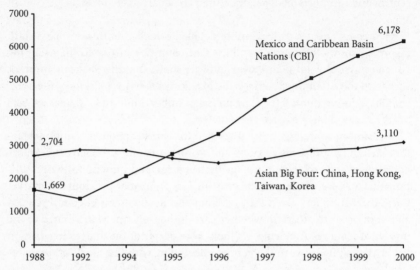

FIG. 2.3. Trend in Apparel Imports: Physical Imports to the United States, 1988–2000 (Volume in million square meters). Source: U.S. Department of Commerce, Office of Textiles and Apparel; data compiled by HCTAR.

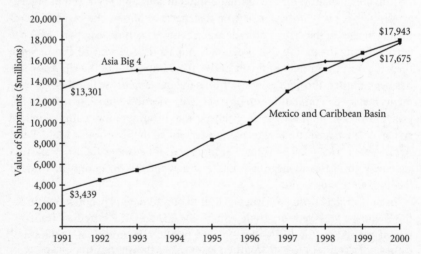

FIG. 2.4. Trend in Apparel Imports: Value of Shipments from Two Regions to the United States, 1991–2000 (Current $ millions). Source: Department of Commerce; data compiled by HCTAR.

percentage of the apparel items for the periods depicted in Figures 2.2 through 2.4. The Uruguay Round of GATT specified that quotas would be removed from apparel categories in three phases between 1995 and 2005.[13] The products selected for quota elimination in the first two phases tended to be those where quotas were not binding. As a result, even by 2001, many of the product categories that constitute large shares of trade remained under quota protection. In addition, even after the final phaseout of quotas under the agreement, tariffs will remain in place between the signatory nations, albeit at lower levels than in 1995. Finally, under the separate Memorandum of Understanding between the United States and China regarding China's accession to the WTO, a bilateral consultation mechanism remains in effect for four additional years beyond the end of quotas for WTO countries (through December 31, 2008).[14] This "safeguard mechanism" would allow the United States to seek to extend quotas with China for specific goods where the elimination of such restrictions would result in "market disruption, threatening to impede the orderly development of trade between the two countries" (U.S. International Trade Commission 1999: 8–12).

Similarly, although the North American Free Trade Agreement formally took effect in January 1994 and requires the eventual elimination of tariffs, many of those tariffs were not phased out during much of the 1990s.[15] For example, in 1998 the top ten product groups from Mexico faced an average tariff rate by U.S. Customs of 11.1 percent.[16] In addition, about 82 percent of the top ten product categories (classified on the basis of SITC codes) were covered by some type of quota restriction in 1998.[17] As a result, one should not conclude that the shift in the country of origin for apparel products arose from the "lifting" of quotas and elimination of tariffs, because much of the system of bilateral agreements that dates back to the MFA remained firmly in place during much of the 1990s.

A more detailed method of examining the role of quotas on the observed shift in sourcing is addressed in a study by Evans and Harrigan (2001). Evans and Harrigan use information on the percentage of quotas for different bilateral trading partners with the United States that were filled in each year between 1990 and 1999 (defined as quota fill rates of 90 percent or higher). For each year, they classify whether a given product had its quota filled for a given trading partner (e.g., China). They then assemble a "basket of products" that were constrained for that trading partner, and those products that were unconstrained. By classifying products on this basis, they can test to see if products imported into the United States by other trading partners track those product categories where other major sources of imports face quota constraints.

If the shift in the sources of imports from the Asian Big Four to Mexico and

TABLE 2.1

*Change in Import Share for Quota Constrained and*
*Unconstrained Product Baskets, China / Hong Kong Quotas,*
*1990–1998*

| Source of Imports to the U.S. market | Unconstrained Product "Basket" by China / Hong Kong Quotas[a] (Percent change in import share[b]) | | | Constrained Product "Basket" by China / Hong Kong Quotas[c] (Percent change in import share[b]) | | |
|---|---|---|---|---|---|---|
| | 1990–98 | 1990–94 | 1995–98 | 1990–98 | 1990–94 | 1995–98 |
| China / Hong Kong | −26.5 | 17.7 | −32.8 | −39.9 | −16.8 | −13.5 |
| Mexico | 463.6 | 28.4 | 130.8 | 510.5 | 132.2 | 79.5 |
| CBI Countries | 188.1 | 125.2 | 13.6 | 116.3 | 68.4 | 14.2 |

*Source:* Evans and Harrigan (2001).

*Note:* Product-level quotas as defined by bilateral agreements between the United States and China and Hong Kong.

[a] Basket of products where the import quota for China / Hong Kong was not exceeded in the year under study.

[b] Import shares are calculated as a percentage of total world imports of the constrained or unconstrained commodity basket.

[c] Basket of products where 90 percent or more of the import quota for China / Hong Kong was reached in the year under study. Note that the basket of goods in each category may shift on a year-by-year basis depending on the level of quota reached for the given year.

the CBI was driven solely by quota limits in China, one would expect to see high levels of growth from Mexico and the CBI in the "quota constrained" product baskets, and much less growth in "unconstrained baskets" where quotas constraints are not binding. Alternatively, if one observed substantial growth in imports in the Mexico and CBI nations even among product categories where constraints had not been reached by China, it would suggest that other factors beyond quotas are present in explaining the shift.

Table 2.1 presents the results of Evans and Harrigan's (2001) analysis of "constrained" and "unconstrained" product baskets, defined on the basis of annual Chinese quota fill rates.[18] They calculate the overall change in import share—defined as the percentage of total imports accounted for by the country for that "basket" of goods—in three time periods: 1990–98; 1990–94; and 1995–98. The first three columns of data provide the overall percentage change in import share for the unconstrained product baskets, and the latter three columns for the constrained product baskets.

The evidence in Table 2.1 shows that there was substantial growth in the import share accounted for by Mexico and the CBI among *both* constrained and unconstrained product baskets during the 1990–98 period. For example, it shows that the import share accounted for by Mexico of all imports to the United States for products unconstrained by Chinese quotas was 464 percent, versus 511 percent for constrained categories. Although this means that Mexico's share of imports in the constrained basket grew more rapidly over the course of the 1990s, the result shows that there was major growth even in those segments where China was not facing quota constraints. During the 1990–94 period, the growth in the Mexican share of imports was more striking among products where the Chinese were constrained by quotas than in the unconstrained categories. However, if one looks at the 1995–98 period, Mexico's share grew more among those product categories where China was unconstrained by its quotas versus the basket of products where China was constrained. Similar patterns can be observed for the CBI nations.

The analysis in Table 2.1 suggests that although quotas certainly play a part in explaining the shifts in import country of origin depicted in Figures 2.2 through 2.4, there must be other factors that contributed to the rapid growth of products "unconstrained" by quota protections. Further analysis of the product composition of import flows provides insight into the role of lean retailing as a contributing factor.

### Composition of Flows: Product Level Analysis

An implication of the model presented above is that the goods coming from Mexico and the Caribbean should be composed primarily of products that are more subject to ongoing replenishment orders by lean retailers. In contrast, those products coming from Asia should be primarily composed of items where replenishment is currently not being practiced, and therefore where traditional cost considerations dominate the issue of variability in demand.

In order to examine this issue, we analyze the product-specific composition of apparel goods originating in China and Mexico (the Appendix provides detailed information on the data used throughout the chapter). If the growth in Mexico as a source of imports during the 1990s arose as a result of broad changes in trade policy (e.g., lowering of tariffs under NAFTA) or from exchange rate shifts, one would expect all product categories to move in the same direction (that is—all product categories should be moving up). Similarly, if national factor productivities rose (or relative wage levels fell), one would expect to find an increase in the volume of imports from that nation, all other things being equal, with the basic composition staying the same. If, on the other hand, replenishment has become a more important factor in sourcing products in Mexico, as we would expect given the rise of lean retailing and growth in product proliferation, one would expect to observe a *shift in Mexico's product composition* from the beginning to the end of the decade. Similarly, if China is not being used as a source of replenishment, and sourcing decisions remained driven by traditional factors, one would not expect to see a broad-based shift in the composition of goods over the study period, except arising from significant shifts in consumer taste.

TABLE 2.2

*Top Ten Imports by Product Category and Volume Shipped: Mexico and China, 1991 and 1999, Ranked by 1999 Shipments*

**MEXICO, TOP 10 PRODUCT IMPORTS AND CORRESPONDING REPLENISHMENT VOLUME, RANKED BY 1999 VOLUME**

| | | 1991 | | | 1999 | | |
|---|---|---|---|---|---|---|---|
| SITC | PRODUCT CLASSIFICATION | Value of Shipments | % of total | Rank, 1991 | Value of Shipments | % of total | Rank, 1999 |
| 84140 | TROUSERS, OVERALLS, SHORTS ETC, MEN/BOYS, NOT KNIT | 212,620,520 | 23.4% | 1 | 1,709,381,769 | 21.8% | 1 |
| 84260 | TROUSERS ETC, WOMEN/GIRLS, TEXTILE FAB, NOT KNIT | 130,444,894 | 14.3% | 3 | 1,280,403,717 | 16.3% | 2 |
| 84540 | T-SHIRTS, SINGLETS & OTH VESTS, KNIT OR CHROCHET | 3,748,684 | 0.4% | 34 | 972,661,347 | 12.4% | 3 |
| 84530 | JERSEYS, PULLOVERS, CARDIGANS ETC, KNIT OR CROCHET | 10,280,935 | 1.1% | 17 | 824,650,916 | 10.5% | 4 |
| 84551 | BRASSIERES, WHETHER OR NOT KNIT OR CROCHET | 63,531,004 | 7.0% | 4 | 307,577,330 | 3.9% | 5 |
| 84521 | GARMENTS, OF FELT & SIMILAR FABRICS, COATED OR NOT | 162,192,679 | 17.8% | 2 | 217,895,090 | 2.8% | 6 |
| 84426 | TROUSERS, OVERALLS, SHORTS ETC, WOMEN/GIRLS, KNIT | 12,951,700 | 1.4% | 11 | 191,405,603 | 2.4% | 7 |
| 84470 | BLOUSES, SHIRTS, ETC, WOMEN/GIRLS, TEXT, KNIT | 12,214,734 | 1.3% | 12 | 169,196,572 | 2.2% | 8 |
| 84324 | TROUSERS, OVERALLS, SHORTS ETC, MEN/BOYS, TX, KNIT | 883,669 | 0.1% | 49 | 149,578,355 | 1.9% | 9 |
| 84482 | BRIEFS AND PANTIES, WOMEN/GIRLS, TEXTILE, KNIT | 29,631,166 | 3.3% | 5 | 126,226,048 | 1.6% | 10 |
| | TOTAL VOLUME IMPORTS | 909,718,506 | 70.2% | | 7,845,262,587 | 75.8% | |

**CORRELATION BETWEEN 1991 AND 1999 PRODUCT SHARES (ALL PRODUCTS)**[*]    0.752

**CHINA, TOP 10 PRODUCT IMPORTS AND CORRESPONDING REPLENISHMENT VOLUME, RANKED BY 1999 VOLUME**

| | | 1991 | | | 1999 | | |
|---|---|---|---|---|---|---|---|
| SITC | PRODUCT CLASSIFICATION | Value of Shipments | % of total | Rank, 1991 | Value of Shipments | % of total | Rank, 1999 |
| 84530 | JERSEYS, PULLOVERS, CARDIGANS ETC, KNIT OR CROCHET | 858,270,426 | 22.3% | 1 | 1,407,626,389 | 19.1% | 1 |
| 84811 | ARTICLES OF APPAREL OF LEATHER/COMP LEATHER | 151,591,228 | 3.9% | 8 | 661,822,800 | 9.0% | 2 |
| 84260 | TROUSERS ETC, WOMEN/GIRLS, TEXTILE FAB, NOT KNIT | 226,639,179 | 5.9% | 4 | 476,004,663 | 6.5% | 3 |
| 84270 | BLOUSES, SHIRTS, ETC, WOMEN/GIRLS, TX FAB, NOT KNIT | 421,827,354 | 11.0% | 2 | 467,765,270 | 6.4% | 4 |
| 84240 | DRESSES, WOMEN/GIRLS, TEXTILE FAB, NOT KNIT | 172,749,363 | 4.5% | 5 | 368,962,376 | 5.0% | 5 |
| 84140 | TROUSERS, OVERALLS, SHORTS ETC, MEN/BOYS, NOT KNIT | 242,821,868 | 6.3% | 3 | 368,278,860 | 5.0% | 6 |
| 84119 | ANORAKS, ETC, WOVEN TEXTILE, MENS & BOYS | 160,850,552 | 4.2% | 6 | 256,525,030 | 3.5% | 7 |
| 84821 | ART OF APPAREL & CLOTHING ACCESSORIES, PLASTIC | 39,276,215 | 1.0% | 20 | 244,475,045 | 3.3% | 8 |
| 84843 | HATS & OTH HEADGEAR, KNIT/CRO, LACE ETC; HAIRNETS | 67,919,136 | 1.8% | 13 | 218,899,049 | 3.0% | 9 |
| 84219 | ANORAKS, ETC, WOVEN TEXTILE, WOMEN OR GIRLS | 152,579,163 | 4.0% | 7 | 196,997,250 | 2.7% | 10 |
| | TOTAL VOLUME IMPORTS | 3,841,192,218 | 64.9% | | 7,355,591,523 | 63.5% | |

**CORRELATION BETWEEN 1991 AND 1999 PRODUCT SHARES (ALL PRODUCTS)**[*]    0.944

*Source:* Value of shipments 1991, 1999, U.S. Department of Commerce.
[*]Calculated as correlation between 96 6-digit SITC product categories in 1991 and 1999. Full product shares by year available from the authors (available at www.hctar.org).

In order to test the above hypothesis, we analyze the import data from both China and Mexico in 1991 and 1999 at the six-digit SITC level. For each country, we calculate the share of total imports accounted for by each product group and rank them based on this share. Table 2.2 presents the top ten imports by product category and volume shipped into the U.S. market from Mexico and China in 1991 and 1999 (ranked on the basis of 1999 imports).

The upper panel in Table 2.2 displays the top ten product imports to the United States from Mexico, ranked on the basis of 1999 volume (far right column). Comparing the rankings of products in 1999 with those in 1991 reveals that only five of the products that were in the top ten in 1999 were also in the top ten in 1991. Further, a number of the products highly ranked in 1999 constituted a very small part of Mexican imports to the United States in 1991. For example, although T-shirts made up more than 16 percent of all Mexican imports in 1999, they constituted less than 1 percent of imports in 1991. This suggests a fair amount of change in product composition over the decade.

This contrasts markedly with the case of China (lower panel of Table 2.2). For China, one finds that eight of the top ten products in 1999 were also in the top ten in 1991. Although there was some movement in the rankings within the top ten, the relative magnitudes of imports are similar across the time periods, suggesting far less change in the composition of imports.

In order to examine the changing relationship in product composition between 1991 and 1999 for the entire set of products imported in each country, we calculated a correlation of product rankings (by the product share of total imports from the country) in 1991 and in 1998 for Mexico and China, using all ninety-six of the six-digit SITC product groups and their corresponding 1991 and 1998 import shares. The results are found in the bold rows in Table 2.2. For China, the correlation between product import shares in 1991 and 1999 was 0.944, indicating that the basic rankings of products between the two periods had changed little. In contrast, the correlation for Mexico is 0.752. Although this suggests that the product composition for Mexico in 1999 still had a strong correlation with that in 1991, it also signifies significantly more shifting of the relative share of products between the two periods.

*Product categories and replenishment*: We can use the data on product composition to take one step further in examining the role of lean retailing in explaining the overall shift in the sources of U.S. apparel imports. In order to do so, we categorized the ninety-six six-digit SITC product categories as to whether or not they are replenishable—that is, subject to replenishment programs by major U.S. retailers. We use a simple dichotomous categorization here, in which replenishability is defined as a product for which lean retailers have been, since the mid-1990s, asking for at least some level of weekly replen-

*Product Composition and Replenishment Status: Mexico and China, 1991 versus 1999*

**MEXICO, TOP 10 PRODUCT IMPORTS AND REPLENISHMENT STATUS, 1991 AND 1999**

| | 1991 | | | 1999 | |
|---|---|---|---|---|---|
| SITC | PRODUCT CLASSIFICATION | Replenished? | SITC | PRODUCT CLASSIFICATION | Replenished? |
| 84140 | TROUSERS, OVERALLS, SHORTS ETC, MEN/BOYS, NOT KNIT | Yes | 84140 | TROUSERS, OVERALLS, SHORTS ETC, MEN/BOYS, NOT KNIT | Yes |
| 84521 | GARMENTS, OF FELT & SIMILAR FABRICS, COATED OR NOT | No | 84260 | TROUSERS ETC, WOMEN/GIRLS, TEXTILE FAB, NOT KNIT | Yes |
| 84260 | TROUSERS ETC, WOMEN/GIRLS, TEXTILE FAB, NOT KNIT | Yes | 84540 | T-SHIRTS, SINGLETS & OTH VESTS, KNIT OR CHROCHET | Yes |
| 84551 | BRASSIERES, WHETHER OR NOT KNIT OR CROCHET | Yes | 84530 | JERSEYS, PULLOVERS, CARDIGANS ETC, KNIT OR CROCHET | No |
| 84482 | BRIEFS AND PANTIES, WOMEN/GIRLS, TEXTILE, KNIT | Yes | 84551 | BRASSIERES, WHETHER OR NOT KNIT OR CROCHET | Yes |
| 84270 | BLOUSES, SHIRTS, ETC, WOMEN/GIRLS, TX FAB, NOT KNIT | Yes | 84521 | GARMENTS, OF FELT & SIMILAR FABRICS, COATED OR NOT | No |
| 84822 | RUBBER GLOVES | No | 84426 | TROUSERS, OVERALLS, SHORTS ETC, WOMEN/GIRLS, KNIT | Yes |
| 84843 | HATS & OTH HEADGEAR, KNIT/CRO, LACE ETC; HAIRNETS | No | 84470 | BLOUSES, SHIRTS, ETC, WOMEN/GIRLS, TEXT, KNIT | Yes |
| 84589 | ARTICLES OF APPAREL, WOMEN'S OR GIRLS'NES, NT KNT | No | 84324 | TROUSERS, OVERALLS, SHORTS ETC, MEN/BOYS, TX, KNIT | Yes |
| 84587 | ARTICLES OF APPAREL, MENS OR BOYS', NES, NOT KNIT | No | 84482 | BRIEFS AND PANTIES, WOMEN/GIRLS, TEXTILE, KNIT | Yes |

CORRELATION BETWEEN PRODUCT SHARE AND REPLENISHABILITY, 1991 (ALL PRODUCTS)  0.242
CORRELATION BETWEEN PRODUCT SHARE AND REPLENISHABILITY, 1999 (ALL PRODUCTS)  0.356

**CHINA, TOP 10 PRODUCT IMPORTS AND REPLENISHMENT STATUS, 1991 AND 1999**

| | 1991 | | | 1992 | |
|---|---|---|---|---|---|
| SITC | PRODUCT CLASSIFICATION | Replenished? | SITC | PRODUCT CLASSIFICATION | Replenished? |
| 84530 | JERSEYS, PULLOVERS, CARDIGANS ETC, KNIT OR CROCHET | No | 84530 | JERSEYS, PULLOVERS, CARDIGANS ETC, KNIT OR CROCHET | No |
| 84270 | BLOUSES, SHIRTS, ETC, WOMEN/GIRLS, TX FAB, NOT KNIT | Yes | 84811 | ARTICLES OF APPAREL OF LEATHER/COMP LEATHER | Yes |
| 84140 | TROUSERS, OVERALLS, SHORTS ETC, MEN/BOYS, NOT KNIT | Yes | 84260 | TROUSERS ETC, WOMEN/GIRLS, TEXTILE FAB, NOT KNIT | Yes |
| 84260 | TROUSERS ETC, WOMEN/GIRLS, TEXTILE FAB, NOT KNIT | No | 84270 | BLOUSES, SHIRTS, ETC, WOMEN/GIRLS, TX FAB, NOT KNIT | Yes |
| 84240 | DRESSES, WOMEN/GIRLS, TEXTILE FAB, NOT KNIT | No | 84240 | DRESSES, WOMEN/GIRLS, TEXTILE FAB, NOT KNIT | No |
| 84119 | ANORAKS, ETC, WOVEN TEXTILE, MENS & BOYS | No | 84140 | TROUSERS, OVERALLS, SHORTS ETC, MEN/BOYS, NOT KNIT | Yes |
| 84589 | ANORAKS, ETC, WOVEN TEXTILE, WOMEN OR GIRLS | No | 84119 | ANORAKS, ETC, WOVEN TEXTILE, MENS & BOYS | No |
| 84811 | ARTICLES OF APPAREL OF LEATHER/COMP LEATHER | No | 84821 | ART OF APPAREL & CLOTHING ACCESSORIES, PLASTIC | No |
| 84159 | SHIRTS, MEN/BOYS, TEXTILE EX COTTON, NOT KNIT | Yes | 84843 | HATS & OTH HEADGEAR, KNIT/CRO, LACE ETC; HAIRNETS | No |
| 84812 | GLOVES ETC, LEATH/COMP, NOT DESIGNED FOR SPORTS | No | 84219 | ANORAKS, ETC, WOVEN TEXTILE, WOMEN OR GIRLS | No |

CORRELATION BETWEEN PRODUCT SHARE AND REPLENISHABILITY, 1991 (ALL PRODUCTS)  0.098
CORRELATION BETWEEN PRODUCT SHARE AND REPLENISHABILITY, 1999 (ALL PRODUCTS)  0.04

*Source:* Value of shipments 1991, 1999, U.S. Department of Commerce; replenishment status, see Appendix.
*Calculated as correlation between 96 6-digit SITC product categories in 1991 and 1999. Full product shares by year available from the authors (available at www.hc-tar.org).

ishment of products.[19] If lean retailing represents a partial driver in changes in sourcing patterns, one would expect to find a relationship between product composition and replenishability for Mexico (particularly in the most recent period) and little of such a relationship for China.

Table 2.3 presents the top ten products from Mexico and China in 1991 and for 1999, and whether that product category was replenishable. Looking first at Mexico (upper panel), Table 2.3 shows that eight of the top ten apparel goods imported from Mexico were replenishable in 1999. In contrast, only three of the top ten goods imported from China (lower panel) were classified as replenishable in 1999.

The changing composition shown in Table 2.2 also is apparent in these results, in particular the growing importance of replenishment as a factor driving sourcing decisions. Table 2.3 shows that for the top ten, the same number of products were replenishable in 1991 and 1999 (three of the top ten). This is consistent with the view that sourcing decisions out of China do not seem to be driven by replenishment throughout the decade—that is, that those products sourced in China tend to be those driven by traditional factors. In contrast, the upper panel of Table 2.3 for Mexico shows that the number of products that were replenishable grew from five of the top ten in 1991 to eight of the top ten products in 1999 (representing some 76 percent of all imports from Mexico).

We can also use the entire set of ninety-six products, classified in terms of product share and replenishability, to further test the relationship. For China and Mexico, we calculated the correlation between the replenishment categorization of the goods and the share of imports made up by the category in 1991 and 1999. The correlations are reported in the middle and bottom rows of Table 2.3. For Mexico, there is a positive and statistically significant relationship between replenishability and product import share for Mexico in both periods. Even more suggestive is the fact that the correlation between the product-level share of imports and replenishment status *increases* between the two time periods, going from a correlation of 0.242 in 1991 to 0.356 in 1999. In contrast, for China (lower panel) there is little correlation between replenishment category and import share by product type in either 1991 or 1999. In both periods the correlations are below 0.1 and are not statistically discernible from zero.

The increase in the relationship between replenishment and product share for Mexico, at the same time that replenishment status remains uncorrelated for Chinese imports, occurs during the time period that lean retailing became a greater driving force in the U.S. market.[20] This evidence is therefore consistent with replenishment considerations becoming a more important driver of sourcing decisions and therefore patterns of global location of production for apparel products.

Separating out the factors underlying global sourcing is a complex matter, since it involves the interplay of product markets and differences in national development patterns in addition to tariff and quota policies. The story above provides a mosaic of evidence, all consistent with the view that replenishment has played a role in the observed shift in the source of apparel products between the two periods. Thus, despite the passage of NAFTA, the devaluation of the Mexican peso, and the start of quota phaseouts under the WTO over this period, we believe that the above evidence suggests that part of the shift in global sourcing witnessed over the past decade can be ascribed to the emergence and spread of lean retailing and its effects on supplier behavior.[21]

## The Illusion and Reality of 2005: The Future of Global Trade in Apparel and Textiles

Major changes will affect the international trading system in coming years. As mentioned above, the Uruguay Round of trade agreements provided that among WTO members all quotas in textiles and apparel would be eliminated by January 1, 2005.[22] Two pieces of recent U.S. legislation also will affect imports from countries in the coming decade: (a) modification of the CBI arrangement to grant Caribbean Basin nations trade status on the same basis as Mexico under NAFTA; and (b) granting countries in sub-Saharan Africa preferred trade status, roughly equivalent to the CBI arrangements.[23]

Many consider the year 2005 as the harbinger of cataclysmic shifts in the global trade of apparel and textiles. Representatives of the U.S. apparel and textile industry have publicly held that the final elimination of quotas will mark the final death knell of the domestic apparel industry, especially with China as a full member of the WTO. Similarly draconian implications have been forecast for other countries that are perceived as beneficiaries of quotas on Asian producers, including those in the CBI.[24] At the same time, other countries that consider the existing quota system as the main barrier to access to the lucrative U.S. market characterize 2005 as the beginning of a new age for their apparel and textile industries.

We have already cited our skepticism of this piece of conventional wisdom. Although traditional factors and the ending of the quota system will impact the sourcing of products, we believe that mainstream predictions miss the mark in several respects. As we noted above, the structure of international trade agreements will not be removed entirely in 2005: tariffs will remain in place, and the U.S./China accession agreement extends procedural safeguards until 2008.

More important, we have argued that replenishment considerations arising from the new economics of distribution and production channels explain an important portion of the shifts in sourcing over the past decade. As lean retailing becomes even more widespread and suppliers more sophisticated in thinking about managing risk, replenishment considerations will factor even more heavily into sourcing decisions.[25] This will make the countries with proximity more competitive for those goods where replenishment is important, and will subject those countries competing along traditional lines to greater competition over a smaller set of apparel products. As these economic factors will not disappear in 2005—indeed, they will intensify—this driver of sourcing location will persist.[26]

We believe that a more nuanced view of the world beyond 2005 is warranted, one that recognizes the "old" factors that have driven part of globalization for centuries but also the "new" factors we have focused upon here. In particular, we would cite four implications regarding the path of globalization in the decade after 2005.

*The future of textiles:* This chapter has not discussed the textile industry, but the set of industries that compose textiles are being affected by much of what we discuss in the chapter. For the portion of the U.S. textile industry that supplies apparel, the shift toward Mexico and the CBI has been very beneficial. Apparel products imported from China and other Asian nations do not contain U.S. fabric. In contrast, CBI and Mexican apparel imports drew extensively on U.S. textiles throughout the 1990s.

This can be strikingly seen in the trade figures on textile exports from the United States to Mexico versus textile exports to China. In 1991, the United States exported $48.8 million of textiles to China. By 1999, those exports had grown only to $82.5 million, or about 1.1 percent of the value of Chinese apparel imports. In contrast, textile exports to Mexico were $542 million in 1991, growing to $2.84 *billion* by 1999, or 36 percent of the value of Mexican apparel imports. Similar patterns can be observed for the decade in terms of textile exports to CBI nations.[27]

A further implication of these trade figures is the opportunity for Mexico to expand its textile sector. Along with increasing Mexican investment in textile production, many major U.S. textile companies have started to move capital there.[28] Yet the obstacles to developing a high-quality, technologically advanced textile sector are much more substantial than for apparel. Textile production is a far more capital-intensive process requiring development of infrastructure, electricity, water, and the management of sophisticated manufacturing processes.[29] Thus, the development of a major textile sector in Mexico and its attendant effects on the U.S. industry will occur over a longer period.[30]

*Development pathways and policies.* The "new" factors in globalization alter the traditional role that apparel and textile industries can play in economic development. The factors considered here do not change the attractiveness of apparel and textile industries for development. But ensuring the success of those industries has become more complex for several reasons. Our analysis suggests that many nations with inadequate infrastructure, distant location from major consumer markets, or political (or even climatic) instability will be at a considerable competitive disadvantage for many apparel products, even if they have low wage rates. Further, for those categories of apparel where replenishment is not a major factor in sourcing, the presence of a large number of countries with extensive apparel capacity means more intense competition among these nations for a smaller market of nonreplenishment products. Together, these forces will make the future of those apparel industries reliant solely on low wages as the source of competitive advantage (e.g., Bangladesh) increasingly bleak and vulnerable to the removal of quotas in 2005.

In discussing prospects for the development of a textile industry in Mexico, we noted that textile production has become very capital intensive, technologically sophisticated, and infrastructure dependent (especially in regard to the need for reliable sources of electricity and water). Combined with the need to have textile production closer to apparel manufacturers in order to reduce lead times and inventory risk, this analysis suggests that nations hoping to use textiles as a focus of development will need to have more comprehensive policies in place—as well as advantageous geographic location—in order to succeed.[31]

*The regionalization of distribution and supply channels*: A common view of apparel trade flows following 2005 foresees products moving from low-wage developing countries to the major consumer markets of the developed world, unimpeded by the system of bilateral quota agreements. The result is a "global" market with limited regionalization.

This perspective does not adequately recognize that retailing models with lean retailing features have been emerging in consumer markets in Europe and in Japan (see Miwa and Ramseyer [2001] on Japan; and Courant and Parat [2000] regarding Europe). Sourcing arrangements are evolving along lines similar to those that have developed for supplying the United States, with Europe drawing on countries in Eastern Europe and North Africa as locations to provide short-cycle production. For example, Turkey has become an increasingly important source for the European apparel and textile market. Turkish manufacturers have improved their lead time performance as a means of taking advantage of major investments in textile capacity in the 1990s (Tan 2000).[32] Similarly, Japan will rely on proximate Asian sources to serve replenishment needs for their market.

As a result, greater regionalization of textile and apparel production is a natural outgrowth of the competitive forces described here. Regional trade agreements along the lines of NAFTA will also play a role in (and in some ways reflect) these developments. Finally, the longer term development of internal retail markets and the growth in income levels and domestic consumption in China and Mexico will focus these major producers on their own markets (Gu 1999; Stiglitz 2000). Instead of a single international market for apparel and textiles, three regionally based models anchored in the United States, Europe, and Japan may better reflect the realities of post-2005 globalization.

## Implications beyond Apparel

From computers to home building-supply products, a growing percentage of consumer products is being sold via distribution systems using lean retailing principles. This means that proximity, inventory risk reduction, and replenishment have a bearing on sourcing decisions for many industries beyond apparel and textiles. Accordingly, the changes underway in this very old chain of industries provide general insight into the major themes that cut across this volume. But we would also argue in thinking about this volume's major themes that one must be careful to delineate what is truly "new" about these changes from more long-standing forces acting on the firms that make up international supply chains.

*Transportation, communication, and globalization:* Falling transportation and communication costs have long affected the growth and development of markets. For example, reduction in shipping costs arising from the growth of the intercontinental railroad system in tandem with the adoption of telegraphy dramatically changed the scale and scope of U.S. retail markets and the industries that supplied them. Similarly, lean retailing represents a marriage of a set of transportation, communication, and business innovations that collectively reduce the transaction costs between the final consumer and the "first mover" in a supply chain. We have shown here that the end result of these falling transaction costs is a distinctive pattern of geographic sourcing that reflects firms' efforts to deal with both "old" and "new" costs of production and distribution.

We believe that supply chains in other industries are increasingly balancing the old costs of supply (labor, factor, and direct transportation) against the new costs associated with managing risk. How particular industries balance these costs will arise from distinctive characteristics of production, technology, industrial organization, and the nature of final consumer markets. For example, the chapter by Curry and Kenney indicates that the current leader of the personal computer industry, Dell Computers, undertakes final assembly in the United States rather than pursuing lower wage assembly opportunities offshore in response to the perishability of PCs and the attendant risk that goes with it.

*Time and speed*: Elapsed time between order and delivery has become far more important as a competitive factor for many of the products provided by apparel suppliers in a world of lean retail distribution. Prior to lean retailing, the presence of large inventories made time a relevant factor in terms of either companies meeting a delivery deadline for an upcoming season, or for the creation of fashion items for a new season. As a result, the relevant measure of time for suppliers was months rather than days. In this sense, time has become a vastly more important issue for supply chains here than in other cases discussed in this volume.[33]

It should be emphasized, however, that lean retailing means that time and speed pertain not only to *median* lead time performance but also to *variance* around that lead time. A supplier that meets delivery targets to demanding retailers on average, but subjects them to high variance in shipments on a week-to-week basis, will not survive long. Traditional global sourcing decisions paid relatively little attention to variance because they were made on the basis of direct costs with lesser attention to risk. Yet predicting how supply chains will evolve—as well as prescribing what policies developing nations should pursue in regard to those supply chains—must take into account the factors that affect variability in time and speed. This places factors such as the reliability of national transportation and communication infrastructures, political stability, and the adequacy of national security systems on increasingly equal footing with traditional factors like input prices and tariff and quota agreements as location determinants.

*Pricing pressure*: Intense price competition has been a fundamental feature of garment production since the emergence of dry goods wholesalers in apparel in the 1850s and 1860s (Chandler 1977). Lean retailing has only intensified pricing pressure at all stages of the channel, from retailing all the way back to fiber markets. Yet the cross-cutting implication from apparel to other industries facing similar restructuring in distribution is not that pricing will remain important in the international location of production: it surely will. More important is how much buyers along the supply chain will be willing to balance price against the "new costs" of production in making their sourcing decisions.[34]

*Proximity to the Customer*: We have argued that the emergence of lean retailing is driving a regionalization of production in major U.S., European, and Asian consumer markets, because of the need to replenish retail stores rapidly. To organize rapid replenishment, some parties in the supply chain undertake the increasingly complicated task of using information on consumer sales to determine the allocation of production across supply chains with different cost, product variety, quality, lead time, and risk characteristics. We believe that similar developments can be expected to emerge in other consumer product industries where replenishment is of growing importance, thereby driving producers to locate closer to their customers.

The relative effects of "old" and "new" factors in the realm of globalization will obviously differ across distribution and supply channels, and with them the manner in which new sourcing patterns play out. But it seems clear that the forces examined in this chapter will contribute increasingly to trade flows and patterns more generally in the coming decade. What is "new" for apparel—one of the oldest industries engaged in global trade—illustrates the forces that will shape globalization across a wider range of industrial sectors.

## Appendix: Sources of Data Used in the Analysis

### Value of Shipment by Country

The import data are taken from the U.S. Department of Commerce, Bureau of the Census, Administrative and Customer Services Division, *U.S. Imports/ Exports History, International Harmonized System Commodity Classification by Country, by Customers District, Historical Summary 1991–95 with updates for 1996–99.* The data is based on information collected by the U.S. Customs Service in its Custom Service Entry Summary forms, which are filed with the Customs Service at the time that merchandise is released to the importer and used to assess tariffs.

The data is organized under the Harmonized Tariff Schedule of the United States Annotated (HTUSA or often termed "HS codes"), which provides a unique ten-digit reporting number for each product imported into the U.S. We used annual data on the value of imports (in current dollars) for the different countries of origin. In order to analyze the data at a more aggregated product level, we use concordance files provided to us by the U.S. Department of Commerce to convert HS codes into the more commonly used Standard International Trade Classification (SITC) system.[35] We use the resulting ninety-six six-digit SITC codes as the basis for the analyses conducted throughout the text.

The dollar values represent the current value of imports as appraised by the U.S. Customs Service in accordance with the legal requirements of the Tariff Act of 1930. The value is generally defined as the price actually paid or payable for merchandise when sold for export to the United States, excluding U.S. import duties, freight, insurance, and other charges incurred in bringing the merchandise to the United States. The price refers to the total payment made or to be made for the imported merchandise by the buyer to the seller. For more details on the definitions of import values, see *www.census.gov/foreign-trade/ guide.*

## Replenishment Classification

The ninety-six product categories were assigned a replenishment status based on a dichotomous variable where: Replenishment = 1 if the product is replenishable given prevailing lean retailing practice, or Replenisment = 0 if the product is not replenishable given prevailing practice. This assessment was based on two sources of information. First, we have available the detailed product records for one of the top ten U.S. retail department stores for sales in a portion of FY 2000. This data contains information on total sales to date for detailed product categories, as well as replenishment sales to date in each of those categories. This allows us to calculate a percent of total sales replenished at a detailed product level. We used this information to provide general guidance on the classification of products. The limitation of this data is that it is grouped on the basis of the retailer's internal product classification system rather than the SITC system for product categorization. We are therefore unable to use it to make the classification directly.

In the cases in which we were not able to use the retail data set for classification directly, we relied upon our qualitative assessment of the replenishability of a product category based on fieldwork and case evidence collected by the authors as part of our larger study of the retail—apparel—textile channel. Although we believe that the combination of the two methods of classification provides us with a reliable overall measure of replenishability, we did not choose to use the actual percentage of replenishment as our metric (although these were available to us in many cases from the retail data set). In future work, we will further refine this measure to provide more precise estimates of the relationships between replenishment and trade flows. The classification is available from the authors.

## Notes

Support for this research was provided by the Alfred P. Sloan Foundation. The authors are very grateful to Carolyn Evans of the Federal Reserve Board for providing us with preliminary results on quota fill rates arising from her research project, as well as broader insights from her work. We also thank Soundouss Bouhia, Scott Garvin, and Muriel Peters for research assistance, and participants at a series of Sloan Foundation Globalization Network workshops for comments on this research. Contact author: David Weil, Boston University School of Management, 595 Commonwealth Avenue, Boston MA 02215, phone: 617-353-4615, FAX: 617-353-6667, email: davweil@bu.edu.

1. Reynolds (1986), p. 130. See also Williamson (1998) for a historical perspective on the "new" issue of globalization.

2. See Gerschenkron (1962) for a seminal discussion of the role of textiles in the economic development of nations.

3. Not all products provided by lean retailers move from suppliers to consumers via

replenishment. There remain a significant, but shrinking, percentage of products ordered well in advance of the selling season based on the assessment of buyers and reflecting the merchandising decisions of retailers. But even those typically fashion-oriented products are moving toward partial replenishment models.

4. This number *excludes* certain combinations of this particular product that Lands' End does not offer. It therefore accurately reflects the number of SKUs that the company must be ready to provide their customers. Example based on shirts offered in the *Lands' End for Men* catalog, June/July 2000, pp. 26–27.

5. The manufacturer in the simulation is described using generic costs, variations in weekly demand, and production cycle time. However, the values used are close to those for casual pants, bras, or an upscale men's dress shirt manufacturer. The average demand for the product is assumed to be constant throughout the year to simplify the data presentation (i.e., we assume no significant seasonality in demand). This assumption would, in fact, be true for men's and women's undergarments, some casual pants, and blazers. For the illustrative example, the total collection of SKUs is aggregated into the three groups shown in the following tabulation:

| Percent of weekly demand | $C_V$ |
|---|---|
| 50 | Low |
| 35 | Medium |
| 15 | High |

Most of the SKUs (50 percent) have been taken to have a low value of weekly variation (0.7), and only 15 percent of the weekly demand is expected in the highest $C_V$ group. This is a typical distribution of SKUs and $C_V$ for a product offered in many styles and sizes by many manufacturers. Details on this example can be found in Abernathy et al. (2000b) and at our research center website, www.hctar.org.

6. The Gap and Nike are just two recent examples of suppliers that have faced major reductions in demand for their products and, as a result, were forced to take large losses because of the need to liquidate inventories.

7. For example, Figure 2.1 is based on a case in which production costs are 20 percent higher in the short-cycle plant; the most profitable position was to have half made in the short cycle plant. Given the same demand and lead-time inputs, when the local production cost rises to be 25 percent greater than that of the offshore plant, the profit is almost the same for all production mixtures up to 50 percent and then falls as more and more is made locally. When local costs are 30 percent higher than those of the offshore plant, then it is always more profitable to concentrate all production offshore. For other simulation results, see www.hctar.org.

8. These countries are often grouped together in trade comparisons because of the significant amount of trans-shipment—where products produced in one country are shipped out of another in order to thwart quota restrictions—between them. Changes in the "nation of origin" instituted on July 1, 1996, attempted to reduce the prevalence of trans-shipment of goods, particularly from China. See U.S. International Trade Commission (1996), p. 87.

9. These Caribbean nations are commonly grouped together in examining apparel and textile trade flows because they are covered by a broad economic development program, the Caribbean Basin Initiative (CBI). The CBI includes trade provisions that pro-

vide preferential trade treatment for CBI nations, including assessing U.S. customs duties on a value-added only basis for apparel products assembled in CBI countries but made of U.S.-formed and -cut materials. In 2000, legislation was enacted by the United States to confer upon CBI nations tariff-free entry for goods made of U.S. materials in order to provide parity with the treatment of goods under NAFTA.

10. The estimated value of apparel imports from different countries varies according to the method used to classify the "apparel industry." There are at least three definitions for defining the apparel and textile industries for purposes of tracking imports: the Standard International Trade Classification (SITC) system promulgated by the United Nations, which classifies on a commodity level basis (with classifications for apparel items beginning with the number 84 in its ten-digit coding system); the U.S. Standard Industrial Classification (SIC) system, which uses industry-level definitions used by the United States from 1940 until 1998 (with apparel items having an SIC code of 23 as the first of four digits), replaced recently by the North American Industrial Classification System; and the U.S. Textile and Apparel Category System, which provides categories for textile and apparel items by fiber and type of product, covered by international textile and apparel agreements. The three systems yield different estimates of total "apparel" imports by country. We use the SITC throughout this study.

11. See the Appendix for information on the data drawn upon for this chapter.

12. The quotas assigned under the MFA for particular products were allocated by agreements to governments rather than to particular producers, and the exporting country's government officials were authorized to distribute the quota among producers. For a thorough examination of the secondary market that emerged within countries for quotas, see Krishna and Tan (1998).

13. Under the terms of the Agreement on Textiles and Clothing, WTO members removed quotas on 16 percent of their textile and apparel trade as of January 1, 1995 (based on their 1990 import volumes); 17 percent more on January 1, 1998; 18 percent in 2002; and the remaining 49 percent on January 1, 2005. In addition to the integration of quotas into the WTO regime, the agreements also require an acceleration of quota growth rates for categories of goods still covered by quotas during the transition period. See U.S. International Trade Commission (1999), pp.8–12 through 8–15.

14. Both countries initialed the Memorandum of Understanding regarding China's accession to the WTO on February 1, 1997.

15. Prior to NAFTA, imports from Mexican assembly plants were covered by the same arrangement covering imports assembled in the CBI (wherein duties are applied only to the value added of goods). Under NAFTA, a growing percentage of goods enter entirely duty free. See U.S. International Trade Commission (1996), p. 43.

16. This represents a weighted average across the top ten products. Tariffs range from 3 percent of the customs import value for men's or boys' trousers, overalls, and shorts of cotton (SITC 620342) to a high of 33 percent of customs import value on sweaters, pullovers, sweatshirts, and similar products (SITC 611030). In many cases, these tariff rates were comparable to those imposed on Chinese imports in the same year. These figures are based on data collected by the U.S. Customs Bureau, Department of Commerce, and are fully described in the Appendix.

17. The comparable tariff figure for the top ten goods from China in 1998 was 11.2 percent. Both estimates represent a weighted average based on the subgroup of each of

the top ten, six-digit SITC categories that were covered by quotas in 1998. These ranged from SITC 620342, where 98 percent of the product group is covered by quotas, to SITC 621210, where none of the product category was covered by a quota. See the Appendix for the source of these estimates. We are grateful to Carolyn Evans of the New York Federal Reserve Board for providing us this detailed information on quota fill rates that is part of her ongoing study (see Evans 2000a, b and Evans and Harrigan 2001).

18. Table 1 is based on Evans and Harrigan (2001), figs. 10 and 11.

19. See the Appendix for a description of the methods employed to classify goods as to their replenishability.

20. The categorization for all ninety-six SITC product groups is available from the authors.

21. Ongoing work by the authors is evaluating the implications of replenishment on global sourcing decisions through modeling the profit/risk trade-offs discussed earlier in the chapter. Continuing work by Evans and Harrigan uses detailed product-level information on factor costs, exchange rates, tariffs, quota fill rates, and replenishability to econometrically estimate their separate effects (see Evans and Harrigan 2003).

22. Although the agreements also call for the overall reduction in tariffs, tariffs will not be eliminated in 2005. Preferential tariff treatment for certain countries also will remain after 2005, such as that specified under NAFTA.

23. Under the Trade and Development Act of 2000, CBI nations will be provided duty-free access to the U.S. (removing the current tariff on the value-added of goods assembled in those countries under the provisions of 9802.00.80 of the Harmonized Tariff Schedule of the United States), provided that the goods are made from textiles produced in the United States. The African Growth and Opportunity Act of 2000 when fully implemented provides for duty- and quota-free entry into the United States for the apparel products from thirty-four sub-Saharan nations, provided that the goods are made of textiles from those nations. See U.S. International Trade Commission (2000), pp. 97–104.

24. This view, for example, was espoused by Laura Rodriguez-Archila, an international trade analyst at the U.S. International Trade Commission. Citing a USITC analysis, she stated: "Once quotas are phased out, the Caribbean Basin is going to lose its advantage." Quoted in Paula Green, "Report: Quota Phaseout to Hurt Caribbean," *Journal of Commerce* (February 11, 2000): 12.

25. Companies that have long specialized in apparel sourcing have, not surprisingly, changed given the new dynamics of global sourcing. For example, Li & Fung Ltd., a company specializing in apparel supply-chain management, began by providing apparel products from Asian manufacturers to retail customers using acquisition of quotas for apparel products in China and Hong Kong as the key source of competitive advantage. Today, the company focuses on "managing the supply chain for high volume, time-sensitive consumer goods" by coordinating a network of manufacturers based in Asia as well as the Mediterranean, Eastern Europe, and Central America in order to be "closer to our customers in Europe and the US" (www.lifung.com). Other companies in the international shipping and transportation industry, such as Sea-Land, UPS, and American Consolidation Services, increasingly are linking traditional transportation activities to the provision of sophisticated logistic services important to both retailers and suppliers (Heaver 2001).

26. Even the most sophisticated efforts to forecast the post-2005 impacts have left out the replenishment dynamic. The USITC models of the effects of China's accession to the WTO on U.S. apparel production and employment are indicative. The USITC models are run at the aggregate rather than commodity level. This undermines the models' ability to capture the types of changes described here, since they have their primary impact through the *composition of products* sourced from different countries. The USITC report indirectly acknowledges this problem: "Finally, the simulations reflect the assumption that the purchasers' willingness to substitute imports for domestic production remains constant throughout the 12-year period [1998–2010]. This may not be the case. For example, if domestic producers were to shift production to specialized subsectors, imports could become less viable substitutes and, as a result, purchasers would be less responsive to changes in import prices" (U.S. International Trade Commission 1999: 8–20).

27. This is based on U.S. Department of Commerce value of imported textiles, SITC 65 (see the Appendix for information on the underlying data). The fall in textile employment in the United States during the 1990s is often mistakenly ascribed to the same factors that reduced U.S. apparel employment. In fact, the textile industry as well as other major end-users experienced growth in production over this period, and much of the employment reduction arose from technological changes and increasing capital intensity of production. See Abernathy et al. (1999), chs. 11 and 12.

28. Among those textile firms that have invested in Mexico since 1994 are Burlington Industries, Cone Mills, Guilford Mills, and Dan River.

29. There is evidence that managerial problems are increasingly affecting performance in apparel and textile production in Mexico. For example, a top executive in one of the largest U.S. textile manufacturers told us that it was managerial capacity that was the primary limitation to the growth of the Mexican textile sector in the next decade. More generally, the advantages arising from Mexico's proximity to the U.S. consumer market can be undermined if suppliers cannot provide short lead times and reliable deliveries to retail distribution centers. If lead times increase and the reliability of shipments decreases, Mexico will become increasingly subject to competition from nations that can provide similar performance at lower cost.

30. It is less clear that the CBI nations will be able to develop a textile sector in the near term for several reasons. First, the NAFTA parity in tariff treatment for the CBI still requires use of textile products manufactured in the United States (unlike NAFTA, where there is no such precondition for apparel imported from Mexico). Second, capital constraints are more substantial in the CBI nations than in Mexico. Finally, the CBI apparel manufacturers currently in operation have specialized primarily in assembly. There is therefore less experience in the management of more complex apparel manufacturing than one finds in Mexico, limiting the supply of skilled managers for textile operations.

31. If in the future relations are normalized with the United States, Cuba may emerge as a growing source for apparel assembly, arising from its proximity to the U.S. market, the availability of a labor supply with skills in this area, and the existence of social and potential business networks between the Cuban mainland and Cuban émigré communities.

32. Indicative of the similarities is the statement of Samir Gandhi, manager of an En-

glish company specializing in sourcing nightwear products for British retailers: "Turkey is very attractive because the quality here is higher and the lead times are significantly shorter. …We are starting to realize that to be competitive in the fast-moving world of fashion, we need to cut down on our lead times. This, in and of itself, justifies the slightly higher price in Turkey." Quoted in Robert Murphy, "Turks Aim to Develop Brands," *Women's Wear Daily* (March 7, 2001): 12.

33. It is important to note that many of the industries described in this book are dealing with the problem of product proliferation that has been an attribute of the apparel industry. Among other implications, the presence of "fashion elements" in the production of computers, electronic components, automobiles, and other consumer goods brings with it the associated problem of product perishability. This constitutes an additional theme common to many of the supply chains described in this volume.

34. Also of interest will be the emergence of other methods for firms along supply chains like apparel to deal with risk exposure in making sourcing arrangements. Commodity markets have long used futures and other options as a means to deal with price risk. As the exposure to risk is pushed back in supply chains, one can imagine the emergence of markets to deal with similar risks in a more systematic fashion.

35. See Feenstra (1996) for a detailed discussion of issues related to data concordance between the HS codes, SITC, and SIC classification systems.

# CHAPTER THREE

# Globalization, Deverticalization, and Employment in the Motor Vehicle Industry

TIMOTHY STURGEON
RICHARD FLORIDA

## Introduction

The motor vehicle industry offers a unique perspective on globalization, because, with its massive employment, huge corporations, and iconic products, it seems to sum up a country's psyche—GM and Ford for the United States, Fiat and Ferrari for Italy, Toyota and Honda for Japan, Mercedes and BMW for Germany, Volvo and Saab for Sweden, and Hyundai and Kia for Korea. In advanced economies, motor vehicle employment is closely watched as a bellwether of manufacturing sector heath, and in many developing countries, creating and nurturing a local vehicle sector is one of the key goals of industrial policy. Moreover, the auto industry was the king of the "Fordist" economy, and when commentators thought of mass production—and its limits—the motor vehicle industry was first and foremost to be praised—and criticized. In terms of regional economies and industrial clusters, Detroit, Stuttgart, and Toyota City exemplified these par excellence, far before the term Silicon Valley was even coined. This chapter examines the tripartite processes of globalization, deverticalization, and modularization in the auto industry with a special focus on one of the most debated issues in policy circles, the impact on employment.

For us, an understanding of globalization in the auto industry cannot be gained solely through an examination of the automobile assemblers; we must also consider the auto parts suppliers, especially since they are producing an increasingly significant part of the value-added of finished vehicles, a process which we refer to as "deverticalization." Parts suppliers are faced with many of the same issues as their customers, and as they capture a larger share of revenues and employment, their decisions will have a significant effect on the overall industry. Globalization and deverticalization are intertwined processes. For all automakers the make-or-buy decision is being complicated by a widening set of locational imperatives and options. More operational and market locations are being considered than ever before, and as they are, the number of firms that might be considered as suppliers has increased geometrically.

Globalization and deverticalization strategies are enmeshed in a movement by various auto assemblers, especially those in the United States, to "modularize" vehicle design and production. Modularity is significant because it facilitates deverticalization: the shift of assembly tasks from the auto assembler's factory to the factories of the first-tier suppliers. This shift has led suppliers to grow in size and scope and improve their R&D capabilities, even while they continue to experience extreme price pressure from their customers. Modularity should be understood not simply as a technical change but also as a change in industrial structure, which also interacts with various spatial changes.

If the impact of the "lean production model" drove change in the 1980s, it is the swirling interplay of globalization, deverticalization, and modularization that has created forces, some favoring localization and others favoring global production and sourcing, that have driven change in the industry during the 1990s. So, locating comparative advantage in the case of the auto industry is an exercise in understanding spatial, organizational, and technological change. These changes are, of course, set against the larger backdrop of technological and market changes, outlined in the Introduction to this volume, that are affecting nearly every industry: reductions in transportation and communications costs, increased price pressure as competition becomes global and more production moves to lower-cost regions, and a clear, continued role for spatial clusters of economic activity, especially in the realm of knowledge creation.

This chapter considers the changing composition of employment in the U.S. auto industry in the context of the dynamics of the globalization and deverticalization of the world's automobile industry. The first section illustrates these changes in the United States. This is followed by a section examining the various facets of globalization. Here, we argue that globalization embodies a variety of processes including intra- and intercontinental trade, factory transplants, and global production and sourcing. These processes are underway simultaneously, but have quite different motivations. The concluding section summarizes globalization in the auto industry and its implications for understanding the reconfiguration of the value chain.

## Trends in U.S. Automotive Sector Employment and Wages

Although manufacturing employment in the United States has been declining steadily during the post–World War II period from a wartime high of 44.5 percent of total nonfarm employment to a mere 14 percent in 2000, motor vehicle sector employment has remained remarkably robust. After dropping from

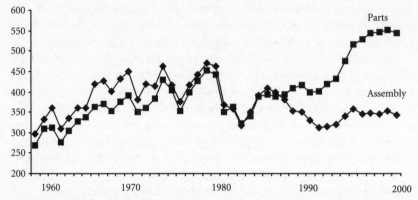

FIG. 3.1. U.S. Motor Vehicle Industry Assembly and Parts Employment, 1958–2000 (thousands of jobs). Source: U.S. Bureau of Labor Statistics, nonfarm payroll statistics from the current employment statistics (national). Note: Assembly includes SIC 3711 (motor vehicles and car bodies), and Parts includes SIC 3714 (motor vehicle parts and accessories).

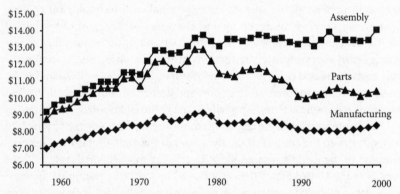

FIG. 3.2. Average Hourly Earnings of U.S. Production Workers in Manufacturing and Motor Vehicle Assembly and Parts, 1958–2000 (in 1983 dollars). Source: See Fig. 3.1.

its precrisis peak of 1,004,900 in 1977 to a twenty-year low of 699,300 in 1982, motor vehicle sector employment rebounded 44.5 percent to an all-time high of 1,010,000 in 1999. Because motor vehicle employment has grown while total manufacturing employment has declined, by 2000 motor vehicle employment's share of total manufacturing employment stood at 5.5 percent, its highest level ever. The commonly held assumption about globalization's impact on employment—that it is eliminating U.S. manufacturing jobs—is not borne out in the case of the motor vehicle industry.

Even so, the structure of the motor vehicle industry, and the characteristics of the jobs within it, have changed markedly since 1986, when the industry's long-time rough employment parity between the assembly and parts sectors began to diverge. Figure 3.1 clearly shows the deverticalization of the industry and reveals that it is the parts sector that has been the real source of job growth in the U.S. automotive industry since the late 1980s. From its low point in 1982, the industry has added only 25,300 jobs in the assembly sector, while the supply sector surged by 220,900 jobs. Automakers are performing far fewer functions within their assembly facilities than they have in the past. Vehicle assembly lines have been streamlined. Assembly workers now bolt together more large sub-assemblies of individual components, or modules, that have been preassembled off-site. Integrated subassembly, or "feeder," lines assembling modules such as seats, cockpits, and climate control systems within vehicle assembly facilities have all but disappeared from the floor of final assembly plants. Modules now arrive fully assembled on loading docks ready to be bolted onto vehicles as they move down the line. The result is more production workers in supplier plants and fewer production workers in final assembly plants.

The shift of manufacturing—and of employment—to the supply base is hardly a panacea for autoworkers. Figure 3.2 clearly shows (in 1983 dollars) that the assembler-supplier wage gap has been steadily widening since the late 1970s. Average hourly wages at suppliers were almost on par with those at automakers between 1958 and 1978, when they ranged from 93 to 97 percent of wages paid by automakers. This rough parity began to erode after 1978, and by 2000 average wages at suppliers stood at an all-time low of 74 percent of those paid by automakers. In 2000, average hourly wages at automakers stood at $24.25 in current dollars, while average wages at suppliers stood at $17.91. Still, production workers at automakers and suppliers alike are paid a significant premium over the average hourly wage of $14.38 paid in 2000 in the U.S. manufacturing sector as a whole.

In the case of the U.S. motor vehicle sector then, the employment data do not support the most basic underlying assumption of the globalization debate, that manufacturing jobs are disappearing. But deverticalization and the attendant shift of jobs to the supply base have meant a fall in the average wage of a worker in the auto industry. So, changes are occurring, but they seem, on their face, to have little to do with globalization. However, by examining the globalization process, it is possible to discover several important trends that may well affect employment in the future.

## The Effects of Globalization

Globalization can be divided into four major dynamics: (a) the globalization of markets, (b) the globalization of production, (c) the globalization of ownership, and (d) the globalization of products. Category (a) can be further divided

TABLE 3.1
*The Eight Effects of Globalization*

| Basic Categories | The Eight Effects of Globalization |
|---|---|
| A) Globalization of markets | 1) Competitive effects<br>2) Trade effects |
| B) Globalization of production | 3) Market seeking investments<br>4) Cost cutting investments<br>5) Constraint breaking investments |
| C) Globalization of ownership | 6) Mergers and acquisitions among automakers<br>7) Mergers and acquisitions among suppliers |
| D) Globalization of products | 8) Commonalization of vehicle platforms, modules, and parts |

*Source:* Authors.

into two subeffects: (1) competitive effects, and (2) trade effects. The globalization of production, category (b), usually entails the relocation of corporate functions through the process of foreign direct investment (FDI) and can be divided to produce three additional subcategories, each of which is likely to have different effects on employment: (3) market-seeking investments, (4) cost-cutting investments, and (5) constraint-breaking investments. Category (c), the globalization of ownership, can be divided into those cross-border mergers and acquisitions that take place at the level of (6) automakers and those that take place at the level of (7) suppliers. Category (d) is the result of automaker consolidation as well as efforts to reduce development costs by sharing parts and vehicle platforms across as wide a range of products as possible as (8) product characteristics are becoming increasingly globalized. (See Table 3.1 for a summary.)

*Globalization of Markets: Competitive Effects*

In the 1960s and 1970s Japanese (and to a lesser extent European) automakers began to penetrate the U.S. market through exports. Although the first "oil shock" of 1973 is often cited as the beginning of a shift toward smaller cars in the U.S. market, the associated rise in gasoline prices was in fact extremely short-lived. The Big Three scrapped plans to build a line of small cars when oil prices fell in 1974. It was not until 1979, when the second oil shock drove gasoline prices up even higher, that American producers embarked on a serious attempt to enter the small car market.[1] By all accounts, Ford's Pinto and GM's Vega were poorly engineered and of notoriously low quality, and so failed to stem the loss of market share to European and Japanese imports (Dassbach 1989). Motor vehicle production in Japan soared from a negligible 300,000 units in 1960 to nearly 11 million units in 1982, growing both on the strength of

Japan's largely protected domestic market of about 5 million units and exports of about 6 million units. In fact, excluding inter-European trade, Japan came to dominate world finished vehicle exports by a wide margin, with the bulk of exports going to the United States (Dicken 1998).

The share of the U.S. passenger vehicle market held by Japanese automakers increased from almost nothing in 1970 to a peak of 25 percent in 1991. The trend was similar, if slightly less pronounced, in Western Europe, where market penetration by Japanese firms reached a peak of 13 percent in 1991 (Ward's Automotive 1996). The competitive pressure applied to the U.S. motor vehicle industry by the success of Japanese imports can hardly be overstated. American automakers had dominated the world motor vehicle industry since the earliest days of mass production, and the success of Japanese firms was at first difficult to accept, let alone respond to, as anything more than a temporary change. But the success of Japanese automakers was not based on short-term fluctuations in gasoline prices or exchange rates; it was based on a fundamentally different production system. The basis of Japanese quality improvements—namely, the "lean" production techniques pioneered and perfected by Toyota—include lower inventories, just-in-time parts deliveries, high-performance work organization (teamwork, job rotation, employee involvement, etc.), heavy reliance on tiers of tightly linked suppliers, and systemwide continuous improvement programs for quality and productivity (Womack et al. 1990). American automakers eventually learned enough about the Japanese production system to begin to graft some of the tenets of lean production to their own system, driving many of the changes that we see in the industry today, including an increasingly deverticalized industry structure that has helped to transfer a growing share of employment into the supply sector.

### Globalization of Markets: Trade Effects

Of all the effects of globalization, finished vehicle trade is perhaps the most obvious. Exports suggest production for demand above and beyond the domestic market, while imports raise the possibility that jobs will be displaced and domestic firms will be threatened. In the motor vehicle industry, finished vehicle imports make the threat of globalization-related job loss most palpable. Each finished vehicle imported and sold is one that might have been produced locally, if local production capacity exists. Of course, exports can offset imports in the overall trade balance.

The success of Japanese automakers' export strategy in the 1960s and 1970s resulted in a gain in market share in the United States that came at the direct expense of Big Three sales. In response, Japanese market penetration sparked a political backlash that resulted in the setting of "voluntary" limits to continued

Japanese market share expansion in the United States via finished vehicle exports. Another stark reality has added fuel to the fire: American automakers have been unable whatsoever to penetrate the Japanese domestic market. The market share of U.S.-badged automobiles in Japan continues to be in the range of 1 percent (Ward's Automotive 1996, 2001).

In a manner similar to what Kenney (in this volume) describes in the television industry, Japanese automakers responded to the "voluntary" quotas by embarking on a wave of plant construction in the United States during the 1980s (Florida and Kenney 1991). Since then the percentage and number of Japanese cars sold in the United States that were built in the United States has steadily increased. From January to July 2001, more than 75 percent of the passenger vehicles sold by Japanese automakers were assembled in the United States (Ward's Automotive 2001). Europe experienced a similar but weaker wave of Japanese "transplants" that began in 1986, with Nissan's plant in the U.K. By 1995, Japanese automakers were locally manufacturing nearly one-third of the passenger vehicles they sold in Europe. In 1986, as "transplant" production ramped up, Japanese exports began declining in percentage terms.

While the establishment of the Japanese transplants seems remarkable from the perspective of post–World War II America, national governments have in fact long played a central role in shaping the geographic expansion of motor vehicle production through the erection of various barriers to trade in finished vehicles. For example, the spread of Ford Motor Company's production to Europe, South America, Asia, and Australia during the 1910s and 1920s was at first driven by a desire to reduce transport costs, but soon national governments the world over were demanding that automakers increase local production and local content to help create jobs and transfer technology (Dassbach 1989; Sturgeon and Florida 1999). By adopting a "build-where-you-sell" approach in the mid-1980s, Japanese automakers simply began to operate according to norms that were established in the industry during the 1920s and 1930s. By taking this long view, the establishment of Japanese "transplants" in the United States and Europe signaled the demise of "export-led" development strategies in the automotive industry. The massive wave of Japanese imports that came to the United States in the 1970s can be seen, in hindsight, as an anomalous historical event that is unlikely to be repeated. Indeed, in our interviews, the mantra of "we build where we sell" was heard from top executives at American, European, and Japanese automakers alike.

### Globalization of Production: Market-Seeking Investments

Although Japanese automakers' investments in North America are discussed above in the context of trade effects—or to put it more accurately, the decline of trade effects—the investments represent an important part of the globalization of production. Japanese automakers established local production in the United States and Europe to retain and continue to expand their participation in markets that had initially been captured through exports. In Japan, the simultaneous decline in exports and stagnation of the local market caused by recession put extraordinary pressure on the production system, resulted in employment loss, mounting debt, and eventually, the transfer of control of several major domestic automakers to foreign firms. For the United States, however, these investments meant the addition of hundreds of thousands of new jobs. The precise number is difficult to judge, but the North American final assembly "transplants" have added at least 35,000 jobs and, according to the U.S. Bureau of Economic Analysis, U.S. affiliates of foreign firms in the entire motor vehicles, bodies, trailers, and parts sector totaled an unlikely 337,600 in 1998—more than enough to account for the overall employment expansion in the U.S. motor vehicle sector since 1982.

In cases in which market-seeking investments have not been preceded by a successful export strategy, such as American automakers' investments in China and Brazil, the impact of new offshore investments on employment at home can be assumed small. Automakers, in general, do not set up plants in emerging economies for the purpose of re-exporting finished vehicles to developed economy markets (except in the case of proximate low-wage countries—see below). In addition to the political risks of such a move, it would make little financial sense as well. In an interview, a manager at one automaker estimated that a 75 percent cost reduction at developing economy plants would be required to offset the added costs of poor infrastructure, low productivity, lack of raw materials, duties, shipping, and the like. Because most of the plants established in emerging economies begin with the assembly of completely knocked down (CKD) kits of imported parts, employment requirements can actually be increased in source plants—most often located in developed economies—where additional working hours are required to process, consolidate, and package vehicle kits destined for CKD assembly plants in emerging economies. In fact, CKD assembly in emerging market locations can help to boost production and employment or alleviate overcapacity problems at home by absorbing some of the output of underutilized domestic assembly plants.

With the gradual and eventual shift to local content, any positive employment impact of emerging market assembly plants for home country employment can be expected to diminish, but that can take a long time. One automaker stated in an interview that the shift to integrated production would come only when annual unit sales reached 50,000 units per year; another thought 100,000 units; and yet another suggested that it would explore integrated production when sales reached 120,000 units per year for two models. Still another automaker stated that a shift from strict kit assembly toward "free-flow" of parts would begin at an annual volume of 20,000 units and become full-blown by 50,000 units. Given the various "crises" experienced by a range of developing nations over the past five years, it is likely that many emerging market assembly plants will not reach such output levels for many years to come. As parts from home constitute a smaller share of the total bill of materials for each vehicle, both local and global sourcing to an emerging market assembly plant can increase.

Of course, with global sourcing, the possibility of home country sourcing and its attendant employment benefits remain a possibility. For items that require a great deal of skill and capital investment, and therefore large-scale production, such as engines and transmissions, home country sourcing is possible even when offshore plants make the full transition to "integrated" production. For example, during our interviews the volume levels necessary to justify engine and transmission production were reported to be about 150,000–200,000 units per year. So, even with a gradual shift from CKD to integrated production, there are likely to be modest long-term employment benefits to advanced economies from emerging-economy investments. There is one major exception to this argument: home country employment is likely to decline when market-seeking investments displace home country exports, as has been already mentioned in the case with Japanese investments in the United States and Europe.

### Globalization of Production: Cost-Cutting Investments

When the flood of Japanese imports radically intensified competition in the United States and Europe beginning in the late 1970s, American and European automakers began to put programs into place to lower operating costs. Of particular importance are regional integration strategies, which have progressively shifted production to lower-cost locations within continental-scale trade arrangements such as Autopact, NAFTA, and the European Union. The integration of lower-cost production sites such as Mexico, Canada, Spain, and Eastern Europe with the largest existing markets and supply bases in North America and Europe has created a powerful operating cost gradient that has influenced key investment decisions by automakers, particularly during the late 1980s and 1990s.

Volkswagen, for example, closed its sole U.S. plant in 1988; it upgraded its factory in Puebla, Mexico—which had long been producing "Beetle" model sedans for the local market—to the manufacture of "Golf" model sedans, almost entirely for export to the United States. Production at the plant increased to nearly 230,000 by 1996. In 1997 and 1998, the factory was upgraded again, this time for the production of "New Beetle" model sedans, a vehicle intended almost exclusively for the U.S. market. The total capacity of the plant complex in 1998 was about 450,000 units.

Chrysler, Ford, GM, and Nissan have all followed similar strategies, upgrading and expanding older car and truck plants in Mexico that had been assembling for the local market for the export of current-model vehicles to the United States. As these new high-volume production capabilities have come onstream, exports of finished vehicles from Mexico to the United States have soared. Finished vehicle exports from Mexico to the United States increased from a mere $244 million in 1989, to $4.6 billion in 1994, to $13.1 billion in 1998. This increase contrasts with the relatively meager increase in the flow of finished vehicles from the United States to Mexico from $1.1 billion in 1994 to $2.2 billion in 1998.

The flow of parts between the two countries, however, reveals a somewhat different story. The transfer of labor-intensive parts production to the Mexican border region began in the early 1980s with the Maquiladora program, and by 1994 it had driven the value of parts exports from Mexico to the United States to $6.7 billion. Perhaps because the bulk of the labor-intensive work had already been transferred from the United States to Mexico, the signing of the NAFTA treaty in 1994 had little impact. Parts exports to the United States grew only 19 percent (to $8.3 billion) between 1994 and 1998.

On the other hand, the flow of parts from the United States to Mexico soared 419 percent, from $1.1 billion in 1994 to $5.3 billion in 1998 (see Table 3.2). Many of these parts were capital intensive items with extremely high minimum scale economies, such as engines, transmissions, and body panel stampings, and so have been supplied by existing plants in the United States. The move to current model production in Mexico also meant that some of the vehicles produced were simultaneously being assembled in the United States, making the reliance of Mexican assembly plants on the U.S. supply base more likely, especially given the underdeveloped state of the local supply base in Mexico.

TABLE 3.2

*Vehicle and Parts Trade Between Mexico and the United States, 1994–98*

|  | 1994 | 1995 | 1996 | 1997 | 1998 | 1994–98 % Change |
|---|---|---|---|---|---|---|
| **Mexico to U.S.A.** | | | | | | |
| Vehicles | 4,633,544 | 7,621,883 | 10,858,953 | 11,661,048 | 13,072,824 | 182.1% |
| Parts | 6,969,265 | 6,887,846 | 7,309,324 | 7,760,585 | 8,306,140 | 19.2% |
| **Mexico to U.S.A.** | | | | | | |
| Vehicles | 1,096,103 | 440,524 | 1,065,100 | 2,018,654 | 2,177,853 | 98.7% |
| Parts | 1,024,167 | 2,501,624 | 4,637,717 | 5,371,234 | 5,323,131 | 419.8% |

*Source:* Data in this table are taken from the COMTRADE database of the United Nations Statistics Division. Vehicles include passenger vehicles (HTC 7812) and good/service vehicles (HTC 7821). Parts include motor vehicle chassis (HTC 7841), motor vehicle bodies (HTC 7842), and other motor vehicle parts (HTC 7843).

TABLE 3.3

*Total and Intra-regional Exports of Finished Vehicles from
Canada, Mexico, Spain, and East Europe, 1994–1998*

(value of shipments in thousands of current U.S. dollars)

| CANADA | Total Vehicle Exports | Vehicle Exports to U.S.A. | U.S.A. Share |
|---|---|---|---|
| 1994 | 30,314,451 | 29,814,444 | 98% |
| 1995 | 32,727,051 | 31,904,068 | 97% |
| 1996 | 32,601,256 | 32,073,902 | 98% |
| 1997 | 34,258,773 | 33,820,566 | 99% |
| 1998 | 35,689,609 | 35,358,624 | 99% |
| MEXICO | Total Vehicle Exports | Vehicle Exports to U.S.A. | U.S.A. Share |
| 1994 | 5,867,920 | 4,633,544 | 79% |
| 1995 | 9,371,855 | 7,621,883 | 81% |
| 1996 | 13,095,236 | 10,858,953 | 83% |
| 1997 | 13,685,097 | 11,661,048 | 85% |
| 1998 | 14,551,983 | 13,072,824 | 90% |
| SPAIN | Total Vehicle Exports | Vehicle Exports to EU 10 | EU 10 Share |
| 1994 | 13,409,250 | 11,035,587 | 82% |
| 1995 | 16,430,312 | 13,311,609 | 81% |
| 1996 | 18,126,965 | 14,887,842 | 82% |
| 1997 | 17,823,480 | 14,667,411 | 82% |
| 1998 | 19,895,227 | 16,389,990 | 82% |
| Eastern Europe 3 | Total Vehicle Exports | Vehicle Exports to EU 10 | EU 10 Share |
| 1994 | 1,444,214 | 793,616 | 55% |
| 1995 | 1,900,444 | 1,122,164 | 59% |
| 1996 | 2,133,988 | 1,424,561 | 67% |
| 1997 | 2,958,940 | 2,005,058 | 68% |
| 1998 | 4,183,812 | 3,046,176 | 73% |

*Source:* Data in this table are taken from the COMTRADE database of the United Nations Statistics Division. Vehicles include passenger vehicles (HTC 7812) and good/service vehicles (HTC 7821).

In regard to employment, it is likely that the blow dealt to U.S. autoworkers by the shift of finished vehicle production intended for the U.S. market to Mexico has been ameliorated to some degree by the reverse flow of parts from the United States to Mexico. Significantly, the jobs that have been retained through parts exports are consistent with the continued deverticalization of the American motor vehicle sector and the shift of jobs to the less unionized, lower-paid parts sector.

The dynamic between Mexico and the United States since the signing of NAFTA is part of a more general ongoing shift toward regional integration in the global economy. Table 3.3 provides additional evidence for increasing regional integration. As Table 3.3 indicates, the share of finished vehicle exports is high and rising in all of the four "peripheral" locations identified—Canada,

Spain, Mexico and Eastern Europe (defined here as the Czech Republic, Hungary, and Poland)—with the transformation being the most notable in those countries that have only recently come on stream within their respective regional production systems—Mexico and Eastern Europe. It should be recognized that in each case the flow of finished vehicles from peripheral countries to their more developed neighbors is offset by a smaller but significant flow of parts into these nations.

While these changes are dramatic, it should be pointed out that the increase in motor vehicle exports from lower-wage locations has been occurring within a more general context of increasing total exports from these countries. Except for Mexico, where passenger vehicles displaced oil as the top export, the relative shares of the top ten exports have not changed very much as total exports have grown. Still, the importance of auto exports is striking. The combined export value of motor vehicles and motor vehicle–related products in the top ten outstrip any of the other top export products by a wide margin in all three countries. This is especially true in Spain, where passenger and commercial vehicles together account for 48 percent of the value of the country's top ten exports.

The modest aggregate employment effects of globalization to date mask the threat to jobs in the United States and Northwestern Europe from the increased flow of finished vehicles from assembly plants in lower-wage peripheral locations. Although jobs do not appear to have migrated away from the United States or other advanced industrial nations in massive numbers, yet the growing reliance on Mexico, Canada, Spain, and Eastern Europe could conceivably shift the industry's center of gravity over the long term. The negative impact of these shifts has so far been mitigated to some degree by the reverse flow of parts from "home" to "host" countries and a powerful boom in auto sales, especially highly profitable SUVs, during the long boom of the 1990s. Yet there is a distinct possibility that employment displacement at home will become severe as more assembly work is relocated and the supply bases in these lower-cost locations continue to upgrade their capabilities over time. This last point is especially pertinent in light of the increased globalization of the supply base, which promises to speed the localization of parts production.

In an earlier work (Sturgeon and Florida 1999) we noted that the emerging low-cost production platforms for the United States and Western European motor vehicle markets had no counterpart in Asia. The Japanese market has been supplied almost exclusively by domestic production. Manufacturing's share of employment in Japan has dropped, but it remains at 20 percent, about 5 percentage points above the United States. Even when the collapse of vehicle sales in Southeast Asia in 1997 put extreme pressure on Japanese affiliates to export, very few such vehicles found their way to Japan (although parts did start to flow). This situation may be changing. According to the *New York Times* (Brooke 2002):

Violating a decades-old taboo, Japanese vehicle companies are starting to sell in Japan vehicles made by their Asian subsidiaries. This year, following the lead of Japanese car-parts makers that export back to Japan from lower-wage countries, Isuzu is to import trucks from China, and Fuji Heavy Industries is to import minivans from Thailand. Toyota plans to phase out pick-up production in Japan by 2004, concentrating its Asian production in Thailand.

While the total volume of finished vehicle exports to Japan is still small, the rise of a low-cost production periphery for the Japanese market could be extremely swift given the substantial capacity that Japanese automakers already have in Southeast Asia. The production capacity of Japanese automakers in China—only one day away from Japan by ocean freighter—remains small, but many Japanese automakers have plans to establish or increase production there. In what could be a mirror of the move of labor intensive auto parts production from the United States to the border region of Mexico in the 1980s, Chinese-made auto parts destined for assembly plants in Japan will likely precede large-scale export of finished vehicles from China to Japan, but many feel that it is only a matter of time before vehicles assembled in China make significant inroads in the Japanese market. According to Andy Xie, Morgan Stanley's Asia economist, "You can make a good quality, modern sedan for sale in Japan for about $5,000," about half the current price (ibid.).

### Globalization of Production: Constraint-Breaking Investments

Automakers, especially American and European automakers, have been able to develop their most advanced modes of production not in their home countries but in the emerging economies. They are able to do so because these new locations offer escape from the path-dependent legacy of previous social and political compromises that have become codified in the organizational and institutional structures that have accumulated at home. Because of the power of labor unions—as well as "outmoded thinking," "cultural blocs," and "management fiefdoms" that our interview subjects attributed to "old-line" managers—automakers find it very difficult and costly to close or to introduce new approaches to assembly at plants in their home bases. As one manager put it, green-field locations provide automakers with "a clean sheet of paper" upon which to implement advanced practices.

American and European automakers are using their newest assembly plants in emerging economies as test-beds to experiment with innovative forms of work and industry organization. There have been and will continue to be attempts to import these lessons to transform existing operations in the traditional centers of the industry, but the process is proving to be difficult. In an approach that demonstrates the lengths to which automakers sometimes must go to transform existing facilities, a manager at an automaker in Europe reported building a new engine line directly alongside an older line to demonstrate new techniques and win acceptance.

The new Daimler-Chrysler plant in Tuscaloosa, Alabama, provides a good example of how quickly "green-field" assembly plants can allow automakers to adopt new approaches. Although Daimler-Chrysler purchases only about 40 percent of the value of its German-built passenger vehicles from outside suppliers, the plant in Alabama had an initial external sourcing ratio of about 70 percent, and plans were in place to increase it to 80 percent. Yet another example is the Volkswagen truck plant in Resende, Brazil, to which suppliers bring subassembled modules directly to the assembly line and then take the unprecedented additional step of attaching them to the vehicles moving down the line. In our interview with IG Metall, the German Metalworkers Union, it was made clear that such practices would be extremely difficult, if not impossible, to implement in Germany.

GM has based its new plants in Thailand and Shanghai, China, on what was learned at their plant at Eisenach, former East Germany, which was opened in 1995. The approach used at Eisenach was blended from the experience gained at NUMMI (a joint-venture with Toyota in Fremont, California), and CAMI (a joint-venture with Suzuki in Ingersoll, Canada), as well as from input from personnel formerly employed by Toyota. Eisenach was GM's first integrated "lean" production system, which was not applied in piecemeal fashion to an existing facility but fully implemented on the first day of the plant's operation. The focus was on teamwork, open communication, short lead times, and continuous improvement (*kaizen*). Quality circles were instituted, break times were allowed to be flexible and mass relief was given between shifts, and job classifications were limited to two. In addition, the plant at Eisenach was configured to have a string of loading docks adjacent to the assembly line to receive parts shipment directly to the line on a just-in-time (JIT) basis.

Eisenach was then used as a model for a recently opened GM truck plant in Brazil, which in turn may be used as a model for a new generation of assembly plants to be established in North America, perhaps within fifty miles of existing plants (agreements with the U.A.W. give autoworkers the right to turn down transfers to work sites more than fifty miles from their existing jobs). GM publicized its intent to invest $21 billion in the United States by 2001, but it was less forthcoming about its plans for expansion in Mexico (Bradsher 1998a, 1998b, 1998c). It is interesting to note that two recent presidents of GM's Brazilian operations were promoted to GM North America (Bradsher 1998a) and that the former president of GM Mexico was installed to manage GM International Operations.

However, greenfield settings are not always a panacea. While it is often easier to implement flexible work organization practices in green-field locations, one automaker we interviewed found "worker empowerment" (e.g., flat hierarchies and employee involvement) hard to implement in (current or former) autocracies such as China, Russia, Vietnam, and Eastern Europe. According to Okada (1998), it has been difficult for automakers in India to get line workers to maintain and clean their own workstations—an element of Toyota-style worker involvement—since sweeping floors has traditionally been a task assigned to the lowest, "untouchable" caste of society. Finally, as a manager from a large automaker noted during our interviews, not all emerging-economy facilities are built from scratch in "greenfields," and plants that are built from existing facilities can initially be a "step backward" in terms of plant design and work organization.

## Globalization of Ownership: Automaker Consolidation

"Mega-mergers" at the automaker level have become a fact of life in the automotive industry. The belief among automakers is that only full-line, global car-makers will survive the transition to a fully globalized economy. There were several problems that transnational mega-mergers have been expected to address. The first is that greater economies of scale could be achieved in parts purchasing. The second is that mergers would permit the auto industry to address the problem of overcapacity by consolidating production in fewer plants. The third is that mergers would help to address the skyrocketing cost of vehicle development. By reusing modules and other design elements across a wider range of vehicle models, particularly those in the underbody and drive train, automakers expect to better recoup development costs and shorten design cycles. For large companies, the acquisition of specialty producers is a way to expand their product lines. So Jaguar furnishes Ford with a luxury marquee suitable for Europe, Chrysler provides Daimler with a full line of midpriced cars without diluting the Mercedes brand name, and so on. Since gaining global-scale manufacturing operations is now seen as a key requirement, mergers can also help to quickly and cost-effectively expand the geographic scope of operations. For example, the Daimler-Chrysler merger means that Chrysler now has access to Daimler's assembly capacity in Europe, Asia, and South America, and Daimler has access to Chrysler's huge production base in North America.[2] Likewise, Mazda and Isuzu have provided Ford and GM with a much larger and badly needed presence in Asia. Besides creating a global-scale network of assembly plants, acquisitions can give automakers access to an enlarged supply base.

Ford's partnership with Mazda, for example, has given it access to Mazda's well-developed supply base in Thailand. Given the difficulty of establishing local supply, and the great pressure that automakers are under to develop local content, such relationships can be a great asset.

Mega-mergers have been wide-ranging. For example, France's Renault took a controlling stake in Nissan, Japan's then financially stressed number two automaker. Germany's Daimler-Benz now owns Chrysler. Ford already controls Jaguar, Volvo, and Mazda; General Motors controls Saab and Isuzu; and BMW produces the Land Rover. By 2001 this merger wave was complete, and there were few small independent firms left.

Still, such combinations do little to mitigate the fundamental problem of overcapacity, which is creating much of the weakness that is allowing the mergers to proceed. The mergers we are seeing in today's automotive industry are between vastly dissimilar companies in terms of product mix and geography, which is why the marriages have been referred to by industry analysts as a "good fit." But it is precisely when companies are similar, are a "poor fit," that mergers lead to the elimination of excess capacity and restored profitability. For consolidation to solve the overcapacity problem, it would somehow have to enable car-makers to eliminate redundant manufacturing capacity, a process that has proved to be difficult, slow, painful, and costly in Korea, Japan, Germany, and the United States alike. Opportunities to reduce capacity through mergers are created when vehicle lines are redundant, not complementary. Complementary production geographies may create global competitors in one fell swoop, but again, this does not address the problem. If the goal is to gain a production foothold in all the world's existing and emerging markets, capacity reductions that decrease geographic reach defeat the purpose of the merger.

The ominous conclusion is that consolidation only helps to alleviate excess capacity if it results in massive rationalization, in effect eliminating redundant plants. But in fact, mega-mergers that involve companies of different national origins might make the process of rationalization even more intractable than it already is. So, while overcapacity invites consolidation, consolidation without rationalization will do little to solve the industry's underlying problem with overcapacity.

### Globalization of Ownership: Supplier Consolidation

*Building a Global Supply-chain.* For automakers that are aggressively adopting modular assembly processes, new plants are going further with collocation with suppliers than existing plants because larger modules are more difficult and expensive to ship long distance and are more likely to be sequenced. For automakers that rely heavily on suppliers, the capability to set up integrated assembly operations in new locations simply does not exist in-house, so they cannot hope to meet local content requirements without the local participation of their key suppliers. But there is great tension between "global sourcing" and "local sourcing." The charter of many automakers' global purchasing organizations is to scan the world for low-cost, high-quality parts. This means that the scope of the supply base is growing beyond national boundaries, and when combined with increased outsourcing, it explains why many automakers have become increasingly dependent on both domestic and foreign locations for parts. However, there are two forces that inhibit unfettered global sourcing. First, there is the need for module suppliers to become involved early in the design process. This limits module sourcing to those suppliers with design facilities close to the vehicle design centers of the automakers, and explains why many world-class suppliers have established design operations within the traditional centers of vehicle design. Second, local content rules can effectively block the shipment of parts from low-cost sources to an automaker's worldwide network of assembly plants. Locally procured parts usually cost more than those obtained through global purchasing organizations, and local content rules obviate the implementation of true low-cost global sourcing strategies. In practice, parts that can be sourced globally tend to be highly standardized, easily transportable, and subject to low tariffs (e.g., electronics, brakes). Parts that are sourced locally tend to be highly specific to particular vehicle models and color sequences (e.g., interior panels), difficult to ship (e.g., seats), or subject to high tariffs (e.g., body panels). Suppliers with truly global operations—that is, design centers near automaker design centers and manufacturing plants near automaker assembly plants—can create a bridge between global and local sourcing (see below).

Thus there is a great tension between the need for supplier collocation with assembly plants, which allows for JIT delivery, and the consolidation of supplier production in large plants that serve multiple customers, which creates economies of scale that drive costs down. There are two factors that come into play: the type of part and the quality and cost of long-distance supply-line infrastructure.[3] In some cases, suppliers locate in industrial parks close to assembly facilities, where modules are built up from parts sourced from their local supply base and their worldwide network of plants and suppliers. On the other hand, where the quality of supply lines is good, such as in Europe, tightly coordinated JIT deliveries can come from a great distance. For example, while GM did not try to resettle suppliers around its new plant in Eisenach, (former East) Germany, because of resistance from their suppliers' works councils, the company found that suppliers do not necessarily need to be clustered around the plant if high-quality supply lines are reliable. Eisenach has "no" inventory and regularly receives JIT deliveries of bumpers, facias, and seats—items that need to be delivered in sequence because of color matching—from suppliers located as far as 1,000 kilometers (621 miles) away.

*The Rise of the Global Supplier.* Globalization is occurring at the same time as increased outsourcing and the move to sourcing modules and systems, and many suppliers are taking a larger role in the globalization process. Companies such as Bosch, Johnson Controls, Lear, Magna, Siemens Automotive, TRW, and Yazaki have become the preferred suppliers for automakers around the world. Many first-tier suppliers have responded by embarking on a wave of vertical integration (through mergers, acquisitions, and joint-ventures) and geographic expansion to gain the ability to deliver parts and modules on a global basis. The entry of GM's and Ford's former component divisions into the merchant market for vehicle components, modules, and systems has, almost overnight, created the world's two largest, most diversified, and geographically extensive automotive suppliers.

As lead firms have outsourced more of the manufacturing, sourcing, and logistics functions that were previously carried out in-house, their preference for dealing with suppliers with international reach has grown. The reasons are several. First, the lead firms are in many cases marketing their products globally, and require engineering, manufacturing, and logistics support in multiple locations. Second, the lead firms often seek to economize on development costs by creating global product platforms that share and reuse many common parts, modules, and subsystems. Partnering with a small number of suppliers, or even a single supplier for a particular part, enables lead firms to exploit these economies of scope more fully, while also avoiding the cost of requalifying new suppliers for each new market. Third, cost pressures require purchasing organizations to scan the world for low-cost, high-quality parts, and to the degree that suppliers are taking on these responsibilities, they too must have global sourcing capabilities. Fourth, suppliers based in protected final markets can combine global sourcing with local sourcing and subassembly to help lead firms meet local content requirements. Fifth, as already discussed, the preference for key suppliers to take on a more active role early in the development process requires these suppliers to be able to collocate at least some of their own design activities with the design facilities of their customers. Some lead firms have given their key suppliers an ultimatum: provide support on a global basis or lose the business entirely. Managers at three global automotive suppliers made essentially the same point during separate interviews:

The industry began to change 5–10 years ago. Today it is a requirement to serve platforms—it is part of the bid. If a supplier doesn't have a global strategy, it can't bid. New projects are no longer seen as an opportunity to expand globally—instead, a supplier must have a global base in place to even make a bid. This forces suppliers to have a global supply system in place.

Suppliers must support assemblers as a sole source for global products lines to support commonalization. We must supply the same part, with the same quality and price, in every location. If [the automaker] says to go to Argentina, we must go or lose existing, not just potential, business. Logistics are becoming a key competitive advantage; we must have the ability to move production to where customers' facilities are.

We want our plants to be present where vehicles are produced. Sometimes customers ask us to locate near offshore assembly plants to provide local content.... We will follow our customer's strategy by establishing local engineering operations in large emerging markets only, such as Korea, Mexico, and Brazil.

Providing this kind of support involves coordinating flows of components, subassemblies, and products across production networks that often span several countries or even continents. It also requires setting up design operations close to the design centers of the lead firms. As will be discussed in more detail below, the great majority of the suppliers that have risen to this challenge so far have originated from the United States and Europe, where the American lead firms have the bulk of their design activities, where there is a deep pool of management talent with long experience in international operations, and where capital has been readily available to finance global expansion, especially during the U.S. stock market run-up in the late 1990s. The pressure for suppliers to expand has been met partly by internal growth but even more so by aggressive merger and acquisition activity. Acquisitions of competitors in similar lines of business have yielded sudden jumps in geographic coverage. Acquisition of firms with upstream or downstream capabilities have broadened the range of products and services on offer. (Frequently, acquisitions have served both purposes simultaneously.)

Unlike the global contract manufacturers in electronics (Sturgeon 2002), a few global suppliers in the motor vehicle industry have emerged from Japan and Europe as well as North America. Still, the trends toward rapid growth, geographic expansion, and consolidation are most pronounced among suppliers based in North America. Bosch and Siemens Automotive, both based in Germany, have tended to remain more focused on their core activities, but since their focus has long been electrical and electronic systems for vehicles, their growth has been in part the result of the increased electronic content in vehicles and in part increased sales to Japanese and especially American automakers. To a lesser degree than their American counterparts, most of the major European suppliers are consolidating and experimenting with a modular approach as well, especially with their American customers. For example, in 2000, Siemens Automotive acquired another German firm, VDO, which added cockpit instrumentation capability to Siemens's climate control and interior plastics capability. This has allowed the firm to bid on completely built-up dashboard modules.

An exceptional case of supplier transformation in Europe is the German tire manufacturer Continental AG, which has long specialized in tires for the retail market and had already established a global manufacturing presence in tires by the early 1990s.[4] As late as 1995, Continental was still concentrated in the retail tires market, and ranked fifty-second in the world in terms of sales to automakers (OEMs). That year, the company established Continental Automotive Systems Group and began acquiring automotive suppliers with a wide variety of competencies and geographic attributes, such as TBA Belting (UK), and ITT Brake and Chassis (United States). The latter acquisition, which was valued at nearly $2 billion, added twenty-three plants and 10,000 employees. To round out the company's global footprint, Continental made a series of additional acquisitions in Argentina, Brazil, Slovakia, Romania, Mexico, and South Africa. In 2001, Continental acquired Temic Microelectronic GmbH, a medium-size ($900 million in revenues) German automotive electronics firm with 3,000 employees and nine manufacturing facilities in Germany, and also a small, newly established global footprint, including 2,800 workers at factories in Mexico, Hungary, the Philippines, China, and Brazil, and two technical centers, one at its headquarters in Germany and a new center in Auburn Hills, Michigan, just north of Detroit and minutes away from Chrysler's new design center. Continental's product strategy is threefold: to leverage competence in synthetic rubber by entering markets for power transmission belts and other rubber parts for motor vehicles; to develop integrated modules from the tire inward, including assembled wheels, brakes, and suspension parts; and to enter the high growth area of vehicle electronics. Today Continental's automotive divisions operate 140 facilities in thirty-six countries and employ 64,000. By 2000, Continental had jumped to number twelve in the global ranking of sales to automakers (see Table 3.4).

As Tables 3.4 and 3.5 show, however, most of the largest and most rapidly growing suppliers providing auto parts and modules are based in North America. Consider the example of Lear. The company's focus is on automotive interior modules and systems that are used in vehicles bearing the nameplates of GM, Suzuki, Hyundai, Isuzu, Jaguar, Mazda, Opel, Ford, VW, Porsche, Mercedes, Chrysler, Saab, Subaru, Fiat, Daewoo, Renault, Toyota, Mitsubishi, Honda, Audi, BMW, Peugeot, Nissan, Volvo, and Rover, among others. Headquartered in Southfield, Michigan, Lear has grown to 120,000 employees working at more than 200 locations in thirty-three countries. Lear rose from the world's thirteenth largest automotive supplier in 1995 to the fifth largest in 2000, with record sales of $14.1 billion.

TABLE 3.4

*Top Fourteen Motor Vehicle Parts Suppliers, 1995 and 2000
Rank by Home Region and Country, 1995–2000 Compound
Annual Growth Rate*

| Home Country/ Region | Company | World Rank 1995 | World Rank 2000 | 1995 World OEM Sales, $M | 2000 World OEM Sales, $M | CAGR 1995–2000 |
|---|---|---|---|---|---|---|
| | | | *North American* | | | |
| U.S.A. | Delphi | 1 | 1 | 26,400 | 29,100 | 2% |
| U.S.A. | Visteon | 6 | 3 | 9,200 | 19,500 | 16% |
| U.S.A. | Lear | 13 | 5 | 4,707 | 14,100 | 25% |
| U.S.A. | Johnson Controls | 15 | 6 | 4,420 | 11,869 | 22% |
| U.S.A. | TRW | 7 | 7 | 6,100 | 11,000 | 13% |
| Canada | Magna | 19 | 8 | 3,223 | 10,099 | 26% |
| U.S.A. | Arvin Industries | 32 | 13 | 1,792 | 5,153 | 24% |
| U.S.A. | Dupont Auto | 18 | 14 | 3,500 | 5,100 | 8% |
| Average North American | | | | 7,418 | 13,240 | 17% |
| | | | *Japanese* | | | |
| Japan | Denso | 2 | 4 | 15,000 | 16,392 | 2% |
| Japan | Aisin World | 5 | 9 | 11,587 | 8,301 | –6% |
| Japan | Yazaki | 10 | 11 | 5,000 | 6,000 | 4% |
| Average Japanese | | | | 10,529 | 10,231 | 0% |
| | | | *European* | | | |
| Germany | Robert Bosch | 3 | 2 | 14,200 | 20,550 | 8% |
| Germany | Continental | 52 | 12 | 800 | 5,500 | 47% |
| France | Valeo | 11 | 10 | 5,000 | 8,200 | 10% |
| Average European | | | | 6,667 | 11,417 | 22% |
| Average top 14 | | | | 7,924 | 12,205 | 14% |

*Source: Automotive News, 1996; Crain's Detroit Business, 2001.*

The spin-off of the internal parts divisions of General Motors and Ford in the late 1990s created the world's two largest and most diversified automotive parts suppliers, Delphi and Visteon, with capabilities to supply complete modules and with global operations from the outset. For example, Visteon has system and module capabilities in chassis, climate, electronics, glass and lighting, interior, exterior trim, and powertrain. The company currently operates forty-two facilities in the United States and Canada, twenty-nine in West Europe, twenty-two in Asia, nine in Mexico, six in Eastern Europe, and four in South America. System and module engineering work is carried out in facilities in Japan, Germany (3), England (3), and the United States (4).

Although outsourcing is an industry-wide phenomenon, our research has

TABLE 3.5

*Top Fourteen Motor Vehicle Parts Suppliers, Percentage of*
*Sales in North America, 1995 and 2000*

| Home Country | Company | 1995 N.A. OEM Sales, $M | 2000 N.A. OEM Sales, $M | 1995 % sales in N.A. Market | 2000 % sales in N.A. Market |
|---|---|---|---|---|---|
| | | North American | | | |
| U.S.A. | Delphi | 21,800 | 23,600 | 83% | 81% |
| U.S.A. | Visteon | 8,140 | 14,400 | 88% | 74% |
| U.S.A. | Lear | 3,373 | 8,600 | 72% | 61% |
| U.S.A. | Johnson Controls | 3,257 | 7,596 | 74% | 64% |
| U.S.A. | TRW | 3,300 | 5,610 | 54% | 51% |
| Canada | Magna | 2,579 | 6,111 | 80% | 61% |
| U.S.A. | Arvin Industries | 892 | 3,252 | 50% | 63% |
| U.S.A. | DuPont Auto | 2,500 | 2,550 | 71% | 50% |
| Average North American | | 5,730 | 8,965 | 72% | 63% |
| | | Japanese | | | |
| Japan | Denso | 2,300 | 3,803 | 15% | 23% |
| Japan | Aisin World | 563 | 664 | 5% | 8% |
| Japan | Yazaki | 1,600 | 2,400 | 32% | 40% |
| Average Japanese | | 1,488 | 2,289 | 17% | 24% |
| | | European | | | |
| Germany | Robert Bosch | 1,576 | 6,200 | 11% | 30% |
| Germany | Continental | 350 | 1,650 | 44% | 30% |
| France | Valeo | 600 | 2,246 | 12% | 27% |
| Average European | | 842 | 3,365 | 22% | 29% |

Source: *Automotive News*, 1996; *Crain's Detroit Business*, 2001.

also identified significant variations in the speed, extent, and nature of deverticalization among automakers. GM and Ford, long among the most vertically
integrated automakers, have been aggressively outsourcing to cut costs and reduce overhead, both by increasing their use of outside suppliers and, as noted,
by moving to spin off their internal parts subsidiaries as independent "merchant" firms. Even so, sourcing is still fairly traditional at GM and Ford, which
have globally centralized and notoriously predatory purchasing organizations.
In the resulting atmosphere of price pressure and mistrust, suppliers are only
slowly and irregularly gaining influence over design. There is some experimentation with preselection of suppliers and involvement prior to project approval,
where suppliers are asked to bid on the parts they would like to design and produce, but the drive toward lowest-cost sourcing and ongoing cost reduction is
still very strong. As a result, there is tension between the purchasing organization, which pushes for lower costs, and manufacturing, which pushes for modularity, local content, and collocation. Daimler-Chrysler's Chrysler Division, by

contrast, has long sourced as much as 70 percent of the value of its vehicles from outside suppliers. Chrysler's relationship with suppliers is far more consultative than GM or Ford, and the company has asked suppliers to perform a significant amount of module design and engineering work.

Japanese automakers are well known for their extensive reliance on multi-tiered supplier networks and high outsourcing levels. The nature of Japanese supplier networks tends to be more "captive" than those that have been developed by American and European firms. In general, Japanese suppliers tend to be more dominated by their largest customer. Japan's largest supplier, a Toyota Group company, generated half of its revenues from Toyota in 1997, and none from Toyota's arch rival, Nissan. Such captive relationships inhibit the buildup of external scale economies and engender financial and technological dependence of suppliers on their largest customers. In this hierarchical system, it is not surprising that the trends toward modularity and the outsourcing of component design and engineering are much weaker among Japanese automakers. As mentioned above, Volkswagen has pursued modularity and final assembly plant simplification largely as an in-house strategy, although its plants outside of Germany appear to be making much greater use of external suppliers. Premium European brands such as BMW and Mercedes have outsourced very little of their component design and engineering.

## Globalization of Products: The Move to Component Modules and Systems

In a trend that is often referred to in the automotive industry as modularization (Baldwin and Clark 1997), automakers are striving to aggregate functionally related or physically continuous parts into subassemblies that are integrated from an engineering point of view. For example, vehicle doors can be delivered with the glass, fabric, interior panels, handles, and mirrors preassembled. Dashboards can be delivered complete with polymers, wood, displays, lights, and switches. Fifteen modules represent about 75 percent of vehicle value. Important modules are suspension (supplied as "corners"); doors; headliners (which can come with grip handles, lighting, wiring, sunroof, sun visors, and trim preassembled); heating, ventilation, and air conditioning (HVAC) units; seats; dashboards; and drive trains (i.e., engines, transmissions, and axles). The logical extension of the trend toward modules would be for suppliers to provide groups of related modules, in what could be called "module systems." For example, seats, interior trim, and cockpit modules could be supplied as a complete "interior system." Figure 3.3 provides a graphic representation of the apparent trend from discrete parts to modules and systems.

It is important to note that some modules comprise continuous subassem-

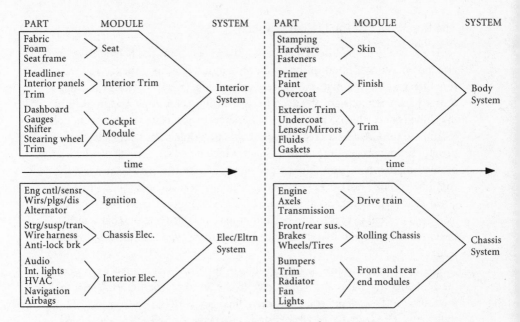

FIG. 3.3. From Part to Module to System. Source: Authors.

blies, while others do not. For example, seats and HVAC units comprise such subassemblies, while vehicle electronics can consist of a variety of discrete components that work together to make up a functional unit. Contiguous subassemblies provide the key benefit of assembly-line simplification, while noncontiguous modules do not. Sourcing noncontiguous modules from a single supplier is practiced because it allows automakers to pass the responsibility for module-level system integration to suppliers. For example, an electronics supplier such as Bosch can make sure that the engine controls work properly with temperature, pressure, r.p.m., and other sensors that provide information to the control unit. In other instances, sourcing noncontiguous modules is a way for automakers to pass warranty responsibility for an entire aspect of vehicle quality, such as engine and transmission sealing, on to suppliers. Some automakers refer to contiguous subassemblies as "modules" and functionally related noncontiguous parts as "systems."

The drive toward modularity often goes hand-in-hand with increased outsourcing and supply-base consolidation. Since automakers are asking their suppliers to provide modules and systems, there has been consolidation in the supply chain as first-tier suppliers buy second-tier suppliers to create systems capability. TRW's recent acquisitions, for example, have given the company the capability to deliver all aspects of occupant restraint systems.

## The Resurgence of the Design Centers

The consolidation of design activities in core locations has helped re-energize the traditional centers of the automotive industry, such as the Detroit metropolitan region, with high-paying research, design, engineering, and administrative jobs. Such jobs are attracted to core locations for good reason. Within the United States, the industry is still remarkably concentrated in its traditional location in the Great Lakes region (see Table 3.6). While there has been a movement of production to the Southern states, which increased their share of automotive employment from only 5.7 percent in 1970 to 16.7 percent in 1992, the continued dominance of the Great Lakes region is clear. Table 3.6 shows that the Great Lakes region decreased its share of U.S. automotive sector employment from 69.4 percent in 1975 to 59.1 percent in 1992. It is also notable that wages in the Great Lakes region maintained a 5 to 10 percent premium during this period.

The largest automotive sector job shift in the United States has been from the Mid-Atlantic States and West Coast to the Southeastern states. Given the proximity and excellent transportation linkages between the Southeastern states and the Great Lakes (Rubenstein 1992), the overall effect has been a reconcentration of the automobile industry around its traditional, albeit expanded core in the American Midwest. Hicks (1994) refers to this reconcentration of the American automotive industry within the wider Midwest region as the formation of a "virtual Detroit." In the 1970s and 1980s, Ford and GM closed almost all of their assembly plants on the East and West coasts, in part because they were too far from the crucial supply base in the Midwest.

The share of nonproduction workers in the sector has shifted to the supply base. Statewide, pay per new job in the supply sector is extremely high, suggesting that most of the jobs added have been in management and engineering. Decreases in the statewide payroll, per job lost in the assembly sector, has been

TABLE 3.6
*Regional Share of Motor Vehicle Sector Employment
and Relative Wages*

| Share of U.S. Employment | South East | Great Lakes | Wages (U.S. = 100) | South East | Great Lakes |
|---|---|---|---|---|---|
| 1970 | 5.7 | 69.4 | 1970 | 78.9 | 104.9 |
| 1975 | 6.8 | 68.7 | 1975 | 72.9 | 106.8 |
| 1980 | 9.4 | 64.1 | 1980 | 73.1 | 109.3 |
| 1985 | 12.5 | 60.9 | 1985 | 73.5 | 111.9 |
| 1990 | 15.6 | 59.4 | 1990 | 75.2 | 112.8 |
| 1992 | 16.7 | 59.1 | 1992 | 79.1 | 110.8 |

*Source:* Bureau of Economic Analysis from Lynch, 1998.

very low, suggesting that most of the jobs shed have been in low-wage segments. Beyond this somewhat vague public data, the revitalization of the Detroit region is obvious to the visitor, with most of the largest European, Scandinavian, and Japanese suppliers establishing their North American headquarters, including substantial engineering staff, in Auburn Hills, about thirty miles north of Detroit.

## Conclusions

While the motor vehicle industry is embedded in the same dynamics of change that is affecting the other industries examined in this volume, there are characteristics that set it apart. Falling transportation and communications costs have increased competition and enabled both automakers and large suppliers to integrate their global operations more tightly than ever before, but the large size and great weight of most vehicles, and many of the materials and modules that go into them, encourage firms to locate production close to consumption in ways that we are not seeing in many other manufacturing industries today. The movement of parts production and final assembly into, or near, final markets, has increased competition and caused prices, relative to the functionality delivered, to fall, but prices have not fallen by half or more, as they have in the PC and television industries. Time to market in the motor vehicle industry is still measured in years, not months. Another difference is in industry organization. In some industries, notably PCs and other electronics gear and even certain semiconductors, a clear split has emerged between those firms that design and market finished products and those that manufacture them. This split has been enabled by the emergence of highly modular product architectures based on open and de facto standards. In the motor vehicle industry, despite a drive to increase the modularity of product architecture and turn more production over to suppliers, automakers have all maintained their deep involvement in manufacturing in the form of final assembly.

Perhaps many of these differences can be attributed to the motor vehicles' place as the most complex—in a physical sense—of all consumer products. As Fine (1998) has noted, motor vehicles have a high degree of dimensional complexity that makes it very difficult to codify design information in a way that can create a market for standardized modules. In the motor vehicle industry, parts and modules are still largely model- or platform-specific. The integral nature of the product means that the procedures surrounding final assembly are critical to the characteristics of the finished vehicle, and to product quality. There are many other large and complex machines that share these characteristics, but none are produced in such high volumes. It is these high volumes that lead us to hold the motor vehicle industry up against the PC industry, which is in many ways an unfair comparison, since the codification of digital designs is a much easier prospect than the codification of designs for power-transferring mechanical systems.

Still, the processes of globalization and industry reorganization are driving significant changes in the motor vehicle industry. The main findings of our research reveal an industry in profound transition: from an older "domestic" model of competition that allowed automakers to compete by exporting from supply bases rooted in their home countries, to an emerging "global" model of competition that increasingly demands that day-to-day production functions be organized on a regional and global basis; from an industry that once treated emerging markets as dumping grounds for old models and production equipment, to an industry that is building leading-edge productive capacity in far-flung corners of the globe; from an export-led industry where firms from different countries competed mainly through markets, to a network-led industry with each major firm producing within each major market.

As the source of competitive pressure shifts from the globalization of markets to the globalization of production, the key competitive advantage in the industry has also begun to shift from excellence at the point of production toward excellence in governing spatially dispersed networks of plants, affiliates, and suppliers. Under this new global model of competition, what matters is not just how effectively cars are produced, but how effectively global-scale production networks are built and managed.

Globalization is shifting the terms of competition in three fundamental respects. First, globalization has meant rapidly entering new and emerging markets. The lure of huge, largely untapped markets in Asia, Eastern Europe, and South America is driving a race among automakers to establish local production. The drive toward investment liberalization and financial integration is continuing, propelling the formerly isolated economies of India, Vietnam, and China to become much more open to foreign investment. Massive exporting of finished vehicles to emerging markets will be unworkable in the face of lingering import restrictions, high transport costs, and nationalistic buying patterns. Automakers believe that local manufacturing builds "corporate citizenship" in each market, which in turn is seen to build consumer acceptance and loyalty. The prize of the Chinese, Indian, and Brazilian markets is indeed large, as car ownership increases in such places with rising incomes.

On the other hand, when the battle for large existing markets intensified radically in the 1980s, many automakers put programs in place to lower operating costs. Of particular importance are regional integration strategies, which have progressively shifted production to lower-cost locations within continental-scale trade arrangements such as Autopact, NAFTA and the European

Union. The integration of lower-cost production sites such as Mexico and Spain with the largest existing markets and supply bases in North America and Europe has created a powerful operating cost gradient that has been tipping key investment decisions toward these "peripheral" locations since the 1980s.

Overcapacity has placed new requirements and pressures on the vehicle and manufacturing design capabilities of automakers. The pressure to manage global-scale operations and produce high-quality vehicles in an increasing number of locations has forced the industry to confront a new set of challenges. As production locations multiply, it is inefficient to construct redundant design, production, and supply infrastructures in each location. While automakers have by no means reached a consensus on how best to build and manage a truly global-scale enterprise, what is clear is that winning at the game of globalization will require new management tools, new efforts to coordinate affiliate and supplier activities, and new modes of corporate governance.

Most automakers are trying to place a greater number of car models on fewer underbody platforms, allowing for greater commonalization of parts while retaining the ability to adapt specific vehicle models to local tastes and conditions. Such strategies call for global sourcing, tighter coordination of worldwide design efforts, and in cases where platform design activities have become geographically dispersed over time, consolidation of project management in core locations. At the same time, the need to respond to unique market requirements has created pressure to localize body design, prompting some automakers to set up regional design centers to cater to local tastes.

Automakers are seeking to mitigate the risks of globalization-induced overcapacity by building a new breed of highly efficient low-volume assembly plants that are easily expandable and very flexible in terms of product mix. The reduction of minimum scale economies is being facilitated by a strong move toward modular assembly, particularly among American and European automakers. The logic is that assembly plants can be smaller and simpler when vehicles consist largely of preassembled modules. When module subassembly is taken off-line, it becomes geographically and organizationally separable from the final assembly plant, making initial automotive assembly investments less "lumpy" and the "deverticalization" of the industry more viable.

Because globalization is occurring at the same time as increased outsourcing and a move to sourcing modules and systems, suppliers are taking a larger role in the globalization process. As a result, we are witnessing the rise of the global supplier. Companies like Bosch, Denso, Johnson Controls, Lear, TRW, Magna, and others have become the preferred suppliers for automakers around the world. Some automakers, particularly American firms, have combined the move to modularity with increased outsourcing, giving increased responsibility to first-tier suppliers for module design and second-tier sourcing. Many first-tier suppliers have responded by embarking on a wave of vertical integration (through mergers, acquisitions, and joint-ventures) and geographic expansion to gain the ability to provide their customers with modules on a global basis. Thus there are simultaneous trends toward deverticalization (by automakers) and vertical integration (among first-tier suppliers) that, in combination with globalization, are helping to create a new supply base capable of supporting the activities of final assemblers on a global basis. More than any other characteristic, it is the simultaneous geographic spread of the supply base, alongside newly established assembly plants, that differentiates the current wave of international investment from those in the past.

One of the most interesting and important aspects of globalization is the ways in which automakers use first-tier suppliers to spread the risk of new investments. First-tier suppliers are being asked to supply new offshore assembly plants locally, shouldering part of the burden of meeting local content requirements and the often onerous task of finding and developing local second- and third-tier suppliers. Automakers are asking suppliers to provide "the same part, for the same price, anywhere in the world." These new demands are putting a great deal of pressure on the first tier, which is responding with massive consolidation and rapid globalization. Global suppliers are growing to the point where operations are beginning to mirror automaker operations, with control and development centralized in core locations and globally dispersed production. Accordingly, global suppliers are facing many of the same challenges that automakers are facing, especially overcapacity risks, coordination and control problems associated with large and spatially dispersed organizations, management of multiple joint-venture relationships, and operation within multiple sets of national and regional regulatory domains. However, because they are usually smaller than automakers, suppliers often lack the resources to deal effectively with these problems.

In summation, this paper has shown how the changing organizational boundaries in the automobile industry, driven by a shift toward product and process modularity, have concatenated with a multidimensional globalization dynamic. One part of this globalization has been a consolidation of the auto industry into a much smaller number of assemblers. This consolidation is being matched by the emergence of a group of parts suppliers that operate globally, producing the modules for the assemblers. In spatial terms, in both Europe and North America, there is a continuing slow shift of finished vehicle production to proximate lower-wage economies that could have a significant impact on the employment of production workers. However, for the most part, white-collar employment remains centralized in a very few major cities. It is our expectation that globalization will continue to roil the auto industry during the next decade as the responses to the last decade of massive change work their way through the value chain.

## Notes

We acknowledge the support of the Alfred P. Sloan Foundation and MIT's International Motor Vehicle Program. Charles Fine, Ken Oye, and Paul Osterman collaborated on aspects of the research. Helpful comments and insights were provided by Richard Lester, Suzanne Berger, Dan Roos, Martin Kenney, Gary Gereffi, Raymond Vernon, Ashish Arora, John Paul MacDuffie, Susan Helper, John Humphrey, Jan Annerstedt, Richard Samuels, Frits Pil, Davis Jenkins, Isaac Makita, Jay Tate, Hirsh Cohen, Frank Mayadas, and the participants in the Sloan Globalization Network, especially Avron Barr, Roger Bohn, Clair Brown, Peter Gourevitch, Bruce Kogut, Robert Leachman, Stephanie Lenway, Greg Linden, Thomas Murtha, Gail Pesyna, and Shirley Tessler. We also acknowledge Eric Wolfe, Aya Okada, Juan Pena Acosta, Kiyoaki Aburaki, Ester Kim, Mike Usowski, Vikram Siddarth, and Austin Gill for providing research assistance. The comments and research assistance provided by Teresa Lynch have been especially valuable. We thank all the participants who participated in interviews or completed survey forms.

1. We note that by 2002, in real terms, gasoline prices had returned to very low levels.

2. Daimler-Benz, although a smaller vehicle company than Chrysler, is the largest industrial firm in Germany by virtue of its diversified businesses in rail transport systems, electronics, aerospace, and military hardware and systems.

3. Of course, if suppliers cannot justify the cost establishing a collocated facility, then automakers must find other means. For example, automakers sometimes ask suppliers to license their designs to indigenous suppliers (this provides an opportunity for indigenous suppliers to upgrade to world-class standards and join global-scale production networks). Since modules are bulky and harder to ship, automakers are pushing their suppliers to collocate with its assembly plants in offshore locations.

4. Continental established a global manufacturing presence in tires largely through acquisition. In 1979, the company acquired the European assets of Uniroyal (USA), a deal that included plants in Belgium, the UK, France, and Germany. In 1985, Semperit Reifen AG (Germany) was acquired, adding plants in Austria and Ireland (since closed). In 1987, Continental acquired General Tire (USA), including four plants in the United States, two in Mexico (since sold), and a series of joint-venture operations in Asia, Africa, and South America. In 1991 a joint venture agreement was signed with Yokohama (Japan) and Toyo (Japan) to make commercial tires for the U.S. market (http://www.conti-online.com/). In 1992, the company acquired the Swedish tire producer Nivis Tyre.

# CHAPTER FOUR

# The Shifting Value Chain

*The Television Industry in North America*

MARTIN KENNEY

Locating global advantage in the television industry is a fascinating task, because it has shifted spatially and in production ownership terms, even while organizationally there has been far less change. As a physical product, a television resembles a personal computer (PC), and yet the organization of its value chain has greater similarity to the automobile industry. In spatial terms, the value chain has exhibited significant plasticity. The U.S. market is ideal for understanding the global forces affecting the industry, because it is the largest single market, and it has been the key competitive battleground for global manufacturers. It also was the first major Fordist industry to fall victim to global competition. This chapter utilizes North America as a case study to understand how the interaction between firm strategies, government actions, and consumer desires has affected the location of competitive advantage in the television industry.

While there can be little doubt that government policy, both Japanese and U.S., influenced the development of the television industry, the fates of the various national television industries were not determined by political initiatives, though location of factories was affected. Rather, these diverging fates rested upon corporate strategy and differing production systems. Still, the relationship between the government and firms also affected the structure of the market. U.S. government intervention in the television industry has a long history, beginning as a procompetition policy in reaction to RCA's use of its patents to stifle competition. Later, the government's major role would be to react to the demands by U.S. firms for protection. Among observers at the time, it was common to attribute Japanese success to clever Japanese and foolish U.S. policy (Prestowitz 1988).[1] This was a gross over-simplification.

There are three distinct segments of the television value chain: picture tube production, other component production and assembly, and final assembly. Each exhibits different dynamics.[2] Each segment has different technical, physical, and personnel requirements: a feature allowing firms to develop complicated and changing spatial divisions of labor. The television industry, like many of the other industries in this book, has faced brutal price competition and, since 1980, constant overcapacity. In contrast to PCs, however, there has been no dramatic curve of improving functionality: there has been a constant increase in screen size for the same price. In response to these changes, firms continually adjusted and readjusted their divisions of labor, globally and regionally. Put differently, the value chain at any moment appeared fixed, but when seen dynamically, change was the rule.

When the television was introduced immediately after World War II, it was a leading edge, high-technology product. However, resembling other electronics products, each new model, even if it incorporated significant new technology, swiftly became a commodity. As the assembly process was routinized and simplified, the value of a television became increasingly embodied in a few components, particularly the picture tube, which is produced by a capital-intensive manufacturing production process.

The television industry was a harbinger of developments in other traditional assembly-intensive manufacturing industries. For example, as the chapter by Sturgeon and Florida indicates, the U.S. auto industry initially lost the low end of the market to the Japanese, but fortunately it regrouped before being annihilated; the television industry did not regroup, and it was annihilated. In this way, televisions were what Fine (1998) termed a "fruit fly" industry—that is, an early indicator of shifts that would affect more significant industries later.

Ultimately, production for the U.S. market was captured by Japanese and European firms producing in North America. The progression of the changing national ownership of the value chain is instructive. The U.S. industry first lost its component supplier industry, followed by the assembly operations, and later the tube industry. The most capital intensive activities were the last to experience a change in ownership and location.

## The Television Industry

In 2003, the global television industry can be divided into six major markets: the United States, Europe, Japan, China, the rest of Asia, and the rest of the world. All the significant firms operate globally. The United States, Japanese, and Western European markets were largely saturated, and purchases were confined to replacement and upgrading. By the late 1990s, the most important growth markets were in the developing countries of Asia, especially China and India, and they were the locus of new investment. Europe remained a protected

TABLE 4.1

*The Ten Largest CTV Manufacturers in the World, 1978*

|  | Company | Country | Number of sets produced (millions per year) |
|---|---|---|---|
| 1. | Matsushita | Japan | 3.60 |
| 2. | Philips | Netherlands | 3.50 |
| 3. | RCA | USA | 2.00 |
| 4. | Zenith | USA | 1.97 |
| 5. | Sanyo | Japan | 1.95 |
| 6. | Sony | Japan | 1.70 |
| 7. | Toshiba | Japan | 1.50 |
| 8. | Grundig[a] | Germany | 1.40 |
| 9. | Hitachi | Japan | 1.25 |
| 10. | Sylvania-GTE[b] | USA | 1.20 |

*Source:* Ruottu (1998: 160)

[a] Grundig owned 25% by Philips

[b] Acquired by Philips in autumn 1980.

TABLE 4.2

*The Ten Largest CTV Manufacturers in the World, 1987*

|  | Company | Country | Number of sets produced (millions per year) |
|---|---|---|---|
| 1. | Philips | Netherlands | 8.60 |
| 2. | Thomson | France | 6.80 |
| 3. | Matsushita | Japan | 4.70 |
| 4. | Sony | Japan | 3.80 |
| 5. | Toshiba | Japan | 3.20 |
| 6. | Hitachi | Japan | 3.10 |
| 7. | Samsung | South Korea | 2.50 |
| 8. | Zenith | USA | 2.30 |
| 9. | Nokia | Finland | 2.20 |
| 10. | Sanyo | Japan | 1.80 |

*Source:* Ruottu (1998: 162).

market served by the major European producers, Philips and Thomson, and the Japanese and Korean firms. Most recently, there have been shifts in Western European production relocating to Eastern Europe. Finally, in Japan there is a continuing shift by Japanese firms of assembly and component production to Asian production sites.

During the last three decades, there have been significant changes in global leadership. As can be seen in Table 4.1, in 1978, U.S. producers were prominent among the top ten global producers. By 1987, Japanese firms were the leaders, but Zenith was still among the top 10 (Table 4.2). The two European producers, Thomson and Philips, had become the world's largest producers; the Finnish company Nokia joined the top 10; and Samsung had just entered the top 10. By 1997, the order had changed again, with the Japanese firms Sony and Mat-

TABLE 4.3
*The Ten Largest CTV Manufacturers in the World, 1997*

|  | Company | Country | Number of sets produced (millions per year) |
|---|---|---|---|
| 1. | Sony | Japan | 15.80 |
| 2. | Matsushita | Japan | 12.70 |
| 3. | LG & Zenith | Korea | 12.20 |
| 4. | Thomson | France | 10.90 |
| 5. | Samsung | Korea | 10.60 |
| 6. | Sharp | Japan | 7.20 |
| 7. | Philips | Netherlands | 7.00 |
| 8. | Daewoo | Korea | 6.80 |
| 9. | Sanyo | Japan | 6.90 |
| 10. | Toshiba | Japan | 5.90 |

*Source:* Author's compilation from various sources.
   *Note:* Chinese makers are unknown.

sushita becoming the leaders (Table 4.3). The two European firms lost ground, while the Korean firms Samsung, Daewoo, and Lucky Goldstar (LG) had become major competitors. In 1999, the sole remaining U.S. manufacturer, Zenith, was sold to LG. Since the Koreans entered the television industry in the 1970s, no other significant global players have emerged (though this might change, as some Chinese firms have begun exporting very inexpensive televisions). In the 1980s, it appeared that Taiwanese television producers, such as Tatung and Sampo, would become global players. However, in the mid-1980s Taiwan opened its consumer electronics market, and Japanese producers routed the local firms. This was not as problematic as it might first appear, as the Taiwanese electronics firms were already shifting to the personal computer industry—a movement that proved to be prescient for Taiwan (see Chapter 5).

## The Fordist World of American Television Manufacturing

After World War II, B/W television sales commenced in earnest, and many new firms entered the industry in the United States, Europe, and Japan. From 1946 to 1948, there were approximately 500 firms assembling B/W televisions in the United States (Teitelman 1994: 52). In 1951, there were 97 B/W television assemblers remaining (*Television Factbook* 1951). By 1960, the number had declined to 27 firms (U.S. International Trade Commission 1977: A4). In 1968, there were 18 firms producing color televisions in 30 factories. The first nadir was reached in 1976, when there were only 12 firms left producing in 15 establishments (ibid.: 13). In 1989, this had increased to 17 establishments because of the Japanese transplants (Robert R. Nathan Associates 1989: 357). After that there would be a terminal decline in U.S. factories.

Since the 1960s the number of U.S. workers employed in SIC Code 3651, which covers radio and television receivers, and SIC Code 3651, which covers vacuum tubes, has declined with only a few respites. For the manufacture of radio and television receivers, employment peaked in 1966 (the middle of the Vietnam War boom) at 130,000. During the next two decades, employment fell to 30,000 in 1987 and then remained relatively constant through 1994. In 2000, employment fell below 20,000 with no indication of recovery.

In the late 1940s, television manufacturing commenced in the U.S. Midwest. At that time, Fordism as practiced in the automobile industry was considered the essence of managerial excellence. Every ill that plagued the U.S. automobile industry surfaced in television production (MIT Commission on Industrial Productivity 1989). Labor relations and product quality were low. According to Porter (1983), between 1970 and 1979 Japanese television makers had between 9 and 26 field calls per 100 sets, whereas U.S. firms had between 100 and 200 field calls per 100 sets. In 1979, Baranson (1980) confirmed Porter's conclusions, finding that the defect rate for Japanese television sets was 0.4 percent, compared with 5 percent for U.S. sets. This greater quality provided important advantages: one of the most important was that when Japanese manufacturers entered the U.S. market, they did not have to establish a costly service network (U.S. International Trade Commission 1992: 4).

The U.S. and Japanese television industries diverged markedly in terms of labor-management relations. The U.S. employees (with the exception of those at Motorola) were represented by industrial unions, whereas in Japan they had enterprise unions (Kenney 1999b). American unionized factories were characterized by intricate job classifications, strict seniority, and bumping privileges; a lack of worker responsibility for inspection; quality control responsibility lodged with inspectors and management; a radical separation of blue- and white-collar workers; and arcane grievance procedures (Kenney and Tanaka 2003). From the 1950s through the early 1980s, the U.S. industry was plagued by strikes, both sanctioned and wildcat. Disruption and disagreement were common and necessitated the use of a just-in-case production system in which inventory was stockpiled in anticipation of difficulties.

Greater efficiency and automation have continuously reduced the labor input in television assembly. An MIT study undertaken in the late 1980s (MIT Commission on Industrial Productivity 1989: 16) stated that "in 1971 the cost breakdown for a 19" Zenith color television was approximately $18 for direct labor ($5 for component insertion), and $168 for materials, of which $70 was for the tube; the suggested retail price was $460. By 1984, offshore labor, automation, and component insertion had reduced direct labor costs approximately six-fold below levels of the early 1970s, making them nearly negligible." Despite the conclusion that labor costs were nearly negligible, there was a continual pressure to reduce costs further.

U.S. assemblers adopted automation reluctantly. One observer attributed this tardiness to a U.S. labor market organization that "inhibits the introduction of automation and other technological change for fear of irreplaceable job loss" (Developing World Industry and Technology, Inc. 1978: 18). In the late 1970s, Japanese firms used less than two hours to build a 21-inch color television, while U.S. and German firms used nearly four hours and the U.K. firm used nearly six hours (Office of Technology Assessment 1983: 238). In 1997, one major Japanese producer had reduced the labor time used to assemble a 20-inch television to only twenty-seven minutes, while the more complicated 32-inch model took eighty-six minutes (Ohgai 1997). This decrease in per unit labor input was directly related to increased automation and component simplification.

Similar to the U.S. manufacturers, the parts and components suppliers also were reluctant to adopt automation. They had endemic quality problems, which adversely affected television reliability. For example, Juran (1978: 10) found that the causes of field service failures for televisions were design and development (20–40 percent), quality of components (40–65 percent), and final assembly (15–20 percent). Inadequate supplier quality had a direct impact on an assembler's quality, hence competitiveness.

The U.S. firms were late in understanding the importance of quality. It was only in the early 1970s that they invested in automatic test equipment, incoming parts inspection, and using burn-in tests for finished receivers (U.S. International Trade Commission 1977: A85). The greatest contribution to reliability was switching from tubes to transistors. Japanese manufacturers, drawing upon their experience with transistor radios, introduced all-transistor televisions in the mid-1960s. In contrast, it was not until the mid-1970s that U.S. manufacturers completely converted to the use of transistors, despite the fact that Fairchild had designed the first all-transistor television in 1962 and demonstrated it to all interested firms (Lecuyer 1999). It was not surprising that U.S. manufacturers garnered a reputation for lack of innovativeness and low quality that was difficult to change.

## The Globalization of the Television Industry

### The 1950s and Early 1960s—Licensing to Overseas Competitors and Component Imports

After World War I, the important radio and receiving tube patents were held by AT&T, GE, and Westinghouse. After complicated negotiations, a newly formed firm, RCA, emerged as the owner of their broadcasting patent portfolio. As a result of a 1930 antitrust indictment against RCA, GE, and Westinghouse, a consent agreement was signed in 1932 and RCA secured its independence. The facilities RCA inherited from GE and Westinghouse made it not only the leading tube maker and radio assembler but also the chief source of research and development (R&D) for the entire U.S. broadcasting industry (Stokes 1982: 3).

From the 1920s onward, inventors and firms in a number of countries raced to perfect televisions. In the early 1930s, U.S. firms demonstrated viable B/W television transmitters and receivers. The onset of World War II interrupted these commercialization plans, but research continued. Moreover, the wartime need for display devices propelled the improvement of high-power vacuum tubes and accelerated the development of mass production techniques for cathode ray tubes. RCA's research laboratory played a central role in many of these innovations. To jump-start the television industry, in 1946 RCA announced that it would include B/W television licenses in the patent package it offered to other companies.

From its experience in radios and as the technical leader, RCA developed a strategy of licensing patents to increase its income, as it could earn greater profits from licensing and selling key components than from only manufacturing receivers (Chandler 2001). Typically, after developing and introducing an innovation RCA would have high market share and profits. It then licensed the technology, and, as new firms entered the market, prices dropped (Graham 1986). Through its licensing strategy, RCA made it uneconomical for the other consumer electronics firms to invest significant sums in research. Conversely, "for RCA, the effect was to make licensing fees the major payoff of its research activity" (ibid.: 41). The handsome profits from licensing and from its tube and component business made RCA successful, but created a potential vulnerability for the entire U.S. industry should RCA ever lag in innovation (Chandler 2001; Graham 1986).

In 1958, RCA's interest in overseas licensing was heightened after negotiating a consent decree with the U.S. Department of Justice requiring RCA to provide royalty-free licenses to U.S. producers. Government success in protecting U.S. producers from RCA had the unanticipated effect of accelerating RCA's efforts to find new licensing income to sustain its R&D operations (Chandler 2001). The decree did not prohibit RCA from charging high license fees to foreign companies. Seeking to expand after the war, Japanese electronics firms needed access to technology, and RCA's licensing strategy provided it. From 1960 to 1968, RCA granted 105 licenses for various radio and television inventions to Japanese firms (Collins 1970: 2924). Once these licensing relationships were established, there was every incentive for RCA to quickly license new innovations to its technology "customers" to ensure a continuing and even swelling cash flow. The result was a dramatic reduction in the lags one would expect in transnational technology transfer (on these lags, see Kogut and Zander 1993).

The licensing rate negotiated between RCA and the Electronics Industry Association of Japan (EIAJ) applied equally to all Japanese firms.[3] The rate on a per-product basis was 0.45 percent of the factory value for each AM radio, 0.9 percent for each FM radio, 1.75 percent for each B/W television set, and 2 percent for each color television set produced. From RCA's perspective the licensing scheme negotiated with the Japanese manufacturers had significant benefits because it was like a tax—profits grew as Japanese production expanded. It was in RCA's interest to encourage Japanese firms to produce as many units as possible. Due to this royalty structure, Japanese firms became the largest single foreign contributor to RCA's income (Bilby 1986: 222). In the late 1970s, RCA received more than $100 million per year in licensing fees from Japan (MIT Commission on Industrial Productivity 1989: 15). One method of increasing revenues was to show the Japanese how to produce. In the 1950s, Japanese personnel visited the United States to inspect RCA's television plants. This was important because Japanese visitors were able to see the production process. Another vehicle was the technology transfer engineering laboratory in Tokyo that RCA established in 1954 (Office of Technology Assessment 1983: 121ff).

From very early on, there were few incentives for U.S. television firms to expand sales globally. European and Japanese markets were small. So the U.S. television firms never evinced great interest in overseas markets, though they did open factories in Brazil and Mexico (Lowe and Kenney 1999). A Zenith executive explained his firm's indifference to overseas markets:

It's hard to explain why a decision is made not to do something. There are a number of reasons behind it—including innate cautiousness. For one, we've always had our hands full with U.S. demand and we've always tended to stick with what appeared to be the biggest payoff and what we knew how to do best. For example, an additional two market share points in the Los Angeles area alone represents more sales volume than there is in most foreign markets. Also, we didn't feel we could compete with the local companies in those markets unless we were willing to sacrifice some of our margin, and we were unwilling to do that. (Porter 1983: 487)

The one firm with global-class technology, RCA was not interested in entering other markets; it was content to license.

The licensing of technology and the transfer of know-how soon had competitive consequences. In the mid-1950s, independent Japanese parts suppliers began selling parts and components, such as tuners, deflection yokes, resistors, capacitors, and vacuum tubes in the United States (MIT Commission on Industrial Productivity 1989: 14). At the time Japanese parts were considered low quality, but U.S. assemblers were price conscious; some began purchasing them. In 1963, Admiral and Zenith, which had previously resisted using imported parts, started purchasing them from the Japanese (Takahashi 1993: 45). Many U.S. consumer electronics firms were not vertically integrated, therefore there was little to prevent them from purchasing the low-cost parts offered by Asian suppliers (Rowe 1970: 2883). The arm's-length relationship that the U.S. assemblers had developed with their U.S. suppliers meant that they were willing to purchase parts from the lowest bidder. The result was that the U.S. supplier infrastructure lost business and began to atrophy.

Japanese firms were not content, however, in the low end of the market. During this period, the Japanese government sponsored measures to improve the quality of electronics components. For example, in the early 1960s the government established a quality-testing program (Takahashi 1993). The major assemblers also extended technical assistance to their suppliers and would not purchase from unapproved suppliers. In the early 1960s, Japanese assemblers inspected all incoming parts. To improve reliability, in the mid-1960s Matsushita launched an effort to achieve 0.01 percent component defects. By the early 1970s, the improvements permitted Japanese assemblers to discontinue inspections. In the early 1970s, Matsushita raised its quality target to 0.001 percent defectives, then in 1985 it was raised to 0.0002 percent. In contrast, in 1972 RCA accepted 1.5 percent defects in the integrated circuits it purchased (Turner 1982: 57).

Using these inspection programs, major Japanese manufacturers began tracing defects to their source and demanding that the supplier remedy the causes (Nishiguchi 1994; Sako 1992). This active effort to manage the supplier chain steadily improved the Japanese supplier base. In contrast, U.S. suppliers had no such relationship with U.S. assemblers and were under price pressure but not quality-improvement pressure. This problem became manifest when U.S. assemblers discovered that imported parts were not only less expensive but also of higher quality. Gradually, they came to prefer Japanese parts.

In this period, U.S. firms, particularly RCA, taught Japanese firms how to become consumer electronics producers. The Japanese purchased and imported technology from the United States and, to a lesser degree, from Europe. In general, only the smaller, less technology intensive parts manufacturers in the United States experienced direct competition, but it did spread to higher value parts. Few finished televisions were being exported to the United States, and most U.S. consumer electronics firms were unconcerned: the B/W television market was growing rapidly, and they were switching to CTV production. However, there were warning clouds on the horizon.

*The 1960s through the Early 1970s—Japanese Imports and Overseas Production*

In the 1960s, the competitive environment changed. The rising imports of low-cost, and increasingly high-quality, Japanese components created serious problems for U.S. suppliers. Then Japanese firms began exporting B/W televisions, and soon U.S. B/W television producers experienced extreme pressure (Curtis 1994: 109; Schiffer 1991). The U.S. firms' strategy of shifting to newer products became increasingly precarious as Japanese manufacturers immediately after capturing the lower end of the market migrated toward the high end.

Japanese entry into the U.S. television market was facilitated by the multiple-channel U.S. distribution system. The system was loosely coupled, and manufacturers, distributors, and retailers operated with changing partners. This was a stable, self-contained system until foreign manufacturers entered. These distributors were independent of the manufacturers and thus would offer any brand capable of generating profits. They supplied radio/television shops and household appliance, furniture, and department stores. Yet another channel consisted of the house brands of general merchandisers, such as Sears & Roebuck, Montgomery Ward, and J. C. Penney. These merchandisers did not actually manufacture the products (Sears was an exception, as it had captive manufacturers); rather, they purchased products from original equipment manufacturers (OEMs) and placed their brand names on them. The general merchandiser offered the manufacturers large orders and, in return, demanded significant discounts (Prestowitz 1988; MIT Commission on Industrial Productivity 1989). They were continually searching for lower-cost producers. The OEM strategy was not universal among Japanese firms entering the U.S. market. Sony, for example, never sold through OEM channels (Morita 1986).

In 1964, through its Warwick subsidiary, Sears received its first OEM color televisions (CTVs) from Toshiba. Sears had approached Toshiba, because RCA and Zenith declined to produce the TVs it required: they were already operating at full capacity because of the Vietnam War–era boom. To assist Toshiba, Sears provided Warwick designs. In 1965, Sears added Sharp as an OEM supplier. As the leading U.S. retailer, Sears's decision to purchase CTVs from Japanese firms confirmed their price competitiveness and quality. With the Sears contract, other retailers soon followed: after 1966, J. C. Penney bought, on an OEM basis, from Matsushita; Montgomery Ward commenced importing televisions from Sharp; and Sears switched from Sharp to Sanyo (Porter 1983: 468). The other smaller retailers also purchased from Japanese manufacturers.

Two critical factors for Japanese success were the favorable exchange rate of 360 yen to the U.S. dollar and low Japanese labor costs. This was significant, as television assembly was still labor intensive. The magnitude of the difference in 1968 can be seen in the hourly wage for production workers. In 1968, the Japanese hourly television factory wage was $.50 per hour, versus $2.72 in the United States. In 1970, the estimated total production costs for a television were about 20 percent lower in Japan than in the United States (Peck and Wilson 1991: 203).

Simultaneously, electronics parts imports increased because of overseas production by U.S. parts makers and the greater use of foreign parts. U.S. assemblers were now dependent upon Japanese parts. These changes seriously affected employment in the U.S. consumer electronics components industry, which fell from the November 1966 peak of 179,000 to 122,000 in March 1970. In 1966, when the U.S. Customs Court ruled that duties on imported Japanese receiving tubes should be raised almost sixfold, U.S. assemblers lobbied Congress to rescind the increase (*Television Digest* 1966: vol. 6, no. 23, p. 7). The U.S. assemblers believed that their fate was separable from that of their U.S. suppliers. The importance and quality of Japanese components prompted *Television Digest* (1966: vol. 6, no. 38, p. 7) to conclude: "Busy Japan is a far cry from low-cost, high-labor content bargain basement of a decade ago. It is now an essential supply station for the U.S. electronics industry." Parts suppliers such as Murata and Toko, which began in the 1950s by innovating new parts for transistor radios, soon turned their attention to TV components (*Television Digest* 1965: vol. 5, no. 44, p. 6). In effect, Japanese parts makers had become integrated into the U.S. assemblers' value chain.

These developments were summed up later by Developing World Industry and Technology, Inc. (1978), which concluded that "it is [the Japanese] evolving capability that has enabled them to move progressively into increasingly complex and sophisticated production and to effectively utilize their widespread network of small-scale parts suppliers to progressively penetrate internationally competitive markets." Japanese TV manufacturers benefited from a supplier infrastructure that evolved with them to become world-class firms.

In the mid-1960s, the U.S. industry began relocating their operations offshore. The movement was propelled by two factors. The first factor, and the one we examine in greatest detail, was the increasing competition from low-priced Japanese imports. A second factor was the labor shortages arising from the fact that the U.S. economy was operating at full capacity servicing the Vietnam War and the Great Society. The first U.S. firms to move offshore were the parts suppliers that were under pricing pressure, because their customers were purchasing from Japanese suppliers. The two countries receiving the greatest investment were Taiwan and Mexico. Other U.S. firms, including assemblers seeking low-cost labor to produce labor-intensive components, soon followed (Moxon 1973; Lowe and Kenney 1999).

The savings from offshore production were only 5–10 percent. For example, in 1977 when Zenith decided to move a major part of its operations offshore and laid off 25 percent of its U.S. workforce, it expected to reduce costs by only $10 to $15 per color television receiver (Porter 1983: 497). And yet, a 5–10 percent reduction of costs could mean the difference between making a profit or suffering a loss. This was especially true in the smaller, less expensive sets that were often loss leaders.

Television subassembly imports increased in value from $23 million in 1971 to $176 million in 1976 (U.S. International Trade Commission 1977: A26–A28), while televisions entering under TSUS (Tariff Schedules of the United States) item 807.00 increased dramatically.[4] In 1971, 33 percent of the completed monochrome televisions sold in the United States were imported under TSUS 807; by 1975 this had reached 53 percent and continued to climb. For color televisions, imports grew from 2.5 percent to 5.8 percent. However, there was one other development—namely, the total percentage of TSUS parts exempted in televisions dropped, indicating that foreign parts were being substituted for exported U.S. parts. Moving offshore to decrease labor costs, U.S. firms discovered that inputs were also less expensive.

Taiwan was the largest Asian recipient of U.S. consumer electronics investment. In the 1960s the only attractant for U.S. firms to Taiwan was inexpensive labor and various government incentives, because there was no infrastructure for electronics production. And yet, U.S. investment grew rapidly. In 1962, the first major supplier to produce offshore, General Instrument Company, commenced operations to produce tuners and other parts in Taiwan with 500 employees. By 1969, it employed 7,200 and paid them an average hourly wage of 10 to 15 cents per hour. Simultaneously, General Instruments closed three factories in New England (Morganstern 1970: 2909). According to the president of a small firm supplying ferrite cores to General Instruments, when General Instruments decided to relocate to Taiwan, his firm's sales declined from $388,000 in 1966 to $240,000 in 1969 to less than $100,000 in 1970 (Stanwyck 1970: 3018).

Even as U.S. firms invested in Taiwan, Japanese firms also moved B/W television production offshore. As prices dropped from 1971 to 1973, virtually all assembly of Japanese B/W televisions relocated to other Asian sites, especially Taiwan (Gregory 1985: 13). Taiwan had an ideal situation because it received investment from the Japanese consumer electronics companies that were winning in global competition and from the U.S. firms that were trying to survive. This permitted Taiwan's infant electronics firms to form technological and marketing alliances with firms experiencing two different industrial logics. Through participation in joint ventures, local Taiwanese firms observed and learned new technologies, internalized new production processes, and participated in the rapidly changing international electronics industry (Zenger 1977). U.S. assemblers increased their parts purchasing from Taiwan's growing supplier base, further encouraging its development. The rising capabilities of Taiwanese suppliers corresponded with and accelerated the decline of the U.S. supplier industry.

*The 1970s through 1987—The Television Transplants*

This period was one during which the pillars of the U.S. television industry, including General Electric, RCA, Zenith, and Magnavox, experienced their

terminal decline because of Japanese competition (see Nevin [1978] for the
Zenith perspective). Given the level of rhetoric and the amount of apparent
activity in Washington, both on Capitol Hill and in the International Trade
Commission, it seemed likely that significant fines, duties, or quotas would be
placed on CTV imports. In 1977, the pressure by domestic manufacturers resulted in an agreement between the Japanese and the U.S. government to create a "voluntary" Orderly Marketing Arrangement (OMA) for three years. Under the terms of the agreement, Japan could export only 1.75 million color
television sets (1.56 million completed and 190,000 unassembled) to the
United States (Gregory 1985: 144). The OMA also restricted imports of nine
basic parts, including color picture tubes (CPTs). According to Robert Strauss,
the U.S. negotiator, the agreement was meant to encourage Japanese manufacturers to invest in the United States. Most certainly, it increased pressure on
other Japanese manufacturers to follow the lead of Sony, Matsushita, and
Sanyo, which had already established assembly facilities in the United States.
A substantial portion of the financial benefit created by the OMA was captured by the Japanese assembly factories in the United States, thus negating
most of the expected positive benefits for U.S. producers (Peck and Wilson
1991: 209f).

In 1971, the fixed dollar-yen exchange rate ended and the yen appreciated—
thereby hampering the competitiveness of Japanese imports. Also, wages increased rapidly in Japan, further contributing to a shift in the economics of exporting to the United States. Still, with the exception of Sony, the Japanese firms
were "reluctant multinationals" (Trevor 1988). Beginning in 1972, Japanese firms
opened—or, in the case of Sanyo and Matsushita, acquired—a total of fourteen
television assembly factories in the United States (See Table 4.4). Initially these
factories were proverbial "screwdriver" factories utilizing production equipment and many components from Asia. For the most part, the CPTs were purchased from U.S. vendors.[5]

Almost immediately after the Japanese OMA was implemented, Taiwanese
and Korean exports to the United States increased, and in 1979 those nations ac-
quiesced to an OMA. The result was that Korean and Taiwanese imports were
stabilized; however, Japanese firms, which had been especially active exporters
from Taiwan, rather quickly relocated their low-end television production to
Southeast Asia. This illustrates the difficulties of using bilateral Orderly Marketing Arrangements; the sanctions were applied to nations, but the exporters
were multinational firms and were able to quickly shift assembly to other nations.

By the mid-1980s, few U.S. consumer electronics firms remained in Taiwan.
Many U.S. assemblers had left the television business. Also, wages in Taiwan had

TABLE 4.4
*The Status of Japanese Television Assembly Plants in the U.S. as of 1999*

| Company | Location | Start of operation | Type of operation | No. of employees, 1999 | No. of employees, 1988 | Products | Maquila | Operations |
|---------|----------|-----------|-----------|------|------|----------|---------|------------|
| Sony[a] | San Diego, CA | 1972 | Startup | 0 | 1,500 | TVs, CTRs, monitors | Yes | TV assembly moved to maquila |
| Matsushita | Franklin Park, IL | 1974 | Acquisition | 0 | 800 | TVs & PTVs | Yes | Closed, moved to maquila |
| Sanyo | Forrest City, AR | 1976 | Acquisition | 400 | 400 | TVs | Yes | Most production in maquila |
| Mitsubishi | Santa Anna, CA | 1977 | Startup | 0 | 550 | PTVs | Yes | Merged with Georgia factory |
| Toshiba | Lebanon, TN | 1978 | Startup | 900 | 600 | TVs & microwave ovens | Yes | Expanding maquila |
| Hitachi | Anaheim, CA | 1979 | Startup | 0 | 900 | TVs & VCRs | Yes | Closed, moved to maquila |
| Sharp | Memphis, TN | 1979 | Startup | 900 | 770 | TVs & microwave ovens | No | Expanding maquila |
| JVC | Elmwood Park, NJ | 1982 | Startup | 0 | 100 | TVs | Yes | Closed, moved to maquila |
| NEC | McDonough, GA | 1985 | Startup | 0 | 400 | TVs | No | Closed |
| Matsushita | Vancouver, WA | 1986 | Startup | 250 | 200 | VCR-TV Combo | Yes | Stable |
| Mitsubishi | Braselton, GA | 1986 | Startup | 0 | 300 | TVs & mobile telephones | Yes | Closed moved to maquila |
| Orion | Princeton, IN | 1987 | Startup | 110 | 250 | TVs | No | Stable |
| Pioneer | Chino, CA | 1988 | Startup | 100 | 0 | PTVs | No | Stable |
| Sony | Mount Pleasant, PA | 1992 | Startup | 800 | 0 | TVs & CRTs | Yes | Large screens only |

*Source:* Electronics Industry Association 1989, Ohgai. 1997, and various sources.
[a] No longer assembling televisions; now producing CRTs and computer monitors and other items.

increased significantly and were soon comparable with those of Mexico. The U.S. television firms had by this time largely discontinued operations in Asia and expanded facilities in Mexico.

## U.S. Assembly Moves to Mexico

By the 1990s, the price wars made it apparent to all assemblers, including the Japanese, that continued production in the United States would be difficult. So even as Japanese and European firms expanded their CPT production in the United States they began relocating assembly to Mexico. During the 1990s, the number of televisions imported from Asia declined as Mexico's production increased. By the late 1990s, an entire production complex in northern Mexico had developed that was capable of producing nearly all the inputs for a television (including some CPTs). In the process, the number of televisions assembled in the United States declined.

The current dominance of Mexico as a site for television assembly was the result of a nonlinear, multicausal series of events. Mexico's Border Industrialization Program (BIP), initiated in 1965, provided financial incentives and freedom from import duties to foreign firms willing to locate factories (that would come to be called maquiladoras) in Mexico's low-wage border region on the condition that all production was exported. U.S. firms used U.S. tariff schedules 806/807 to avoid duties on the inputs exported from the United States. Under the BIP, cities along the U.S.-Mexican border, and later those in Mexico's interior, could establish free trade zones (Lowe and Kenney 1999).

These plants were located close to the U.S.-Mexican border because of the initial requirements of Mexican law (Sklair 1993). Yet, even after the entire country was opened for investment, consumer electronics operations opted to stay close to the border. The reasons for this were superior access to U.S. suppliers and infrastructure, proximity to customers, and the firms' focus on the U.S. market. The U.S. consumer electronics firms used their Mexican production facilities to produce components (forty-three of forty-seven consumer electronics maquiladoras focused on components from 1966 to 1973). Four television assemblers, Warwick, GTE, Magnavox, and Teledyne, also joined this first wave of investment, but initially they undertook only subassembly (*Television Digest* 1974: vol. 14, p. 49).

Because of these investments, Mexico rapidly became an important parts supplier to the United States. Often these imports were entirely intrafirm—that is, a U.S. firm sent a set of parts to its maquiladora, where they were assembled and then shipped back to its U.S. factory. The dimensions of this trade were large. For example, from 1968 to 1977, Mexico was the largest source of television tuners. Similarly, in the early 1970s, Mexico was the number one exporter of tantalum capacitors to the United States (*Television Digest* 1971: vol. 11, no. 6, p. 4). Sears's Warwick subsidiary was one of the first television assemblers to aggressively exploit inexpensive Mexican labor. Warwick was partially owned by Sears, and its production was almost entirely dedicated to Sears and Roebuck. Despite the close relationship, Warwick faced constant price pressure because Sears purchased from other vendors (in this period, the other vendors were Japanese, and later they would be Korean).

In 1966, Warwick was the first U.S. manufacturer to open an assembly plant in Tijuana to produce for the U.S. market. In this factory Warwick assembled 12-inch B/W televisions (a product under severe competitive pressure from Asia). In 1968, it opened a second plant in Tijuana to produce television parts (ibid. 1969: vol. 9, no. 12, p. 7; Sklair 1993: 51). A third Warwick plant was opened in 1974 in Reynosa, Mexico (Sklair 1993: 51). Although Warwick had only 7 to 9 percent of the U.S. market share, it was the largest assembler in Mexico until the mid-1970s. With increasing costs in Taiwan, other important firms including General Instruments, Motorola, RCA, and Zenith opened plants in Mexico. And yet, until 1973, these new plants (the exception being Warwick) produced only components. For example, RCA opened a deflection yoke plant in Ciudad Juarez in 1969, and Zenith opened two parts plants in Matamoros in 1971.

Mexican production gradually shifted away from simple component assembly as many U.S. parts suppliers exited the industry. Also, the number of final assembly plants increased. By the late 1970s, Mexico's role had evolved from being a parts supplier and exporter of B/W televisions to assembling both the CTV chassis and television kits. Companies such as RCA, Sylvania, and Zenith had their Mexican plants assemble incomplete sets. This was determined partially by import restrictions requiring U.S. producers to assemble the final product in the United States to avoid high tariffs.

The U.S. and Mexican tariff regulations affected the spatial organization of production. In Mexico, U.S. firms could secure Japanese and Taiwanese parts duty-free, because of tariff laws written to protect U.S. firms assembling overseas. Higher tariffs were placed on many parts and components rather than preassembled or semiassembled televisions shipped into the United States. For example, the duty on a television tube was higher than on a finished television. Therefore, U.S. firms would purchase the tubes in Asia, assemble much of the television in Mexico, and do final assembly in the United States (Ohgai 1996). These purchases strengthened the Asian infrastructure. Trade rules that had been developed to protect high-value items, particularly the television tube, had the ultimate effect of accelerating the erosion of the U.S. parts infrastructure.

By the early 1980s, a new shift in the global television value chain was underway. For the most part, U.S. manufacturers had relocated television assembly from Asia to the Mexico-Texas border. For the remainder of the 1980s and into the 1990s, U.S. manufacturers (and those acquired by European firms) continued to move assembly operations into Mexico. During the 1980s, pricing pressure on Japanese manufacturers increased, as did trade friction. In response, the Japanese followed the American firms to Mexico.

Mexico was attractive to Japanese firms, also. Most obviously, Mexico offered inexpensive labor coupled with free trade zone status. There were other benefits, such as a fairly lax taxation system, and less stringent environmental, health, and safety regulations. For the Japanese, Tijuana had significant advantages over the Texas border, where the U.S. firms had clustered. First and foremost, it was close to the Pacific Ocean shipping lanes, allowing easy access for many parts imported from Asia. These parts landed in Los Angeles or Long Beach, where duties were paid (or not paid and trans-shipped) and then re-exported to Mexico. Moreover, the Southern California area already hosted Sony, Hitachi, and Mitsubishi Electric. Also, San Diego was a much more desirable domicile for the Japanese expatriates who would establish and manage the maquiladoras. Still, at that time, Tijuana's industrial infrastructure was poor, and there were few trained workers—but the advantages outweighed the disadvantages. Curiously, Warwick had been operating chassis assembly factories in Tijuana since 1966, but the operations were closed in 1977, when Warwick was purchased by Sanyo (Kenney and Florida 1994; Lowe and Kenney 1999). So, in 1980 there was little electronics production in northwestern Mexico.

In 1980, Matsushita opened a small chassis assembly operation in Tijuana that would be the seed of what evolved into the largest cluster of television assembly operations in the world. In the early 1980s, Sony, which had a television assembly and CPT factory in San Diego, used a subcontractor in Tijuana to undertake labor-intensive activities. The initial activities in Tijuana involved low technology and were labor intensive. And yet, the Tijuana factories were not static; they would evolve. During this period, often, there was a division of labor between the United States and the Mexican factories known as the "twin plant" arrangement. However, twin plant proved to be a misnomer, because the overwhelming tendency was for the U.S. plants to shrink while the maquiladoras grew. Frequently this resulted in the closure of the U.S. factory in favor of its Mexican counterpart, though that was not always the case. For example, the Sony San Diego factory began by assembling televisions, then gradually transferred its various assembly operations, first to its Tijuana facilities and later also to Mexicali. Sony San Diego graduated to cathode ray tube (CRT) production, R&D, and the assembly of various other Sony products.

The Japanese assemblers were not the only firms to relocate. After their abortive attempts to begin assembling televisions in the United States, the Korean assemblers, driven by rising wages in Korea, the rising value of the won, and ferocious competition in the U.S. market, also opened factories in northern Mexico (Choi and Kenney 1997). In these factories the Korean firms assembled televisions on an OEM basis for various U.S. retailers and also supplied smaller televisions to their Japanese and European competitors.

The Japanese and Korean assembly plants opened in Tijuana with only a few accompanying suppliers. Their operations were geared to receive components, either from Asia or the United States, assemble them, and then ship them to their U.S. counterpart plants for final assembly. But given the labor cost advantages and continuing trade friction with Asia, the transplants deepened their production, and in the process offered opportunities for Japanese or Korean suppliers to relocate to Mexico to supply them.

The first foreign assemblers to leave the United States were the Taiwanese. For the Taiwanese, this marked their abandonment of the global television business. Korean firms followed the U.S. and Japanese manufacturers and established assembly factories in Mexico. While Japanese firms established Mexican factories, they tenaciously tried to retain their U.S. factories. But by the early 1990s, most Japanese firms concluded that television assembly in the United States would never become profitable; most closed their U.S. factories and transferred the remaining production to their Mexican factories.

Zenith, the final U.S. manufacturer, succumbed to competition in 1998, when the Korean firm LG (Lucky-Goldstar Electronics) increased its ownership to a majority position. But even this investment was insufficient, and Zenith filed for bankruptcy in late 1998. LG absorbed the remainder of Zenith and closed its manufacturing facilities in the United States and in Mexico, with the exception of one Mexican assembly operation. The Zenith closing cost approximately 2,000 U.S. jobs (Wolinsky 1998; Zenith Electronics 1998).

The two major European producers, Thomson and Philips, had large U.S. operations. Thomson Electronics of France had the largest North American market share, as the result of its 1987 acquisition of GE's television operations (GE had purchased RCA's operations in 1985). The acquisition was meant to build sufficient scale to compete with the Japanese.[6] This scale was reached, but both the newly purchased GE operations and Thomson's European operations continued to lose money and market share. During the 1990s, to offset these losses, the French government repeatedly provided subsidies to Thomson. In 1996, wearying of the seemingly endless subsidies, the French government accepted a bid from Daewoo and the French defense contractor Lagerdere. This bid intended to split Thomson's profitable defense electronics operations from the money-losing consumer electronics division. In order to accomplish this the defense operations would be merged with Lagerdere and the consumer electronics division would be absorbed by Daewoo. Because of French public pressure and union concerns, which centered upon the threat that Daewoo would lay off French workers, the proposed sale was blocked and Thomson remained French.

In 1998, in an effort to lower costs, Thomson closed the former RCA television assembly factory in Bloomington, Indiana, which was once the world's

TABLE 4.5

*Television Assembly Plants in the U.S., by Location, Product, and Employment, 1999*

| Firm | Location | Products | Employment |
|------|----------|----------|------------|
| GC Capital | Knoxville, TN | All sizes | 800 |
| Matsushita Kotobuki | Vancouver, WA | TV/VCR Combo | 500 |
| Orion | Princeton, IN | All sizes | 110 |
| Sanyo | Forrest City, AR | All sizes | 300 |
| Sharp | Memphis, TN | All sizes | 900 |
| Sony | Mount Vernon, PA | Projection televisions | 300 |
| Toshiba | Lebanon, TN | All sizes | 900 |

*Source:* Author's compilation.

largest color television factory, and where mass production of the color television first began. The closure cost 1,100 jobs (Nickell 1997), and came despite the fact that Thomson controlled approximately 20 percent of the U.S. market. After 1999, all Thomson televisions sold in the North American market were assembled in Mexico. Finally, in 2001, Thomson's television operations returned to profitability on the basis of its large share of the U.S. market and global cost cutting.

Philips's U.S. operations were the result of its purchases of Magnavox in 1974 and GTE/Sylvania in 1980. Through these purchases, Philips acquired assembly facilities and a CPT factory in Ottawa, Ohio. With the purchase of Magnavox, Philips inherited a large assembly complex in Ciudad Juarez and a complex of factories in Chattanooga. In the late 1990s, Philips also fell victim to the difficult environment. Curiously, its response differed from that of most firms: rather than closing its U.S. facilities, it spun them off to their managers and provided them with medium-term contracts. These factories no longer produce televisions, and Philips production is now all in Mexico.

By 2002, only seven U.S. assembly factories remained in operation. Of these only three were large facilities (see Table 4.5). The Sanyo facility in Arkansas had shrunk to a minimum economic size, and remained open at the insistence of Sanyo's most important customer, Wal-Mart. With the exception of the Sony large-screen television factory in Westmoreland County, Pennsylvania, serving the East Coast, all the remaining U.S. factories had sister plants in Mexico. Given the difficult competitive environment, the U.S. factories' survival seems dubious, particularly because the Mexican plants were profitable and could draw upon a growing transplant supplier base.

The 1990s were difficult for CTV manufacturers. Low-cost imports from Southeast Asia and Korea were joined by imports from rapidly expanding Mexican factories, driving prices down. This was exacerbated by the increasing importance of electronics superstores, such as Circuit City and The Good Guys, and retailers such as Wal-Mart and Target that demanded large discounts in exchange for large volume. High wages and benefits made the U.S. factories uncompetitive, and these factories relocated to Mexico to take advantage of the maquiladora program.

*Suppliers*

With little support from either the government or U.S. assemblers, U.S. suppliers collapsed. In contrast, Asian and especially Japanese suppliers captured increasing market share as they supplied Asian and U.S. assemblers. Only a few of the Asian suppliers followed their customers to North America, preferring to ship parts from Asia. However, a continuing increase in the value of Asian currencies made labor costs in Mexico ever more attractive. Also, the assemblers demanded cost savings and rapid responses to demand. Thus as Mexican television assembly increased, Japanese suppliers began relocating to Mexico.

With a few exceptions, Japanese parts suppliers had not made extensive investments in the United States. For those that had U.S. factories, they were often unprofitable. The initial response was to subsidize the U.S. operations, but as the assemblers relocated to Mexico it was pointless to remain, so all activities were consolidated into the maquiladoras. For example, a plastic parts maker, Kyowa Electric, had operated a factory in Anaheim, California, since 1986 to supply local Hitachi and Mitsubishi plants, but in 1994 it felt compelled to open a factory in Tijuana, Mexico. In 1998 it closed its Anaheim factory and moved its remaining operations to Mexico, and then opened a branch factory in Mexicali. In another case, a Japanese plastic molder had established a factory in Dalton, Georgia, to supply Mitsubishi in Georgia and Thomson in Indiana. When these factories announced their closure, the plastic molder also closed and moved to Tijuana. Other Japanese suppliers repeated this pattern as they followed their customers.

Suppliers' locational decisions are always contingent upon a variety of factors. However, all factors being equal, proximity to customers is beneficial. For the most part, the U.S. television maquiladoras in the Ciudad Juarez area operated integrated facilities, so suppliers were not as significant. In contrast, Asian producers were far more dependent upon their suppliers. In other words, U.S. manufacturers did not mind operating internal parts operations. Japanese firms, on the other hand, were more comfortable outsourcing such operations. The initial Japanese assembly operations did not attract parts suppliers; however, in 1986 a new wave of Japanese assemblers relocated operations to Tijuana, and Matsushita upgraded its chassis production (i.e., stuffing a printed circuit board) to full television assembly. Chassis production does not require many local suppliers, because the components are small and can simply be delivered in bulk. However, the television assembly has different logistical requirements.

For example, plastic and wood cabinets are bulky but relatively low value-added, meaning that transportation costs can be prohibitive. Fortunately, a factory for their production is relatively inexpensive ($5 million). In contrast, other components such as the CPT are not only bulky but are also high value-added and must be produced in capital- and scale-intensive facilities. CPT production benefits from economies of scale, and, unlike cabinet production, the capital investment for a new factory is high.

In 1987, the initial wave of independent Japanese parts suppliers arrived in Tijuana. The cabinetmakers were in this group; often they relocated because of encouragement and even pressure from the assemblers. Wire harness producers also began operations, as their production is extremely simple but labor intensive. Even a Japanese firm producing the shaped styrene foam used in packaging televisions began operations. This first wave of supplier investment created a rudimentary division of labor.

The difference between Tijuana and Ciudad Juarez was striking. Ciudad Juarez received far less supplier investment, either American or Asian. In 1987, Murata Electric established a maquiladora to manufacture deflection yokes replacing U.S. and Asian imports. In 1988, Taisho Electric built a factory in Ciudad Juarez to build television coils, and in 1989, TDK established a factory to build coil components for autos and televisions; few other suppliers arrived, however, and they were in insufficient numbers to create the synergistic clustering effects that would be experienced along the California border.

An important deepening of the Tijuana parts infrastructure occurred in the early 1990s, when two of the largest television component manufacturers in the world, Sanyo Industrial Components and Matsushita Industrial Components, established operations in Tijuana. They produced deflection yokes, flyback transformers, and many other television-related parts, not only for their own assembly operations but also to supply other television assemblers. They would soon be joined by another global giant, Samsung. These operations did not displace U.S. production, which was already minimal, but rather replaced Asian imports.

The Korean assemblers arrived in the late 1980s and began their operations using parts imported from Korea. In the early 1990s, they began purchasing some components locally from Japanese suppliers, even as they established their internal component-making operations and encouraged their Korean suppliers to relocate to Mexico. Almost paralleling a process that Japanese assemblers had begun five years earlier, the Koreans began warning their suppliers that production would be moved out of Korea, and it would no longer be economically feasible to use components imported from Korea.

In 1991, the rudiments of an industrial cluster were apparent in Tijuana;

however, it proved to be only the beginning, as the number of televisions produced increased further. The 1994 ratification of NAFTA accelerated a general relocation to North America, because it stipulated that all televisions must contain 62 percent North American content to be accepted for duty-free status. NAFTA also had a clause effective in 2002 discontinuing the Mexican policy of allowing the import of CPTs duty-free provided they were then re-exported in a television. These requirements pressured Asian television firms to increase their North American content. For the Japanese firms, this was not so difficult because they already had begun producing CPTs in the United States and were purchasing other CPTs from Thomson and Philips. For the Korean firms, which were importing many parts from their Asian factories, NAFTA's passage required more dramatic action, if they did not want either to pay high import duties or purchase parts from their competitors.

The Korean response was to deepen their operations by building CPT factories in Mexico. Each Korean firm established an integrated production complex producing all the television components except for sophisticated integrated circuitry. This strategy meant that the Korean firms made investments an order of magnitude larger than they had in their initial assembly facilities. Samsung invested over $500 million in its Tijuana television production complex, which now manufactures CPTs and components and assembles televisions. LG invested $300 million and Daewoo invested $260 million so they could also produce CPTs, components, and televisions.

During the 1990s, the number of Japanese and Korean television parts suppliers swelled. Soon they began establishing operations in Mexicali because of the lack of new factory space and increasing wages in Tijuana. In 1999, there were at least twenty-one Japanese and eight Korean television parts suppliers in Tijuana, and twelve Japanese and nine Korean television parts suppliers in Mexicali. The suppliers were not the only firms to relocate operations to Mexico. When Matsushita closed its Chicago facility (which it had purchased from Motorola) in 1995, a U.S. plastic parts firm, Mulay Plastics, also moved to Tijuana.[7]

Employment in the consumer electronics maquiladoras can only be estimated, because growth has been rapid and there is no single reliable source for employment. However, in 1998, Thomson, Philips, and Toshiba employed approximately 22,000 Mexicans in their factories along the Texas border. The Japanese and Korean firms employed another 30,000, mostly along the California border. In total, the consumer electronics assembly maquiladoras employed approximately 52,000 Mexicans. Another significant source of employment were the no less than sixty-seven parts suppliers that, with a conservative estimate of 200 employees each, hired another approximately 13,400 persons for a total of more than 65,000 employees.

Television assembly in North America shifted to Mexico, while imports from Asia continue to decline. In 2001, Mexico produced more TVs than the United States; however, the average cost of the televisions produced in the United States was higher (in large part, because they were larger). Similar statistics by tube size were not available for other years. However, in 1997, North American television demand was for 27.2 million units; of these 21.4 million were produced in Mexico, 3.8 million in the United States, and 2 million in Asia (BAN-COMEXT 1999). With the 1998 closure of the Mitsubishi factory another 700,000 mostly large-screen televisions shifted to Mexico. The 1998 opening of a Sharp television factory in the Tijuana area further shifted production to Mexico, though the Mexican factory has not led to the closure of the Sharp factory in Memphis, Tennessee.

In 2000, it was possible to purchase nearly all the components needed for assembling a television in northwestern Mexico. Moreover, for most components there were multiple sources. In other words, the environment became richer and more complex, thereby increasing its attractiveness. The only components not available locally were the sophisticated digital signals processing chips and some CPTs, but the situation for CPTs was changing. In other words, the region had become the center of television assembly in North America, and it has developed many of the agglomeration economies associated with an industrial cluster.

## Color Picture Tubes

The single most critical and highest value-added component in a color television is the CPT, which is also the last tube left in the television—and as Murtha et al. argue in Chapter 7, will be phased out over the next decade. The location of CPT facilities is determined by a matrix of the following considerations: proximity to glass production, TV assembly plants, and transportation nodes; availability of skilled labor; and decent utilities. Increasingly, as in the case of televisions, CPTs are no longer being transported between continents, even while trade between countries in the same macro-region has increased. Global-class CPT factories were concentrated in Europe (France, Holland, and the UK), North Asia (Japan, Korea, Taiwan, and China), Southeast Asia (Singapore, Malaysia, and Thailand), and North America (U.S. Midwest and northeastern Mexico). In North America, the concentration of operations in Ohio and Pennsylvania was the remnant of the U.S. television industry, which had been clustered in the Midwest.

The capital investment in a CPT factory was determined by a number of variables including size, the number of production lines, the type of tube (direct view or projection), and the size of the tubes produced. Smaller tube sizes, in general, required less expensive factories. The initial investment for larger screen televisions (25-inch and greater) was between $200 and $300 million, and a typical factory employed between 500 and 1,000 persons. For example, in 1988 it cost Matsushita $150 million to build its Troy, Ohio, factory with an annual capacity of 2 million tubes. In 1986, Toshiba spent $220 million to refurbish and expand the Horseheads, New York, CPT factory (Khurana 1994: 89). To be viable, the operational capacity of a new plant should be more than 1.5 million tubes per year. The most expensive lines were required for tubes larger than 30 inches and with rectangular screens (16 x 9 aspect ratio) and ultraflat face panels. The larger CPTs are more difficult to produce because there is a greater defect probability. As in any capital-intensive process, high yields are the key to profitability.

Corporate strategy regarding the building of new CRT production facilities is complicated by the seemingly inexorable erosion of market share by Flat Panel Displays. The FPD will eventually make the CRT obsolete, and in the process will result in a shift of production to Asia. Thus these U.S. factories are probably doomed to closure in the next decade.

In contrast to television assembly, CPT production is automated, capital intensive, and requires a skilled labor force including significant numbers of technicians and engineers. Because of the large capital investment and required technical capabilities, there were fewer firms producing CPTs than assembling televisions. The picture tube was an important part of the total cost of a television. Through time this percentage has increased because the tubes were being improved to have flatter faces, more nearly perfect rectangular shapes, and shorter necks, while most of the other components declined in price. Profitability for the smaller tubes was low, because they were easier to make and there was price competition; gradually, Japanese and European manufacturers abandoned those segments.

The CPT production geography differed from that of television assembly. In contrast to the large number of television assembly plants globally, in 2001 there were only twenty-three companies producing CPTs of any kind, and only ten producers were significant. In total, there were approximately fifty major CPT production facilities globally. With the exception of Southeast Asia, Taiwan, Korea, and, most recently, China, there were no leading-edge CPT production facilities in developing countries, though in the late 1990s Korean manufacturers and Mitsubishi had begun operations in northwestern Mexico. Globally, of the factories operating in 1999, more than 60 percent were owned by Japanese companies, an increase from 10 percent in 1970 (ibid.: 67), though by 2001 Japanese firms were abandoning production facilities on account of

Korean competition. In 1985 there were more than twenty CPT factories in the United States (ibid.: 66), compared with only eight in 1999; the sole factory in Canada closed in 1998.

In the 1970s prior to foreign producers' entry into the United States, RCA, GTE-Sylvania, Zenith, and National Video Corporation controlled the U.S. color tube market (MIT Commission on Industrial Productivity 1989: 48). U.S. CPT industry employment peaked in 1967 with total employment of 27,600. In 1999, U.S. CPT factories employed approximately 11,000 persons—a significant decline from the 13,000 employed in 1997. The most recent losses were due to the 1998 closure of the Zenith factory. In March 2002, Hitachi announced that it would end CPT production in its Greenville, South Carolina, factory (Landers 2002). Total employment will continue to decrease, because no new CPT factories will be built in the United States, and older ones will close as consumption shifts to FPDs.

In the last twenty years, there has been a significant shift in the world's leading television tube makers that has mirrored the changes in television assembly (see Table 4.6). In 1981 three U.S. makers and five Japanese makers were in the top ten. By 1995 the rankings had changed dramatically, as there were no longer any U.S. firms in the top ten, and the Japanese maker Mitsubishi had fallen out of that group. During the last three decades, some U.S. factories have closed, and foreign firms acquired the others. The most notable development has been the growth of Korean manufacturers (Kenney 1999a).

The three Korean tube producers Samsung, LG, and Daewoo are also television assemblers, and they did not cross-source tubes, though they all supplied non-Korean firms. Taiwanese firms entered the television tube market in the 1970s, but with the exception of Chungwha (a company related to Tatung) dropped out or switched to computer monitor production in the mid-1980s. So entry into CPT production has been limited. Korea was successful because its companies had access to massive low-interest government loans and captive in-house television assembly operations that guaranteed a market for a portion of the capacity. Finally, their most significant competitor, Japan, was hobbled in the low end of the market because of rising labor costs and an appreciating yen. These conditions permitted Korean firms to capture market share and expand operations (ibid.).

In the late 1990s, a number of CPT factories were opened in northwestern Mexico. These were an important deepening of the Mexican television production infrastructure. Samsung's aims were particularly ambitious: it built the largest CPT factory in the world in Tijuana. Further, a joint venture of Corning, Samsung, and Asahi Glass established a glass bulb and faceplate factory in Tijuana. Also, NEG, the largest Japanese producer of television tube glass, built a

TABLE 4.6
*World's Largest Television CPT Producers in Units, 1981 and 1995*

| 1981 Rank | Company | 1995 Rank | Company | 1995 Production in million units |
|---|---|---|---|---|
| 1 | Philips (Neth) | 1 | Samsung (K) | 30.5 |
| 2 | RCA (U.S.) | 2 | Philips (Neth) | 19.5 |
| 3 | Hitachi (J) | 3 | Toshiba (J) | 17 |
| 4 | Toshiba (J) | 4 | Thomson (F) | 14.7 |
| 5 | Zenith (U.S.) | 5 | Sony (J) | 11.9 |
| 6 | Matsushita (J) | 6 | Orion (K) | 11.8 |
| 7 | Sony (J) | 7 | Chunghwa (T) | 10.4 |
| 8 | Mitsubishi (J) | 8 | LG (K) | 9.6[a] |
| 9 | ITT (U.S.) | 9 | Matsushita (J) | 8.8 |
| 10 | Videocolor (F) | 10 | Hitachi (J) | 6.9 |

*Sources:* Turner 1982; Fukushi 1995.
  *Note:* Countries omitted included CIS, India and Poland
  [a]LG purchased 60 percent of Zenith that had production of 4.4 million tubes

neck, funnel, and faceplate factory in Mexicali to serve Mitsubishi, LG, and Daewoo's CPT factories. The investments in these factories are in the range of $200 to $300 million. These glass factories increase the richness of the Mexican infrastructure.

If the past is prologue, the current electronics investment in northwestern Mexico will create a deeper and more powerful infrastructure as the existing firms expand and relocate even more production from Asia and the United States to Mexico. The number of TV imports to North America from Asia (2 million in 1997) should either decline or remain stagnant. Mexico, which already assembles nearly 20 percent of the world's televisions, should continue to increase its exports until FPD TVs displace CPT TVs (BANCOMEXT 1999).

*Tube Components and Glass*

The television tube glass industry makes the glass neck, funnel, and faceplate that are joined together at the tube factory. The glass industry was globally oligopolized, and there were only a few exits and even fewer entries over the past two decades. The three major independent glass producers were Corning Glassworks, Nippon Electric Glass (NEG), and Asahi Glass. European CPT glass production was integrated within the large television producers, Philips and Thomson. The two major Japanese producers developed their technology through long-standing technical relationships with U.S. glass producers.

In 1980, there were three major U.S. producers, Corning, Owens-Illinois (OI), and Lancaster Glass, supplying glass picture tube bulbs and panels. RCA operated its own tube glass production, though it also purchased from external vendors (Levy 1981: 107). The U.S. industry was concentrated in Ohio, Pennsylvania, and New York. The history of Japanese glassmakers was nearly the inverse of that of the U.S. firms. After World War II there were no major Japanese tube glass manufacturers. In response to the necessity of importing the glass, the entire tube, or the glass blanks from abroad, Japanese companies entered the growing market for homegrown tube makers. Toshiba (with Westinghouse technology) and Matsushita (with Philips Technology) began producing glass internally. As in the United States, Japan quickly realized that glassmaking was quite different from electronics, and the independent glassmakers displaced the in-house glassmaking operations of CPT and television makers, such as Toshiba, NEC, Matsushita, and Mitsubishi Electric. The two dominant Japanese producers would be Asahi Glass and NEG. Asahi imported technology from Corning Glass. NEG, utilizing technical assistance agreements with Owens-Illinois, began production of B/W CPT funnels and panels in 1965. In 1968, with technical assistance from OI, NEG began production of color bulbs and panels (NEG n.d.).

Asahi and NEG had quite different strategies for responding to the movement offshore of Japanese television assembly and then later CPT production. In 1988, Corning and Asahi formed a U.S. joint venture, Corning Asahi Video Products Company, to produce CPT bulbs and panels (Asahi Glass 1992: 26). For this joint venture, Corning contributed its CPT glass facility in College Station, Pennsylvania (Mathew 1993: 11). However, in April 2003 Corning announced it would increase production of CPT glass in North America. In 1995, Asahi, Sony, and Corning created a joint venture to produce glass for Sony's Pittsburgh area television tube facility. In 1988, NEG concluded an agreement with OI to create a 50–50 joint venture, called Techneglass, to manufacture CPT bulbs and panels in the United States. Then in 1993, NEG purchased OI's share of the joint venture, making it a wholly owned subsidiary (NEG 1995). After purchasing OI, NEG embarked on a major investment program to improve the quality and capabilities of its acquired plants, all of which were in Ohio. In 1996, Techneglass supplied glass for nearly 70 percent of North American televisions (Salmon 1996).

There are no statistics available regarding employment in TV tube glass production, and the companies do not provide information. Employment is difficult to calculate because of Corning's secrecy. In 1996, there were approximately 1,600 employees at the NEG Columbus plant, 1,400 of which were union members and the rest salaried (ibid.), though in Ocober 2002, the number had decreased to 750 because of the closure of one production line (Newpoff 2002). Total U.S. factory employment in the CPT glass industry has declined during the last forty years. The proportion of the decrease related to imports and that related to technological change is uncertain. However, there must have been some displacement of U.S. tube glass production, because of the foreign-made tubes imported either in unassembled form or as part of finished televisions. Even though U.S. firms may have decreased CRT production, the total volume of glass processed probably increased in the 1990s as Japanese manufacturers began CPT production and imports dropped. Also, television screen sizes increased, requiring larger bulbs and thus more glass.

## Conclusion

The U.S. television industry is often pointed to as an example of the catastrophic consequences of globalization. The reasons for the collapse of the U.S. television industry and then the relocation of the foreign firms out of the United States are complicated. The structure of the U.S. industry with its arm's length relationships with suppliers and loose relationships between manufacturers and retailers is often portrayed as the Achilles heel that permitted Japanese manufacturers to enter the market. This is undoubtedly correct, and when Japanese firms were able to offer less expensive products, both components and completed televisions, U.S. retailers and consumers were willing to purchase them. Whether correctly or incorrectly, the U.S. response was to retreat to higher value-added areas. The difficulty with this strategy was that it meant that improvement in terms of functionality, quality, and production efficiency was mandatory. However, U.S. firms failed in all three improvement areas.

U.S. government protectionism was unable to save the U.S. manufacturers. Protectionism did encourage Japanese firms to establish or purchase factories in the United States. However, the difficult competitive environment meant that Japanese transplants also found it impossible to retain their competitiveness and relocated their assembly factories to Mexico. The attraction of proximity to the assembly plants and the general competition facilitated by a constantly ongoing process of production routinization encouraged the establishment of tube factories and other higher valued-added component production in the United States. However, tube production also gradually relocated to Mexico. By 2000 the locus of the North American television assembly, tube, and component production had shifted to northern Mexico.

For the larger understandings of globalization, the television industry provided interesting insights. As we demonstrated, despite their apparent stability at any given moment, the spatial location of various nodes in the value chain was constantly in flux, though the organizational structure was invariant. Interestingly, the United States never had a clear television or consumer electronics cluster; rather it was dispersed from the East Coast through Chicago. Organizational competitive advantage continued to be located in the integrated firms, because of their control over branding and distribution channels. In contrast to the PC industry, the television never became a modular product produced by a disintegrated value chain.

Although the television has some resemblance to the PC in terms of components, it does not experience the same pressures of obsolescence. In this respect, television assembly has greater resemblance to the automobile. The production process never was as disintegrated, and there was never an open market for components, despite the fact that television assembly is almost as modularized as PC assembly. The most important threat to the current global configuration of television production is the possible replacement of CPT by the FPD as the viewing device of choice. As the Murtha, Lenway, and Hart chapter indicates, the FPD is rapidly declining in cost and appears to be on a trajectory to replace the CPT. This technology shift could alter the geography of television production, because at this time substantially all FPD production is in Asia—and there is no guarantee that FPDs will ever be produced in North America. It is possible that this architectural shift will transfer substantially all television production to Asia.

## Notes

The author thanks the Alfred P. Sloan Foundation for funding this research. He also thanks all of the managers who gave willingly of their time. Special thanks to Shoko Tanaka for translating during the many trips to Japan. Also, the author thanks "Frank" Ohgai for his encouragement and door-opening introductions.

1. For another version of this shibboleth, see Murtha et al. in this volume.

2. For a discussion of value chains, see Porter (1985). For the commodity chains formulation, see Gereffi and Korzeniewicz (1994).

3. Traditional wisdom says that the EIAJ and MITI bargained on behalf of the Japanese industry, and therefore was able to achieve a much lower price. However, this arrangement was also convenient for RCA, as the EIAJ and MITI policed the agreement and ensured that the fees were paid, thereby simplifying the collection process.

4. TSUS 807 is the customs category permitting U.S. parts to be exported overseas for assembly and then be reimported with duty paid only on the value-added incurred overseas.

5. These CPTs continued to have quality problems even in the late 1980s.

6. "Overnight, Thomson Has the Stuff to Take on the Titans." *Business Week* (August 10, 1987): 36–37.

7. Mulay Plastics is interesting because it also supplies the Sanyo television factory in Forrest City, Arkansas. The relationship with Sanyo can be traced back to Warwick, which was a subsidiary of Sears, based in Chicago. Similarly, Motorola was based in Chicago and sold its television operations to Matsushita.

PART TWO

# The Organizational and Geographic Configuration of the Personal Computer Value Chain

JAMES CURRY

MARTIN KENNEY

Frederick Jameson (1991), in one of his ruminations on postmodernism, remarks that the personal computer (PC) comes up short as a visual emblem in an era that is, at least, in part defined by digital technology.[1] Notwithstanding the potent symbolism of the beige (or black) box, the PC falls short as an art object. And yet, the installed base of 500 million PCs worldwide not only provides desktop computing to hundreds of millions but also makes the PC the device that enabled the Internet to become more than just a curiosity for research scientists affiliated with universities and government laboratories. Even if it is not iconic, the PC has in some way touched every other industry discussed in this book, as it has become the ubiquitous information appliance, and the Dell business model has become universally admired. The production and distribution of the PC illustrates, nearly perfectly, the dynamics discussed in the Introduction.

The tension between the global and the local suffuses the PC industries and is derived from the modular design of the personal computer system. The physical components of the greatest value and technical virtuosity are the semiconductors and the hard disk drive. We omit the monitor in this statement, though as Murtha, Lenway, and Hart show in Chapter 7, the flat panel display (FPD) is certainly worthy of placement in this group of components. As Leachman and Leachman and McKendrick show, these two classes of components experience extremely rapid improvement, while the value of earlier generations decreases accordingly (Curry and Kenney 1999). For example, newly introduced semiconductors and hard disk drives (HDDs) experience a rate of technological obsolescence that decreases their value at up to 1 percent per week. Outside the electronics sector, as Abernathy et al. show, it may only be fashion-forward clothing that experiences a similar rate of value erosion. For the PC assemblers, mastering this pace of change is vital for success. Excess inventory or transit time, delays of expensive components, or any finished or semifinished product containing them, anywhere in the value chain, results in value loss. A PC is like a "hot potato." Anyone holding it experiences value loss, while those holding it for less than the average time experience value preservation, which is captured as profit. Thus logistics capabilities are a central competency in the PC industry.

The desktop PC is the ultimate modular product (Langlois 1990; 1992).[2] Nearly every major component is a module (there are about ten to fifteen, including peripheral devices such as keyboards and monitors); this facilitates the disintegration of the value chain into separate firms. This modularity reinforced by open interface standards allows producers from low-cost environments to enter PC production absent other barriers to entry. In the competitive environment of component production created by modularity, the only firms to consistently make a profit have been Intel and Microsoft, precisely because they have been able to prevent entry (Borrus and Zysman 1977). This makes possible a second dynamic: a PC assembler is, in many ways, more a logistics coordinator than a manufacturer (Fields 2003). For example, with the exception of Dell and Gateway, all the major PC firms actually assemble only a fraction of their PCs; the remainder are outsourced to contract assemblers. But, more fundamentally, the assembly process adds little value, and the process is so routinized that proprietors of small shops and even individuals in their homes can undertake it. There are some exceptions to the disintegrated structure of the PC industry. Companies like IBM, NEC, Fujitsu, Samsung, and some other integrated computer makers do have internal operations that produce HDDs, memory chips, and other components. These firms are not dominant. Internal integration has not assisted their competitive status, and may, in fact, have hurt it. A more important form of integration is Microsoft's continuing strategy of integrating all PC-related software and Intel's use of its power in microprocessors (MPUs) to dominate the PCI bus chipset market, to become a significant producer of motherboards, and to begin to integrate other functions such as graphics into the microprocessor.

The speed of change is one source of pricing pressure. To illustrate, it is not unheard of for Intel to declare that it will cut prices for a group of MPUs effective immediately or very soon by, say, 20 percent—or as much as 54 percent (Spooner 2001). This immediately devalues the MPUs in a PC firm's inventory by 20 percent, leading to a write-down. An equally important source of pricing pressure is the commodity status of the PC. There is little or no difference between a Dell, Hewlett Packard, or a no-name clone. The components and soft-ware are from the same sources, and are all available in the open market.

For a simple assembled product, the PC value chain is quite disintegrated. A PC assembler can produce an entire PC from scratch (very few do this cur-rently), it can source an almost fully completed box, or it can ask a contract manufacturer to assemble the entire box and place the assembler's label on the box. And, in fact, many firms use a combination of these strategies. For exam-ple, Dell sources its least expensive computers directly from a Taiwanese firm that has a contract manufacturing operation in China, while assembling its higher-end PCs in its own factories around the world for that specific region. For other firms, such as HP and Compaq, contract manufacturers do the bulk of their production, mainly offshore.

Three articles (Leachman and Leachman; McKendrick; and Murtha, Len-way, and Hart) in this book deal directly with PC components, and, as they in-dicate, these are sourced globally. And yet, as we will show, much final assembly for the U.S. market is done in the United States or Mexico. The PC epitomizes globalized production in which development, design, manufacturing, and dis-tribution are interlinked across vast distances—but which all operate on a time frame that seems more appropriate for firm clusters. In contrast to the clusters from which the component makers benefit, the geography of PC assembly is determined by the need to get the assembled unit to widely dispersed cus-tomers as quickly and as inexpensively as possible. By necessity the movement of large quantities of different parts and components from numerous, widely separated suppliers must be coordinated, even while operating under extreme time pressure. The PC must be delivered to markets whose variegated segments demand a variety of configurations and "solutions" to specific needs or prob-lems.

It is not crucial for most suppliers to manufacture their product near the as-semblers, nor for the assemblers to concentrate in any region, though Dell re-quires that its suppliers have warehouses (supply logistics centers) within twenty minutes' driving distance of its assembly operations. Also, where possi-ble Dell sites its overseas assembly operations close to Intel's final testing and packaging operations.[3] However, what is most important is availability of a so-phisticated multimodal delivery system capable of reliably moving time-sensi-tive components quickly and non–time sensitive products more slowly and in-expensively. The size and weight of the finished product, the downward pressure on both component and finished PC prices, and the complexity of the market all give an advantage to those assemblers who are, in terms of time and space, close to the final consumer.[4]

From the previous discussion, one might conclude that U.S. firms should have difficulty competing as PC assemblers. However, despite the fact that the PC is a highly standardized product, much of the manufacturing of the components occurs in Asia, and assembly is done by a variety of subcontractors in the United States and abroad. U.S. assemblers, especially the specialists, dominate the global market.

## Modularity, Speed, and Build-to-Order

In the 1990s, the PC contributed three ideal-typical concepts to thinking about business: modularity, speed, and build to order (BTO). In the case of modularity, it was scholars that were most influenced (Baldwin and Clark 2000; Langlois 2002). In the case of speed, many managers came to realize its significance, both in terms of speed-to-market, and the speed of change in components, their own products, and their markets (Fine 1998; Curry and Kenney 1999). For BTO, it was management thinking that was most affected (in the case of autos, see MacDuffie and Helper 2001; for garments, see Hammond and Kohler 2001).

The open-system modularity of the PC was, in large measure, due to a strategic mistake by IBM (Chposky and Leonsis 1988; Ferguson and Morris 1993; Langlois 1992; Steffens 1994). In the process of developing a microcomputer on a crash schedule, IBM decided that it needed to outsource many components including floppy disk drives (Tandon), power supplies (Zenith), circuit boards (SCI Systems), and the two critical components: the operating system (Microsoft) and the microprocessor (Intel). In the case of the first three components, most production would relocate to Asia. However, the two critical components would remain under the control of Microsoft and Intel.[5] IBM's decision to outsource the operating system and the microprocessor caused it to lose control of the PC, as all of the components became available in the marketplace. Microsoft negotiated an agreement with IBM that essentially gave Microsoft ownership of the operating system software, and Intel's microprocessor became the electronic core of the IBM PC. As merchants, therefore, Microsoft and Intel were both willing and able to sell to all customers, American and foreign. Although the PC was initially very profitable for IBM and for its first fierce competitor, Compaq, over time the PC became a commodity with the value-added captured by those making components protected by either insurmountable barriers of entry or intellectual property restrictions. Moreover, the standardized interfaces used throughout the PC made it easy to interchange components and peripherals. This was quickly exploited by Taiwanese manufacturers who were capable initially of doing only the lowest level of assembly work—but through this they could enter the industry and gradually upgrade their capabilities (Dedrick and Kraemer 1998; Levy and Kuo 1991). Modularity with open interface standards meant that for most modules there were no non-market barriers to new entrants.

Modularity ignited what Bresnahan and Richards (1999) termed "vertical competition," in which every firm in the value chain strives to commoditize the other segments of the value chain. The much-vaunted Wintel duopoly is not an exclusive arrangement.[6] Microsoft gladly qualifies other MPUs to run its software, such as the new Transmeta MPU, while Intel is anxious to support other operating systems such as Linux. Because lower prices encourage greater sales, every firm would like the overall price of a PC system to drop; their only wish is that the cost reduction occurs at other segments in the value chain. This means that new entrants can emerge from almost anywhere in the world. As long as they conform to the publicly available standards, have adequate quality, and deliver as promised, even the world's largest PC vendors might purchase from them.

The PC industry operates in a condition of constantly declining component prices, with constant model turnover. The falling price and time constraints are caused by both rapid technological change and the diverse market-driven nature of PC component production. If PC production were completely vertically dominated by a few large companies, then it might be possible to contain rapid change and introduce new innovations in an orderly fashion. In a market characterized by vertical competition, high profitability is possible only in the high end of the market, but any given performance level is at the high end only transiently before being commoditized and rapidly losing value. This dynamic is halted only when the product is sold to the final consumer (and does not come back as a return). There are two implications of the value erosion dynamic that are important for this chapter. The first implication is that powerful advantages will accrue to any firm that can shorten the period during which it holds inventory. The second implication is that rapid transportation of product containing high-value components is vitally necessary, so low production cost cannot be the only criterion in cost calculations. Time is a vital dimension influencing the location of various production activities.

Given these dynamics, there were a number of responses, most of which were a variant on outsourcing. However, another model emerged that has been termed the BTO direct marketing model as practiced by Dell Computer and Gateway Computer. The BTO model is predicated upon a population of experienced consumers willing to purchase a computer on the basis of a series of specifications without in-person examination—in other words, consumers who treat a PC as an entirely standardized commodity; in the case of Dell, this represents close to 80 percent of its total sales. These consumers permit the

BTO practitioners to build computers only after they have been ordered. Therefore, Dell orders the components only after receiving an order. For this reason Dell carries little inventory, because it has contracted with its suppliers to pay for components upon arrival at Dell's factory. Even better, Dell has already locked in the price. Also, since the consumer has ordered the computer, it is likely that they will keep it and not return it, thereby substantially reducing the amount of returned (and hence greatly devalued) product. What the BTO firms have developed is a model designed to exploit the PC's modular design and its concomitant value erosion dynamic.

It is useful to view the component supply system from the perspective of the assembler. The PC as a final product is relatively bulky and heavy. This is in part because it was designed for ease of assembly and thus was not as compact as it could have been (see the early Apple IIs, Macs, or notebook computers for the alternative tight physical design). The valuable components in a PC (MPU, DRAMs, HDD, and chipset) occupy an area that is only some 10 percent of the total volume of the box. If the motherboard and the high-value graphics cards are added, the total space occupied might be one-fifth of the box. The small size of these valuable components allows them to be inexpensively shipped by air to any location. The larger and heavier components and peripherals with lower value compositions, such as cases and keyboards, can be shipped by cargo container. Since the assemblers are concerned with both supply *and* distribution logistics, and the most important components are shippable by air, physical proximity to suppliers is not critical, though it might be convenient. For example, Dell's European assembly operations in Ireland are located close to Intel's Irish factory.[7] However, assurance that all components (including those of low value) will arrive as scheduled is vital. Dell has tackled this problem by requiring all of its suppliers (except Intel) to have a warehouse within twenty minutes of its assembly facilities.

## The Personal Computer Industry

The PC, in its manifestation as a beige box, is the result of one of the simplest assembly processes in contemporary manufacturing. Modularity and internal standardization has proceeded to such an extent that an assembler with minimal training can assemble a PC in fifteen minutes with little more equipment than a screwdriver and a socket set. The most sophisticated moving device is the HDD, which is a sealed box that is inserted into the computer to be held in place by four screws and has a power socket and a data cable socket. The power supply is attached prior to the assembler's receiving the case, and the various power supply wires emanating from it need merely be plugged into the appropriate module. With the integration of some subsystems onto the mother-board during the 1990s, and the introduction of USB ports in the late 1990s, assembly became even simpler. In terms of manufacturing, the PC firms merely purchase and assemble the components and install the software.

Given the simplicity of the final assembly process, the consumer desiring a new PC has numerous options: it is possible to build it yourself. It can be built by the local PC store. It can be purchased at a computer chain store from a mass producer such as HP or eMachines who either assembled it or had a subcontractor assemble it, or it can be purchased by telephone or over the Internet from one of the build-to-order, direct marketers such as Dell or Gateway, which then assembles it and delivers it to your door. Each channel contains essentially the same product, and all have one thing in common—nearly all of the manufacturing is done elsewhere by the component firms, and sometimes all of the assembly is done by another firm. For example, in 2002, IBM announced that it would no longer manufacture any desktop computers—that is, the only physical relationship IBM has with the computer is the IBM badge that the subcontractor places on the machine. Given the lack of differentiation and the simplicity of assembly, the only areas available for differentiation by the PC firms are more efficiently organizing their supply chains, more effectively managing their marketing channels, and managing their brand.

As a condition of survival, PC firms must incorporate the latest technology (innovated elsewhere and available simultaneously to competitors) and assemble and deliver the PC to the market as quickly as possible. The only other ways for these companies to generate value beyond that which they derive from the boxes they sell is diversification, or in an ancillary strategy, to outsource their PC assembly work and concentrate on marketing and downstream logistics. Virtually all the major PC assemblers have pursued variants of this; examples are Compaq's acquisition of DEC and HP's successful entry into the market by using their marketing skills, brand name, and existing distribution channels while producing very few of their own PCs. Other examples of change are HP's recent acquisition of Compaq, and IBM's retreat from manufacturing PCs and decision to stop selling consumer PCs through standard retail channels, while converting most of its marketing efforts to business users and Internet sales. The companies that have had the most success dealing with the problematic nature of the PC as a commodity have been the direct marketers, most notably Dell and, until recently, Gateway.[8]

The key components in a PC, with the exception of the software, lose value as rapidly as fresh produce, prompting the founder of Acer, Stan Shih (1996), to compare the PC industry to the fast food industry. Like a fast food hamburger, the final assembly of the PC should take place as close as is economically feasible to the final consumer. The perishable components can be produced in distant locations as long as they can be economically airlifted to the final assembly site. The logic of the PC industry seems to turn conventional geographical patterns of production upside down. Unlike many electronic products, which are assembled or fabricated in low–labor cost regions and then shipped to market in high–labor cost regions, the low value-added operation of assembling a PC is undertaken in relatively high–labor cost areas. While some PC production for the U.S. market has shifted to Mexico (Acer in Ciudad Juarez for example), or to contract manufacturers in the U.S. South, it is still relatively close to the intended market—and labor costs are much higher than those in China, to where a significant amount of board-level component manufacture and low-end PC assembly is being relocated. There is one exception to this pattern: the cheapest machines using components that are almost entirely depreciated are now built in China.

*Business Models*

The PC industry is curious, because nearly twenty years after its introduction, though there has been consolidation, there is as of yet no dominant model for firm organization—though recently Dell is, perhaps, becoming the dominant firm. In Table 5.1, we parse the PC industry into seven basic business models, though it should be recognized that these are ideal types and there are other variants, and there has been significant experimentation with yet other models, especially in the area of employing the Internet (Kenney and Curry 2001). These models provide insight into the different organizational configurations that PC assembly can adopt and how differently they may organize assembly, distribution, and marketing. Therefore, it should not be surprising that there were a wide variety of entrants with differing strategies, both spatially and organizationally. Some of the most critical decisions assemblers had to make were whether to make or buy the PC, where to locate their assembly facilities, and how to organize their finished product distribution. Finally, given the component devaluation dynamic, assemblers had to consider how long they held inventory—so spatial location was not irrelevant because a temporally inefficient location can lead to excess devaluation.

Another issue is how to interact with the final consumer. This decision is important, because it has contributed to different make-or-buy and location decisions. The traditional distribution method had the PC firm undertake final assembly in its own factory or in a subcontractor's factory and then deliver the PC to a retailer. The mass assembler interacted with customers through the retailer, a common method, yet one that presents difficulties for interorganiza-

TABLE 5.1

*PC Assembler Business Models*

| Category/Model | Characteristics | Main value leverage | Examples |
|---|---|---|---|
| 1. Retail assemblers (value-added re-sellers) | Small local shops ("screw-driver guys"); some with fairly large accounts; collectively account for 25% market share | Know local market; best at customer service; low production overhead | |
| 2. Standard mass assemblers | Inputs shipped to central facility; long-term production planning; marketed through standard retail/VAR channels | Traditional scale economies; brand identity. More recently, OEM from Categories 3, 4, and 5 | IBM, Compaq, HP, Siemens, Sony, NEC, Fujitsu, Samsung |
| 3. Contract manufacturers | OEM assemblers for large branded marketers (standard mass producers) | Efficient production, enable large branded assemblers to expand production while minimizing risks | Solectron, SCI Systems, Jabil Systems |
| 4. Global logistics producers | Assembled at dispersed logistics centers; monthly or weekly production planning; direct shipment to channels bypassing OEM customer | Input and distribution logistics on global scale, provision of OEM and ODM services | Acer, FIC, Mitac, Tatung |
| 5. Channel assemblers | Quasi-logistics centers for standard mass producers; handle excess capacity for mass producers; handle service, integration, configuration for large accounts; alternate retail channel | Distribution logistics, service to customers, system integration | Ingram Micro, Microage, Tech Data |
| 6. BTO/direct marketers | Inputs assembled at central facilities; production planning on per-order basis; direct shipment to customer | Mass customization; protected from price declines | Dell, Gateway, Micron (defunct) |

*Source:* Authors' compilation.

tional information flow. This can be further exacerbated when there is a subcontractor for final assembly, making informational transparency issues even more complicated. The BTO model has a direct relationship to the customer; there are no other intermediaries, thereby providing the BTO firm with the most contemporary and unmediated information.

PC producers exhibit only limited apparent clustering or agglomeration. The major producers' central production facilities are located in a variety of places: Texas (Dell and Compaq), and South Dakota (Gateway). They also rely on numerous original equipment manufacturer (OEM) electronics contract manufacturers scattered around the country. Two global logistics firms, Tai-wanese PC producers FIC and Acer, have located plants in Austin, Houston, and El Paso, Texas, and Ciudad Juarez, respectively. The global contract manufac-turers Solectron, Sanmina, Flextronics, SCI Systems, and Jabil Circuit have nu-merous locations around the world. These companies produce both compo-nents and assembled PCs. The mass assemblers also use the services of various distributor-VARs. One of these, Ingram Micro, operates an assembly/integra-tion center in Memphis, Tennessee. Ingram's six other distribution centers, dis-persed throughout the United States, also engage in some assembly and config-uration activities. While some of the OEM assembly facilities are located near the major assemblers, there is no specific reason for them to be, since the as-sembled PCs are shipped directly to retailers and VARs—and in some cases to the final customer. Distributors like Ingram also perform some assembly func-tions by collocating at an assembler's plants. As for the major assemblers them-selves, three of them (Compaq [now HP], Gateway, and Dell) had their main assembly facilities, and two of the three (Compaq and Dell) had their head-quarters, in the cities in which their founders lived at the initial startup. Gate-way was founded in North Sioux City, South Dakota, and has an assembly fa-cility there; in 1998 its headquarters moved to San Diego, though it has no production facility there.

Since the core components are small and can be shipped in from distant lo-cations, and finished PCs are large enough to incur significant transport costs, there is no driving logic to locate suppliers in vertical production clusters. Component supplier or distributors' representatives can be stationed at the as-sembler's plant in order to coordinate the inflow of components from more distant locations. There are instances where suppliers have set up facilities near their major customers, but it is far more likely for companies that engage in downstream configuration functions to locate operations in or near a major as-sembly facility. The dispersed location of large-scale PC assembly reflects the dispersed nature of PC assembly in general. More significant than having sup-pliers in close proximity is proximity to adequate transportation hubs, espe-cially air cargo. For example, Ingram Micro located their assembly and config-uration facility near the Memphis airport, which is the hub for Federal Express. In the United States there does not appear to be any benefit in large assemblers locating in close proximity to each other, and there are no clusters.

*Retail Assemblers*

To understand the industrial dynamics of PC assembly, it is useful to begin with the retail assembler category that is invisible, but continues to supply at least 25 percent of the entire market. Given the ease of assembly and the wide availability of components, it is easy to enter the PC industry, as Michael Dell proved by beginning his business assembling PCs in his University of Texas dormitory room. These small local shops, once referred to by Steve Ballmer of Microsoft as the "screwdriver guys," can be found in almost any city and in many small towns. Collectively, these local "beige" or "white box" producers (also known as value-added resellers, or VARs) have a 25 percent market share in the United States and an even greater share in many other countries.[9] According to *Reality Research and Consulting* (2000), an estimated 5.62 million white box PCs were sold in North America in 2000. These systems were sold by a motley collection of some 28,800 solution systems integrators, consultants, and value-added resellers. They range from small shops that might produce only a few PCs per week to much larger operations that have contracts to supply local businesses with PCs and other computer-related equipment. These producers operate with lower overhead than the large assemblers and deal directly with customers without the costs of maintaining a large, geographically dispersed technical-support staff or support call centers. The VAR category also consists of numerous other firms that do some kind of assembly or configuration work and are situated in the distribution channel either as technology distributors or integrated information technology service providers.

These firms have survived for two main reasons. First, because of the open market for parts and components, they are able to offer systems similar in quality and price to those of the large assemblers.[10] One major distribution channel for parts is firms such as MicroAge, Ingram Micro, and Tech Data, which also provide channel assembly services. While the retail assemblers do not have the ability to negotiate lower prices for volume purchases, they also do not have the high overhead (including transportation) that large firms do. The second reason is that they are close to their customers. That is very important. Many of these customers demand more than assembled boxes; quite often they are looking for vendors able to provide design, coordination, consultation, and ultimately, complete specially configured systems. The VARs and system integrators, which do this kind of work, may provide completely assembled systems from the major assemblers, as-is or reconfigured, or they may assemble their own systems. The services provided by local and regional VARs are particularly important for smaller enterprises that may not be willing pay the high fees that the larger consultancy firms charge. Moreover, when there are problems, the customer can go directly to the provider and need not deal with large, impersonal service departments (a number of which have also been outsourced). These small assemblers form the base of the industry, and have proved remarkably persistent.

*Mass Assemblers and the Contract Manufacturers*

The traditional competition for the retail assemblers was the mass assemblers exemplified by IBM and Compaq. These firms operated on a quarterly plan that estimated the number of PCs in every category that the market could bear, and then built (or subcontracted) to the plan. The product was built, pushed into the channels, and then the assembler hoped that the plan was accurate. If the plan was too optimistic, the resulting inventory gluts were eliminated by massive discounting. If the plan underestimated demand either in an overall sense or in certain models, there were general product shortages or shortages of a particular model.

The mass assemblers relied heavily upon three other models listed in Table 5.1—that is, contract manufacturers, global logistics firms, and channel assemblers—to undertake some or much of their actual assembly. The involvement of these other assembly models was not confined to subassembly. Significant percentages of the mass assemblers' entire production were completely subcontracted to OEMs. Thus, in many respects, for some models in their product lineup, the mass assemblers, especially HP and IBM, are merely mass marketers, and their most important contribution to the product is their brand name.

To illustrate how important subcontracting has become, in 2000 Compaq Computer imported $9.5 billion worth of components from Taiwan alone. This compared with Compaq's total sales, which were $35.6 billion in fiscal year 2000. In 2000, Compaq was Taiwan's top PC OEM client, outsourcing everything from motherboards and monitors to power supplies and notebook systems. The number of Taiwanese firms providing Compaq was remarkable. One Taiwanese firm, Inventec, made Compaq's Armada business notebooks; Arima Computer produced most of the Presario consumer notebooks; and Quanta was considered as a potential notebook supplier. Mitac and FIC produce desktop PCs, and cathode ray tube (CRT) and FPD monitors for Compaq globally. To service Compaq, FIC has a major assembly complex in Texas (Custer 2001).

The mass assemblers and contract manufacturers are dispersed throughout the United States. The one firm assembling PCs along the border, Acer in El Paso and Juarez, mostly produced PCs on an OEM basis for IBM. When IBM cancelled its Aptiva line, the Acer Mexican facility was adversely affected, and the El Paso factory was closed (Bloomberg News 2000b). The contract manufacturers produce a variety of PCs, workstations, and servers for large PC mass assemblers such as Compaq, IBM, and Hewlett Packard, as well as numerous smaller brands and "beige box" nonbranded PCs. U.S. mass assemblers produce a significant number of PCs for the U.S. market in Guadalajara, Mexico. There, major brand-name firms like IBM and Hewlett Packard produce finished PCs, along with workstations/servers and notebooks, for export. They are also joined by the U.S. contract manufacturers, most of whom have established facilities in Guadalajara in the past few years; from there they supply not only finished PCs to the mass assemblers but also components to the U.S. assembly facilities of Dell, Compaq, and various other firms.

During the mid 1990s, there was a general movement of the Taiwanese Global Logistics Producers to locate final assembly in North America as part of an effort to meet the demand for speed to market and to decrease the retention time of a PC. However, from 2000 onward, Taiwanese firms began shifting assembly from bases closer to end markets (the United States and Europe) to low-cost areas such as China. For example, in 1999, 30 percent of all the PCs produced by Taiwanese firms were assembled in North America, but this shrank to 25 percent in the first quarter of 2000. China increased to second in the first quarter of 1999 with 27 percent of Taiwanese assemblies, and rose to first place with 37 percent in the first quarter of 2000 (Computex Online 2001). The reason for this is that the constant cost pressure combined with the fact that for a low-end machine that cost, say, $600 retail, even if it declined in value at 1 percent a week, it lost only $18.00 in three weeks. There are other advantages to production in China beyond labor costs. The most important of these is that a finished Chinese computer can be shipped directly to its retail outlet in the United States, whereas final assembly in North America requires all the components be shipped to the North American factory, to then be unpacked and assembled. For low-end systems, the savings on depreciation may not outweigh the extra shipping costs and the higher cost of labor in Mexico or the United States. So it is possible that final assembly for the traditional retailers could, once again, shift overseas.

The mass assemblers have outsourced production of the entire PC to contract assemblers in a bid to lower costs and to displace risk. This strategy has permitted them to lower costs; however, the PC and its components are still subject to devaluation as they progress through the value chain to the retailer and then the final consumer. Nevertheless, the temporally based devaluation continues, and even assembling in the low-cost Chinese environment cannot circumvent this reality; therefore a business model that overcomes the temporal devaluation dynamic will, ceteris paribus, have a profound advantage.

*Build to Order*

The BTO model pioneered by Dell and Gateway directly addressed the temporal devaluation dynamic.[11] Here, computers were assembled only after the consumer's order was received. This reduced risk substantially, because it was no longer necessary to build to a projection of consumer demand, ship the inventory into the channel, and then wait to see what sold. In the BTO system, the

PC assembler receives immediate consumer feedback on what is selling and thus can adjust projections immediately. This information can be transmitted directly to suppliers, thereby providing them with near real-time information on sales. That permits the supplier to adjust more rapidly to market changes, creating greater overall transparency in the entire production chain. As with the retail assemblers, the BTO firms assemble all of their desktop PCs, and do not use any contract assemblers for final assembly. Internal assembly provides them with complete control of the customer order fulfillment cycle, eliminating dependence on external organizations.

The BTO model exposes the reason that clustering is not a powerful dynamic in the PC industry. Proximity to the customers, who are widely dispersed, is the most important competitive advantage. The whole point of the BTO model is to bring assembly as close to the customer as possible. This is not limited to proximity in the physical/geographical sense; it also refers to proximity in the organizational sense. One of the BTO firm's most important advantages has been the fact that they interact directly with the consumer and assemble the system only upon a customer's order. This means they have disintermediated all of the distributors and retailers standing between conventional assemblers and customers (Curry and Kenney 1999).

## The Globalization of the U.S. PC Firms

One might expect that in a commoditized industry and with many powerful Asian competitors, U.S. firms would be at a disadvantage. However, the opposite is actually true. U.S. PC assemblers have been gaining global market share (in terms of units sold) at the expense of their overseas competitors. In Europe, U.S. firms have gained market share and driven local vendors from the marketplace. Today, in most nations outside of Asia, the competition is increasingly among U.S. PC firms. In Asia, the competition is between various national firms and the globalized U.S. firms.

The first global PC vendor, not surprisingly, was IBM, which used its global network to market PCs. Until the early 1990s, in most foreign markets IBM did not face the U.S. clone makers; rather it faced national computer firms and some—though far fewer than in the United States—white box assemblers. In Europe its primary competitors were the various national champions such as Olivetti in Italy, Groupe Bull in France, Siemens in Germany, and ICL in Britain. In the Japanese market, the competition was more severe, because IBM faced the entrenched Japanese computer firms such as NEC, Fujitsu, and Hitachi, to name the most prominent. In Korea, IBM faced a closed market that was reserved for domestic manufacturers. So, until the early 1990s, IBM was the most global of the PC vendors. Korean and Japanese firms made repeated efforts to penetrate the U.S. market. However, after some initial success, except in notebook computers they invariably failed to consolidate their gains and were forced to retreat.

The success of the U.S. firms in global markets is best illustrated in Table 5.2. As did Compaq earlier, Dell gained market share in the United States and then went on to capture the global market share crown. The increased rank of Fujitsu/Siemens and NEC in 2002 is due to the HP/Compaq merger. They are continuing to lose global market share. With the U.S. market saturated, all the PC assemblers looked to foreign markets for growth. Table 5.3 indicates how far-flung these operations are. But it also shows that Gateway was forced to close its overseas operations because of competition from Dell and HP/Compaq. For the European market, the primary assembly location has been Ireland and Scotland. The reasons for this were a combination of government subsidies, relatively low wages, and a preference for locating in English-language environments. In Latin America, the pattern was different, with Brazil and Mexico being the two largest hubs. HP and IBM have their most important Latin American production facilities in Guadalajara, a legacy of an earlier local origin requirement that Mexico imposed on the computer industry. However, business was so difficult that in 2000, IBM sold its Brazilian manufacturing operation to Solectron (Solectron 2000).

The first major U.S. PC start-up to enter foreign markets was Compaq,

TABLE 5.2

*Global Ranking of PC Sales by Units, First Quarter*
*2003, 2001, 1999, 1997, and 1990*

| Ranking | 1Q, 2003 | 2001 | 1999 | 1997 | 1990 |
|---|---|---|---|---|---|
| 1 | Dell | Dell | Compaq | Compaq | IBM |
| 2 | HP/Compaq | Compaq | Dell | IBM | Apple |
| 3 | IBM | HP | IBM | Packard Bell NEC | NEC |
| 4 | Toshiba | IBM | Packard Bell NEC | Dell | Compaq |
| 5 | NEC | Fujitsu/ Siemens | HP | HP | Toshiba |
| 6 | | | Gateway | Gateway | Olivetti |
| 7 | | | Apple | Apple | Groupe Bull |
| 8 | | | | Acer | Fujitsu |
| 9 | | | | Fujitsu | Unisys |
| 10 | | | | | Commodore |
| 11 | | | | | HP |
| 12 | | | | | Dell |
| 13 | | | | | Packard Bell |
| 14 | | | | | Gateway 2000 |

*Source:* Various journals.

TABLE 5.3
*Global Location of U.S. PC Firms' Factories*

| Company | U.S. factories | Compaq direct | Asia factories | Configuration centers | Latin Amer. factories | Europe factories | Australian factories |
|---|---|---|---|---|---|---|---|
| Compaq[a] | Houston, TX; Fremont, CA | Ontario, CA; Omaha NE; Indianapolis IN; Swedesboro NJ | Singapore | Bangalore, India; Akiruno-City, Japan; China | Sao Paulo, Brazil | Ayr, Scotland; Erskine, Scotland | Sydney, Australia |
| Dell | Austin, TX; Nashville, TN | | Penang, Malaysia; Xiamen, China, | | Eldorado do Sul, Brazil | Limerick, Ireland | |
| Gateway | North Sioux City, SD; Hampton, VA; Salt Lake City, UT | | Malacca, Malaysia (defunct) | | | Dublin, Ireland (defunct) | |
| Hewlett Packard[a,b] | | | Singapore; China | Bangalore, India | Guadalajara, Mexico | Netherlands | |
| IBM[b] | North Carolina | | Japan; China | | Guadalajara, Mexico | Scotland | |

*Source:* Authors' compilation

[a] With the merger of HP and Compaq, we expect many of these will be closed. However, this has not yet been announced.

[b] There was insufficient information for a complete listing as large integrated firms do not report their PC factories separately.

which began selling PCs in Europe in April 1984, less than two years after its formation. In November 1987, Compaq opened its first overseas manufacturing facility in Scotland. However, as in the United States, Compaq's operations gradually evolved from relatively integrated production to one in which it outsourced even more of their global operations. So by 2001, Compaq and HP had the Taiwanese firm FIC producing hundreds of thousands of desktops a month in the Czech Republic (Hung 2001).

Dell also moved into the global markets relatively early. Beginning in 1987 it opened a sales subsidiary in the United Kingdom, and followed that in 1990 by opening a manufacturing center in Limerick, Ireland, to serve European, Middle Eastern, and African markets. In 1996 an Asia-Pacific manufacturing center was opened in Penang, Malaysia, followed in 1998 by a production center in Xiamen, China. In 1999 a manufacturing facility in Eldorado do Sul, Brazil, was established to serve Latin America. In relative terms, Dell lagged Compaq in globalizing. However, the important point is that like IBM, Compaq, and HP, Dell now operates globally.

The Asian market is the most interesting from the perspective of globalization, because it is the home of a number of powerful computer firms, ranging from the Japanese and Korean mass assemblers to the Taiwanese global logistics producers. Finally, the fastest growing PC market in the world is China, and its leading firm, Legend Computer, is growing rapidly and may soon enter the ranks of world leaders. However, even in China, Dell now ranks seventh in sales.

With the exception of IBM, U.S. PC makers benefited from two attributes of the U.S. market. The first was its huge size. Probably more important was the fact that almost invariably, key hardware and software, especially the new killer applications, were developed—or, as was the case for the World Wide Web, were adopted—most rapidly there. So, U.S. PC makers were privy to the latest trend. This was not the only advantage. As Microsoft and Intel integrated the world under one standard, U.S. makers were able to penetrate new markets on their heels. For example, Microsoft unified Japan under the Windows standard, and made the NEC 9800 DOS standard obsolete (West and Dedrick 2000). This stratagem provided an opportunity for U.S. vendors such as Dell and Compaq to enter the Japanese market; though Fujitsu retains the greatest market share, U.S. vendors achieved a foothold.

Although the U.S. firms are not dominant in Asia, they hold such a commanding lead in the rest of the world that they are becoming globally dominant. The globally dominant position of the U.S. PC firms is not difficult to understand, as they were able to use the knowledge and brand name recognition gained from operating in the competitive U.S. markets. Also, as they grew in size they were able to reap the benefits of volume discounts that were much greater than any other national firm could achieve. These advantages have allowed them to gain market share even in Asia, a region in which many strong PC firms already exist.

## The Globalization of PC Component Markets

The market for PC components is global, but the geography of PC component production is essentially Pacific and includes the U.S. West Coast, Northern Asia, China, Southeast Asia, and, to a lesser degree, Mexico.[12] The remainder of the world is largely irrelevant. However, within this Pacific realm, locations undertake both the production of different components and parts of the value chain, as is shown so well in the chapters on HDDs, FPDs, and semiconductors. Moreover, as these chapters indicate, the location of many of these activities has been shifting through time. Remarkably, other activities, especially design, as some of the other chapters indicate, have remained rooted in places such as Silicon Valley.

The PC consists of a hierarchy of components, each with its own value composition and its own vulnerability to obsolescence. While there is a great variation and complexity in the actual production linkages, it is possible, at least for

TABLE 5.4
*The Value and Time Sensitivity of Personal Computer Components*

| Key components | Value | Time sensitivity |
|---|---|---|
| Proprietary | | |
| Operating System | High | Low |
| Microprocessor | High | High |
| Commodities | | |
| FPD | High-Medium | High |
| Memory (SRAM, DRAM, EPROM, etc.) | Medium | High |
| Hard Disk Drives | Medium | High |
| Monitors | Medium | Medium |
| Secondary Higher Value Components[a] | | |
| Video/Multimedia Chips and Card | Medium | High |
| Mainboard Chipset and Mainboard | Medium | High |
| BIOS Chip | Medium | Medium |
| Communications Chips and Card | Medium | Medium |
| Commodity Components | | |
| Floppy Disk Drive | Low | Low |
| Keyboard and Mouse | Low | Low |
| CD-ROM Drive Assemblies | Low | Low |
| Cases | Low | Low |
| Power Supplies | Low | Low |
| Connectors, Cables, etc. | Low | Low |

*Source:* Compiled by authors from *Electronic Business Asia* (August 1996).

[a] The value of these printed circuit boards is almost entirely in the chips in the previous category.

illustrative purposes, to conceptualize four levels of components (see Table 5.4). Each component reflects either an international or regional spatial division of labor, or both. Also, as we indicated above, in terms of components there is an organizational division of labor, because only a few of these firms have integrated the disparate parts of the PC value chain. As mentioned earlier, IBM and the large multidivisional Asian computer/electronics firms such as NEC, Fujitsu, Toshiba, Hitachi, and Samsung do or did produce a variety of capital-intensive components such as HDDs, DRAMs, monitors, and FPDs in a variety of locations around the globe. The competencies for component manufacturing have not translated into success in the PC industry. The converse seems also to be true—that is, PC assemblers in general do not appear to have been successful in integrating into component production. For example, Compaq produced a number of its own components during the 1980s, but then in the early 1990s it had to retreat. Similarly, Acer believed it could produce components for its PCs, but these efforts had limited success.

### Key Components—Proprietary

The first level of components, the operating system and microprocessor, are "proprietary." By this we mean that the product is strongly defended by various forms of intellectual property protections, or also in the case of Intel, manufacturing scale-related barriers to entry, that have been persistent and difficult to overcome. The production (or development) of PC operating systems for the mass market is dominated by one firm, Microsoft, whose operations are predominantly in the United States. As of June 30, 2000, of the 39,100 people Microsoft employed on a full-time basis, 27,000 worked in the United States and 12,100 were employed overseas, a significant number of which were in sales and marketing related positions (Microsoft 2000). Even more important, Microsoft

TABLE 5.5

*Financial Results for Selected Firms in the PC Value Chain, 2000*

| Company | Net revenues | Operating income | OI/NR | Products |
|---------|-------------|------------------|-------|----------|
| Microsoft | 23,845 | 9,624 | .4036 | OS/apps. |
| Intel | 33,726 | 10,535 | .3124 | Microprocessor, chipsets, mainboards |
| AMD | 4,644 | 1,029 | .2216 | Microprocessor, SRAMs |
| Samsung Elect. [a] | 27,145 | 4,762 | .1741 | DRAMs, FPDs, CRTs, etc. |
| Micron Tech. [b] | 7,584 | 1,515 | .1998 | DRAMs |
| Seagate | 6,448 | (561) | N/A | HDDs |
| Quantum | 4,749 | 180 | .0379 | HDDs |
| Western Digital | 1,961 | (98) | N/A | HDDs |
| Maxtor | 2,705 | 32 | .0118 | HDDs |
| VIA Tech. [c] | 950 | 201 | .2116 | Chipsets |
| Asustek | 2,136 | 473 | .2214 | Mainboards/graphics boards |
| Creative Tech | 1,369 | 150 | .1069 | Graphics chips/boards |
| ATI Tech. | 1,309 | 139 | .1062 | Graphics chips/boards |
| NVIDIA | 735 | 100 | .1361 | Graphics chips |
| Accton Tech.[d] | 296 | 15 | .0507 | Comm. chips/boards and hubs |
| Logitech | 761 | 48 | .0631 | Input devices |
| Dell | 31,888 | 2,310 | .0724 | PCs |
| Compaq | 42,383 | 569 | .0139 | PCs |
| Gateway | 9,601 | 242 | .0252 | PCs |
| Acer | 4,761 | 205 | .0431 | PCs, OBM/OEM |
| Legend | 3,490 | 110 | .0315 | PCs (China) |
| Trigem Comp. | 3,176 | (13) | N/A | PCs (Korea and export) |
| Mitac | 4,983 | 74 | .0149 | PCs OEM |
| Quanta Comp. | 2,511 | 259 | .1031 | Notebook PCs OEM |
| FIC | 2,308 | 7 | .0030 | PCs OEM |
| Ingram Micro | 30,715 | 226 | .0075 | Distri. and OEM assembly PCs, parts etc. |

*Source:* Compiled by authors from *Electronics Business* (August 2001).

[a] DRAMs accounted for only 25 percent of total sales, though this was the most profitable area for Samsung. 1999, Samsung's DRAM sales were $10.6 billion.

[b] Micron Technology had PC sales in 2000 of $1.066 billion with a net loss of $146 million. If these were removed from Micron's results its profit rate would be significantly higher (Micron Technology 2000).

[c] Original earnings were in NT$; these were converted to U.S.$ at NT$ 32.5 = $1.

[d] These are 1999 earnings, which are the latest available. U.S.$ 1 = 32.5 NT$.

is the most highly profitable firm in the PC value chain and has no strong competitor (see Table 5.5). It does little subcontracting, preferring to integrate as much of its process in-house as possible. It even undertakes its disk duplication internally in a facility in Humacao, Puerto Rico (ibid.). Microsoft is integrated both organizationally and spatially, undertaking most of its value-adding activities, as opposed to sales and marketing activities, in the Seattle area.

Intel dominates the PC MPU market, though it does experience competition from Advanced Micro Devices (AMD). As the chapter by Leachman and Leachman indicates, the MPU value chain is more dispersed than that of Microsoft. However, the headquarters for Intel, AMD, and a new competitor, Transmeta, are all in Silicon Valley.[13] According to Intel, 70 percent of its wafer production is conducted within the United States, in New Mexico, Oregon, Arizona, California, and Massachusetts. Another 30 percent is undertaken in Israel and Ireland. Intel also manufactures microprocessor- and networking-related board-level products and systems at facilities in Malaysia, Oregon, and Washington. "A substantial majority of [Intel's] components assembly and testing, including assembly and testing for microprocessors, is performed at facilities in Costa Rica, Malaysia, and the Philippines" (Intel Corporation 2002). They also are expanding a component assembly and testing facility in China. Subcontractors are used to assemble chipsets, but not the core microprocessors. According to Intel, a substantial majority of the design and development of components and other products is performed in the United States at their facilities in California, Oregon, Arizona, and Washington. Outside the United States, Intel has significant product development facilities in Israel and Malaysia (ibid.). AMD has substantially the same profile. Because of its smaller size, it has fewer production sites, though it does have one in Europe. These firms, though their operations are globalized, continue to draw upon their Silicon Valley roots.

The strength of Intel and Microsoft can be seen from Table 5.5 in two ways. First, though these are crude measurements, it is clear that these two firms capture as much profit as all the other firms in the PC industry do. In addition to capturing the largest mass of profits, Intel and Microsoft profit rates of 31.2 percent and 40.4 percent of revenues, respectively, are significantly higher than those of other firms. There are differences between Microsoft and Intel. Most important, Intel does have competition, while Microsoft experiences none. Also, whereas Intel's MPUs do experience dramatic price declines over their life cycle, Microsoft is able to hold the price of its software steady during the entire product cycle! More remarkable, as the average price of a PC has been declining, the operating system price has remained constant, thereby increasing as a percentage of the entire system cost. In terms of globalization, it is apparent that these two U.S. firms realize the lion's share of the profit in the entire value chain, and respectively are the most profitable software and semiconductor firms in the world.

### Key Components—Commodities

The second level of key components varies in their level of technological sophistication. As McKendrick shows, HDDs contain precision-machined moving parts and solid-state integrated circuitry. Memory modules consist of DRAMs mounted on small, pluggable circuit boards. FPDs are hybrid solid-state devices that have been difficult and expensive to manufacture but are rapidly decreasing in cost (see the chapter by Murtha, Lenway, and Hart). CRT-based computer monitors are based on television tube production (for a further discussion, see the chapter by Kenney). The difference between these products and the prior level is that though they are high-technology commodities, they experience brutal price competition. Therefore profits are both cyclical and concentrated among the first movers with the most capable products and greatest production efficiencies.

The globalization of FPDs and HDDs is explained in other chapters. In the case of DRAMs, as Leachman and Leachman point out, the only U.S. manufacturer left in the industry is Micron Technology. Micron is also globalized, though its main operations remain in Idaho. Micron operates a fabrication facility in Avezzano, Italy, and a module assembly and test facility in Scotland. Finally, in Asia it acquired its Japanese joint venture fabrication facility and operates an assembly and test facility in Singapore (Micron Technology 2000). The only major European-owned DRAM producer is Infineon, which was spun out of Siemens. Infineon also has DRAM operations in Europe; Richmond, Virginia; and Hsinchu, Taiwan, with a number of assembly and test facilities scattered around the world (Infineon Technologies 2000). With the exception of Micron and Infineon, the remainder of the DRAM producers are headquartered in Asia, especially Japan and Korea and, to a lesser degree, Taiwan. The world's leading producer is Samsung, and it is profitable when DRAM prices are strong. However, the most interesting thing about DRAMs, as Leachman and Leachman indicate, is how difficult it is to remain consistently profitable. For example, in the twelve months that ended in August 2001, the cost per megabyte of DRAM dropped 90 percent. Most of the Japanese firms have been shifting their product mix away from DRAMs or consolidating their operations. For example, Hitachi and NEC created a joint venture in an effort to cut costs. In Korea, LG and Hyundai merged into the Hyundai-operated Hynix, which in 2003, despite subsidies, hovers close to bankruptcy. In spatial terms, most leading DRAM producers have fabrication facilities in Asia, North America, and Europe, though Europe has the fewest.

Monitors based on CRTs are a declining industry because of the competition from FPDs (see the chapter by Murtha, Lenway, and Hart). Traditionally, CRT monitors run the gamut from high-quality ($1,000) to low-end ($150), but, in general, they are a medium-value product that experience a medium-level of price erosion. There are no U.S. firms producing either CRTs or monitors. Japanese firms originally dominated the industry, although competitors from Korea and Taiwan have captured ever-greater market share and overcome the Japanese lead even in high-end monitors. This contrasts with televisions, where Japanese firms continue to dominate large-size television CRT production.

The geography of CRT monitor production differs from that of FPDs, in the sense that CRT components are produced globally, roughly mirroring the production of CRTs for televisions (see Kenney in this volume). During the two decades Asian firms have inexorably gained market share from Western firms. In 2001 Samsung was the largest monitor CRT producer in the world, while LG Electronics was number two. Samsung has factories in the United Kingdom, Brazil, Mexico, China, Korea, Malaysia, and in 2000 it announced that it would build a factory in India (Bloomberg 2000a). Though the factories are scattered throughout the world, the bulk of production is in Asia. More recently, the move to FPDs is decreasing monitor production. For example, in 2001 one major competitor, Hitachi, announced that it would close its CRT monitor production facilities in Japan and Malaysia, preferring to concentrate upon FPDs (Reuters 2001). In general terms, it is safe to say that CRT production is being phased out in developed countries, while it is still growing in the developing nations, especially China.

Despite the Korean strength in monitor CRT production, Taiwanese firms and Taiwan are the center of monitor production. In 2000, Taiwanese firms shipped 59.6 million CRT monitors, which accounted for 53.7 percent of global CRT monitor shipments. However, the data indicate that monitor assembly has moved offshore from Taiwan (see Figure 5.1). One important factor was the desire by assemblers to reduce their monitor inventory. This is possible because the monitor can be delivered in a separate package. For example, a PC ordered from Dell actually triggers two shipments: Dell's shipment of the PC and a monitor producer's shipment of the monitor. Immediately prior to final delivery, the shipment is integrated at a local delivery center operated by UPS or FedEx. This eliminates the need for Dell to carry monitors in inventory and a redundant shipment of the monitor from the monitor factory to Dell's warehouse. However, to effectively undertake this strategy, the monitor assembler must be able to reliably fulfill Dell's order. If the monitor firm is importing the monitor from Asia, then it must carry sufficient inventory. To achieve proximity the Taiwanese monitor manufacturers opened factories in Northwest Mex-

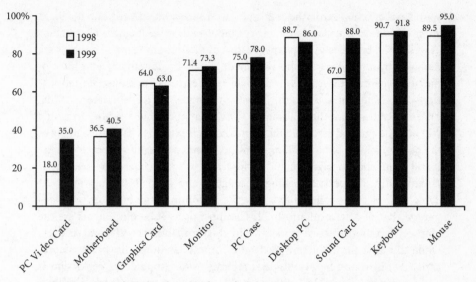

FIG. 5.1. Taiwan's IT Hardware Industry's Overseas Production, 1998 and 1999.
Source: Information Technology Information Services 1999.

ico, where Samsung, LG, and Mitsubishi built monitor CRT factories (Sony also has a monitor CRT plant in San Diego, though in 2002 its low-end monitor production was transferred to Asia). From 2000 onward, these factories came under severe pricing pressure because of the extremely low production costs in China. In 2001, Taiwanese monitor producers MAG and Acer closed plants in Mexicali, while Tatung never began production at a plant it had constructed in Tijuana in 1999. In general, CRT monitor production was under pricing pressure globally because of the cost advantages in China, which has been steadily increasing its global market share (*Electronic Engineering Times* 2001).

These four key components differ from MPUs and the OS in the sense that they are commodities, and, in general, it is difficult to extract significant profit unless the firm is the market leader—and even then continuing profitability is a struggle. In three areas, CRTs, FPDs, and DRAMs, north Asian firms are the global leaders. As McKendrick explains, it is only in HDDs where the U.S. firms have retained their leadership position, though Japanese and Korean firms continue to be competitors.

*Secondary Components*

A third tier consists of secondary components and revolves around other important semiconductors and their accompanying printed circuit boards. These components are the motherboard and its chipset, the multimedia chips, and sound and graphics cards, the communications chip and its card, and the BIOS chip. Taiwanese firms are extremely competitive in supplying these logic chips as well as the board-level implementations of these components. The chips are designed by a number of firms—some of which are Taiwanese, with most of the others being American. As Leachman and Leachman demonstrate, fabrication is then subcontracted to the Taiwanese semiconductor fabricators, TSMC or UMC, and yet another Taiwanese firm often operating a factory in China will both design and assemble the printed circuit board (PCB). While many of the processes that go into making a finished board are highly automated, there is still hand labor involved, including insertion of some chips into boards, machine tending, inspection, testing, packaging, and so forth (Barnes 1997). As Table 5.5 indicates, profitability is superior to commodities but does not compare to that of Microsoft and Intel. The most profitable components are the chipsets and motherboards, as shown by the profitability of VIA and Asustek, while the least profitable are likely the communications chips and adapter cards, as illustrated by Accton Technology.[14] Motherboard chipset design is done either in Taiwan (VIA, SIS, and ALI), or Silicon Valley (Intel). Graphics and sound chip design is done in Taiwan (SIS and RealTek), Canada (ATI), Silicon Valley (e.g., ESS Technologies, NVIDIA, and Cirrus Logic), and Singapore (Creative Technologies). Here, Taiwan has been able to move from the commodities described in the next section to these more sophisticated products. These firms often do their own design work, and, in many cases, sell their products under their own label. New sophisticated graphics chips and motherboard chipsets can provide good returns, but especially in graphics chips commodification is a constant threat, because the technology changes rapidly and, because of the PC's standardized interfaces, there is little protection against a superior chip. It is not unusual to see branded graphics cards that only a year previously might have sold for $300 to $400 each now retailing at between $20 and $30.

The motherboard and the core logic chips on the motherboard (most important among them being the one or two chips referred to as the motherboard chipset) implement the PC's main bus, which controls the exchange of electronic pulses (data) through the various parts of the system. Counter to the general logic of disintegrating the value chain, the chipset and motherboard are of such importance that Intel produces chipsets and in the mid-1990s began producing some motherboards. Constantly improving chipsets are necessary if the PC is to derive all of the benefit of new MPUs. Chipsets are not as profitable as MPUs, but Intel can use its chipsets to force the pace of technology adoption. In 2001, Intel controlled about 40 percent of the chipset market, a sufficient market share to be able to control the pace and direction of its evolution.

Motherboard production is far more strongly dominated by Taiwanese firms. In 2000, Taiwanese firms accounted for nearly 75 percent of total world-wide motherboard production (Wilcox 2001). The Taiwanese producers' motherboard value chain has increasingly become more geographically dispersed as Taiwanese firms have moved the assembly of basic boards to low-wage areas, mostly to China but also to Thailand and the Philippines. Of Taiwan's total motherboard production, 39.9 percent was produced "offshore" in 1996, accounting for 29.6 percent of worldwide production. By 2000, Taiwanese firms produced 84 percent of all motherboards, of which 48 percent were produced offshore, so offshore Taiwanese production was 42 percent of total global production (Taiwan Technology 2001). Intel accounted for most of the remaining production. The Taiwanese leader, Asustek, supplied about 50 percent of the Taiwanese production and also had the good profit margins that accrue to the leader. In 1996, motherboard production was quite globalized, but China is rapidly increasing its share of global production as factories in other parts of the world close.[15]

The logic chips on the other cards in a PC are designed in various countries, but particularly important design locations are Silicon Valley and Taiwan. These firms are less profitable than the chipset producer VIA and the motherboard producer Asustek. Wherever these chips are designed, almost invariably they are fabricated by either TSMC or UMC. Perhaps even more so than is the case with motherboards, these various boards are produced either in Taiwan or China. As in the case of motherboards, in response to severe price pressures production is being relocated from Taiwan to China.

### Commodity Components

The most commodified components in the PC are power supplies, keyboards and other input devices, the case, cables and connectors, floppy disk drives, and so forth. With the possible exception of high-end keyboards and input devices, these are largely unchanging and experience minimal improvement in functionality. Because they experience little price erosion, they can be manufactured anywhere. The only significant trade-offs are between labor costs, material costs, and cargo container shipping costs. With little new design input, the vast majority of these components do not experience significant price erosion. There is one interesting twist, however: as the price of PCs decreases, these items will likely become a greater portion of the total cost, because most of the cost savings have already been wrung out of them.

The commodity component that does have some opportunities for design input and improvement that can increase profitability is input devices. For the most part this is in the after-market, where consumers wish to upgrade their keyboard, mouse, or gaming device. The two most significant firms in this field are Microsoft and Logitech. Microsoft's division selling input devices has been very profitable. The federal government's Microsoft antitrust case indicates that the peripheral's division benefited significantly from Microsoft's pressure on PC assemblers to use or, at least, offer Microsoft's peripherals as an option. Another significant input device firm is the Swiss firm Logitech, which commits 4.8 percent of its revenues to R&D and has relatively strong profits (see Table 5.5). Logitech competes on the basis of design and its strong marketing channels. Whereas Logitech operates its own factories in China, Microsoft simply outsources its production to Asian firms. There is also some production of input devices in Mexico by Taiwanese firms, but the vast majority of the mice, keyboards, and so forth are produced on an OEM basis for firms such as Compaq, Dell, and HP in low-wage locations in Asia, especially China, and then shipped in cargo containers to the United States.

The remaining components include computer cases (the proverbial beige box), cables, connectors, screws, fans, and miscellaneous other parts. These are commodities and experience little innovation or change. The production locations for these parts are difficult to trace, however; if they are small, almost invariably they are produced by Taiwanese firms in Asia. Computer cases are produced by Taiwanese firms in Taiwan or, more recently, China, though some of these Taiwanese firms have established Mexican factories to supply their U.S. customers.

The market for low-value, standardized components is largely supplied by Taiwanese firms that have lower cost structures than their Western or Japanese counterparts. The only barrier to entry is having industry standard quality and having the lowest price, resulting in intense pricing pressure and very low profit rates. Design, engineering, and greater scale can wring incremental costs out of these items, but the major cost savings have come from lowering labor costs. The question is whether, after moving production to China, even lower labor cost environments can be found.

Reflections

Two features of the PC determine the configuration of the PC industry. First, the architecture of the PC, which has allowed the development of an extreme version of modularity, has given rise to its vertically disintegrated value chain. Second, the rapid decline in value of its semiconductor and hard disk drive components emphasizes the importance of situating the final segment of the value chain in close proximity to the final consumer. For the PC assembler, controlling logistics is critical for commercial success. Few products experience the ravages of delay-induced devaluation as palpably as the PC. Dell Computer's business model is based on managing and even benefiting from the technical speed of change in the PC value chain.

Global supplier chains in the PC industry use air freight for the high value-added items while using slower conveyances to transport the lower value-added items. The PC and garment industries both suffer from having perishable products—in one case because of the exigencies of changing fashion, and in the other case because of the speed of the technical improvement of certain key components. Inventory of these key components is subject to a relentless destruction of value. Dell Computer's success is due to its logistics system and the BTO business model that allows it to manage the depreciation dynamic.

Most interestingly, there is little spatial clustering among PC assemblers, nor is there any significant clustering of supplier production activities close to PC assemblers. Dell is the exception, because it demands that suppliers have a warehouse within a twenty-minute commute of the assembly plant. However, the suppliers' production facilities can be located anywhere. This lack of clustering can be explained by the fact that the PC is a modular product with rigidly specified component interfaces with a very high degree of interchangeability. In effect, for desktop computers all of the knowledge necessary for assembly is already codified, and very little tacit information is required. This means that the assembler-supplier relationship can be entirely market-based.

The only important global cluster is located in Taiwan, where the assemblers are close to each other and to component suppliers. As we have shown, many of the components used around the world are sourced from these Taiwanese firms; however, they never controlled the key components including the operating system, the microprocessor, and the HDD. Therefore, despite the considerable success that Taiwanese firms have experienced, it has been difficult for them to capture high levels of value added. In both spatial and organizational terms, advantage has been captured by two firms: Microsoft and Intel garnered a disproportionate share of the value chain profit.[16] Having inherited the crown jewels of a near monopoly position from IBM, each had greater profit margins than any of the other firms in the chain and, though no comprehensive accounting is available, probably captured greater profits than all the assemblers combined. Thus power is concentrated in these two standard-bearers.

U.S. assemblers dominate global sales of the world's PCs—a commodity with low profit margin—despite the fact that Taiwanese firms produce approximately half the total supply. U.S. assemblers have significant advantages. First, they have enormous volumes that permit them to extract the greatest volume discounts from suppliers. Second, and probably most important, they benefit from being in the world's largest and most advanced market, where new "killer" applications first emerge and become standardized—for example, the general use of the Internet (Kenney 2003), or using PCs as MP3 burners. U.S. firms are in a position to learn from the market and have tomorrow's globally desirable products today. This "proximity to the market" is as important as production efficiency, as generations of Asian producers trying to enter the U.S. market have discovered.

Globalization in the PC industry has transferred much of the manufacturing of PCs and their components to Taiwan and now China. However, this has not been a zero-sum game for the United States. Microsoft, Intel, and, increasingly, Dell have been the greatest beneficiaries of the PC industry.

## Notes

The authors thank Gary Fields for valuable suggestions and comments.

1. This paper refers only to PCs using the Microsoft operating system and an x86 microprocessor, which account for 95 percent of the world's PCs.

2. In terms of the software standards-based interaction of the various components, notebook computers are interesting, because they are, for all intents and purposes, as modular as desktop PCs. However, because of the tight tolerances arising from attempts to decrease the weight and dimensions of the machine, it is difficult to fully black box the components. This frustrates modularity by creating physical interdependencies (Baldwin and Clark 2000). So, for example, the heat given off by the microprocessor is not easily vented to the environment; this affects other components, thereby creating an interdependency.

3. We thank Gary Fields for pointing out these attributes of Dell's overseas operations. See also Fields (2003).

4. For the modern electronics industry, physical proximity is not always as important as what might be called "hyperspatial proximity"—that is, easy access to transportation nodes. Thus, in Mexico for example, Guadalajara has a distinct advantage over Tijuana in large-scale electronics contract manufacture. In the United States, Tennessee became a center of PC assembly, because of the large UPS hub in Nashville and the Federal Express hub in Memphis. In Mexico, even though Tijuana is closer to many U.S. markets, it lacks the air cargo transport infrastructure capabilities that Guadalajara has. As Kenney (this volume) shows, northern Baja California has a distinct advantage in televisions, a large product characterized by a slower rate of technological change that can be efficiently shipped by road or rail.

5. IBM had retained the BIOS chip as a lever of control, however Compaq was able to reverse engineer it. Once Compaq had done this, others did also, and the final lock was broken, enabling other firms to enter. Without recognizing it at the time, IBM gave Microsoft and, to a lesser degree, Intel the control that it had exerted in other classes of computers.

6. For a further discussion of the control of the Wintel standard, see Borrus and Zysman (1997).

7. We thank Gary Fields for pointing this out. For further discussion, see Fields (2003).

8. Gateway has recently seen sales slump as its core customers, U.S. consumers, have lengthened their upgrade cycle.

9. In the first quarter of 2003, the largest branded assembler, Dell, had captured 30.7

percent of the U.S. market, an increase from 20.7 percent in the same quarter a year earlier (Gartner Inc. 2003).

10. Dell's effort to gain market share created an extremely difficult pricing climate in 2001. The local retail assemblers are under severe pressure, because the largest manufacturers are able to secure larger discounts from suppliers and during the price war are passing these discounts on to consumers.

11. For a detailed discussion of the Dell model, see Curry and Kenney (1999) and Fields (2003).

12. For the sake of clarity and brevity we limited this discussion to common desktop PC components. Technologies usually associated with notebook PCs such as PCMIA cards, FPDs, and peripheral PC components such as printers, speaker systems, and so forth, are not considered.

13. It should be noted here that Transmeta's microprocessor products, while compatible with Intel/AMD chips in running Microsoft software, are predicated on an entirely different technology. Unlike AMD, which could be characterized as essentially a quasi-cloner of Intel chips and as such is a direct competitor to Intel, at this juncture at least, it seems that Transmeta may end up as a niche competitor in the low-power device market.

14. The reason for Accton's relatively low profitability is that most desktop PCs use Ethernet adapter cards. The chip technology for Ethernet is nearly twenty years old, and there is little new innovation.

15. The data in Table 5.3 is based on the author's 1996 survey covering roughly 80 percent of mainboard producers worldwide.

16. See Borrus and Zysman (1997).

# CHAPTER SIX

# Leveraging Locations

*Hard Disk Drive Producers in
International Competition*

DAVID G. MCKENDRICK

American firms dominate the hard disk drive (HDD) industry. This chapter argues that a central reason for their success has been that U.S. producers configured the industry into two kinds of industrial clusters. They established technological clusters in only a few locations in the United States, which are sources of these remarkable innovations. They also set up complementary operational clusters, concentrated in Southeast Asia, where they source and make the components and products. Indeed, the offshore manufacturing operations of American HDD producers have been no less important in preserving their leadership than the innovations they generate in the United States.[1]

The experience of the HDD industry thus offers a counterexample to some prevalent assumptions about industrial clusters, globalization, and competitiveness. First, on the surface the industry seems to fit perfectly the localized competition model emphasized by researchers who study industrial clusters: clustering promotes innovation. The industry is among the most technologically innovative industries of the last fifty years. Hard disk drives are also the quintessential "Silicon Valley industry" so often the subject of studies of regional development, industrial districts, and economic geography. The industry was born in San Jose, California, and the region hosted more disk drive start-ups than any other place on earth. But in fact, the industry is nested in a larger international industry structure. Industries can create clusters not only at home but also abroad. I suspect that many studies of industrial clusters would observe similar structures if viewed more broadly.

Second, HDD firms demonstrate that companies can go offshore for manufacturing without losing ownership, expertise, or control. All of the surviving major HDD firms own and manage their own manufacturing facilities abroad.

Thus, going abroad is not synonymous with outsourcing. Moreover, the HDD industry also shows that firms can separate product development and manufacturing over long distances and still thrive. Although this approach requires investment in learning to handle international product transfer (Terwiesch et al. 1999) and supply chains, the investment itself can develop into a core competence that can be used repeatedly in exploiting overseas location-specific assets.

Third, going abroad does not mean the hollowing out of industry, nor necessarily an aggregate loss of employment. On the contrary, the disk drive industry shows how foreign direct investment can create a division of labor that permits a strengthening of certain home-based activities. There can be little question that the initial move of manufacturing to Southeast Asia incurred transitional costs for workers in the industry. But had the U.S. industry not shifted assembly to Southeast Asia, it would not have enjoyed its subsequent success. As a result, there would be far fewer highly paid, skilled jobs in the United States in various stages of the industry. In 1995, for example, workers in the United States received nearly 40 percent of *all* wages paid in the industry, while 62 percent of the wages paid by U.S. firms went to their U.S.-based workers (Gourevitch et al. 2000). As I describe below, the speed and depth of American firms' move from Silicon Valley to Singapore was not a sign of weakness or prelude to its exit from the industry but a central factor behind industrial leadership.

To frame the discussion, I begin by briefly summarizing some central characteristics of the industry. Section two describes in a general way the relationship between industry evolution and industry location, including the globalization of operations. The next section explains the research approach. The fourth and fifth sections present the empirical story. Section four provides an historical account of the location of the disk drive industry since its inception in 1956 until the present, detailing how U.S., but not Japanese, HDD firms were aggressive in shifting their operations to Southeast Asia while keeping their technological core at home. Section five analyzes the dynamics of industry location from the perspective of Southeast Asia, describing how the region's location-specific assets evolved to accommodate the HDD industry's changing competitive requirements. The sixth section considers why American and Japanese firms adopted different locational strategies, and why Japanese firms were slow to copy the American push into Southeast Asia. I conclude with some observations about the implications of the HDD experience for the book's five cross-cutting themes.

## Industry Background

Hard disk drives (HDD) are remarkable devices. A critical technology behind the spread of the Internet, they permit companies and individuals to offer and access billions of web pages and are now finding markets in a variety of even newer applications including TV recording, digital cameras, hand-held computers, home appliances, and automobiles. This is, of course, in addition to their traditional role as the primary medium for online computer storage.

Extraordinary and almost unparalleled innovation has made these applications possible. Consider the growth in storage capacity of a drive, as measured by its areal density.[2] Between 1956, when IBM shipped the world's first HDD, and 1991, areal density increased at an annual rate of 30 percent. From 1992 to 1997, however, it grew by 60 percent per year, a faster rate of progress than for semiconductors, and by an astounding 100-plus percent annually since 1997. This makes disk drives an unusual industry in that technological change has actually *accelerated* with industry age. Rapidly increasing areal density has translated directly into dramatically falling prices that consumers pay for each megabyte of storage. A little more than a decade ago the average per-megabyte cost of a disk drive was $11; in 2000 it was a penny.

In addition, disk drives are challenging to produce. Embodying diverse technical disciplines, they are composed of a number of components and subassemblies, many of which are rapidly moving mechanical parts and subject to extraordinarily tight manufacturing tolerances. The value chain is also complex, with head subassemblies, disks, motors, and electronics constituting the four main subchains, in addition to sales and service, tools and equipment, and research and development. Contemporary producers have broken these steps of the value chain into many discrete pieces, analyzed the economics of each, and sought to locate them around the world at the most cost-efficient sites (ibid.). Yet, despite the demanding manufacturing requirements and complexity of the value chain, 196 million disk drives were made in 2001 by eight companies that made no money. Unit prices of disk drives have fallen even as each drive stores more than its predecessors. In early 2001, Western Digital advertised a 30-gigabyte disk drive for a retail price of $119; in 1985, an 80-*megabyte* drive cost almost $1,000 if ordered in quantities of 1,000. Industry competition is so intense that industry revenues increased by less than one-third between 1994 and 1998 even as unit shipments more than doubled.

Few, if any, industries face the same combination of rapid technological change, intense cost pressures, value chain complexity, and short product cycles. Surviving firms have thus had to manage a number of pressures that required strength in both R&D and manufacturing. In response to demanding and volatile markets, technological changes, and intense competition, producers have reduced costs and moved technologically sophisticated products quickly to market and to volume production.

Moving HDD assembly from the United States to Southeast Asia, while preserving research and development at home, enabled American firms to maintain their industrial leadership. Consider that, in 1999, American firms made almost 80 percent of the world's hard disk drives. In that year, they assembled fewer than 1 percent of their drives in the United States and roughly 70 percent in Southeast Asia; in 1985 almost all drives made by U.S. firms were assembled at home. In 1995, 29 percent of the employees who worked for American firms in the HDD value chain worked in the United States; 55 percent worked in Southeast Asia (ibid.). One American disk drive company, Seagate Technology, became the largest employer in Thailand and Malaysia, and the largest private sector employer in Singapore. It was also the largest single exporter from China in 1998, with almost $1 billion in exports. Two American disk drive companies, IBM and Seagate, were the largest exporters in Thailand in both 1997 and 1998.

Today, the Japanese disk drive industry appears almost as globalized as the American, with most assembly taking place in the Philippines. But such appearances hide crucial differences in both the timing of globalization and the degree to which firms developed and exploited location-specific assets overseas. American HDD firms were not only much quicker than their Japanese counterparts to shift assembly and manufacturing to Southeast Asia; they also embedded their activities more deeply into the fabric of host countries. The American style of globalization was profoundly different from that of the Japanese. The experience of the disk drive industry strongly suggests that studying industrial leadership now requires understanding the role of location in international competition.

## Industrial Clusters and Globalization

Historically, industries have shown signs of both geographic dispersion and regional clustering during their early development. In the case of the U.S. automobile industry, for example, firms were widely dispersed (Ellinger 1977), but three clusters appeared early in the industry's development in New England, the Midwest, and the region around New York City (Bigelow et al. 1997). Although Silicon Valley became the center for the semiconductor industry, important early entrants—Motorola, Texas Instruments, Philco, General Electric, Hughes Aircraft, Sylvania—were dispersed across the United States (*Electronic News* [July 8, 1968]).

Where a firm establishes itself can affect its survival chances (Lomi 1995). In industries that compete nationally or internationally, one or more industrial clusters gradually begin to gain an evolutionary advantage. Not all locations hosting the industry continue to do so; firms residing there exit the industry, or else the location does not attract new entrants. Firm entry is important to the competitive strength of a cluster; it replenishes the location's knowledge stocks through the introduction of new technologies and business practices. Silicon Valley's dynamism and longevity is generally attributed to the entrepreneurial spin-off through which new technologies and industries emerged (Freiberger and Swaine 1984; Angel 1990; Saxenian 1994; Cringely 1996; Kaplan 1999). Over time, these locations generate *agglomeration economies*, and as isolated firms exit, the number of locations hosting the industry diminishes.

Agglomeration, or external, economies are a central part of industrial life, and accrue to firms that locate close to one another. They exist when the net benefits to being in a location with other firms increase with the number of firms in the location (Arthur 1986). Agglomeration economies enable proximate firms to be more innovative, seize opportunities faster, produce at lower cost, and respond to market changes more quickly than firms that are not clustered. Although difficult to measure (Audretsch and Feldman 1996; Hayter 1997), these economies result from any of three elements (Arthur 1986; Krugman 1991, 1993; Head et al. 1995): (1) a pooled market for workers with specialized skills; (2) specialized intermediate inputs and services; or (3) informational spillovers, including technological ones (Arthur 1986; Krugman 1991; Hayter 1997). Firms from the same industry will continue to invest in the same location up to the point where the costs to the collocation of activities exceed these benefits. Companies can thus benefit from the proximity of a greater number of companies in the same activity, in spite of the tendency among managers to decry the intensity of competition, higher input costs, and difficulty in retaining employees.

So far, I have described the location of industry, and the benefits of agglomerating, in a general way, without distinguishing among different activities carried out by the firm. But by keeping the focus at the level of the firm, researchers may miss much that is important in the dynamics of location, and in the globalization process in particular. An important but seldom studied question is: *What* is clustered? As a first cut, it is analytically useful as well as realistic to distinguish between technological activities and operational ones (O'hUallachain 1989). As an industry ages, the two sets of activities begin to have separate locational requirements that lead them to be organized into often distinct geographic configurations.

During an industry's early development it is likely that firms collocate product development and production. Products and processes are uncertain and undergo extensive experimentation. Production processes are often quite artisanal. At the plant level, producing more units generates experience in the manufacturing process and greater understanding of how to produce additional units even more cheaply—the learning-by-doing phenomenon. Feedback loops between product development and manufacturing can enable a firm to design and produce new products incorporating similar or related technologies and serve as a strong force to concentrate both sets of activities. These clusters thus become self-reinforcing both for innovation and for methods of production, thus increasing their dominance (Pred 1965; Webber 1972). Theoretical models that characterize the emergence of an industry cluster emphasize increasing returns, path dependence, and cumulative causation without distinguishing between innovation and manufacturing (e.g., Arthur 1986; Krugman 1991).

But there is little reason to think that the agglomerative forces enhancing innovation and those making operations more efficient are the same. Innovative activity, such as patenting, which is much more prevalent for products than for production processes (Levin et al. 1987), tends to cluster in places where knowledge spillovers are high (Jaffe et al. 1993; Audretsch and Feldman 1996); proximity facilitates the communication and absorption of highly contextual or uncertain knowledge. Yet "production is remarkably concentrated in space" (Krugman 1991: 5) because clustering facilitates economies of scale and lower-cost production. These two sets of activities are subject to different locational requirements and may not need to be collocated. In fact, it is not clear that any single location has the requisite assets to satisfy the competitive requirements of both sets of activities as an industry evolves and competition intensifies. The skills to design something are not the same as those needed to make it. Indeed, over time we might expect industries to begin to organize themselves into separate technological and operational clusters.

### Technological Clusters

Technological clusters refer to the collocation of activities that lead to the recognition of new market opportunities, the development of new technologies, and the design of new products.[3] The term refers to places where "innovation" occurs (Storper 1993; Jaffe et al. 1993; Powell and Brantley 1992; Feldman 1994; Harrison et al. 1996). Technological clusters form primarily at an industry's home base, and their durability is conditioned by new entry, repeated intra- and interfirm coordination in product design, and technological diffusion.

Although new entry contributes to the ongoing competitiveness of a region, it does not explain why a firm continues to concentrate technical activity in that location for an extended period. One might instead expect a firm to search for less expensive R&D talent and shift product development work to that lower cost location. But in most industries there are enormous amounts of tacit knowledge associated with product development, making proximity desirable among members of design teams. Tacit knowledge is also important at the community level. Close engineering-level relationships among stages in the value chain are often necessary for a company to win a "design-in" for a particular product. Firms also have a need to keep up with external technology developments, and diffusion of technical knowledge can be especially rapid and effective within industrial clusters. Even in highly global industries, "more rapid (or more complete) diffusion is arguably more likely to occur in places where there is a relatively densely packed community of organizations with shared interests in a particular innovation than in less institutionally rich or densely packed locales" (Harrison et al. 1996).

### Operational Clusters

Producers of many types of assembled products acquire a wide variety of inputs. To the extent that the assemblers and their suppliers are physically proximate, they constitute "operational clusters" based on the economies of proximity in input-output relations: lowered transport, logistics, and even packaging costs; speed of throughput; product changeovers; increasingly specialized process engineering and assembly labor; and economies of scale. Where technological clusters develop and disseminate information critical to product innovation, operational clusters effectively develop or disseminate methods of manufacturing, assembly, or logistics, as well as information on how to operate in the particular political and legal jurisdiction.

Clustering in operations offers several benefits. Indeed, operational clusters are typically what economists have in mind when they define economies of scale as a principal agglomeration externality (e.g., Krugman 1991; Paul and Siegel 1999). In this view, clustering minimizes transportation costs and facilitates specialization and scale, by which ancillary firms can spread their output across large local customers. Clustering also enables risk pooling by which a concentration of suppliers constitutes a "depot" of specialized inputs, whether components, services, or labor with industry experience. Through second-sourcing strategies, assemblers can drive prices down and obtain supplies in time to meet changing demand. Clusters of manufacturing operations also facilitate the diffusion of best practice through information spillovers, thereby making plants within the operational cluster more productive than isolates.

### Globalization of Operations

This characterization of collocation and clustering raises a critical puzzle. Models and empirical studies of agglomeration typically focus on why clusters persist, and it is true that the HDD industry's technological cluster has been remarkably durable. But many industries have experienced global movements in the location of production over time. Why would a firm embedded in an operational cluster shift production elsewhere, seemingly forgoing the benefits of agglomeration? If agglomeration arguments have merit, we might expect that both HDD product development and assembly would have remained in Japan and the United States, or that these clusters would dissipate only gradually. As detailed below, however, the American HDD industry moved offshore very rapidly, initially to Singapore, later elsewhere in Southeast Asia. To understand why this occurred, one must analyze the dynamics of the industry's location. Before doing so, however, it is necessary to explain our research approach.

## Research Approach

Despite the importance of industrial clustering to competitive advantage, it is surprisingly difficult to find empirical work that links patterns of location, including the globalization of economic activity, to industry performance over time. This is not because of a paucity of research on industrial location, including its international dimensions. It is, rather, because scholars in the fields of geography, economic geography, and regional planning have generally sought to explain other economic phenomena.

In attempting this task, the research reported here made several methodological choices. First, it examines firms within an industry, as opposed to larger aggregates that lump together diverse and often unrelated firms. A long tradition of research on urbanization and regional development, for example, addresses the rise of cities and regions and incorporates into the analysis the full range of manufacturing and services within those locales. An industry focus, by contrast, looks at location through a different lens and reveals different processes. Even the four-digit SIC code encompassing hard disk drives is too aggregated: it is for "data storage," which includes optical storage, tape storage, floppy disk drives, disk drive arrays, as well as disk drives. Each of these segments has different competitive ecologies and geographic configurations.

Second, it seeks to explain how location affected the performance of the American HDD industry vis-à-vis its foreign rivals. Most studies invoking location seek to explain the performance of a particular firm, or other outcomes such as patenting, incomes, or urban and regional growth.

Third, it examines the industry from its inception rather than at a particular point and traces its development over time. Specifically, it encompasses the entire population of firms that ever made a hard disk drive, tracks almost all suppliers that made two critical components (heads and media), and covers most firms in other parts of the value chain since 1980.

Finally, not only does it track the headquarters of all firms in the HDD industry, it also identifies the location of their R&D and production worldwide. Thus, its focus is global, rather than attending to only one or several locales, and it differentiates between R&D and production, which have different geographic requirements.

While single-industry studies have obvious limitations, this approach has at least three advantages over other studies of industries, globalization, or particular regions. First, this approach avoids a bias in many industry studies that favors large firms and those that survive. By including all firms, this study was able to observe small firms pioneering and leveraging locations to their advantage, while most large firms paid a price for being slow to change their location strategies. Multinational corporations are not typically characterized as small, nor is foreign direct investment generally thought a vehicle for small firms to grow.

This approach also allows us to observe the globalization process in a somewhat different way than most studies. As Michael Porter (1990) has argued, industry and industry segments are the best focus for analyzing competitive advantage because specialized and commercially valuable skills and technologies emerge from a competitive struggle within industries. I would add that a focus on an industry from its inception would provide an even stronger basis for drawing conclusions about the sources of competitive advantage. Longitudinal studies may identify causal factors that might not otherwise be observed if only one or a few years of an industry's evolution are considered; they may also avoid problems associated with cross-sectional snapshots when the process under study is not stable.

Thus, a third and related virtue of tracing an entire industry through both space and time is that it captures the *dynamics* of industry location. I have identified the location of each hard disk drive assembler—its R&D facilities and assembly plants—over the entire life of the industry. I also have detailed the history of the industry's movement into Southeast Asia, including the buildup of supporting stages in the value chain. This portrait allows us to distinguish those activities that moved (assembly) from those that did not (product development). Analyses that focus only on manufacturing or on R&D, on the locations of a few of the largest organizations, or that look at only some locations for a short period—no matter how intensively—can easily miss the changing role played by industry location in competition within the industry as a whole.[4]

## From Silicon Valley to Singapore: The Development of Offshore Operational Clusters

The disk drive industry took a decade to develop recognizable clusters. In the United States, drive activity was initially quite dispersed geographically. By the late 1960s, industry clusters appeared first in Northern and Southern California, later in Massachusetts and Minnesota. In Japan, it similarly took a decade for a cluster to emerge around Tokyo. By contrast, Europe never attracted sufficient entrants to generate a homemade cluster. In each case during the industry's initial twenty-five years, firms generally collocated production and innovation.

*1956 to 1980: The Collocation of Technology Development and Production*

A variety of captive and independent firms entered the disk drive business between 1956 and 1980. Most were computer system manufacturers and diversified industrial enterprises, some were specialists in peripherals or other types of magnetic storage, but few were start-ups. One group of entrants consisted of computer systems manufacturers. In the early 1950s, IBM's San Jose lab was searching for a capacious storage device. IBM was lagging behind Remington Rand, which had announced magnetic drum storage for its Univac File Computer in 1954. IBM responded with the first prototype disk drive, which was delivered to a customer site in June 1956. The following June, the first production unit came off the line (Bashe et al. 1986). IBM's drive was an immediate commercial hit, and other systems manufacturers began to develop disk drives. By the early 1970s, General Electric, Control Data, NEC, Hitachi, Fujitsu, Honeywell, Burroughs, NCR, and Toshiba had all begun to offer disk drives with their mainframe systems. These companies usually collocated their disk storage and systems development groups: GE in Arizona, Fujitsu in Kawasaki, CDC in Minnesota, Burroughs and NCR in Southern California, and Digital Equipment in Massachusetts.[5]

A second group of entrants included machinery and computer peripheral companies serving computer system manufacturers that had not yet made their own disk drives. These firms placed a wide variety of different technological bets, experimenting with various disk and recording head technologies. They were also geographically dispersed. Bryant Computer Products (Michigan) and Data Products (initially Minnesota, later moving to Southern California) were the first two companies to enter the industry after IBM. While IBM's first disk drive used disks 24 inches in diameter, Bryant's were 39 inches and Data Products's were 31 inches. Other early entrants among this group came from Northern California (Friden) and Massachusetts (Anelex). In Europe, Sperac, a creation of France's Plan Calcul, and Data Recording Instruments (England) served their national computer firms.

A third group consisted of "second generation" producers of disk drives. Engineers and managers from IBM left to start their own disk drive companies; others would reverse engineer IBM drives; and some firms relied on technology transfer agreements.[6] Two Northern California firms, Information Storage Systems, an IBM spin-off, and Memorex, a tape drive manufacturer that hired a team of IBM engineers to design its first disk drive, made drives completely plug-compatible with IBM's. Another set of second-generation firms came from the electronics and defense industries and for the most part reverse engineered IBM disk drives. Many of these firms were located in Southern California, which after the end of World War II became the home to technology companies, especially aerospace and defense firms. The western part of the San Fernando Valley into southern Ventura County was often thought of as a smaller version of what was becoming known as Silicon Valley, but disk drive activity also emerged in Orange County, to the south of Los Angeles. Century Data Systems, Marshall Industries, Pertec, and Data Products were four prominent disk drive companies with headquarters, product development, and manufacturing in Southern California.

The two most successful entrants outside of California were Control Data and Digital Equipment Corporation (DEC). Control Data was for many years the leader in original equipment manufacturers (OEM) production and the source of Minnesota's present-day capabilities in magnetic recording. DEC was one of the most successful of the captive drive makers, for a time second only to IBM, with operations in Massachusetts and later in Colorado. General Electric invested in storage technology in Arizona, moving it to Oklahoma City in the late 1960s. Potter Instrument Company (Melville, New York) leveraged its know-how in tape drives to enter the disk drive business. Although a leader in magnetic drum storage, Univac had a brief and unhappy experience designing disk drives for its mainframes at its Blue Bell, Pennsylvania, facility. Storage Technology, an IBM spin-off that originally made tape drives, helped to establish Colorado as a center for data storage technology, although its disk technology originated in Silicon Valley.[7]

Whether measured by number of firms or revenue, disk drive activity was considerably spread across the United States, although most of the largest HDD producers between 1960 and 1980 were based in California.[8] Almost all production was carried out in the United States as well, in the same location as product engineering and development. Product development was similarly proximate to assembly among European and Japanese producers.

High transportation costs should have encouraged dispersion of assembly to locations closer to overseas markets for firms seeking to expand internationally. Disk drives introduced before 1980 were very large and very expensive. The original IBM disk drive had fifty platters that were 24 inches in diameter.[9] In the late 1960s, Control Data offered a disk drive that was 3 feet deep, 6 feet tall, 10 feet wide, weighed 1,000 pounds, stored 50 megabytes, cost $300,000, and needed a crane to deliver it to any customer residing above the first floor. Even the IBM 3380, introduced in 1981, stood almost 6 feet high and 4 feet wide and deep. Moreover, the minimum efficient plant size was small by today's standards. The number of HDDs built for mainframes and minicomputers numbered less than 100,000 annually during the early 1970s, and only 500,000 disk drives were shipped in 1980 (Disk/Trend 1981). Century Data Systems, for example, one of the leading OEM producers during the early 1970s, produced only 500 drives per month.

Nonetheless, only the largest companies assembled drives or manufactured disk drive components overseas. During the 1960s and 1970s, the largest overseas markets were in Europe, where Burroughs, IBM, Honeywell, Control Data, and Memorex operated assembly facilities. In fact, of the forty-six U.S. entrants into the disk drive industry before 1980, only these five assembled drives abroad. IBM assembled drives in Germany; Burroughs in Scotland, Canada, and the growing Brazilian market; Control Data took over Honeywell's German HDD assembly facility; and Memorex assembled drives in Belgium for a short time. Among Japanese and European companies, only BASF (Germany) assembled drives overseas, making 8-inch drives in Los Gatos, California.

## Changing the Logic of Location: The Globalization of Production

At some point, the benefits of keeping manufacturing operations within an existing cluster at home diminish relative to other opportunities. Firms may decide to grow through geographic expansion. New organizational or technological innovations may prompt firms to reconsider their existing locations. Competitive pressures change and can force firms to relocate production, or changes in the external environment such as more liberal trade and foreign investment regimes open up additional locations for investment. In the case of disk drives, the introduction of the desktop computer, and its requirement for a small storage device, completely upended the geographic status quo. The IBM personal computer in particular and the subsequent explosion of the PC market in the 1980s drove demand for mass production of small storage devices. This need was initially met by floppy disk drives. But shoe box–size 5.25-inch hard drives soon relegated floppies to a backup role, and the hard drive became the PC's principal mode of storage.

Initially, producers of the smaller disk drives, like their predecessors, collocated technology development and assembly. Between 1980 and 1985, forty companies entered the industry. Many of the companies that pioneered the new desktop market were spin-offs of firms that made larger disk drives (especially IBM), and these new entrants set up business in the same region. But because Control Data (Minnesota) and DEC (Massachusetts)—the other market leaders during the 1970s—spawned no new entrants, disk drive development and manufacturing gradually became more concentrated in California, with some additional clustering in Colorado. By 1991, Northern California was the headquarters of the five largest companies: IBM, Seagate Technology, Quantum, Conner Peripherals, and Maxtor. While fewer in number, firms based in Southern California, such as Tandon, Computer Memories, Peripheral Technology, and Microcomputer Memories, were founded by engineers with experience at other Southern California disk drive firms, including floppy disk drive companies. The pioneers of smaller disk drives came primarily from these two regions.

Through the early 1980s, home-based production remained the dominant strategy for American, Japanese, and European firms, and assembly of small disk drives occurred in locations proximate to product development. Virtually all of the production of hard disk drives in 1983 was concentrated in two countries, the United States (72.3 percent of worldwide shipments) and Japan (12 percent of shipments). With almost 5 percent of global shipments, Europe produced more disk drives than Asia outside Japan. U.S. firms produced some 93 percent of their drives in the United States, while Japanese firms produced all of theirs in Japan.

However, some HDD firms began to consider offshore production. PC makers were putting enormous cost pressures on their HDD suppliers at the same time that a wave of new HDD entrants emerged. For many young companies, winning early contracts from computer makers was a make-or-break situation. As the largest PC producer, IBM, in particular, had enormous leverage. In 1982, it paid $600 for each 5.25-inch drive it purchased; in 1984 it bought about a million 5.25-inch drives at $400 each (*Electronic News* [June 4, 1984]). Although some HDD firms did not think such price cuts were sustainable, others were less sanguine. Looking to lower its operating costs, Seagate became the first company to experiment with taking production to a low-cost offshore location, starting with subassemblies in 1982 and final assembly in Singapore in 1983. Seagate and a few other American manufacturers discovered they could reduce the share of labor cost in assembly from almost 25 percent to 5 percent, thereby significantly cutting unit costs.

Thus, while the relentless pace of innovation tended to concentrate technological development into a few home-based clusters, American—but not Japanese—disk drive firms began to shift assembly overseas to achieve lower costs. A handful of pioneers demonstrated they could physically separate volume manufacturing from product and process development, and as other American HDD firms copied this model, the industry achieved a considerable competitive advantage.

*The Emergence of Singapore as the Center of Production: 1983–90*

The experiences of Seagate, Tandon, and Computer Memories in Southeast Asia began to influence other American HDD firms. The perceived success of Seagate's Singapore facility, in particular, spurred several other HDD producers to adopt a similar cost-based location strategy. Although Seagate's president noted that offshore assembly made transportation costs soar, communication between U.S. engineers and foreign plants more difficult, and quality control more challenging (*Business Week* [March 16, 1987]), company sales jumped from $51 million in 1982 to $222 million in 1983, its first year of Singapore-based assembly, and $302 million in 1984, establishing Seagate as the leader in desktop disk drives. Computer Memories also experienced rapid growth over this period, with sales jumping from $41 million in 1983 to $150 million in 1985.

Many American firms followed Seagate's lead and chose Singapore as their first overseas manufacturing site. In addition to Computer Memories and Tandon, both Maxtor and MiniScribe began to ship drives made in Singapore plants in 1984, followed by Micropolis (in 1986), Conner Peripherals (in 1987), and Cybernex Advanced Storage Technology (in 1987). In 1992, Integral Peripherals and MiniStor also began to ship from Singapore soon after they were established. American HDD companies also opened overseas facilities in other low-cost Asian locations such as Taiwan (Microscience International and Priam in 1987), and Hong Kong (Ampex in 1983).

Gradually, a dramatic change in the locus of assembly occurred. Manufacturing in low-cost assembly locations in Asia, particularly Southeast Asia, became the norm among a large proportion of American firms. By 1990, Singapore was the world's largest producer of hard disk drives, accounting for 55 percent of global output, measured in unit shipments, and significant operational clusters were emerging in parts of the value chain in Thailand and Malaysia as well.

Although the firms that moved abroad during this period were American, they were similar in additional ways. Every American assembler that went to Asia made desktop disk drives, and almost all of them also made only the smaller form factors. Companies that made larger disk drives for minicomputers and mainframes were much less likely to shift, even if they also made the smaller drives. In addition to specializing in desktop drives, the early adopters of the Southeast Asian assembly strategy were also medium-size and relatively new to the industry at the time of their move. Some 75 percent of these firms fell into the middle third of the size rankings at the time they started up production in Southeast Asia: Seagate was the twenty-second largest company when it began to ship from Singapore; Tandon was ranked twenty-fifth; Computer Memories was twenty-seventh. Similarly striking was the disparity in age between early and late adopters of the Southeast Asia assembly strategy. The average age (duration in the HDD industry) of the firms assembling drives in Southeast Asia was below that of the rest of the American industry until 1994, when the older disk drive manufacturers made the move.

Yet while American firms with similar organizational characteristics and strategic focus tended to adopt the Southeast Asian assembly strategy during this period, the Japanese firms that focused on the desktop drive segment did not. The revealed global strategies of American and Japanese firms could not have been more different. Not one of the new Japanese entrants into the desktop market (and which made drives only for the desktop) copied the American strategy, nor did any Japanese assembler of desktop drives make the move. After they entered the desktop markets in 1985, for example, Fuji Electric, JVC, Seiko Epson, and Alps Electric all confined their manufacturing to Japan. And while the average duration of American and Japanese firms in the HDD industry during this period was quite similar, not a single new Japanese entrant copied its American counterparts. By 1990, eight years after the first HDD was produced in Singapore, American firms assembled two-thirds of their disk drives in Southeast Asia. In contrast, Japanese companies continued to manufacture predominantly in Japan, where they produced 95 percent of their disk drives.

As a group, Japanese firms were clearly hesitant to abandon a strategy that appeared to be working up until the mid-1980s: exporting from Japan. In 1984, for example, TEAC Corp. was shipping almost 60 percent of its output to the United States. Even as late as 1989, both Matsushita and Hitachi invested in Japanese manufacturing capability for 3.5-inch drives, judging that applying more automation to drive assembly would enable them to overcome the otherwise higher costs of manufacturing in Japan. As the yen strengthened against the dollar and they turned their attention abroad, the United States, not Asia, was the site of their first overseas manufacturing investments. Fujitsu opened a U.S. plant in 1986, NEC followed in 1987, and Toshiba entered in 1992. At one point, Fujitsu reportedly intended to manufacture nearly all of its disk drives in the United States (*Computerworld* [December 9, 1985]). Toshiba explained that its strategy in HDDs was proximity to the market: to respond to market needs by designing and building products closer to their point of sale (*Los Angeles Times* [August 6, 1991]). While the low-cost Asian manufacturing strategy had been selected by American firms, Japanese firms pursued a strategy more consistent with industries under less cost pressure.

An analysis over time of the share of U.S. and Japanese HDD firms with facilities in low-cost Asia highlights these different national strategies. U.S. firms invested in low-cost Asia much earlier than their Japanese counterparts. By 1989 more than one-third of U.S. companies had facilities in low-cost Asia, almost all specializing in desktop products, while none of the Japanese were assembling in the region. Only in 1996 did the share of Japanese companies in low-cost Asia exceed the U.S. share, by which time all surviving Japanese companies had adopted the dominant strategy (McKendrick et al. 2000: 103).

*Industry Convergence on Southeast Asia: 1990–97*

For high-volume, low-priced, and low- to medium-capacity drives, where cutting costs was paramount, Southeast Asia was clearly the location of choice for American companies, and their strategy increasingly confined the Japanese to niches in the high-capacity segments. This was a surprising switch, since high-volume, low-cost manufacturing is an area in which the Japanese had traditionally excelled. But eventually the success of the American firms forced the Japanese to follow. Between 1991, when Fujitsu began production in Thailand, and 1996, all the principal Japanese HDD firms gradually shifted manufacturing to Southeast Asia, specifically the Philippines. But the lag in doing so placed them behind the American leaders.

By 1991, Fujitsu had reached maximum capacity at its Yamagata, Japan, HDD facility and was searching for ways to expand production capacity of its desktop drives (*Computergram International* [January 3, 1992]). Rather than expanding its existing Japanese or American facilities, Fujitsu invested in Thailand and retooled an existing facility for production of low-capacity 3.5-inch drives (IDC Japan Report [February 28, 1991]). But in response to the market downturn, it stopped all Thai production shortly thereafter.[10] In 1994, Fujitsu restarted Thai HDD assembly and by the end of 1995 was doing nearly all of its volume manufacturing in Thailand and at a new facility in the Philippines. The CEO of Fujitsu Computer Products of America cited the move to Southeast Asia as one of the prime factors behind the company's rapid growth in 1996, when Fujitsu doubled its worldwide hard drive revenues and enjoyed a 123 percent growth in unit shipments (*Business Wire* [June 17, 1997]).

NEC, Hitachi, and Toshiba soon joined Fujitsu in Southeast Asia. NEC completed its own HDD facility in the Philippines in 1995 and increased its offshore production to 75 percent of total HDD output (*COMLINE Daily News Computers* [October 9, 1995]). Hitachi also made its first HDD investment in the Philippines in 1995 and by 1998 had 90 percent of its 2.5-inch disk drive production in the Philippines.

By 1995, more than 70 percent of the word's disk drives were produced in Southeast Asia, generating nearly 61 percent of the industry's revenues. HDD production in the United States fell to 5 percent of world shipments, accounting for less than 9 percent of world revenues, while production in Japan fell to

10 percent of shipments and 13 percent of revenue. Japanese firms had greatly increased their presence in Southeast Asia, producing nearly 55 percent of their HDDs in the region. Virtually all of the remaining drive production by Japanese firms remained in Japan, compared with only 13 percent produced by U.S. firms in the United States and Japan. By the mid-1990s, then, the geographic distribution of Japanese assembly had begun to resemble that of their American competitors. But the damage caused by being late to adopt the global strategy had already been done. Japanese firms were left in the unenviable position of playing catch-up.

*Deepening Globalization: The Value Chain Follows*

Through continued investment in the region, nearly every part in the HDD value chain is now produced in Southeast Asia in some quantity, reinforcing its preeminence as the center of HDD and components production. In almost every year since its initial investment in 1982, Seagate has reinvested in Singapore—upgrading existing facilities or building new ones. Seagate also invested heavily in Thailand and Malaysia in upstream activities like motors, recording heads, and printed circuit board assemblies. These investments transformed Seagate into the largest private employer in both Singapore and Thailand, and among the largest in Malaysia. Independent manufacturers of critical components, such as media and heads, also moved into the region, further reinforcing it as the industry's production location of choice.

Although the value chain is not completely organized along national lines, there remains a distinctly national dimension to the pattern of globalization. Japanese HDD assemblers and their suppliers moved offshore roughly in tandem, reinforcing the Philippines as an attractive assembly site for Japanese producers (Tecson 1999). By contrast, American suppliers mostly ignored the Philippines.

In summary, American HDD assemblers initiated the move to Southeast Asia, and much of the manufacturing aspects of the value chain followed. The technical imperatives of the industry ultimately led to a convergence of American and Japanese strategic posture, as can be seen by the percentage of firms adopting a low-cost assembly strategy. This convergence is further reflected by the fact that by 1987, a short five years after initial investment in low-cost Asia by an HDD firm, noncaptive firms assembling in low-cost Asia controlled 55 percent of the HDD market, measured in revenue terms. By 1996 the market share for HDD firms with assembly facilities in low-cost Asia had increased to 98 percent.

## The Dynamics of Location-Specific Assets: Industry Requirements and Southeast Asian Capabilities

As we have seen, at some point the benefits of keeping manufacturing operations within an existing cluster at home diminishes relative to other opportunities, and a new locational logic emerges. The value of a location thus depends not merely on conditions at one point but also on its ability to meet an industry's changing technological and organizational needs. The experience of the disk drive industry demonstrates that location-specific assets *outside* an industry's home base can do that, while complementing its technological resources at home.

The investments made by the American HDD firms in Southeast Asia not only transformed the geography of the disk drive industry; over time they completely altered the kind of assets the industry leveraged at each location. Southeast Asia initially provided a combination of low factor costs and generic public policies, such as tax holidays and liberal rules governing trade and investment. Yet these did not remain the primary contribution to U.S. competitiveness. Constantly chasing cheaper factors would have nullified any initial advantage, as Porter (1990, 1998) has rightly observed. Over time, foreign investment, economic growth, learning and changing public policies altered the very nature of these locations. Local assets became more sophisticated and came to encompass more industry-specific public policies that complemented firm-specific advantages and agglomeration economies. These diverse location-specific assets also became linked together into regional production networks that exploited the distinct advantages, including agglomeration economies, at each location.

Changes in the industry's competitive ecology demanded new kinds of location-specific assets. Industry competition has gone through three periods since 1980, when the first desktop disk drive was produced: 1980–85, 1986–92, and 1993–99. During each period, the industry's competitive requirements grew more demanding, and Table 6.1 summarizes how the region's locational assets evolved to meet them.[11]

During the first phase (1980–85), the industry was obsessed with cutting costs, largely by squeezing labor rates and reducing tax liabilities. Disk drive quality was not as high as it is today, and firms could realize considerable savings from having lower paid employees rework defective drives. In addition, firms began to squeeze the costs out of their components by developing a set of indigenous suppliers for making relatively basic parts. Most industry activity was concentrated in Singapore, with Thailand beginning to host the most laborious tasks and feeding the output back to Singapore.

TABLE 6.1
*Dynamics of Industry Location and Benefits: HDD in Southeast Asia,
1980 to the Present*

| Competitive pressures | Southeast Asia role in disk drive assembly | Singapore | Thailand | Malaysia |
|---|---|---|---|---|
| | | *1980–85* | | |
| Cost | Produce new product in the U.S., transfer mature product to Singapore | Labor costs<br>Generic incentives<br>Non-industry specific infrastructure<br>Pre-existing managerial and technical personnel | Labor costs<br>Generic incentives<br>Proximity to Singapore | |
| | | *1986–92* | | |
| Cost; time-to-market | Ramp new product in the U.S., transfer to Singapore for volume production after process has been stabilized. Mature product later transferred from Singapore to Thailand to Malaysia | Moderate agglomeration effects (specialized labor, intermediate inputs)<br>Some industry specific incentives<br>Generic incentives | Pre-existing managerial and technical personnel<br>Labor costs<br>Proximity to Singapore | Pre-existing managerial and technical personnel<br>Labor costs<br>Proximity to Singapore |
| | | *1993–present* | | |
| Cost; time-to-market; time-to-volume; yield improvement | Pilot production in the U.S., products transferred directly from the U.S. to Southeast Asia for ramp | Strong agglomeration effects (specialized labor, intermediate inputs, technological spillovers)<br>Strong industry specific incentives<br>Proximity to Thailand and Malaysia<br>Generic incentives | Generic incentives<br>Moderate agglomeration effects (specialized labor, intermediate inputs)<br>Proximity to Singapore and Malaysia<br>Labor costs | Generic incentives<br>Moderate agglomeration effects (intermediate inputs)<br>Proximity to Singapore and Thailand<br>Labor costs |

*Source:* Adapted from table 3.2 in McKendrick et al. 2000, p. 60.

During the second phase (1986–92), competition intensified as hard disk drives became an increasingly common feature in personal computers (PCs), and HDD firms began to focus much more on selling disk drives directly to PC assemblers. PC producers generally required state-of-the-art products and imposed more demanding time-to-market cycles on HDD firms, as well as thinner profit margins.[12]

American firms responded to these pressures not by shifting to other locations but by reinvesting in the region and building a strong supplier base. By 1990 three-fourths of the parts needed to produce a disk drive could be purchased in Asia (*Los Angeles Times* [June 25, 1990]; *Business Times Singapore* [May 3, 1993]). Singapore began to generate some agglomeration economies, while Thailand and Malaysia offered U.S. firms an increasingly skilled technical labor force for doing more sophisticated subassemblies. The three countries together represented an interdependent system, with most drive assembly being done in Singapore, fed by subassemblies from its neighbors: proximity to Singapore minimized coordination and transportation costs. Public policies in Singapore also evolved to offer more industry-specific benefits.

With the most recent phase, roughly beginning in 1993, the industry competed along multiple dimensions: unrelenting pressure on costs, time-to-market, as well as time-to-volume and yield improvement. Manufacturers vied for contracts with even fewer major-volume customers, led by Compaq, Dell, Hewlett-Packard, and Apple. Economies of scale became even more critical, along with better quality control, faster ramp (from zero to 2 million drives in a quarter for one product, and the larger firms offer several products concurrently), and better control over the supply chain. Profit margins increasingly depended on achieving high manufacturing yields and uninterrupted access to high-quality components.

During this phase, the U.S. HDD industry developed operational clusters in all three countries, each generating at least moderate agglomeration economies. Singapore continued to stand apart: it produced the highest performance disk drives, had the industry's deepest process engineering skills, hosted the most suppliers, and offered the strongest institutional base. By the time the Japanese HDD firms had finally developed their own production system centered on the Philippines, they merely preserved their small share of the worldwide market.

The Southeast Asian operational clusters and their integration into a production system emerged to complement U.S.-based technology development. While product innovation usually grabs most of the credit for industrial leadership, manufacturing programs must also be capable of rapid change to new products, with fast, smoothly executed production ramps. The U.S. disk drive industry developed strong operational assets in Southeast Asia with the ability to evolve quickly to new products. As much as product innovation, this regional production system sustained America's industrial leadership in disk drives.

### Seagate Technology: The Dynamics of Location in Microcosm

The experience of Seagate Technology illustrates how firm capabilities and Southeast Asia's location-specific assets coevolved to contribute to America's competitiveness in disk drives. Consider Figure 6.1, which suggests how Seagate

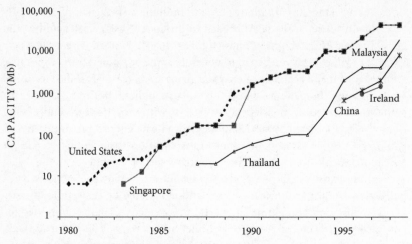

FIG. 6.1. Seagate: Highest Capacity Drive at Each Production Location, 1980–98.
Source: McKendrick et al. 2000, p. 144, fig. 64.

used different locations to make different kinds of disk drives. The lines in the graph depict the most capacious drive Seagate assembled at each of its production locations in each year. Within two years of beginning drive assembly in Singapore, Seagate was making its highest capacity disk drives there. In 1987, Seagate began to assemble drives in Thailand, but Singapore and Thailand played two distinctly different roles. Singapore received new drives from the United States, ramped them up to volume production, eliminated bugs, and stabilized yields. Once the process had matured, Seagate saved on costs by transferring the mature product from Singapore to Thailand for its end-of-life manufacture. For example, in 1990, after Seagate had absorbed Control Data's HDD operations and shifted all assembly offshore, Singapore made Seagate's highest capacity drive, which was 1.65 gigabytes, while Thailand made the older 60-mb models.[13]

Until 1995, only Singapore and Thailand assembled Seagate drives, with Singapore doing the more skill-intensive processing.[14] Twice a day, after Thailand completed head-disk assembly, the drives were flown to Singapore for final assembly and test. But merely focusing on low costs was no longer a viable strategy in the early 1990s. During the 1980s Seagate was able to sacrifice time in getting to market in exchange for high-volume, low-cost production. But the industry's requirements had changed in the late 1980s and early 1990s, and Seagate paid a heavy price for being late to the market. The company restructured its engineering department in the United States to reduce the time-to-market cycle, and its Southeast Asian operations responded. Seagate was late to market with a 3.5-inch disk drive but subsequently caught up and offered a full menu of products. The company began to equal the time-to-market pace of its competitors, *and* at lower cost. The relatively close proximity of Seagate's operations within the region, and those of its suppliers, facilitated the execution of the time-to-market strategy.

In 1995, the company opened additional assembly plants in China and Ireland, both investments intended to hedge against potential constraints on market access to China and Europe. And through its 1996 acquisition of Conner Peripherals, Seagate inherited additional drive assembly operations in Singapore, Malaysia, and China, as well as Italy, which Seagate promptly closed.

As time-to-volume pressures mounted, and with too much capacity in the industry, Seagate found itself in possession of too many HDD assembly plants. It closed its Ireland facility, which had the highest cost per drive in the company, relocated drive assembly from Thailand to Singapore, and consolidated its three Singapore drive plants into one massive operation. Each remaining location played a distinct role. Singapore remained the core of Seagate's drive operations, making the company's highest performance disk drives and performing the most demanding process and product engineering outside the United States. Singapore also had responsibility for product development and production of Seagate's very successful low-cost disk drive for the sub-$1,000 desktop PC market. Malaysia was responsible for Seagate's desktop products, which by 1998 included the assembly of a 28-gigabyte drive; the Malaysian facility received products directly from the United States for production. China was used in ways that took advantage of its lower labor costs, making the drives that were initially launched in Malaysia and Singapore.

The geographic proximity of Seagate's other stages of production supported drive assembly. Table 6.2 shows the geographic configuration of Seagate's employment since 1981. It helps to illustrate how the company benefited from both the heterogeneity of assets offered by the different countries and the flexibility it gained by locating some activities in more than one country. In the early 1980s, the company's focus was on Singapore, where it began printed circuit board assembly (PCBA) and drive assembly, and by 1984, Singapore already accounted for more Seagate employees than the United States. But the company quickly used Thailand to assemble its heads. Having the most labor intensive activities in Thailand while doing the more engineering intensive activities in Singapore leveraged the assets of both locations while minimizing oversight and coordination costs. Note, too, that after a brief dip, Seagate's U.S.-based employment increased as the company globalized; its high-volume production offshore generated the resources that supported R&D in drive design, recording heads, disks, motors, and specialized semiconductors.

TABLE 6.2

*The Geographic Pattern of Employment in Seagate, 1981–98*

| Ranking | Total | U.S. | Singapore | Thailand | Malaysia | Indonesia | China | Europe |
|---|---|---|---|---|---|---|---|---|
| 1981 | 1,000 | 1,000 | | | | | | |
| 1982 | 1,600 | 1,200 | 400 | | | | | |
| 1983 | 2,350 | 1,600 | 1,000 | 50 | | | | |
| 1984 | 4,100 | 1,300 | 1,700 | 800 | | | | |
| 1985 | 4,200 | 1,000 | 2,000 | 1,200 | | | | |
| 1986 | 9,500 | 1,000 | 5,000 | 3,500 | | | | |
| 1987 | 14,300 | 1,300 | 8,000 | 5,000 | | | | |
| 1988 | 28,450 | 23,000 | 14,000 | 12,000 | | | | 150 |
| 1989 | 35,150 | 9,000 | 10,500 | 14,000 | 1,000 | | | 650 |
| 1990 | 39,950 | 11,000 | 12,000 | 15,000 | 1,500 | | | 250 |
| 1991 | 40,550 | 9,500 | 12,400 | 16,600 | 1,500 | 300 | | 250 |
| 1992 | 43,550 | 9,500 | 12,400 | 16,600 | 3,700 | 1,000 | | 250 |
| 1993 | 43,250 | 9,000 | 13,000 | 16,000 | 4,000 | 1,000 | | 250 |
| 1994 | 54,050 | 9,500 | 13,900 | 22,000 | 7,000 | 1,000 | | 650 |
| 1995 | 65,200 | 9,500 | 15,000 | 26,000 | 12,000 | 1,500 | 500 | 700 |
| 1996 | 91,850 | 11,000 | 18,000 | 34,000 | 20,000 | 1,500 | 5,000 | 23,500 |
| 1997 | 106,150 | 9,500 | 19,400 | 44,000 | 23,000 | 1,500 | 5,100 | 3,150 |
| 1998 | 88,750 | 9,000 | 15,000 | 39,000 | 18,000 | 1,500 | 4,000 | 2,250 |

*Source:* McKendrick et al. 2000, p. 146, table 6.10.

*Notes:* 1989 employment includes CDC acquisition; 1996 includes Conner acquisition. U.S. numbers include overseas marketing and sales staffs not otherwise captured. Numbers are generally for midyear. In cases where figures were unavailable, they have been interpolated.

As Seagate grew, it expanded its operations in Southeast Asia, again pairing Thailand's cheaper labor with Singapore's more skilled engineering. It opened a second PCBA plant in Singapore and reinvested in its Thai heads assembly operations, adding a plant to make recording head subassemblies in 1989. And as Seagate became more vertically integrated, it shifted additional stages there as well, in particular motor production to Thailand, making it Seagate's motor supply center. In 1989, with head-disk assembly, motor, and heads subassembly operations concentrated in Thailand, Seagate's Thai employment surpassed Singapore's to become the company's principal component production and subassembly center. By the late 1980s, Seagate had also helped to develop a range of local suppliers in Singapore that possessed greater experience in electronics manufacturing than firms in neighboring countries. These local firms cut component costs by 40 percent or more over what Seagate had been paying to import them from the United States or Japan. Although vertically integrated, by the late 1980s, Seagate was buying far more components in the region than it was making (*Electronic Business* [November 15, 1988]).

By the early 1990s, Seagate's regional production system had become even more self-sufficient, with multiple suppliers, including in-house production, located in Singapore, Thailand, and Malaysia. Seagate expanded production with investments of $100 million per year from 1989 to 1991, most of it in Southeast Asia (*Chilton's Electronic News* [December 24, 1990]; *Business Times Singapore* [March 18, 1994]). Not only did Seagate benefit from the variety of locational assets in the region, it had more sourcing options across the region that increased its flexibility. Seagate made heads subassemblies in Malaysia and Thailand, and it had added printed circuit board assembly in Indonesia and Malaysia to complement its Singapore PCBA operations. Seagate also sourced base plates, actuators, and other components from a choice of suppliers in Singapore and Malaysia, many of which it helped to develop.

This geographic configuration of activities offered Seagate a number of advantages over the course of its history. In the early 1980s, its operations in Singapore and Thailand were a key reason that Seagate was the low-cost leader in the desktop drive business. It won critical high-volume production orders from IBM, which at the time was making its own desktop drives at its Rochester, Minnesota, plant. Because of its locational choices, Seagate was thought to have a minimum 20 percent cost advantage in producing the same 20-megabyte drive that IBM was producing (*Electronic News* [April 29, 1985]).

As it became more vertically integrated in the late 1980s, Seagate's mix of plants in the region gave it even greater cost advantages. According to Seagate's CEO, between 1983 and 1994 Seagate had "improved its cost/performance ratio by nearly 2,000 times, making it the lowest cost producer of heads in the industry. Since the start of production, the cost of the heads has been reduced by a factor of 25 times and the areal density of the heads has increased 75 times" (*Business Wire* [November 1, 1994]). Since heads subassemblies are a significant part of a disk drive's bill of materials, this gave Seagate tremendous competitive advantages. Proximity among facilities also reduced the company's supply line and gave it more control over delivery times.

As labor rates became relatively less important (though certainly not trivial) to competitive success, and time-to-volume more critical, Seagate began to reconsider the geographic configuration of its operations. Instead of considering only the cost of a particular component or process, Seagate began to consider whether a given location could meet the industry's time-to-volume pressures. Some of its components were more costly to *move* than to manufacture, and the physical separation delayed schedules. Following a cyclical downturn in the industry in 1997, Seagate began to consolidate its operations. The company closed a number of redundant facilities in Ireland and the United States. In late 1999, it began to evaluate whether to combine different steps of the heads subassembly process under one roof in order to improve speed of operations.

Proximity within Seagate's regional production system has given the company advantages in cost, speed, and flexibility. Proximity within the region has enabled Seagate to capture significant economies in coordination, transport, component, labor, and other managerial costs. Singapore has been the company's manufacturing headquarters, with the highest product and process engineering skills. Lower labor costs in Thailand made the country Seagate's center of assembly, and Thailand's proximity to Singapore reduced the company's supply lines and gave it more control over delivery. Malaysia has responsibility for the assembly of desktop drives and for transferring production to China. Malaysia is also Seagate's global center for the machining of sliders (heads), which are then sent on to Thailand for assembly.

## Explaining the Differences in the Strategies of American and Japanese Firms

I have argued that the U.S. HDD industry strengthened its competitive advantage by developing and exploiting offshore location-specific assets. It is puzzling why the Japanese disk drive industry took so long to imitate this strategy. Their slowness in doing so suggests that firms in a given industry in one nation may behave differently than their competitors from other countries, and that these behavioral differences can lead to different competitive outcomes.

Why would firms in the same industry but from different countries respond differently to the same environmental, technological, and competitive changes? I argue that the reason is that an industry's competitive dynamics are shaped both by the strategic focus of firms in an industry and by the "mental models" managers develop to interpret and make sense of the competitive environment (McKendrick 2001). Typically, a new global strategy will be pioneered by only a small set of national firms sharing some similar characteristics. Through processes of competitive mimicry, firms from the same nation will initially adopt similar global strategies—in this case, overseas assembly—but over time the industry as a whole converges on the same strategy. The result is that first-mover advantages apply both to the firms that pioneer the new location strategy and to the national industry of which they are a part.

What explains such mimetic behavior? One possibility is the rational calculations made by managers in trying to imitate good performers or economize on search costs. But because the source of another organization's performance is often ambiguous, mimicry may arise from more social aspects of organizational life, such as shared understandings of the situation or of what is considered to be "appropriate" behavior. One important mechanism that motivates mimicry and that appears to account for the early and rapid shift of the American disk drive industry to Southeast Asia is "observational learning" (Greve 1995) of salient competitors. As put to us in an interview with the former president of Seagate: "Everybody follows everybody in our industry." Observational learning explains why imitation within industries takes place even when it is unclear whether there is any communication among the adopters or when the sources of information are diffuse (ibid.).

Which firms are salient to others? Salience arises from the models managers use to understand their strategic situation (Porac et al. 1989; Porac et al. 1995; Nath and Gruca 1997; Greve 1998). In their decision-making, managers group together organizations that are similar along important dimensions (such as size, sales growth, or the products they offer), monitor these organizations (Porac et al. 1995; Greve 1998), and define unique product positions in relation to them.[15] Indeed, organizations are likely to mimic only their salient competitors because of over-reliance on information about them (Porac et al. 1989; Greve 1996). Regulations, taken-for-granted norms, market competition, financial analyst reports, and the business press are all important sources of information about appropriate behavior, providing blueprints for managers by specifying or reporting the forms and procedures required to be a member-in-good-standing in that industry (DiMaggio and Powell 1983; Abrahamson 1996).

Nationality—even regional proximity—also shapes mental models and determines which firms are salient. A variety of empirical evidence suggests there are cross-national differences in the direction and timing of foreign investment. National level data on outward foreign investment show that firms from the same country tend to invest in neighboring countries or in those countries with which they have close political or cultural ties (UN 1993). Bartlett and Ghoshal (1989) note the persistence of national characteristics in the global strategies of firms in the same industry. Hu (1995) contends that the differences between national "qualities" are likely to be more important than the differences between firms based in the same country, so that national advantages usually outweigh firm-specific advantages.

These findings suggest that strategic behavior cannot be explained entirely by reference to technological and economic factors; in response to pressures for locational change, firms in the same industry but from different countries may behave differently. Managerial ideologies and cultural norms in effect limit the range of an organization's choices and channel its behavior. As a result, as a nation's firms begin to extend their operations internationally, they carry with them national business practices and principles (Kogut 1992; Dunning 1993).

Behavioral differences in internationalization can have competitive consequences. In the first stage, global strategy favors one nation's firms over others. While imitation of the "right" strategy is an obvious way for competitors to undermine an initial advantage, inherited organizational structures, practices, and relationships constrain their ability to adopt superior practices quickly. Because these kinds of practices are difficult to observe directly or are strongly interdependent with other routines, they take much longer to diffuse across national borders than do more observable phenomena like product innovations (Armour and Teece 1978; Kogut 1991). The result can be differences in timing and direction of strategic action: one nation's industry develops a more effective strategy relative to its competitors than those of another nation. And because of agglomeration economies and the development of a regional production system, those advantages can be difficult for second-movers to match quickly.

This is precisely what we observe in the disk drive industry. Not only did the American industry globalize extensively, it did so much earlier than the Japanese. The firms that led the shift abroad were similar along several dimensions, including making the same kinds of disk drives and being of similar size and age; in addition, many of them came from California, making them more observable and hence more salient to one another.[16] In addition, the business press and financial analysts began to associate Southeast Asian production with success, and came to expect American HDD firms to conform to that industry model.

By contrast, Japanese firms appeared to follow a different competitive logic. Through 1985, Japanese HDD firms benefited from a strong dollar, but as early as 1986 they began to complain about the strong yen and had every incentive to move assembly offshore. Japanese HDD executives noted that their disk drives were not as price competitive as they had been (*Electronic News* [July 7, 1986]). Seagate was undercutting their prices in Japan by 15 percent with drives shipped from Singapore (*Business Week* [March 16, 1987]). Conner Peripherals trumpeted that it had strong sales to the computer divisions of NEC and Toshiba (*Electronic Business* [May 14, 1990]). Moreover, all of the Japanese disk drive companies were already experienced multinationals and had plants making other products in the region; and both Fujitsu and NEC shifted the production of *other* cost-sensitive components to Singapore in 1986 because of the strong yen (*Financial Times* [November 3, 1986]). Yet none of them, including new Japanese entrants into the desktop market, shifted disk drive assembly to lower cost Asian locations. Instead, both Fujitsu and NEC, for example, set up assembly in the United States. As a Fujitsu executive commented in 1987, referring to Fujitsu's efforts to reduce its costs by 50 percent: "It is cheaper to build drives in the U.S. for export than in Japan" (*Electronic Buyer's News* [May 18, 1987]). He made no mention of Southeast Asia. Although aware of the movement of U.S. desktop drive production to Southeast Asia, and facing

competition from U.S. firms in their domestic market, Japanese firms nonetheless did not follow.

Although I cannot say with certainty why the Japanese HDD industry was so
late in shifting assembly to lower cost locations, conversations with Japanese
managers and a reading of the business press suggest three reasons. First, Japanese managers did not consider the U.S. pioneers as necessarily viable competitors; it took a few years before Seagate and other new American disk drive firms
began to be salient to the Japanese. Rather, key strategists in Japanese firms
identified other Japanese HDD firms as their immediate rivals. Second, Japanese industry continued to follow a model that emphasized the importance of
producing close to the customer; several firms in fact began to produce small-
diameter drives in the United States at the same time that U.S. firms were moving production to Southeast Asia. While this logic might have been compelling
in the era of large-diameter disk drives, it was completely inappropriate for the
production of desktop disk drives. Finally, Japanese managers also had a sense
that souring U.S.-Japan trade relations might lead to the establishment of trade
barriers against Japanese disk drives; as in other industries, Japanese production in the United States was thought to mitigate that threat.

What finally drove adoption of the global strategy among Japanese firms? In
an important respect, these late movers behaved just like their older American
competitors, which were also slow to shift assembly to Southeast Asia. IBM,
Unisys (the old Burroughs and Memorex drive operations), DEC, and Hewlett-
Packard had all competed in the predesktop era. Like the Japanese, each of
them also competed across multiple form factors throughout the 1980s (and in
some cases into the 1990s), including the smaller form factors. More important,
each of these late movers relied to a considerable extent on an internal market.
As captive sales as a share of total sales diminished, each made a greater commitment to assemble in lower cost locations. Their internal market concealed
the higher operating costs of assembling in "legacy" locations.

While these shared characteristics acted to delay adoption of the emergent
global strategy, nationality still influenced the choice of location. The Japanese
followed one another to the Philippines, but Control Data, DEC, HP, Unisys,
and IBM all drew on the infrastructure and personnel previously constructed
by American disk drive manufacturers in Singapore, Thailand, and Malaysia.

Table 6.3 summarizes the characteristics of the firms that shifted assembly to
Southeast Asia. American disk drive firms were the early movers into Southeast
Asia. They tended to compete in the same market segments (small disk drives
for the OEM market), were of similar size (medium) and age (young), and emulated successful firms with similar characteristics (Seagate, Computer Memories, MiniScribe). Of course, none of the new Japanese entrants to the desktop

TABLE 6.3

*Summary Chararacteristics of Firms Assembling in Southeast Asia*

| | Early adopters, 1982–90 | | Late adopters, 1991–96 | | Profile of late adopters in 1989 | |
|---|---|---|---|---|---|---|
| | U.S. | Japan | U.S. | Japan | U.S. | Japan |
| Number of adopters | 17 | 0 | 10 | 6 | 5 | 5 |
| Noncaptive firms | 15 | 0 | 7 | 2 | 2 | 1 |
| Captive firms[a] | 2 | 0 | 3 | 4 | 3 | 4 |
| Types of drives produced | | | | | | |
| Small | 12 | 0 | 10 | 4 | 2 | 1 |
| Large and small | 5 | 0 | 0 | 2 | 3 | 4 |
| Ties with other adopters[b] | 7 | 0 | 3 | 0 | 1 | 0 |
| Firm size | | | | | | |
| Small | 1 | 0 | 4 | 2 | 1 | 1 |
| Medium | 12 | 0 | 3 | 2 | 0 | 1 |
| Large | 4 | 0 | 3 | 2 | 4 | 3 |
| Firm age | | | | | | |
| Younger than average | 14 | 0 | 6 | 2 | 1 | 1 |
| Older than average | 3 | 0 | 4 | 4 | 4 | 4 |

*Source:* McKendrick et al. 2001, p. 328, table 5.

[a] Any captive sales.

[b] Equity links, spinoffs from prior adopters, other personnel movement.

market mimicked the moves of American firms competing in the same market segment. The firms that were late to Southeast Asia, in contrast, tended to be in the industry the longest, were the largest, had operated across market segments, and had a degree of captive sales (see Table 6.3, far right columns).

## Implications for the Book's Five Themes

During 2001 and 2002, competition in the disk drive industry intensified as the PC industry and its disk drive suppliers experienced as bad a slump as participants can remember. Worldwide disk drive employment declined precipitously, and several more HDD companies exited the business. The most prominent casualty is IBM, the company that created the world's first disk drive and possessed more technological resources than any other company. In mid-2002, IBM announced it will fold its HDD operation into a joint venture with Hitachi: Hitachi will own 70 percent of the joint venture, even though IBM will contribute three times the employees and four times the revenue. The expectation is that Hitachi will become the sole shareholder in a few years. Despite this dramatic and, to many, sentimental event, American firms continue to dominate, as well as invest in and exploit, the location-specific assets as described in this chapter.

*Pricing Pressure*

The industry's competitive ecology is the most significant catalyst for the globalization of production, limiting the ability of the industry's leaders to control pricing or the length of product life cycles. Computer manufacturers and distributors make buying decisions largely on price and on the ups and downs of the computer industry business cycle. As a consequence, the industry is often whipsawed, with periods of rapid growth leading to overcapacity, followed by price wars, losses, and shakeouts. As in other industries, disk drive companies strive to avoid the pitfalls of the price-sensitive, high-volume low end of the market by differentiating product and moving into higher capacity segments, such as drives for file servers and network storage. But the fact is that, historically, there has been little ability for firms to sustain a product differentiation strategy. While one or two firms have been the capacity leaders for a year or two, trying to grab a more profitable position, no company in the history of the industry has survived solely by making small quantities of high-capacity drives.

Absent this pressure, manufacturers would have had less incentive to cut costs, and thus be less likely to shift the geographic locus of production.

*Time and Speed*

HDD firms fundamentally compete on price, but no other industry simultaneously operates under more time pressure. Product cycles have shortened to less than nine months, while product ramp-ups and ramp-downs need to occur quickly to avoid being late to (and out of) market, since prices—and hence revenue per product—erode over time. Thus, firms face the challenge of achieving speed of execution at competitive costs.

This requirement suggests trade-offs between speed and cost in terms of the location of economic activity. The importance of speed in international competition implies that geographic dispersion of activity should in fact be minimized, since distance between activities can slow lead times, product ramp-up, and throughput. Speed is generally facilitated when stages of production are adjacent. Ease of transport to and from all the locations employed at the adjacent stage maximizes speed. Speed is also facilitated when exchanges are conducted between people that share a language and culture. The requirement of speed should thus tend to concentrate activity geographically. But when costs also matter, as in hard disk drives, firms also face pressure to adopt a geographic configuration in an attempt to minimize overall costs. This likely means dispersing production to lower cost locations. What to do?

The disk drive industry resolved the tension between these two pressures by developing complementary industrial clusters.

*Knowledge, Capabilities, and Clusters*

Cost, price, and speed interact with knowledge and capabilities in dynamic, often unforeseen ways. Together they directly affect a value chain's geographic configuration, including its propensity to cluster. As described in this chapter, pricing and cost pressures can serve as a wedge to separate the collocation of design and manufacturing. One might therefore expect, as Michael Porter (1990) has argued, that chasing cheaper factors nullifies any initial advantage, and does not generate any but transitory new ones. This may be true for some industries, but American disk drive firms did not constantly chase cheaper factors. Rather, they reinvested in the region, stimulated the formation and growth of local suppliers, and created strong operational clusters that complemented the technological clusters at home.

Over time, operational clusters acquire their own specific knowledge and capabilities. Operational clusters stimulate the development and facilitate the dissemination of manufacturing, assembly, or logistics methods.

*Transportation, Communications, and Globalization*

As in other industries, HDD firms exploited advances in communications and transportation and became adept at coordinating activities dispersed across a number of international locations. Because the HDD industry relies primarily on air transportation, perhaps the most important feature was the physical and regulatory improvements made at airports in Southeast Asia—Singapore especially—to enable the import and export of components and final products to flow quickly in and out of the country. Although electronic communication and web-based tools have improved the ability of firms to manage over long distances, neither played a role in the shift of assembly from the United States or Japan to Southeast Asia in the 1980s and early 1990s.

*Proximity to the Customer*

Every firm would prefer to locate product development, marketing, sales, and manufacturing near each of its customers. This is, of course, impossible, and firms must instead make difficult choices about where to locate particular functions or activities. In HDD product development and assembly, proximity to customers has seldom played a leading role in location decisions, and only then because of concerns about market access rather than a need for close technical interaction. As I described above, proximity to component designers and other technological expertise has influenced locations in product development. HDD product development teams develop close engineering-level relationships between stages in the value chain. By contrast, technical interactions with individual customers are less frequent and do not necessitate physical proximity. In HDD assembly, the need for customer proximity had some influence on decisions to locate assembly abroad during the industry's first 20 years, when HDDs were heavy and expensive to ship. But it has had a negligible effect in shaping contemporary patterns of HDD assembly. Instead, proximity to key suppliers and competitors has been much more important, as I described in this chapter. If proximity to the customer was a motivating factor behind location decisions, we would expect HDD firms to locate production where the vast majority of HDDs are consumed, either by computer manufacturers or final consumers. The world's largest markets—the U.S. and Japan—have very little HDD assembly, while Taiwan, a leader in computer assembly along with the U.S. and Japan, hosts no disk drive assembly. With a high value-to-weight ratio and low barriers to trade, disk drives—and many other high tech commodities—are easily and cheaply shipped by air throughout the world from a very few locations.

## Notes

1. A more complete discussion can be found in McKendrick et al. (2000).

2. Capacity is determined by the number of bits that can be squeezed onto a square inch of disk, otherwise known as the HDD's areal density.

3. The idea behind a technological cluster is similar to what Storper (1992) calls a technological district, except that the unit of analysis is the industry rather than multiple industries that compose the district. Important in the distinction is the relatedness of innovative work or interdependence of specific firms within the industry-based technological cluster.

4. The literature on economic clustering, for example, emphasizes the proximity of competitors and related firms but generally without attention to different activities and the precise functions a cluster performs from the perspective of the firm. Researchers study either manufacturing (e.g., Head et al. 1999) or innovation (Audretsch and Feldman 1996), or else refer to "firms" clustering together without specifying the activities that are clustered (e.g., Krugman 1991).

5. IBM and Honeywell were exceptions: IBM's San Jose lab was set up in 1952 in order to tap the engineering skills in California, far from the company's New York–based mainframe operations. Honeywell's storage operations were initially in Massachusetts rather than collocated with its Minnesota systems groups.

6. Internationally, disk drive design and production were mainly diffused through technology transfer arrangements with U.S. firms. NEC, Hitachi, and Hokushin had technical tie-ups with Honeywell, Bryant Computer Products, and Diablo Systems, respectively. In Europe, Compagnie Internationale de l'Informatique had a license to make Control Data drives, and BASF acquired technology from Century Data Systems. In the late 1970s, Brazilian firms acquired licenses from Ampex, Control Data, and Pertec, among others.

7. Storage Technology's entry into disk drives was through its 1973 purchase of Disc Systems Corporation, a Santa Clara, California, start-up formed by former Memorex

engineers. Storage Technology acquired Disc Systems before it had shipped any drives, and in late 1974 it moved the operation to Colorado (*Electronic News* [December 2, 1974]).

8. By "based" I mean the center of a firm's disk drive operations, not necessarily its corporate headquarters. For example, the core of IBM's disk drive operations is in San Jose, California, not Armonk, New York. Burroughs's disk drive headquarters were near Los Angeles, not Detroit.

9. IBM switched to 14-inch-diameter disks in 1963, which became the de facto standard for almost twenty years.

10. Interview with Fujitsu manager, July 21, 1999.

11. For a visual illustration of the companies operating in Southeast Asia during each of these three periods, see McKendrick et al. (2000: 121–36).

12. As one example of the industry's increased emphasis on time-to-market, Micropolis improved its rate of new product introduction from two disk drives in 1988 to five in 1989, and six in 1990.

13. Note that the dotted line in the figure refers to U.S. production. At the time Seagate acquired Control Data's HDD operations, CDC's highest capacity drives were made in the United States. The steep slope of the dotted line between 1988 and 1989 reflects the fact that Seagate obtained much higher capacity products with the acquisition. The steep slope of the solid line between 1989 and 1990 reflects the rapid transfer of all volume production of CDC drives from the United States to Singapore.

14. Seagate quickly shut down Control Data's German assembly facility after its 1989 acquisition, as well as CDC's small Singapore HDD plant and its component operations in Portugal.

15. As Greve (1998: 968) summarizes: "Organizations in a strategic group occupy similar market positions, offer similar goods to similar customers, and may make similar choices about production technology and other organizational features."

16. Of the seventeen firms that went to Southeast Asia between 1982 and 1990, ten were headquartered in Silicon Valley.

# CHAPTER SEVEN

# Industry Creation and the New Geography of Innovation

*The Case of Flat Panel Displays*

THOMAS P. MURTHA

STEFANIE ANN LENWAY

JEFFREY A. HART

The growing knowledge-intensiveness of global economic activity demands new ways of thinking about industry, competition, and strategic management. This need presented itself to us dramatically in the research on the flat panel display (FPD) industry that we describe in this chapter. Our project started out as an investigation of an emerging high-technology industry that for many observers, including ourselves, represented a crisis of competitiveness for U.S. companies. The genesis of the thinking we present here occurred in our discovery that we were wrong. We had focused on the accumulation of physical plant and equipment, at the time concentrated in Japan, as the essential dynamic that defined new industry creation and its management challenges. In fact, the essential dynamics to be managed were global learning and knowledge creation processes that necessarily engaged an international community of companies.

Along with Japanese competitors, alliance partners, suppliers, and customers, U.S. companies with strong organizational capabilities in Japan played essential roles in commercializing the technology and creating the product application that sparked the FPD industry's high-volume takeoff. This technology is called thin-film-transistor liquid crystal display (TFT LCD, or TFT for short), and the product application was color displays for notebook computers. Color TFTs were first manufactured in a size, volume, and format suitable for use in notebook computers in the early 1990s. As the decade progressed, increasing workforce mobility, pervasive Internet use, and graphics-rich computer operating systems interacted to create explosive growth in demand for the color screens.

When a new technology commercializes first and draws significant capital investment in a particular country, as FPDs did in Japan, conventional wisdom assumes that local companies gain a potentially insurmountable lead over companies from elsewhere. But that did not hold true for TFTs and the flat panel display industry. At best, it represents a misleading assumption for strategy in new, knowledge-driven industries. The FPD industry emerged as a complex global network of relationships among companies and people. Each encompassed distinctive, complementary advantages and needs. Companies succeeded when their managers challenged assumptions traditionally used to formulate new industry strategies. Access to technology and market knowledge outweighed ownership and national location of manufacturing facilities as a determinant of business performance. Companies needed to reassess strategy processes that biased managers' thinking in favor of managing projects rather than people, building physical assets rather than creating knowledge assets, producing at home rather than learning abroad, and analyzing financial results rather than managing time.

During most of the twentieth century, a company on the brink of entering a new industry faced the moment of truth when management decided whether or not to commit funds to build a factory large enough to produce goods at minimum cost (Chandler 1962). Companies commercialized innovations by establishing manufacturing in their home countries. They projected their organizations outward to the rest of the world as market opportunities arose, and to seek minimum costs of capital, labor, and materials. Vertical and horizontal integration were prescribed internationalization modes to protect firm-specific knowledge from competitors and potential competitors by sharing it only within company boundaries. Similar reasoning motivated most international companies to center scientific leadership, research, and development at home.

As the high-volume FPD industry took off in the 1990s, many companies succeeded with strategies that seemed to invert these principles. Other companies tried to play by the rules and failed. When companies entering the FPD industry chose Japan over the United States to establish plants, they chose distance over proximity to the U.S. notebook suppliers that would become their biggest customers. Other countries besides Japan showed equal or greater promise as economic sources of materials. The companies invested before managers identified the high-volume product market opportunities that would bring the industry to critical mass. Some accepted relatively high costs of land, plant and equipment, labor and materials in order to locate at what appeared to be the geographic center of new industry developments. Many entered into codevelopment, production, and marketing alliances that required them to share vital, firm-specific knowledge, not only with suppliers and customers but also with powerful international competitors. These successful companies moved decisively to create knowledge stakes in a new display functionality that offered myriad prospects in future product markets. They mobilized knowledge assets from around the world while centering their businesses in Japan, where the new industry was approaching critical mass. Their technologies and manufacturing processes had reached advanced stages of development when high-volume, mass product markets emerged.

The factors underlying the industry's emergence seem emblematic, in retrospect, of the "dynamics propelling globalization" that Kenney identified in his introductory chapter. Leading producers established their fabs in Japan, relying on advanced transport and communications to meet globally dispersed customers' requirements for physical product as well as continually evolving FPD functionalities. The industry's early geographic concentration in Japan arose and was reinforced because of the demands of knowledge creation in circumstances of extremely rapid market and technology evolution.

Yet it is important to acknowledge that the globalization dynamics that seem so powerfully reflected in this industry's early history did not initially unfold in a self-evident or deterministic fashion. Managers made a variety of strategic choices, with performance implications for their firms that varied from bankruptcy to market leadership. Successful firms created and then leveraged the dynamics, though not always with foreknowledge of the more difficult long-term implications for their own operations as these dynamics gathered force and assumed lives of their own. Unrelenting cost pressures, for example, emerged at least in part from the founding firms' determined strategies to simultaneously advance the technology and at the same time introduce manufacturing economies. They were determined to create a mass market that could rapidly repay their enormous gambles on capital equipment. Geographic patterns of location emerged and were reinforced early in the industry's history because of firms' successful knowledge-creation strategies under conditions of rapid change. These patterns were recast when new firms in new countries bought existing knowledge to establish their own learning foundations for innovation. But not all senior managers of firms that tried to enter the industry saw or availed themselves of these cross-border learning opportunities. Some saw dangerous dependence rather than fruitful interdependence, limited their global ties, and as a consequence made enormous losses.

In this chapter, we explain how U.S. companies that succeeded in becoming leaders in the flat panel display industry adopted strategies that allowed managers and engineers to engage in critical knowledge-creation processes at the geographic center of the industry. Successful U.S. companies located the headquarters for their display businesses in Japan and leveraged their companies' global technology and market resources to build their presence in the industry. U.S. companies that failed adopted strategies that focused on domestic collaboration among FPD fabrication equipment and materials makers to create a new, U.S.-origin toolset for FPD production on U.S. soil. The U.S. government policies that encouraged these strategies evoke Duguid's distinction (in this volume) between "physiocratic" and "new economy" as a way of characterizing policy-makers' mindsets. U.S. policy-makers focused on trade in goods, while the industry's emergence was fundamentally driven by trade in knowledge. We focus in this chapter on the firms that successfully exploited this reality. Our book *Managing New Industry Creation* (Murtha, Lenway, and Hart 2001) offers a more complete FPD industry history, along with general frameworks for strategy derived from the top performers' experiences.

We argue here that U.S. companies needed to leverage organizational capabilities and physical locations in Japan in order to create the knowledge necessary to build globally competitive manufacturing facilities. After large-format TFT LCDs commercialized in the early 1990s, FPD manufacturing equipment and process technology evolved across multiple generations at a pace that, up to that time, had never been seen in high-technology industries. Managing transitions to new generations required engineers and equipment operators who could draw on their experience and understanding of previous generations to solve problems in bringing new manufacturing facilities on line. This reservoir of experience was critical to improving yields, which drove manufacturing costs down and helped to reduce prices to increase consumption. The pace and specific configuration of each generational shift emerged from intimate, first-hand interactions among people representing FPD manufacturers, equipment providers, and materials producers. Physical proximity played a critical role. The pace of generational shifts increased after IBM introduced its first portable computer with a color display, the ThinkPad, which triggered an explosion of demand for TFT LCDs. After the ThinkPad's introduction, TFT production also started up in Korea, where companies began their own knowledge creation processes after first acquiring and learning to use earlier generations of process technology and manufacturing equipment.

## The LCD's Beginnings

On May 28, 1968, at RCA's Rockefeller Center headquarters in New York City, company officials held a press conference to unveil a "very crude prototype" of a liquid crystal display. Many people present—both media and company representatives—hoped the new technology would soon replace the cathode ray tube (CRT) as the world's dominant image-engine and transfigure into the first flat TV. This tiny TV of the future was the first flat panel display presented to the general public. It used the new technology to show a black-and-white image of two moving lines.[1] RCA engineers demonstrated other LCD applications as well, including an electronic clock that was widely shown in print and on TV news programs around the world.

The demonstration culminated years of work at RCA's David Sarnoff Research Center. Liquid crystals were, at the time, a relatively obscure family of materials. Richard Williams had demonstrated at Sarnoff around 1960 that a liquid crystal substance in its transparent state turns opaque, and scatters (or reflects) light instead of transmitting it, when charged with an electric current (Johnstone 1999: 96). Starting in 1964, George Heilmeier led some of the first experiments that harnessed this property to create an image-capable display, fueling the research program that ultimately led to RCA's announcement. Sarnoff's engineers discovered liquid crystal material that retained its crystalline properties over a wide temperature range, and they used transparent electrodes and a polarizer to electrically control the liquid crystal's optical properties. They called their method "dynamic scattering." With the dynamic scattering breakthrough, commercial release of the first flat television entered the range of feasibility, the company asserted in response to journalists' inquiries.[2] But many technical problems remained to be resolved before flat TV could become a reality. Most serious among these, researchers needed to find cost-effective, manufacturable means to electronically address the complex mosaic of tiny picture elements, or pixels, that would be needed to display a well-defined, moving image.

Within a few years, however, RCA began to diversify away from consumer electronics. After RCA's visionary founder, David Sarnoff, died in 1971, CRT replacement fell off of the agenda for the corporate managers who succeeded him. In 1973, the company made a brief foray into LCD manufacturing for point-of-purchase displays and later watches. But within a few months of starting operations in Somerville, New Jersey, RCA sold the plant to Timex, the watch company (see Brinkley 1997: 51; Johnstone 1999: 35, 102–5; and Harrison 1973). RCA's 1975 annual report made no mention of its LCD program, which had disappeared some time the previous year.

In Japan, engineers at Sharp Corporation had watched news reports of the RCA press conference with interest. Sharp set out promptly to incorporate the new technology, complete with warts, into a commercial product: the hand-held calculator. The company, then known as Hayakawa Electric, had pioneered the business in 1964 with the Sharp Compet, the first fully electronic calculator to be manufactured at commercial scale.[3]

Sharp engineers initially asked RCA to manufacture LCDs for their calculator. RCA's management decided that the technology was not sufficiently mature to manufacture. Instead, RCA licensed its dynamic scattering LCD technology to Sharp in 1970. In April 1973, Sharp introduced the EL-805, the first calculator with an LCD display. The LCD calculator was followed within a few months by the first LCD watch, introduced by Seiko.

Both Sharp and Seiko began early to seek outside customers for their displays. The companies found that engagement with outside customers not only brought in revenue but also diversified and invigorated their R&D efforts. The companies continued to upgrade their FPD technology to meet their own future product needs and to meet customers' needs and specifications. Apple Computer, in particular, acted as an early, influential Sharp customer for its pioneering notebook and personal digital assistant. Its graphical user interface operating system preceded Microsoft Windows by a number of years. The visual demands of Apple's operating system added great impetus to FPD producers' initial quests for color, high resolution, size, and smooth video motion.

As the industry's potential grew increasingly evident from the middle 1980s up until the notebook computer's takeoff in the early 1990s, joint efforts among manufacturers, equipment suppliers, and materials manufacturers were needed to enable the transition to high-volume production of the largest, most advanced displays. Sharp was again involved, along with Toshiba and IBM as FPD producers, and Applied Materials and Corning in equipment and materials. Several of these companies competed with each other in related fields. Cooperative relationships with downstream system integrators such as Apple Computer and Compaq played a role, even as some FPD producers began to compete with them for notebook market share. Without these cooperative relationships, the high-volume FPD industry would have emerged eventually, but not as rapidly as it did.

## IBM Japan Wins a Mandate

In the mid-1980s, IBM assembled a number of task forces to examine alternative FPD technologies and their prospects for replacing the CRT. IBM had for many years researched and manufactured large, flat, black and white Plasma Display Panels (PDPs) for industrial use (primarily financial markets), and sourced large quantities of CRTs to incorporate in its popular line of computer monitors. The task forces identified color reproduction as a critical display characteristic for users, and TFT LCDs as the technology with the most promising future. The cost of developing color PDPs appeared prohibitive at the time, although the technology has since surmounted that obstacle to gain status as a leading contender for dominance in large, flat home televisions (see Murtha, Lenway, and Hart 2001: 46–48, 71–77).

IBM senior managers decided to locate a new TFT LCD development project in Japan with IBM Japan in the leadership role. The project was established as an alliance with Toshiba. Both companies contributed capital, people, and facilities for the project, which set a goal to develop the largest TFT LCD color prototype possible, as quickly as possible. The researchers on the project team received support from experienced LCD researchers at IBM's Thomas Watson Laboratories in Yorktown Heights, New York, and Toshiba's corporate R&D staffs. The companies agreed to each host the project for one year in their respective facilities in Japan, starting at Toshiba, where a rudimentary R&D line was to be erected as soon as possible. At the end of the project, each company would be free to independently pursue further research or manufacturing plans. The contract was officially signed and work began on August 1, 1986. Sharp, which was ramping up high-volume production of a 3-inch color TFT display at the time, also decided to vault ahead to something much larger.

By summer 1988, both Sharp and IBM/Toshiba had developed TFT LCD prototypes measuring around 14 inches diagonally, demonstrating a potential for flat video reproduction that had seemed only remotely conceivable in the time immediately following RCA's LCD announcement twenty years earlier.[4] Neither company paused for long to debate the question of which had arrived first at the starting line in the race to commercialize large-format TFTs. Both had arrived at a turning point that offered the sobering opportunity to place far greater resources at risk building high-volume facilities and proving a high-volume production process. Managers and engineers in all three companies knew that fashioning large prototypes individually represented R&D achievements, but building them in quantity represented a serious manufacturing challenge.

The 14-inch color TFT LCD prototype developed by the IBM/Toshiba team was presented to IBM's top management in 1988 at a meeting in Japan. Web Howard, a senior IBM physicist, made the case to IBM's top management that the portable personal computer market would grow sufficiently large to warrant high-volume TFT LCD production. He predicted that users would be willing to pay up to five times more for a TFT LCD than a CRT monitor because "they provided a new platform for taking work anywhere" (Howard 1996).

## Managing Intra-industry Interdependence

According to a respected former industry analyst in Japan, "an atmosphere of euphoria" prevailed as prospective TFT LCD manufacturers faced production investment decisions in 1989. Other companies besides Sharp, IBM, and Toshiba—most notably NEC—had pursued TFT research for large-format color TFT LCD displays for many years. The 14-inch prototypes suddenly raised the stakes. The announcements altered perceptions of what could be achieved in the short term and thereby changed assessments of the pace at which commercialization of large-format TFTs would proceed. Published estimates of industry potential mushroomed to $10 billion for 1995 and $40 billion in 2000.[5] FPD industry possibilities received more mass media attention than RCA's original 1968 LCD announcement. TFT production planning appears to have moved from the back burner to the fast track in a number of firms.

Nearly one year after the IBM/Toshiba prototype announcement, on August 30, 1989, the two companies announced their agreement to form a manufacturing alliance, Display Technologies, Inc. (DTI). The alliance was structured as a 50–50 percent joint venture between Toshiba and IBM Japan. The partners initially capitalized DTI at about $140 million,[6] earmarking $105 million for a high-volume TFT LCD fabrication facility. DTI's headquarters and first fab would be located in Himeji City, next to one of Toshiba's manufacturing facilities. DTI officially started up on November 1, 1989. Sharp management also decided sometime between 1988 and 1989 to go ahead with large-format color TFT manufacturing. Both companies announced plans to initiate production on Generation 1 lines in fall 1991.

At Toshiba and Sharp, managers anticipated that the new large-format color TFT LCDs would sell at high volume only if the market was globalized at the instant of its creation. Sharp prospected for global customers such as the U.S. computer makers Apple and Compaq. Toshiba's managers did the same, but also concluded that collaboration with IBM would help globalize the Japanese company's insular management culture.[7] Tsuyoshi Kawanishi, a senior Toshiba executive who was instrumental in forming the DTI alliance, anticipated that the United States would play a big role in the market for final goods in any long-term TFT LCD scenario. His experience with the semiconductor trade wars of the mid-1980s alerted him to the possibility that similar tensions could arise with the U.S. government over concentration of FPD manufacturing in Japan. He hoped that establishing TFT manufacturing as a joint venture with a U.S. company would help defuse the impact on the business of any such development.[8]

Creating a high-volume manufacturing process would also require close partnerships with equipment and materials suppliers who could contribute specialized expertise, technologies, and research muscle. Many potential suppliers, such as Canon, Nikon, Toray, and Anelva, were Japanese, and they enjoyed long-established relationships with the companies considering TFT manufacturing. Several U.S. electronics equipment and materials suppliers with operations in Japan were considering the opportunities that mass production of large TFTs might offer. Toshiba approached Applied Materials to design and manufacture chemical vapor deposition (CVD) equipment, although the companies did not reach agreement in time to equip the first generation of TFT LCD fabrication facilities. Corning had played an indispensable role in TFT development from the beginning, having followed up on unanticipated small orders for its specialty glasses from large Japanese corporate electronics laboratories in the early 1980s. By the middle of the decade, it was already well established as the leader in manufacturing specialty glass for smaller TFTs.

In September 1989 the business press in Japan heralded optimistic projections for large format TFT LCD production. Beginning in April 1991, Toshiba and IBM partners expected DTI to begin a ramp-up that would quickly bring production to a rate sufficient to produce 200,000 TFT LCDs a year, or roughly 16,000 displays per month, with an increase to 1,000,000 displays per year in 1994.[9] In early October 1989, Sharp announced a less ambitious target of 3,300 to 5,500 units per month for its planned autumn 1991 production startup.[10] Several months later, NEC managers announced that it would also jump into the market in 1990. In the months prior to the 1991 production startups, the consensus view among the pioneering manufacturers held that by 1995, large TFT LCD screens would reach price levels attractive in the mass market, less than $500.[11]

## Yield Wars

On May 15, 1991, DTI announced that production had started up earlier in the month, with the first TFT LCDs scheduled for shipment within a week or two.[12] But the ramp-up did not go smoothly. DTI engineering director, Hidenori Akiyoshi commented, "We actually started from nothing. Nobody, us included, had any experience with large-format TFT LCD production. Although a test production run had been carried out by Toshiba's laboratory, a lot of unexpected problems were waiting as we ramped up. When we started production, the overall line yield was far below 10 percent, primarily due to equipment problems" (West and Bowen 1998: 6).

Corning had anticipated the movement toward large-format TFT LCD production with its early 1988 decision to build fusion glass production facilities in Shizuoka. Just before the first high-volume plants ramped up in Japan, Corning established its glass substrate business as Corning K.K., a distinct, global business unit with authority and accountability centered in Japan, headed by President Satoshi Furuyama. The organizational processes that led to these decisions, which anticipated TFT demand by more than three years, proved fateful for Corning's market position. When the new Sharp and DTI facilities initiated production in 1991, they required a sufficient supply of substrates to operate at full capacity, despite low yields. Even if most production ended up as waste, the rate of process learning to increase yields varied directly with throughput. As IBM's Bob Wisnieff said, "It takes an awful lot of glass flowing through a line, really just acting as a pipe cleaner."[13]

In September 1991 yields at DTI reportedly hovered around 8 percent.[14] In other words, fewer than one in ten displays coming off the new line could actually be sold. Other companies were experiencing similar frustrations. By the March 31, 1992, conclusion of Japan's 1991 fiscal year, DTI had shipped a total of 30,000 displays, or about 4,200 per month. But as Sakae Arai, senior manager of LCD marketing at Toshiba said, finding working units to ship "was like picking through the garbage."[15] At costs running $2,000 to $3,000 per working display, the manufacturers were shipping money out the doors.

The yield problems emerged because the earliest high-volume manufacturing equipment and process generated particle contamination at a rate far greater than anyone had anticipated. The process developers had refined the methods and equipment for creating thin film transistors—particularly large-area chemical vapor deposition (CVD)—from amorphous silicon technology perfected for solar energy panels.[16] Solar energy panel performance is indifferent to particles introduced in the manufacturing process. Not so with TFT LCDs, where a single microscopic particle can cause pinhole dropouts or color variations on the final product. Improved CVD equipment emerged as one of the most important challenges among many in the struggle to improve yields.[17]

After much persuasion, Toshiba and Sharp convinced Applied Materials of Santa Clara, California, to leverage its semiconductor equipment-making experience to develop a CVD tool for second-generation TFT LCD fabs. The company formed a new unit, called Applied Display Technologies (ADT), which developed the new tool. After forming an alliance with Komatsu, Ltd., the renamed AKT established its worldwide headquarters in Kobe, Japan, with Applied Materials Japan chairman Tetsuo Iwasaki as president. The company delivered its first product, the AKT-1600, in mid-1994. The new tool's contribution to yield enhancement helped span a productivity gap that impaired the TFT LCD's promise as the first FPD technology to challenge the CRT for display market dominance. It rapidly established AKT as the leading force in CVD. Since reverting to 100 percent Applied Materials control in 1998, AKT has retained this leadership as well as its U.S. manufacturing base.

The problems, however, could not be attributed to any one piece of equipment. DTI's Akiyoshi explained that yields suffered from electrostatic charge buildup, contaminants introduced in CVD operations and on panel carriers, glass panels chipping or cracking, inferior seals in panel assembly, and out-of-spec materials.[18] "Unless we change the current production concept," com-

TABLE 7.1

*Main Commercial Generations of Color TFT LCD Substrates*

| Generation | Typical substrate size | Optimized for display size (qty.) | Earliest adoption: startup dates, adopters |
|---|---|---|---|
| 0 | 270 x 200 mm | 8.4-inch (2) | 1987 Sharp |
| 1 | 300 x 350 mm | 9.4-inch (2) | 3rd Quarter, 1990 NEC |
| | 300 x 400 mm | 10.4-inch (2) | 2nd Quarter, 1991 DTI |
| | 320 x 400 mm | 8.4-inch (4) | 3rd Quarter, 1991 Sharp |
| 2 | 360 x 465 mm | 9.5-inch (4) | 2nd Quarter, 1994 Sharp |
| 2a | 360 x 465 mm | 10.4-inch (4) | 2nd Quarter, 1994 DTI |
| 2.5 | 400 x 500 mm | 11.3-inch (4) | 3rd Quarter, 1995 Sharp |
| 3 | 550 x 650 mm | 12.1-inch (6) | 3rd and 4th Quarters, 1995 Sharp, DTI |
| 3.25 | 600 x 720 mm | 13.3-inch (6) | 1st Quarter, 1998 Samsung |
| 3.5 | 650 x 830 mm | 17.0-inch (4) | 3rd Quarter, 1997 Hitachi |
| | | 15.0-inch (6) | 3rd Quarter 2000 Samsung |
| 3.7 | 730 x 920 mm | 14.1-inch (9) | |

*Sources:* Business press and interview materials.

mented Kouichi Suzuki, general manager of Toshiba's LCD division, "we won't be able to cut prices" to achieve mass-market penetration.[19]

Substrate size increases contributed to enhanced productivity, but created a new set of challenges as companies needed to qualify and ramp up new generations of manufacturing equipment for each new size. The evolution from generation to generation unfolded at an unprecedented pace. AKT top management has suggested that the rate of change in FPD technology between 1990 and 2000 exceeded the rate of change in semiconductor technology from the mid-1970s to 2000 by a factor of eighteen, measured according to substrate area (Law 2000). Another way of looking at expanding substrate sizes (see Table 7.1) suggests that TFT LCD makers endured at least five generational changes in half the time the semiconductor industry endured the same number of transitions.[20]

The Generation 1 fabs had cost around $150 million in plant and equipment. Within months, legend had it, mountains of broken glass from unacceptable products piled up behind the fabs of the pioneering manufacturers, who were also piling up materials costs for process creation and refinement that closely approximated their investments in capital equipment. Discussions with equipment and materials manufacturers about a next generation of high-volume process technology started even before the Generation 1 fabs went on line. Success in the second generation of production equipment, however, would depend on the companies' abilities to create and retain knowledge in waking up the first.

Increasing yield figures represented the most visible measure of knowledge creation and accumulation. In effect, each company's fab acted as a laboratory, seeking successful outcomes to experiments that would shape the next and subsequent generations of production technology. DTI president Toru Shima described the problem: "In order to take advantage of the best materials and equipment, we need first to deal with internal barriers to high yields."[21]

Invested in a fixed stock of capital equipment, managers in each company soon acknowledged that successful yield management would depend more than anything else on the people involved. Companies could not address this dependence solely by promoting learning, as a company might do, for example, by improving operator training. Training assumes an existing body of knowledge. The process was unsettled, and not working very well in any case. The scientists, engineers, and operators were identifying problems and inventing critical process refinements in real time, as they did their work. The companies faced a challenge in finding ways to enhance these individualized and team-based knowledge creation processes. They also needed to find ways to generalize the resulting knowledge, diffuse it within their organizations, and channel it into creating the next generation.

NEC's engineers spent months working in the fab with counterparts from equipment and materials manufacturers, drawing comparisons that might help explain why any one machine should achieve different yields from another of the same type. Methodologies were invented to study operators' movements, in hope of identifying specific behaviors that might contribute to performance differences among different individuals using the same machine. To facilitate this monitoring, operators attached bar codes to each other, each piece of glass, and each machine, and submitted one and all to computer monitoring. Draconian as these measures may have appeared at the time, the operators discovered surprising sources of particle pollution in otherwise mundane behavior. Shigehiko Satoh, engineering manager at NEC's LCD fab in Izumi, expressed his hope to a touring visitor that cleanroom operators would refrain from sitting down, as doing so would release a cloud of invisible particles sufficient to destroy thousands of dollars worth of products.[22] By late fall of 1991, as other companies struggled to push yields to 25 percent, NEC claimed industry leadership by announcing that it had achieved 50 percent. Some months later in mid-April 1992, DTI had reportedly reached yields of about 40 percent, while NEC claimed yields well above 50 percent, on the way to 80 percent.

*The Face of a New Machine*

In November 1992, IBM Personal Computer Company (PCC) introduced a product line that would transform skeptics' views of the company's TFT program from high-risk gamble to prescient vision. Model 700C, the first in a long line of ThinkPad notebook computers, attracted immediate attention not only for its computing functionality but also as a marvel of industrial design. The DTI 10.4-inch color TFT LCD, the largest, brightest ever available, transformed 700C owners into targets of their coworkers' envy. The unit also incorporated a small trackpoint embedded within the center of its full-size keyboard to perform cursor functions. The 700c's computing capabilities were built around an Intel 80486 processor and 120 Mb hard drive. The 10.4-inch display offered up to 50 percent more screen space than other color TFT LCDs on the market.[23]

The product's combination of performance and design values attracted attention, but the price triggered shock waves. The 700c listed at $4,350. Toshiba reacted by replacing its $5,499 T4400SXC with the $3,999 T4400C, also a 486 notebook, but with a 9.5-inch display.[24] Prices on 80386-based notebooks tumbled. TFT LCDs had found an application that was expected to grow at 70 percent per year, and at the time, 10.4-inch displays appeared likely to establish themselves as a dominant design. Due to ongoing yield problems at DTI, IBM would need to buy quite a few of them from its competitors.

This proved difficult. By the end of 1992, IBM's ThinkPad success had triggered display shortages that rippled across all notebook suppliers. IBM struggled against a two-month backlog.[25] In early 1993, Microsoft introduced Windows 3.1, which displayed 256 colors. This added fuel to the color display fire, particularly for IBM-compatible computers, which used the Microsoft operating system. IBM PCC tried to translate its notebook market smash hit into FPD buying power, offering to source 10.4-inch displays from Sharp. Sharp's facilities were optimized to fabricate four 8.4-inch displays per 320 by 400 mm substrate. The engineers declared that the Gen 1 line had achieved yields of 60 percent, with monthly output of 90,000 displays. Sharp was offering these to high-volume customers for between $800 and $900.[26] If the company switched to 10.4-inch displays, throughput would fall to two units per substrate, resulting in wasted materials, reduced productivity, and increased costs.

## Size Wars

In the wake of the ThinkPad introduction, Sharp, DTI, and NEC revived investment plans that had languished as yield improvements started to expand output more rapidly than demand could absorb. NEC hoped to quadruple production from 24,000 to 96,000 displays per month by the end of 1993 with a Generation 2 line. In July 1993, DTI's parents announced that they would invest 30 billion yen, or $280 million, to triple capacity with a Gen 2 line at Himeji. DTI slated the new line to start up in the summer of 1994. DTI expected the TFT LCD market to continue the 70 percent yearly growth that began in 1992 through 1995.[27] Consistent with this forecast, Sharp also planned two Gen 2 lines to start up in mid-1994 to manufacture 10.4-inch TFTs.

After the ThinkPad popularized the high-end notebook computer, screen size stepped to the forefront of product features as a source of brand differentiation. This surprised many marketers. In the early 1990s, Sharp engineers had focused on minimizing power consumption to extend battery life. Sharp stuck with 8.4-inch displays, in part, because the smaller size consumed dramatically less power than a 10.4-inch display. Weight had also been an issue for most companies. NEC and Hitachi officials believed that customers ranked price above size.

IBM was perhaps the first notebook supplier to explore product attribute preferences with focus groups of users. Subsystem Technologies and Applications Lab director Steven Depp articulated the findings at a University of Michigan College of Engineering industry forum in November 1994. "You ask people what they like in our ThinkPad notebook, and one thing they like is the screen. . . . [W]hat you carry around for your mobile computer is basically the display." Users focused on brightness, image quality, and size. In the wake of these studies, IBM and Toshiba decided to invest in Gen 3 equipment for a DTI fab that would manufacture 12.1-inch displays. This size appeared especially promising because it offered a viewable area equivalent to that of a 14-inch CRT. As 10.4-inch prices continued to slide during the second half of 1995, Sharp and DTI people worked to bring up Generation 3 lines. The Sharp teams faced the added challenge of bringing up an intermediate generation (referred to as 2.5) based on stretching Generation 2 equipment to its absolute limits in substrate-size handling. Generation 3 lines carried automation, already an added feature of Generation 2, to a level of pervasive robotization. The substrates were too large for an operator to handle. Full cassettes used to transport substrates between manufacturing stages weighed about 80 pounds.

Because fewer humans were needed to operate Generation 3 lines, Sharp and DTI management expected the new fabs to achieve high yields rapidly. This proved true for DTI, but not for Sharp. At DTI, experienced engineers from the Gen 1 and Gen 2 lines transferred from Himeji to the new Yasu location to bring the new line up. The reduced requirements for human intervention allowed DTI to redeploy its knowledge in this way without diminishing yields on the existing lines. In fact, DTI had maintained a stable headcount since 1994.[28] At Sharp the effort to bring up two lines at once, along with a new array process to increase the displays' aperture ratio, appeared to have too thinly spread its experienced engineers and operators. By May 1996, Sharp had conceded publicly that the Gen 3 line had proven itself a "major technical challenge," and that progress was slow. DTI's Gen 3 line was by then operating at full yields,[29] having started up sometime in the fourth quarter of 1995.

In April 1996, Sharp, Fujitsu, and Samsung announced that they would phase out 10.4-inch TFT LCDs as a result of plunging prices, after the size hit a low of $300 per unit in March. Yet 12.1-inch displays were in short supply.[30] Many Gen 2 lines were switched to manufacturing two-up 12.1-inch displays. Merchants were getting spot prices of $950 to $1,450 for 12.1-inch displays, and offering volume prices of $850 per unit to long-term customers. They could generate more revenues by producing two larger displays per substrate than four smaller ones.

## Efforts to Establish Production in the United States

While the first high-volume, large-format TFT fabs were under construction in Japan, industry attention in the United States turned to the political arena rather than the factory floor. On July 17, 1990, the Advanced Display Manufacturers of America (ADMA) filed an antidumping petition[31] with the U.S. Department of Commerce and the U.S. International Trade Commission (ITC). Established earlier in the year, ADMA's founding members included Optical Imaging Systems (OIS), Planar, Plasmaco, Photonics Technologies, Magnascreen, Cherry Corporation, and Electroplasma. All of the founding companies had received R&D contracts from the U.S. Defense Department's Defense Advanced Research Project Agency (DARPA). None had reached a decision to establish high-volume, large-format FPD production facilities.

The petition charged thirteen Japanese companies, including Sharp, Toshiba, Hosiden, and Hitachi, with predatory pricing of FPDs. The ITC authorized an investigation of the Japanese companies' production costs. Taking into account low production yields, the investigators concluded, fair market value for some of the companies' products exceeded the FPD prices on offer in the U.S. market (Hart 1993). Steep antidumping duties were authorized for several Japanese companies' TFT LCDs on August 15, 1991, at just about the same time Sharp and DTI were bringing up their first Generation 1 lines. But in November 1992, OIS, which had been recently purchased by Guardian Industries and was the only U.S. domestic TFT LCD producer, requested that the duties be removed. On June 21, 1993, the U.S. Department of Commerce complied.

Despite its apparently innocuous conclusion, the antidumping petition permanently affected the course of FPD industry development within the U.S. Notebook producers, faced with the prospect of paying tariff-laden prices for the most advanced displays, immediately moved their assembly operations offshore. U.S. customs officials had ruled that the duties could not be levied on screens already incorporated into assembled goods. The duties also placed an artificial price floor under TFT LCDs at a time when the plants in Japan were struggling to move enough panels to drive production learning processes. Companies ramping up new fabs in Japan found they could charge close to the tariff-burdened price for displays selling there and to notebook assemblers producing in third markets. "This was an unexpected windfall," a respected former FPD market analyst later suggested. "The TFT manufacturers were able to put together quite a war chest, which allowed them to expand capacity more rapidly than expected."[32]

The petition also validated a bias in many U.S. companies toward framing the industry knowledge race in terms of international rivalry among countries rather than global competition among firms. Many continued to look to government for the resources to compete. The widespread impression among U.S. industry participants held that the government needed to step up its involvement in the industry to counter Japanese government investments. In fact, Japanese government investments were minimal,[33] having directed companies' resources to a technological dead end that was subsequently abandoned.[34] The U.S. Public Television documentary series *Frontline* offered a one-sided assessment of the antidumping case and its aftermath, asserting that Japanese government support had played an important role in establishing the industry in Japan.[35] One defense industry journal reported with expansive inaccuracy in May 1993 that "the Japanese cornered LCD manufacturing capability by government investment of almost $4 billion."[36] None of these reports reflected first-hand experience of industry circumstances in Japan. But in retrospect, they evoke the atmosphere of national urgency in which AT&T, Xerox, Standish, OIS, and the members of the ADMA entered negotiations with DARPA in 1993 to jointly fund an R&D consortium to help jump-start the industry in the United States.[37]

The discussions concluded with the establishment of the U.S. Display Consortium (USDC) on July 20, 1993, as a nonprofit, public/private consortium with a primary mission of supporting the development of an FPD manufacturing infrastructure in the United States.[38] During its first six years of existence, the organization consisted of FPD producers, users, and equipment and materials suppliers with at least 50 percent U.S. ownership. The group based its structure on that of SEMATECH, another public/private consortium formed by DARPA and U.S. semiconductor producers and equipment makers in August 1987. According to one of several press releases issued to announce the consortium, however, important differences existed between the two programs. Unlike SEMATECH, the USDC would not establish an R&D and pilot manufacturing facility in which to test new equipment and materials.[39] This approach had not worked well for SEMATECH, because semiconductor manufacturers that were engaged in their own equipment development programs were reluctant to share a common factory floor (Young 1994). USDC development programs called for member manufacturers to test new equipment and materials in their own commercial fabs.

The absence from the membership rolls of high-volume manufacturers who could fulfill this role,[40] however, undermined the USDC's mission to "build the U.S. infrastructure required to support a world-class, U.S.-based manufacturing capability." As the centerpiece of its programs, the consortium identified U.S. industry development needs and invited proposals from members for projects to meet these objectives. Development teams consisted of equipment and materials suppliers working with an FPD producer that would serve as project coordinator and beta site. The USDC provided grants to defray project costs out of its DARPA funding, which the winning bidders matched at equal or greater value.[41] But the USDC membership framework did not provide members with development partners who could qualify and integrate their equipment and materials innovations in the global, high-volume manufacturing context. No high-volume TFT LCD manufacturers existed on U.S. soil. Even if one had existed under foreign ownership, USDC practice would have proscribed contracting with it.[42]

The issues that interposed between many U.S. equipment and materials manufacturers and high-volume producer/development partners reflected managerial mindsets as well as consortium policy and practice. Industry officials with influence over the consortium's project selection process did not believe that interdependence among equipment, materials, operators, and R&D scientists differed in any meaningful way between low- and high-volume production lines. Some did not regard the matter of line integration as important at all in designing new equipment, asserting that new pieces of equipment could, in principle, be qualified for high-volume production with data generated by "running them by themselves for a few days in a room."[43]

But the question was not one of principle, but rather one of practice. In practice, Generation 1 high-volume production lines were already running at high yields by the time the USDC's programs were established, and their operations had for some time been contributing vital knowledge to the design of Generation 2. Competing with existing equipment and materials makers would require companies to demonstrate a capability to integrate into existing production line systems, while making a clear contribution to both product features and yield enhancement. Participants in USDC development programs might have greatly benefited from opportunities to integrate new tools and materials into lines that incorporated process solutions reflecting the international state of the art. This would have required beta-siting in a production context with equipment and materials of diverse international origins.

U.S.-based producers, however, gave priority to U.S.-origin equipment when they established their fabs. At OIS, executives apologized for the few Japanese-origin tools on the production line.[44] Executives at Hyundai's ImageQuest affiliate in Fremont, California, expressed pride in creating a production line and process using equipment originating almost entirely in the United States. "We're more American than the USDC," president Scott Holmberg commented during a fab tour, noting as well that USDC ownership rules at the time precluded ImageQuest from membership.[45] USDC members wishing to qualify their project outcomes in a state-of-the-art production context needed their own international contacts and resources to do so. Photon Dynamics, whose project ranks as the USDC's most significant global success, was already working closely with Japanese and Korean customers as well as investors, when it accepted the USDC's first contract for a TFT LCD visual inspection system.[46] Few other members enjoyed similar advantages.

## The FPD Industry Jumps to Korea

As demand for FPDs took off in the early 1990s, managers in the large, diversified Korean companies known as *chaebol* identified the FPD industry as an opportunity to leverage their existing semiconductor manufacturing capabilities. They also perceived a need to insulate their notebook computer businesses from TFT LCD supply shortages. Although Korean government guidance suggested an alliance to establish TFT production in Korea, management at Samsung, LG, and Hyundai chose to enter the industry independently and compete with each other. Distinctive approaches to international collaboration provided sources of competitive advantage for all three entrants, and helped two of them—Samsung and LG—win the two leading global market share positions by 2000. These independent international relationships took three forms: technical cooperation, strategic alliances, and long term contracts. Some relationships contained elements of all three.

*Technical cooperation* included equipment and materials supplier relationships, customer relationships, and R&D partnerships, including licensing. Technical cooperation relationships helped companies establish a knowledge base in current generation production technology, move rapidly into production, and create a foundation for continuous learning in ramping up successive new generation facilities. The Korean companies' positions as close followers to companies that had established high-volume production in Japan offered both advantages and challenges. Unlike U.S. companies that started up in the same time frame, they purchased equipment, process recipes, and extensive consulting services from the successful producers, equipment manufacturers, and materials makers. As a consequence, at Samsung and LG, Generation 2 installations came on-line and reached commercial yields relatively quickly—but not quickly enough to take advantage of the profits available to first movers.

Samsung and LG gained critical knowledge advantages by ramping up their Gen 2 lines, however, even in the face of price declines. Already committed to Generation 3 investments in the range of $600 to $800 million, both companies needed to leverage the knowledge gains from Generation 2, particularly experienced operators, to move rapidly forward. Samsung entered Generation 3 in late 1996, reaching commercial yields in early 1997, hot on the heels of DTI and Sharp. LG followed with its Generation 3 line in the second half of the year, but running a slightly larger substrate that offered cost economies while optimized for slightly larger displays.

Technical cooperation relationships as well as *equity-based strategic alliances* also helped the companies to cut costs in the face of continuous price declines, and to differentiate their products. Samsung's alliance with Corning, Samsung-Corning Precision Glass Co., placed it alongside the leading substrate supplier in the forefront of glass innovation. Samsung-Corning opened its first fusion glass plant in Korea in 1995.[47] The relationship contributed to increased efficiency and helped Samsung approach generational transitions with confidence and foresight. In 1995, Samsung entered into a cross-licensing agreement with the Japanese firm Fujitsu, a fellow late TFT LCD entrant. Fujitsu provided its wide viewing–angle technology in exchange for Samsung's high-aperture ratio, brightness-enhancing technology.[48]

LG management regarded technical cooperation as an even more central element in strategy, in part as a means of compensating for the company's size difference with Samsung and Hyundai. "Our philosophy is not to try to do everything for ourselves," said Choon-Rae Lee, managing director of LG's LCD Division. "We will work with anyone who can add a cost or differentiation advantage."[49] Management also set a goal to excel in particle control and yield enhancement. At least two technical cooperation agreements significantly contributed. In 1994, LG entered a $30 million joint venture with Alps Electric, a

Japanese components firm, to develop ultraclean manufacturing technology at Alps Central Laboratory in Japan. LG implemented the technology for the first time on its Generation 3 line at Kumi.[50] Its work with Photon Dynamics on TFT array test equipment proved crucial to meeting LG's zero-defect objective,[51] and helped the company gain a five-year, $1 billion contract to supply 12.1-inch displays to Compaq, despite having only one year of volume production experience.[52]

The Korean entrants set strategic objectives to profitably seize both differentiation and cost leadership advantages by establishing primacy or at least close followership in the transitions to Gen 3, and subsequently Gen 3-plus high-volume production technology. They also pushed process technology forward through other productivity enhancements, including increased array testing, inspection, and cleanroom particle control.[53] Running state-of-the-art Gen 1 and Gen 2 lines at pilot quantities, the companies began to accumulate experience to selectively enter equipment and materials manufacturing as well as high-volume Generation 3 production. Samsung, for example, achieved commercial yields on its first high-volume line, a Generation 2, in July 1995,[54] at approximately the same time as Sharp and DTI were starting up their Gen 3 lines. The company started up the industry's next Gen 3 line in October 1996,[55] and it broke ground for a Gen 3-plus line to handle 600 by 720 mm substrates in January 1997.[56] During the same period, the company developed independent materials and equipment capabilities in several components including glass substrates in its Samsung-Corning joint venture.

*Long term contracts* as well as equity-based alliances with customers played an important role in sustaining continuity. Only Hyundai delayed ramping up its Generation 2 line, which it had installed by the end of 1995, hoping for stabilization in 10.4-inch prices.[57] Technical cooperation tied to a long-term sales agreement with Toshiba helped the company to overcome subsequent delays in achieving commercial yields,[58] and to reduce further delays in moving to Generation 3. Hyundai's transition to Generation 3-plus, like that of all of the Korean producers, was complicated by external events of global significance.

Financial crisis gripped Asia in the late 1990s, placing the Korean TFT LCD producers' ambitious expansion plans at the mercy of an investment capital crunch. Long-term contracts assumed increasingly vital roles in helping to continue next generation investments, while at the same time ensuring notebook computer companies of an increasing supply of the most advanced display components to sustain their growing businesses. In November 1999, Hyundai concluded contracts with four notebook manufacturers—including IBM, Compaq, and Gateway—for five years' sales of $8 billion.[59] In March 2000, Hyundai announced that it hoped to start up a next generation fab at Ichon, raising the company's planned production capacity to 1.5 million TFT LCDs annually.[60]

In July 1999, Apple Computer revealed plans to invest $100 million in Samsung in order to speed the construction of new production capacity for TFT LCDs.[61] In October 1999, Samsung signed a five-year contract worth $8.5 billion to supply TFT LCD displays to Dell Computer Corporation.[62] Having doubled capacity in 1999, Samsung was on track to open the world's first fab to utilize 730 by 930 mm substrates.[63] Industry sources differed on what number to designate the new generation. One called it "Generation 3.7" (see Law 2000), others 3.5-plus. Samsung preferred "Generation 4." Many industry participants still waited for a fabled one-meter-square substrate to bear that designation.

Management decisions to expand production and continue TFT LCD generational progressions in the face of the Asian financial crisis surprised industry observers. But these decisions thrust Samsung and LG well ahead of more cautious producers in Japan as well as the United States, and created two very profitable businesses.

LG's TFT LCD business was so profitable, in fact, that management struck a defiant pose when government's crisis plans for restructuring Korean industry demanded the combination of LG Semiconductor with Hyundai's semiconductor business. Unhappy about any such plan, management made it clear that the LCD Division's assets, with a book value of about $1 billion, were not on the table.[64]

International markets ratified management's decision with the May 1999 announcement that Royal Philips Electronics of the Netherlands would acquire 50 percent of LG's LCD unit in exchange for an investment of $1.6 billion in the joint venture. LG.Philips LCD was established in July 1999, and officially began operations in September 1999.[65]

In 1999, Samsung's global FPD market share, ranked first, stood at 18.8 percent. LG.Philips's share, ranked second, stood at 16.2 percent. Korean companies, staffed by many U.S.-educated engineers and managers, had broken Japan-based sources' short-lived near monopoly over high-volume, large-format color TFT LCD production. Furthermore, the Korean companies did it with the cooperation of equipment makers, materials producers, and TFT LCD producers centered in Japan. Philips established a European presence in high volume even more rapidly, seizing opportunities for TFT LCD production partnership that every U.S. company except IBM had neglected for years.

## Conclusion: Cluster Busting

Many managers and public policy makers believe that when a scale-intensive high-tech industry concentrates in one country, companies from other countries get easily locked out. Debates about how countries should respond to high-tech industry concentration in other countries have centered on either building countervailing industry concentrations (known as clusters) at home or establishing facilities within the foreign cluster itself. Public policy-makers and business strategists have turned for guidance to economic geography, which offers a research tradition that explains why certain industries develop great centers of creativity and productivity in particular world regions but not others (e.g., Porter 1990, 1998). Attention has focused on the importance of country- or region-specific management or innovation systems (see Kogut, this volume), path-dependent historical developments, institutions such as great universities and national research laboratories, and the importance of knowledge spillovers that occur among companies through common suppliers, consultants, customers, job changers, and the social and professional networks that emerge as part of the local industry community.

The FPD experience demonstrated how easily these ideas can be misappropriated as guides to corporate strategy and public policy, particularly in the early days of a new high-technology industry. Much U.S. thinking about the FPD industry has foundered on the notion that the vitality of the FPD industry in Japan somehow arose when factors intrinsic to Japan combined (illegitimately!) with a U.S. invention. The proposed factors ranged widely across well-known Japanese business institutions and country capabilities, including the availability of patient capital, the coordinative power of government, and the meticulous rigor of Japanese engineers and production workers. None of these factors can explain the collision of individual creativity with the global innovation system that catalyzed the beginnings of LCD research in Japan.

Cluster thinking confused many observers of the FPD industry's emergence, because it draws attention to stable internal institutions and knowledge that may offer countries some degree of autonomy in world markets. The Northern Italian high-fashion textile industry, for example, may well have enjoyed an ability to dictate important trends in high-end fabric design for a time. But such autonomy is increasingly short-lived. Even traditional industries like high-quality fabric have diffused to Asia in recent years because of globalization. Focusing on clusters can create a false sense of permanence for business strategy.

More important, high-technology industries increasingly emerge from a convergence of local with global factors and knowledge that catalyzes rapid accumulation of new knowledge. In terms of Kenney's five dynamics (Chapter 1), FPDs represented a principal but volatile focus of value creation in the segmented supply chain for notebook computers. The high-volume FPD industry originated in a convergence of knowledge drawn from a variety of countries. The knowledge moved in global markets through the transport of people, equipment, and materials, and the communication of ideas both within and across national borders. The industry's concentration in Japan in its early phases was a consequence—not a cause—of the rapid acceleration of knowledge accumulation around FPD technology in the 1980s. As the mass consumer market for notebook computers emerged in the 1990s, industry learning continued to be catalyzed by global forces, including the Internet, growing demand sparked by firms' continual efforts to reduce costs, and continually changing consumer markets for technology products that incorporated FPDs.

State-of-the-art business strategy prescriptions for entering the FPD industry in the early 1990s would have suggested establishing operations in Japan. But potential market entrants that waited until the FPD industry's strength in Japan had become widely evident were already too late to play leadership roles in that phase of the industry's development. Leadership was important, because only leaders made any money. As a consequence of the financial stress that many companies in Japan experienced, it later became possible to buy in using an acquisition strategy. Only one company, Philips, was wise enough to do so, by entering an alliance with Hosiden, a small, merchant producer, which it ultimately acquired. The foundations for Philips's visionary move were established years earlier in its close post–World War II relationship with Matsushita, which had played an important advisory role in the establishment of Hosiden. Philips had also gained timely industry awareness in an expensive, but ultimately unsuccessful, effort to establish FPD manufacturing in Europe. In general, if a company discovers the attractiveness of an industry because a cluster has emerged somewhere, its management has already experienced a fatal failure of foresight.

U.S. public policy prescriptions for the FPD industry focused on finding government-led strategies to remedy the U.S. market's presumed failure to offer incentives for local firms to establish facilities on U.S. soil. In economic theory, market failure offers one of few justifications for government economic intervention in markets. International markets can fail for many reasons. Knowledge markets are especially prone to failure because one firm's ownership of knowledge does not preclude other firms from having it, whether or not they pay for it. Firms face difficulties in negotiating knowledge exchanges: price-setting by nature involves some degree of disclosure, and disclosure of information reduces incentives to pay (Arrow 1971). Particularly in the United States, these difficulties have predisposed managers to focus on strategies that restrict outsiders' access to their firms' knowledge, rather than on ways of profitably sharing what they know with competitors, collaborators, suppliers, and customers. These concerns intensify for most companies when they manage international businesses.

The heated pace of high-technology competition inverted this conventional logic for some U.S. firms. As a consequence, they became key players in the FPD industry. But the U.S. government fell behind by implementing policies to encourage domestic FPD industry cooperation in preference to international market activity. These efforts to create a countervailing FPD presence in the United States created incentives for U.S. companies to cut themselves off from the suppliers, customers, complementary assets, and knowledge streams that were creating the industry. U.S. taxpayers and some entrepreneurs in the FPD industry paid a heavy price for these failed policies in the 1990s. Instead of establishing high-volume FPD manufacturing in the United States, another generation of progress was lost.

Intensive research on the evolution of the global FPD industry has persuaded us that high-tech industry concentration in one country or world region does not lock companies from elsewhere out unless they close the door on themselves. New high-technology industries often bubble under the surface for many years in several countries before they suddenly achieve critical mass and commercialize at global scale in one or more of them. Once a new industry emerges, continuity in knowledge accumulation, the pace of technical advance, and the commercial and social relationships that drive knowledge creation in the industry reinforce one another.

It is impossible to predict the exact timing and location in the world where any given technology will commercialize and a global industry emerge. But it is possible for companies to design management processes that positively affect their probabilities of participating. Companies with affiliates in a country or region where an industry emerges have as good a shot as local companies at taking integral positions, provided their managers can fully leverage local organizational capabilities with global technological capabilities as these opportunities arise. In the successful companies in our study, local managers functioned in peer networks as global managers. Local initiatives served as primary means to identify and go after global opportunities. Long-standing corporate research traditions in underlying technologies combined with strong local operations to establish these companies' stakes in the rapid accumulation of knowledge assets associated with the FPD industry's emergence. Developing such a knowledge stake formed a necessary condition for successful physical asset deployments anywhere in the world, including at home.

## Notes

This research was funded by a project grant from the Alfred P. Sloan Foundation Industry Studies Program. We also wish to acknowledge the Berkeley Roundtable on the International Economy (BRIE), Michael Borrus, Bala Chakravarthy, Hirsh Cohen, Steven Depp, Yves Doz, Martin Kenney, Tadao Kagono, Greg Linden, Frank Mayadas, David Mentley, Gail Pesyna, C. K. Prahalad, Myles Shaver, Jennifer Spencer, Ross Young, the Tokyo office of the Asian Technology Information Program (ATIP), the United States Display Consortium (USDC), and the managers and officials who participated in our research. We retain accountability for errors.

1. "RCA Develops a New Visual Display Means Using Liquid Crysta," *Wall Street Journal*, May 29, 1968, 4.

2. Johnstone's (1999) account conveys an optimism that may have been privately expressed by the researchers, particularly Heilmeier, whom he interviewed in March 1994. Most of the contemporary published journalistic accounts we accessed conveyed cautious or neutral assessments of the technology's likely time-to-market in television form. See, for example, "Liquid Crystals," *Science Digest*, December 1968, 32–34. Yet journalists who were working in the field of consumer electronics around the time of the announcement and in the years following remember a sense of immediacy and excitement that contemporary journalistic style may have tempered in print. Telephone discussion, Robert Angus, former senior editor of *Consumer Electronics Monthly*, August 5, 2000.

3. According to Johnstone (1999: 38), an earlier fully electronic calculator by Sony, the SOBAX, never advanced beyond the prototype stage.

4. "Sharp Develops Thin, 14-Inch TV Monitor Light Enough to Hang on Wall," Asahi News Service, June 17, 1988; "Toshiba, IBM Claim Largest Color Liquid Crystal Display," Japan Economic Newswire, September 21, 1988, accessed via Lexis-Nexis, September 18, 2000.

5. Interview, Norihiko Naono, director of business development, Rambus K.K., (former Nomura analyst), Tokyo, Japan, October 17, 1996.

6. "Toshiba, IBM Set Plant for Large LCDs," *Los Angeles Times*, August 30, 1989, Business Section, Part A, 3.

7. Interview, Kanro Sato, general manager, Liquid Crystal Display Division, Toshiba Corporation, Tokyo, Japan, June 12, 1997.

8. Interview. Kawanishi was executive vice president and head of Toshiba's worldwide electronics components and semiconductor businesses and later held the title of senior executive vice president for partnerships and alliances. When the authors met with him on November 15, 1996, at Toshiba's Tokyo headquarters, he held the title of "senior advisor," and played a visible emeritus role within the company.

9. "Toshiba, IBM Japan Link to Make LCDs," *Nihon Keizai Shimbun* (*Japan Economic Journal*), September 9, 1989, 13.

10. "Sharp Up for Volume Color LCD Production," Jiji Press Ticker Service, October 12, 1989, accessed via Lexis-Nexis, September 18, 2000.

11. Yuko Inoue, "Market Slump Snags Color LCD Venture; Toshiba, IBM Revise Targets but Remain Optimistic," *Nikkei Weekly*, April 25, 1992, 8.

12. "Toshiba-IBM LCD Venture Firm Goes On-Line," Japan Economic Newswire, Kyodo News Service, May 15, 1991, accessed via Lexis-Nexis, September 26, 2000.

13. Interview, Robert Wisnieff, manager, flat panel display fabrication, International Business Machines Corporation (IBM), Thomas J. Watson Research Center, Yorktown Heights, New York, July 22, 1996.

14. Steven Butler, "The Art of Perfection: Steven Butler Explains How a Single Speck of Dust Creates Havoc with the Way Liquid Crystal Displays Are Made," *The Financial Times*, London, April 16, 1992, Technology Section, 14.

15. Bill Snyder, "Full Speed Ahead: Toshiba Corp. Plans Ambitious Expansion," *PC Week*, November 7, 1994, A1.

16. CVD tools coat extremely thin films of metals and chemicals on glass as part of the procedure that forms the millions of transistors built into a TFT LCD.

17. Yuko Inoue, "Production Woes Stall Mass-Market Hope for Color LCDs," *Nikkei*

*Weekly*, September 21, 1991, 8. The article reported that Nomura analysts had identified color filters and CVD efficiency as "two major headaches for LCD parts makers, partly due to limited competition." Color filters were expensive and in short supply, and CVD inefficient, causing production bottlenecks.

18. Brooke Crothers and Jack Robertson, "IBM/Toshiba LCD Unit Sees Yields Rise to 50 Percent," *Electronic News*, July 6, 1992, accessed via Lexis-Nexis, July 1999.

19. Yuko Inoue, see note 17.

20. This represents a conservative interpretation. The outcomes of such analyses depend critically on how many generations the analyst judges to have passed. This is in part an issue of industry politics, as companies may claim territory by referring to their own incremental changes as generation changes, or by discounting the generational claims of others.

21. Interview, Toru Shima, president, Display Technologies, Inc. (DTI), Himeji, Japan, June 2, 1997.

22. Steven Butler, see note 14.

23. "Color Display, Built-in Pointing Device Lead IBM ThinkPad Line," PR Newswire, October 5, 1992, accessed via Nexis-Lexis, August 15, 2000. One month after the product announcement, the editors of *PC/Computing* presented IBM with the "Most Valuable Product" (MVP) award at the annual "Best Hardware and Software of the Year" award ceremonies in Las Vegas before the opening of COMDEX/Fall '92. "IBM ThinkPad 700C Named Best Color Notebook Computer," PR Newswire, November 16, 1992, accessed via Lexis-Nexis, August 1999.

24. Kristina Sullivan, "Color Notebooks Also Hit by PC Price Wars," *PC Week*, November 16, 1992, accessed via Lexis-Nexis, August 15, 2000.

25. Adam Greenberg, Brooke Crothers, and Jonathan Cassell, "Notebook Shortage Blamed on LCDs," *Electronic News*, December 14, 1992, 1.

26. Brooke Crothers, "Sharp Sticks to Displays with High Yield Record," *Electronic News*, April 12, 1993, 15. The source quoted regarding the IBM PCC overture to Sharp was Norihiko Naono (see note 5), at the time a Nomura Research Institute analyst.

27. "Toshiba-IBM Japan Venture to Boost TFT LCD Output," Japan Economic Newswire, Kyodo News Service, July 8, 1993, accessed via Lexis-Nexis, September 26, 2000.

28. Toru Shima (see note 21) gave DTI employment as 1,451 in June 1997.

29. Jack Robertson, "FPD Players Split over Glass Mfg. Strategy—Can't Decide on Shift to Larger Screens," *Electronic Buyers' News*, May 20, 1996, accessed via Lexis-Nexis, September 26, 2000.

30. Jack Robertson, "Suppliers Phase Out 10.4" Displays," *Electronic Buyers' News*, April 22, 1996, 1.

31. Dumping is defined as selling abroad at prices below fair market value in the home market.

32. Interview, Norihiko Naono (see note 5).

33. Norihiko Naono, "Japan FPD Market: Industry at Large," *Electronic News*, September 7, 1992, 10. This point was reiterated repeatedly in our research by most U.S. and all Japanese government officials, although some U.S. officials had the opposite impression.

34. In 1989, MITI encouraged FPD producers to form the Giant Technology Corporation with a funding level of about $28 million to pursue nonlithographic printing

techniques to fabricate very-large-format TFTs. The formula of cost sharing between business and government is subject to dispute (see also Borrus and Hart 1994). This program proved itself a major misdirection of corporate resources, according to Steven W. Depp, director, Subsystem Technologies and Applications Laboratory, International Business Machines Corporation (IBM), Thomas J. Watson Research Center, Yorktown Heights, NY. Telephone discussion with Lenway and Murtha, November 14, 2000.

35. Martin Koughan, writer/producer/reporter, and David Ewing, director, "Losing the War with Japan," first broadcast on U.S. Public Television's *Frontline*, November 19, 1991.

36. Sheila Galatowitsch, "LCDs Run Away with Military Flat Panel Market," *Defense Electronics*, May 1993, 25.

37. "Pentagon Picks Partner for Flat Screens," *San Francisco Chronicle*, February 5, 1992, F3. The discussions reflected the companies' response, submitted January 18, 1993, to a request for proposals issued by DARPA nine months earlier.

38. "SEMI Forms FPD Division to Serve U.S. Display Consortium," *Business Wire*, July 20, 1993, accessed via Lexis-Nexis, summer 1994.

39. Ibid.

40. IBM was a member of the consortium's user group, but not the producer group.

41. By 1998, projects budgeted at more than $95 million had been funded in this way.

42. For a discussion of the critical role of practice in learning and knowledge creation, see Brown and Duguid (2000a), esp. chs. 4 and 5.

43. Interview, industry official with Murtha and Lenway, Silicon Valley, summer 1996.

44. Interview, Rex Tapp, president and CEO, Optical Imaging Systems, Inc. (OIS), Northville, Michigan, May 7, 1996.

45. Interview, Scott Holmberg, president and CEO, ImageQuest Technologies, Inc., Fremont, California, June 25, 1996.

46. Photon Dynamics raised capital in Japan with the help of the Nomura and Daiwa Securities firms beginning in 1991. Bob Johnstone, "Research and Innovation: Spot the Mistake," *Far Eastern Economic Review*, July 16, 1992, 66. The Korean company LG also took a position in the company, according to Choon-Rae Lee, managing director, LCD Division, LG Electronics, Inc., Seoul, Korea, December 6, 1996.

47. Samsung and Corning established their first joint venture in 1973 to manufacture CRT glass. See www.samsungcorning.co.kr, accessed November 16, 1996.

48. Samsung website: www.sec.samsung.co.kr, accessed November 16, 1996.

49. Interview, Choon-Rae Lee (see note 46).

50. "South Korea, Taiwan Firms Raid Japanese Staffs, Buy Technology," *Nikkei Weekly*, March 3, 1997, 20.

51. De facto industry standards permit shipping goods with as many as five defective pixels.

52. "LG to Supply $1 Billion Worth of TFT LCDs to Compaq," *Korea Economic Weekly*, December 12, 1996, accessed via Lexis-Nexis, June 1997.

53. "Korean TFT LCD Producers Expected to Match DRAM Share by End of the Decade," *PR Newswire*, August 27, 1997, accessed via Lexis-Nexis, July/August 2000.

54. Interview, Jun H. Souk, executive director, AMLCD R&D, Semiconductor Business, Samsung Electronics Co., Kiheung, Korea, December 5, 1996.

55. Ibid.

56. "Samsung Breaks Ground on Third TFT LCD Production Line," *Business Wire*, January 7, 1997, accessed via Lexis-Nexis, July/August 2000.

57. "South Korea Close to Production of Large LCDs," *Dempa Shimbun*, August 31, 1996, 1.

58. "Display Technology to Buy Hyundai Displays," *Dempa Shimbun*, October 24, 1996, accessed via COMLINE, October 25, 1996; also interview materials.

59. Yoo Choon-sik, "Hyundai Elec in up to $50 Bln Chip, LCD Deals," Reuters, November 15, 1999, accessed via AOL November 17, 1999.

60. "Hyundai to Boost LCD Business," *Korea Herald*, March 17, 2000, accessed at http://www.nikkeibp.asiabiztech.com, September 29, 2000.

61. "Apple Going Big-Time Flat," CNNfn, July 28, 1999, accessed at cnnfn.com/1999/07/28/technology/apple/, August 1999.

62. Yoo Choon-Sik, "Hyundai Elec."

63. Alan Paterson, "What's Wrong with This Picture?" *Electronic Business Asia*, April 2000, accessed at eb-asia.com, April 10, 2000.

64. B. H. Seo, "Defiant LG Hints at Compromise," *Electronic Engineering Times*, January 4, 1999, accessed at www.edtn.com/news/0199/0199/010499bnews3.html, October 16, 1999.

65. See www.lgphilips-lcd.com.eng/company/lcd_history.html, accessed October 16, 1999.

# CHAPTER EIGHT

# Globalization of Semiconductors

## *Do Real Men Have Fabs, or Virtual Fabs?*

ROBERT C. LEACHMAN

CHIEN H. LEACHMAN

Real men have fabs.
— W. Jerry Sanders III, CEO, Advanced Micro Devices, Inc.

We are your virtual fab. It's just like having your own fab, only we treat you better.
— From a Taiwanese semiconductor manufacturing corporation's advertisement

In many ways, the semiconductor is the quintessential industrial product of the second half of the twentieth century. Increasingly, semiconductors are contained in every assembled product. For nearly every product, electronics are the key to its functionality and often its value added. Every product discussed in this book is touched by electronics, be it a direct connection with its functionality, as in the case of the PC and the television; an increasingly valuable component, as in the case of automobiles; in the case of garments, indirectly in the production machinery and information systems that make possible the coordination of the entire chain; or, as in the case of flat panel displays, because semiconductor manufacturing equipment could be redesigned to accomplish their manufacture. So, in some profound way, the semiconductor has infiltrated every part of the economy.

From the spatial and organizational dynamics of the semiconductor design and production value chain, we can understand much about the changing spatial dynamics of commerce and industry during the last half-decade. We shall profile the changing geography of semiconductor fabrication, which is the highest value-added aspect of IC manufacturing. We note the rapid rise of Taiwan as a global center for the manufacture of semiconductors. This may appear to be a story then of how an industry globalized and left the United States. However, as will be shown, such a simplistic view overlooks the rich tapestry that is being woven by this industry as it becomes more complicated and speciated with both vertical and horizontal divisions of labor populated by different organizations. For certain kinds of logic chips, a sophisticated division of labor between specialized design houses located in Silicon Valley and specialized manufacturers located in Taiwan has developed that would not have been possible without the introduction of sophisticated computer-aided design software. For contract manufacturing of digital logic chips, Taiwan has managed to establish itself as the leader.

There are other areas of the semiconductor industry, such as commodity memory and the most sophisticated microprocessors and digital signal processors, where thus far it has proved ineffective to partition design and fabrication into separate firms, though after qualification the newly designed chips can be produced at different factories around the world. Rather than simply argue that outsourcing is the inevitable way in which semiconductors will be made, we show that the industry is far more variegated, consisting of several segments organized differently. In the segment of the industry comprising general digital logic, the fabless semiconductor design firm located anywhere in the world (but most commonly in Silicon Valley) partnering with a contract fabrication firm located in Taiwan has become the preferred organizational methodology for manufacturing. In other segments, particularly commodity memory and sophisticated microprocessors and digital signal processors, the integration of design and manufacturing is the more successful organizational format. This paper explores the spatial and organizational outcomes of the choices by firms in different industry segments.

The distribution of semiconductor manufacturing capacity has shifted markedly during the last two decades. At the start of the 1990s, the United States and Japan collectively accounted for three-fourths of worldwide fabrication capacity, but by the second half of the 1990s fabrication capacity shifted to the Asia Pacific region,[1] a trend that seems likely to continue. This is the result of not only varying business strategies and levels of success enjoyed by semiconductor firms in different regions but also a reorganization of firm boundaries and geographic locations for different parts of the value chain. The most salient of these changes is the increased use of contract manufacturers for chip fabrication.

## Producing an Integrated Circuit

The semiconductor value chain can be divided into three distinct activities: design, wafer fabrication, and device packaging and test (P&T). These activities can be undertaken in spatial proximity to each other, or they can be geographically dispersed. Moreover, it is possible to integrate all three activities in one organization or separate them into different organizations. The relative wisdom of separation or integration is contingent upon technical, economic, and strategic factors that differ by product.

Fabrication and P&T differ dramatically and usually are undertaken in separate facilities in locations with very different labor market and infrastructural endowments. Relative to fabrication, P&T have been far more labor-intensive and much less technology-intensive, though recently they have become much more automated. The physical location of P&T has varied by firm, but early in the history of the industry much of this segment of the value chain was relocated from the developed nations to Southeast Asia.[2] The pioneers in moving P&T offshore were the U.S. merchant semiconductor producers that were founded in Silicon Valley, especially Fairchild. In fact, many of these merchant producers employed larger work forces in Asia than they did in the United States (Scott and Angel 1988).[3] Since the early 1980s, roughly 85 percent of worldwide P&T capacity has been located in Southeast Asia.

The P&T portion of the value chain has remained relatively stable in terms of location and corporate boundaries, with a few exceptions such as Intel's recent establishment of a P&T facility in Costa Rica. Therefore, this chapter concentrates on the changing location of fabrication operations and the reasons why firms producing different types of semiconductors exhibit varying strategies and organizational configurations.

The development of advanced fabrication process technology is a formidable undertaking requiring considerable engineering talent. Repeatability and controllability must be achieved for each of the hundreds of delicate fabrication steps performed at an unobservable microscopic scale. Wafer fabrication is the most capital- and technology-intensive aspect of the semiconductor manufacturing process. In 2001 a state-of-the-art wafer fabrication facility (hereafter, fab) cost approximately $2 billion, making it one of the most expensive types of factories in the world. On a per-chip basis, the capital investment requirement for fabrication was roughly ten times that for P&T. This means that industry dynamics are primarily a function of fab capacity decisions. To complicate the business environment, the fabs depreciate very rapidly as new generations are introduced.

A typical piece of wafer fab processing equipment is useful for three or four generations of process technology, where each generation involves a 50 percent reduction in the minimum feature size from the previous generation. Further, each succeeding generation typically requires replacement of between 25 and 35 percent of the processing equipment used in the previous generation.

Over the life of the industry, the time between chip generations has averaged two to three years, and recently it has been compressed to one and a-half to two years. In 2001, 0.25-micron process technologies were widely operated at high volume in the industry, production volumes of 0.18-micron technologies were being ramped up, and 0.13-micron process technologies had just been qualified for production at a number of wafer fabs.

The final link in the semiconductor value chain is the design process. Semiconductor design originally consisted of laying out the design by hand on paper. As semiconductors became increasingly complicated, it became necessary to computerize chip design layout. This computerization had an unexpected side benefit—namely, it allowed the easy transference of designs through computer networks to anywhere in the world. Coupled with standardized fabrication process technology whose parameters could be specified in the design software, this made it feasible in the case of many (but not all) products to uncouple design from manufacturing. The detachability of design from manufacturing created the potential for the emergence of the fabless semiconductor firm and its binary, the semiconductor foundry (i.e., a contract manufacturer performing fabrication). In effect, the value chain was decomposed into three organizationally separable functions. Firm strategy then could disintegrate or integrate these functions.

## To Foundry or Not to Foundry

The semiconductor industry encompasses a great variety of products which, while produced by a common manufacturing process, exhibit radically varying value propositions. The value of chips performing logical or communications functions ("logic chips") reflects the software and software architectures supported by them. For example, an Intel microprocessor enables the Microsoft operating system, whereas a Motorola microprocessor does not, so the latter is priced at a lower level. There are formidable barriers to entry into specific logic businesses, and so prices are relatively high. On the other hand, chips performing solely memory functions ("memory chips") are flexibly usable in any software architecture. The value of a memory chip basically reflects the amount of memory capacity packed into the small slice of silicon. With no architectural barriers to market entry, the memory chip business experiences commodity pricing pressures.

The following comparisons concretely illustrate the variety of organizational configurations in the semiconductor industry. We compare three products from three different industry segments: an Intel Pentium IV microprocessor, a 64 Megabit dynamic random-access memory (DRAM), and a niche communications chip marketed by a fabless semiconductor company. All three products were fabricated using 0.25-micron process technology during the period be-

TABLE 8.1

*Comparison of Revenue per Wafer in Different Segments of the Industry*

|  | Intel Pentium IV | 64 megabit DRAM | Niche communications chip |
|---|---|---|---|
| Net good chips per 8-inch wafer (0.25μm technology) | 80 | 400 | 2,000 |
| Average selling price | $400 | $4 | $4 |
| Revenue per wafer | $32,000 | $1,600 | $8,000 |

*Source:* Authors' data.

*Note:* Typical March 2001 foundry price per wafer (0.25-micron process technology): $1,800.

tween 1998 and 2001. The Pentium IV market could fill roughly eight large fab lines; the 64M DRAM market could fill about twenty large fab lines; but the niche communications chip had a market much smaller than the capacity of a single fabrication line. The approximate net chips per wafer, rough average selling prices, and consequent revenue per completed wafer are displayed in Table 8.1. Noted at the bottom of the table is the typical foundry price per wafer in early 2001.

As can be seen, the foundry option seems hopeless for the DRAM merchant. Wafer cost must be driven lower than the typical price charged by the foundries, motivating in-house manufacturing expertise and investment (the Korean, U.S., and pre-1996 Japanese approach)—or at least dedication of a foundry fab to the merchant's products and transfer of key technology and engineering expertise (the post-1996 Japanese approach). The foundry option is also unattractive for Intel, but for quite a different reason. The average selling price is very high primarily because of Intel's monopoly power—that is, no one else (except perhaps AMD) simultaneously has a comparable device, a comparable process technology, and a manufacturing capacity sufficient to significantly erode Intel's market share. If Intel chose to outsource its fabrication and supply its leadership process technology to the foundries, it would become vulnerable to losing its extraordinary franchise.

On the other hand, the foundry option is quite attractive for the niche communications chip merchant. Sales of its chip would not be nearly great enough to fill a fab. Given the small chip size, revenue per wafer is very good, so the foundry-level manufacturing cost is not a problem. For the firm that designed the chip it is better to tap the market as early as possible, rather than spend the time to develop a lower-cost alternative to contract manufacturing—if that is even financially and technically possible. By using a foundry fab, lucrative niche markets can be tapped quickly with very little capital investment, and sales can be completed before prices seriously erode from inevitable technological obsolescence.

*Geographical Distribution of Fabrication Capacity*

There are a number of possible metrics of fabrication capacity—for example, number of wafers that can be processed per month, the total wafer surface area that can be processed per month, number of factory workers, amount of installed processing equipment, and so forth. The changing pattern of globalization can be best understood by examining the total capacity to produce integrated circuits. We measure fab capacity in terms of the estimated number of electrical functions that can be produced per month, where a function could be a memory bit or a logic gate. Capacity measured this way is very large. When summed across the fabs in the regions of North America, Japan, Europe, and Asia Pacific, the resulting regional capacities are expressed in hundreds of quadrillions ($10^{15}$) of electrical functions per month.

We used 1998 data for 1,175 fabs worldwide from statistics gathered by Semiconductor Equipment and Materials International (1998) to create a database. This database indicates, for each existing or announced fab, the wafer capacity, minimum feature size, type of products, location, and location of ownership. It was updated with data collected by the Competitive Semiconductor Manufacturing (CSM) Program at the University of California, Berkeley. Based on direct information from firms in the industry, data was obtained for fabs missing from the database, inaccuracies were corrected, and historical records for the evolution of feature sizes at each fab were improved (Leachman and Leachman 1999).

Figure 8.1 displays the percentage annual growth in worldwide fabrication capacity during the period between 1980 and 2000. Over these two decades, fabrication capacity grew at the average rate of 37 percent per year. Exceptional years include 1983–84, when capacity grew by 60 to 63 percent, and 1995, when capacity grew by 56 percent. Both these periods of rapid growth in capacity triggered deep industry recessions. The extraordinary expansion in 1983–84 was concentrated in Japan, while the extraordinary expansion in 1995 occurred mostly in the Asia Pacific region (which omits Japan).

Even when total wafer output is not increased, there is a tremendous increase in capacity afforded by each succeeding generation of technology (because of the increase in circuitry per wafer that the new generation affords). Thus in our methodology, because of the rapid technological evolution, old capacity investments account for little of current capacity. Consequently, as Table 8.2 indicates, the regional shares of total industry capacity can change remarkably rapidly, even though older fabs continue to operate. Throughout the 1980s, about 75 percent of world fabrication capacity was located in North America and Japan. At the beginning of the decade, the North American share of capac-

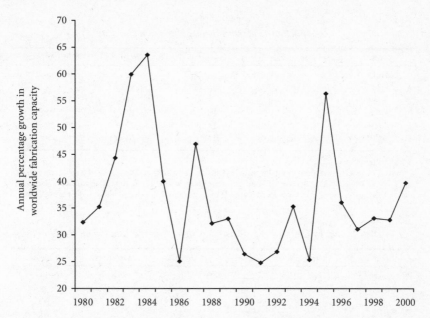

FIG. 8.1. Growth of Worldwide Semiconductor Fabrication Capacity. Source: Authors' data.

ity was more than 40 percent, but it dropped to 30 percent during the decade and stayed at that level throughout the 1990s. The European share of fabrication capacity declined slightly over the two decades, falling from 16 percent to 13 percent. Japanese capacity surged to a 47 percent share during the early 1980s, but then it declined sharply through the 1990s to a level of only 20 percent in 2000.

Perhaps the most arresting trend in Table 8.2 concerns the Asia Pacific region. From a share of world capacity below 5 percent in 1980, the Asia Pacific share rose to almost 40 percent twenty years later. This tremendous growth occurred after 1990, and the trend appears to be accelerating. In Table 8.3, Asia Pacific fabrication capacity is divided by country. During the 1990s, Taiwan and South Korea accounted for more than 80 percent of fabrication capacity located in the region, in the range of 86 to 89 percent during the second half of the decade. Singapore has the next largest share during this period, about 9 to 11 percent. During the first half of the decade, South Korean capacity was greater than Taiwanese capacity, but in the second half of the decade, Taiwanese capacity grew faster and surpassed South Korean capacity.

At the beginning of the 1990s, other countries in the Asia Pacific region ac-

TABLE 8.2.

*Regional Shares of Worldwide Fabrication Capacity*

| Year | Asia Pacific | Europe | Japan | North America |
|------|------|------|------|------|
| 1980 | .04 | .16 | .38 | .42 |
| 1985 | .06 | .16 | .47 | .30 |
| 1990 | .12 | .13 | .45 | .30 |
| 1995 | .20 | .15 | .37 | .29 |
| 1998 | .31 | .14 | .27 | .29 |
| 2001 | .38 | .13 | .20 | .29 |

Source: Authors' data.

Note: All figures are fractions of total worldwide fabrication capacity and may not add to 1.0 due to rounding. The Asia Pacific region includes all Asian countries except Japan. The Europe region includes Russia, Israel, and Turkey. Fabrication capacity located outside the four regions shown above was negligible in all years.

TABLE 8.3

*Distribution by Country of Fabrication Capacity in the Asia Pacific Region*

| Year | Other | Malaysia | Singapore | South Korea | Taiwan |
|------|------|------|------|------|------|
| 1990 | .11 | — | .06 | .42 | .41 |
| 1995 | .02 | .00 | .09 | .51 | .38 |
| 1998 | .01 | .00 | .11 | .38 | .50 |
| 2001 | .02 | .03 | .10 | .25 | .61 |

Source: Authors' data.

Note: All figures are fractions of total fabrication capacity located in the Asia Pacific region. Figures may not add to 1.0 due to rounding. The "Other" category includes Australia, China, Hong Kong, and India.

counted for more than 10 percent of fabrication capacity, but since 1995 fabrication capacity located in Hong Kong, India, Australia, and China has been negligible. Fabrication investments in Australia, Hong Kong, and India before 1990 were not followed up with any significant investments in the 1990s. As of 2001, fabrication capacity in Malaysia accounted for about 3 percent of the regional total, resulting from the start-up of two advanced-technology contract manufacturing firms.

When the distribution of capacity by region of ownership is examined, a somewhat different picture emerges. In Table 8.4, capacity is tabulated by the region in which the owning firm is located, rather than the region in which the fab is located. The fractions in each row of the table sometimes add to a larger total than unity, particularly in later years. The reason is that when a fab has more than one owner, we have credited the entire fab capacity to each owner. There were two reasons for this. First, we were unable to secure information on the ownership shares of jointly owned fabs. Second and, more interesting, one of the most common forms of joint ownership over the past two decades involves one partner contributing the process technology and operation of the facility, and the other partner(s) contributing the design and marketing of prod-

TABLE 8.4

*Distribution of Worldwide Fabrication Capacity by Region of Ownership*

| Year | Asia Pacific | Europe | Japan | North America |
|------|-------------|--------|-------|---------------|
| 1980 | .03 | .15 | .37 | .44 |
| 1985 | .05 | .10 | .46 | .40 |
| 1990 | .12 | .09 | .45 | .36 |
| 1995 | .20 | .12 | .37 | .36 |
| 1998 | .33 | .10 | .31 | .38 |
| 2001 | .39 | .08 | .24 | .38 |

*Source:* Authors' data.

*Note:* The shares of capacity sum to greater than unity in some years because the capacity of jointly owned fabs is credited to all owners.

ucts produced by that fab. The other partner(s) are guaranteed rights to a certain portion of fab capacity in consideration of their investment. Should one partner not fully utilize its share, the unused capacity is offered to the other partners or marketed to others. Thus it is common for one or several partners from the same region to have access to the entire fab capacity. The figures in this table may be thought of as indicating the amount of capacity potentially *accessible* to owners in each region. This illustrates the phenomenon of various types of partnerships that are coming to characterize most of the industry and will be discussed in greater detail below.

As of 2001, Asia Pacific firms accounted for the largest share of ownership of fabrication capacity. Upon comparison, it can be seen that the shares of worldwide capacity wholly or jointly owned by North American and Japanese firms did not decline as much as did the shares of capacity located in those regions, although the decline in the Japanese ownership share was substantial. North American, Japanese, and European firms increased their investments in foreign-located capacity during the second half of the 1990s, mostly in the form of investment capital or process technology furnished to Asia Pacific contract manufacturers. On the other hand, Asia Pacific firms made only relatively minor investments in fabrication capacity located outside the Asia Pacific region. The result is a concentration of both fabrication activity and ownership of fabrication capacity in the Asia Pacific region.

Another way to categorize fabrication capacity is by the amount that is operated by contract manufacturers vs. the amount that is operated by firms that also design and market the devices produced using that capacity. Following the industry vernacular, we use the term "foundry" to designate a fab that is engaged to produce devices designed and marketed by firms that are not owners of that fab. If one or more of the fab's owning firms is solely engaged in contract manufacturing and has no semiconductor products of its own, we term it a "pure-play" foundry. We also use the term "fabless" to describe semiconduc-

TABLE 8.5

*Distribution of Fabrication Capacity by Product Type*

| Year | Foundry | Logic | Memory | Memory/Logic |
|------|---------|-------|--------|--------------|
| 1990 | .08 | .51 | .20 | .21 |
| 1995 | .08 | .31 | .31 | .31 |
| 1998 | .16 | .27 | .33 | .24 |
| 2001 | .25 | .29 | .28 | .18 |

*Note:* All figures are expressed as fractions of world-wide capacity. Figures in certain years may not add to 1.0 due to rounding.

TABLE 8.6

*Distribution of Pure-Play Foundry Capacity*

| Year | Asia Pacific | Europe | Japan | North America |
|------|--------------|--------|-------|---------------|
| 1995 | .70 | .10 | .14 | .06 |
| 1998 | .76 | .08 | .06 | .09 |
| 2001 | .89 | .03 | .02 | .05 |

*Source:* Authors' data.

*Note:* All figures are expressed as fractions of total world-wide pure-play foundry capacity. Figures in certain years may not add to 1.0 due to rounding.

tor merchants that outsource their fabrication needs to the foundries. Firms that carry out the full suite of design, manufacturing, and marketing functions are termed "integrated" manufacturers. Classification of the industry into integrated, fabless, and foundry companies is not entirely clear-cut. Integrated firms may offer idle capacity for the fabrication of products marketed by others, thereby becoming a foundry as well as an integrated company. On the other hand, by curtailing investments in fabrication capacity and outsourcing manufacturing to others, an integrated firm can become increasingly fabless.

There are two broad product categories, memory and logic, that divide semiconductor production. Our database classifies each fab as a producer of logic products owned by an integrated firm, a producer of memory products owned by an integrated firm, a producer of both memory and logic products owned by an integrated firm, or a pure-play foundry. In Table 8.5, we summarize worldwide fabrication capacity by these categories. As indicated in the table, the percent of worldwide fabrication capacity accounted for by pure-play foundries has risen from 8 percent in 1990 to 25 percent in 2001. All of this growth occurred after 1995. Of course, the total share of worldwide capacity devoted to foundry production is likely much higher than this figure, because an unknown portion of the capacity at fabs operated by integrated companies is devoted to foundry services—and this capacity is included in the nonfoundry categories (because it is not reported).

In Table 8.6 the regional distribution of pure-play foundry capacity is detailed. The most important trend is that the share of worldwide foundry capacity located in the Asia Pacific region has risen from 70 percent in 1995 to 89 percent at present. Most of this capacity is located in Taiwan.

## Regional Strategies

The semiconductor firms in different regions have developed very different strategies and experienced differential success. These strategies and their success explain the concentration of world fabrication capacity in the Asia Pacific region that occurred during the late 1990s. We briefly summarize these strategies as they relate to fabrication capacity. As will be discussed, these strategies and success levels resulted in two key trends. The first trend was for DRAM production to become concentrated in the Asia Pacific region including Japan, though increasingly the locus shifted to Korea. The second trend was a rapid growth during the second half of the 1990s of foundries located in the Asia Pacific region, especially Taiwan.

### Japanese Strategies

The rise of the Japanese share of worldwide fabrication capacity from 38 percent in 1980 to 47 percent in 1985 reflects the MITI-led push into very large scale integration (VLSI) by the large integrated Japanese electronics firms and their capture of much of the vast DRAM market. During the 1990s, Japanese domination of DRAMs steadily eroded because of the entrance into the industry and strong growth of the Korean chaebols (discussed below).

The 1996–98 industry downturn, combined with especially poor market conditions in Japan, created trying conditions for the Japanese semiconductor manufacturers. During the mid-1990s, Japanese firms lagged Korean and American firms in their development of process technology and investments in fabrication capacity needed to produce the 16M and 64M DRAM generations.[4] By the time the Japanese had ramped up for volume production, the market had collapsed. After experiencing large losses caused by the steep decline in DRAM prices and the relatively high cost of fabrication capacity in Japan, most Japanese DRAM merchants curtailed capacity investments and DRAM production. As a result, the DRAM market share accounted for by Japanese companies declined significantly. Japanese companies continuing to market DRAMs have by and large opted to pursue joint ventures, technology licensing, and contract production of DRAMs in Taiwan in lieu of in-house production. Fabrication of specialty memory and logic products, however, has been retained in Japan.

A number of foundries in Japan were established in the late 1980s and early 1990s. These firms were mostly subsidiaries of Japanese steel companies. They also suffered heavy losses in the late 1990s. Unlike foundries in the Asia Pacific region (discussed below), the Japanese foundries did not secure a significant customer base outside Japan. One of the most important of the Japanese foundries had been established by Nippon Steel, but in 1998 it sold a majority interest in its facilities to the UMC Group, one of the leading Taiwanese foundry companies.

In spatial terms, most Japanese firms did not locate significant amounts of fabrication capacity outside Japan. The notable exception was NEC, which for many years has operated a sizable fraction of its fabrication capacity overseas. The all-in-Japan policy of the other Japanese producers began to change after the 1996–98 downturn, and since that time there has been a sharp increase in Japanese investment in fabrication capacity located in the Asia Pacific region. The vehicles for this increased ownership were joint ventures or technology licensing arrangements with firms in Taiwan and Singapore, and to a lesser extent, South Korea.

*Korean Strategies*

Korean entry into the semiconductor industry was driven by their "follow-Japan" strategy. Beginning in the 1980s, the Korean chaebols (Samsung, Hyundai, and LG) received massive government support in the form of loan subsidies to enter into the DRAM business. Finding certain U.S. and Japanese firms willing to license their DRAM technologies, they invested heavily, initially incurring massive losses while they were learning about the industry (Kim 1997; Kenney 1999a; Mathews and Cho 2000). The ultimate result was that by 1996, the Koreans had captured about 40 percent of the DRAM market, mostly at the expense of Japanese firms.

In the wake of the 1996–98 industry downturn, the three large Korean DRAM companies were reduced to two (Samsung and Hynix, the latter a renaming of Hyundai Electronics after it absorbed the semiconductor business of LG). This is consistent with the need for very large integrated firms to compete in the DRAM business. In the late 1990s, Samsung and Hynix each operated a single DRAM fabrication facility in the United States, but the remainder of their vast fabrication capacity was located entirely within South Korea. By the year 2000 the financial condition of Hynix had become precarious, and in early 2002 Hynix was acquired by Micron Technology, the American DRAM manufacturer. The demise of LG and Hynix are also results of the uncontrolled investment that caused massive overcapacity and a near collapse of the Korean economy.

Since 1998 there have been two foundry start-ups in South Korea. In a bold shift of business strategy, Anam, once the world's largest packaging and test foundry company, sold all its manufacturing facilities in order to finance the construction of an advanced wafer fabrication plant. Texas Instruments, which guaranteed to utilize a certain portion of the capacity, supplied the process technology. Anam's 250nm-logic foundry fab has been operational since 1999. Dong-bu, another industrial group, also has recently constructed an advanced-technology foundry fab. Dong-bu has licensed advanced process technology for this fab from Toshiba. The ultimate success of these initiatives is not yet clear.

## Taiwanese Strategies

The Taiwanese strategy for entry into the semiconductor industry is typical of their industrial strategy of finding niches to exploit. In the 1970s and 1980s, the Taiwanese government established a research facility to develop CMOS process technology licensed from RCA (Mathews and Cho 2000). Taiwan Semiconductor Manufacturing Company (TSMC) and the United Microelectronics Company (UMC, later the UMC Group) were the first two major fabrication foundry companies, and in 2002 were the world's two leading foundry companies. In some ways, this success was accidental, since these companies entered into the foundry business not because they recognized it as a superior business strategy but rather because it was the most feasible avenue for the development of a business. As TSMC chairman Morris Chang stated in an interview for *Business Week*, "We were lucky."[5] The key discovery of the Taiwanese firms was that success in product design and marketing was much more difficult to develop than was skill at manufacturing, but that there were significant profits to be secured in contract manufacturing. These two firms entered the pure-play foundry business in two different ways. TSMC began with the pure-play vision. However, UMC strove to become an integrated company, with little success, before concentrating upon foundry work.

These companies and other subsequent foundry start-ups were not started by large, industrial firms (as was the case in Korea and Japan), but by organizing a variety of investors, each of whom made relatively small investments. For example, the largest initial TSMC investor, at 27.5 percent, was a customer: Philips. At each firm, the by-laws call for generous distribution of profits among all employees as well as the investors. As a result, management, engineers, and production workers in some of the Taiwan foundries are better compensated than in almost any other semiconductor manufacturing company in the world. This has enabled them to attract top-flight talent. For example, a significant percentage of the senior management consists of Asian-born U.S. doctorates with substantial U.S. industry experience.

The Taiwanese foundry companies have grown very rapidly, as they were able to secure much of their capital needs for new fabrication plants by pooling investment funds from their Japanese, American, and European customers. Toward the end of the 1990s, TSMC and the UMC Group made major additions of fabrication capacity located in North America and Japan, respectively, but the lion's share of their capacity remained in Taiwan. Moreover, they announced ambitious expansion plans featuring numerous large fabrication plants to be built in the new Science-Based Industrial Park located in Tainan, Taiwan. The financial success of TSMC and UMC has prompted other foundry start-ups in Taiwan as well as Singapore and Malaysia. There are now several significant foundry fab operations in Singapore, involving significant investments from U.S. and Japanese customers or joint venture partners. There are also two major foundry start-ups in Malaysia and two in South Korea.

During the 1990s, the Taiwanese government encouraged the establishment of DRAM companies in Taiwan, reportedly as an effort to protect Taiwanese electronics manufacturers from periodic DRAM shortages. As a result, several DRAM operations were started in Taiwan, some with the (reluctant) backing of the logic foundries. By and large, these operations have not been very successful, as their manufacturing performance lagged that of the major DRAM manufacturers in Korea and the United States. Because of their marginal performance, some were converted to foundry production or sold to the foundry companies. For example, Acer sold its fabs to TSMC in 1999. In the same year, WSMC, a joint venture of Winbond, Toshiba and various Taiwanese investors, was sold to TSMC. Power Chip, a joint venture of Mitsubishi and Taiwanese investors that initially produced DRAMs marketed by Mitsubishi, also was converted to foundry production.

The Taiwanese semiconductor industry curiously found success through a series of experiments and failures. What it discovered is that there was significant success to be garnered by manufacturing for other firms. Moreover, the customers were willing to advance capital toward construction of fabs. For the Taiwanese firms the only caveat was that they should not compete with their customers. However, the foundry model would never have succeeded had there not been a group of ready customers. In the next section, we discuss the emergence of these customers in the context of the U.S. semiconductor industry.

## U.S. Strategies

The U.S. invented the transistor and the integrated circuit, and was the first to manufacture both. The rapid growth of U.S. companies through the 1970s and the emergence of Silicon Valley were envied throughout the world. However, beginning in the early 1980s, U.S. market share declined precipitously as Japanese competition eroded the U.S. advantage in market share by dint of their superior manufacturing prowess. By the late 1980s, there was near panic in U.S. government circles and a drumbeat of demands for protection against supposed unfair Japanese trade practices (see, for example, Borrus 1988).

In subsequent years, the U.S. integrated producers improved their manufacturing performance considerably. Benchmarking results from the UC Berkeley Competitive Semiconductor Manufacturing Program indicate that by 1997 there had been considerable closure in manufacturing performance between the best performers in the United States and those in the Japan and Asia Pacific regions (Leachman 2002). However, the share of worldwide capacity located in the United States has not increased since 1985. The lack of growth was the result of major shifts in the structure and organization of the U.S. industry.

The first reason is that U.S. firms, with the exception of Micron Technology, gradually exited the DRAM market. Since DRAM fabrication accounts for such a large percentage of total circuitry, the abandonment of their production retarded U.S. growth by our measure. Most of the U.S. merchant semiconductor firms such as Intel abandoned DRAMs in the late 1980s. Later, other U.S. integrated companies also exited the DRAM business. The last to retreat were IBM and Texas Instruments, which left after the 1996 downturn. IBM sold its remaining DRAM capacity to its foreign joint venture partners, Toshiba and Infineon. Micron purchased Texas Instrument's DRAM fabs in 1998, changing overnight from a company with 100 percent of its fabrication performed within the United States to a company operating large fabs in Europe, Japan, and Singapore as well as the United States. As noted above, in 2002 Micron acquired Hynix. As a result of its acquisitions, Micron's plans to build additional fabrication facilities in the United States were postponed, as it elected to upgrade and re-equip its newly acquired foreign fabs. Thus DRAM production by U.S. firms has both declined and become more globalized. Considering the fact that the Asia Pacific DRAM companies keep the vast majority of their fabrication capacity within their home region, the share of worldwide memory capacity that is located within the United States was reduced.

The second significant change in the U.S. industry has been to emphasize logic devices. However, what has occurred is a complicated set of changes. U.S. firms have enjoyed considerable market success, but this was accompanied by increased outsourcing of the fabrication to foundries located in the Asia Pacific region, especially Taiwan. Beginning in the mid-1980s there was a steady increase in newly established firms, especially in Silicon Valley, whose business model was that they would design and market semiconductors and contract out the manufacturing. In effect, they planned to benefit from the fact that the greatest value added in a semiconductor is in the design stage. Moreover, even at that time the cost of a fab was far greater than any startup could afford, and, at least initially, a startup could not utilize the entire capacity of an efficient-scale fabrication plant. Effectively, the startups planned to use their expertise in designing innovative digital logic and mixed signal products. Already, at that time, integrated firms often offered foundry services in an attempt to secure a return on otherwise idle manufacturing capacity. So, foundry production itself was not an original strategy. Over the years, securing capacity for producing devices, particularly those that needed only older process technologies, was possible. However, the new firms from their inception planned to take advantage of the excess capacity in other firms' fabs and then do the marketing themselves.

This was made possible because owners of excess capacity were always willing to produce for noncompetitors. The more interesting question is why there has been such remarkable business growth for pure-play foundries—that is, why the fabless firms have not made greater use of foundry services offered by integrated firms. One answer is that the fabless firms were naturally reluctant to share their designs with competitors or potential competitors, particularly when it came to the designs for their most advanced products. Moreover, anticipating the "silicon cycle," the fabless firms, quite appropriately, feared that the integrated firms would withdraw their foundry services during cyclical upturns. In other words, the integrated firms would elect to utilize the production capacity for their own products, especially those requiring advanced process technologies. However, a foundry that had no intention of becoming an integrated manufacturer with design and marketing activities could alleviate such fears. Moreover, the contract manufacturer would not see the fabless firms as simply a "temporary capacity filler." Rather, the foundry would be much more likely to provide excellent customer service to its patrons. As it turned out, the Asian pure-play foundries indeed provided excellent customer service and became trusted business partners of the American fabless companies.

As these fabless companies succeeded and grew, they needed to secure uninterrupted access to more fabrication capacity. Beginning in the early 1990s, many foundry customers were increasingly willing to supply capital to foundry companies in Taiwan and Singapore to aid in the construction or expansion of fabrication plants, in return for first rights to utilize a corresponding portion of the fab capacity. In other words the industry found a collective action solution to the capital cost problem. If the investor/customer could not fully utilize its portion of capacity, the foundry sold the surplus capacity to other customers. Consequently, a substantial amount of U.S. investment in fabrication capacity flowed into the Asia Pacific region during the second half of the 1990s.

The model became so successful that formerly integrated U.S. semiconductor companies began to increase their use of foundries in the late 1990s. For example, in 1998 Motorola announced that it intended to outsource 50 percent of its semiconductor fabrication needs within five years. Hewlett Packard abandoned plans to build a new fabrication plant in Colorado and outsourced fabrication of many of its advanced technology semiconductors to foundries or joint venture firms in the Asia Pacific region. Former integrated stalwarts such as National Semiconductor, Conexant, and Cypress Semiconductor increased their use of Asia Pacific foundries. Contract fabrication enabled them to tap markets without waiting for the completion of new fabs or to shift older products out of in-house fabs to make room for new products requiring more advanced process technology.

Today, the only major exceptions to this trend to outsource fabrication are Intel, AMD, IBM Microelectronics, and Texas Instruments. The reason for this is that the microprocessors, digital signal processors, and other sophisticated semiconductors they are producing exploit the most advanced process technologies. The foundries offer process technologies that are state-of-the-art, but not quite capable of achieving the density, speed, or reliability requirements of their products. For these firms, outsourcing their flagship products is not possible without revealing or licensing their strategic process technology. There also has been resistance to the use of foundries by the major American ASIC (application-specific integrated circuit—i.e., custom product) vendors, including LSI Logic and Agere Systems. However, some of these firms probably cannot afford to finance the next generation of fabrication plants without partners. For example, AMD announced in 2001 that it was seeking a partner for its next major fabrication plant, and in 2002 it announced a joint venture with UMC to construct and operate an advanced fabrication facility in Singapore. Whether or not the others can continue to eschew use of the foundries remains to be seen.

Given these kinds of arrangements, the U.S. semiconductor industry has become the most sophisticated and complicated in the world. Although a number of the integrated producers operate fabs abroad, it is the U.S. fabless semiconductor firms that made possible the foundry firms in the Asia Pacific region. But then the evolution of the foundry business model proved so powerful that foundries began to attract business from some of the integrated firms. So, the innovations in the U.S. industry made possible this further disintegration of the semiconductor value chain.

*European Strategies*

The three major European semiconductor firms are ST Microelectronics, Philips, and Infineon (formerly Siemens). Philips and Infineon make significant use of foundries or joint venture fabs in Taiwan, as well as carrying out in-house fabrication, the latter at sites in both Europe and the United States. ST Microelectronics emphasizes signal-processing devices using in-house process technology. ST's fabrication capacity is distributed among Europe, the United States, and the Asia Pacific regions. Because of the globalization of manufacturing by the three European firms and the relative perception among most foreign firms that there is no pressing need to produce in Europe, the share of worldwide fabrication capacity within Europe has declined.

## Economic Forces and Technological Innovations

As we demonstrated in the previous section, the most notable development in the semiconductor industry during the 1990s was the symbiotic emergence of the fabless firm-foundry firm division of labor. This was the impetus for the rapidly increasing fab capacity in Taiwan and, to a lesser degree, Singapore. This section discusses the economic forces and technological developments that made this possible.

The two overarching economic forces in the industry are (a) the rising capital costs of fabrication facilities, and (b) the large economic rewards for early market entry. Both of these forces contributed to the reorganization of the industry. For the last twenty years, the capital cost of a 25,000-wafer-per-month fabrication facility able to accommodate leading-edge digital process technology has been doubling every four years, and in 2001 it was in excess of $2 billion—beyond the financial reach of most firms in the industry. If such firms were to build new manufacturing facilities on their own, the facilities would have to be sized for much smaller wafer output. However, wafer fabrication is characterized by substantial economies of scale, arising from the indivisibility of process machinery and engineers. A UC Berkeley study of fab economics demonstrates that a 10,000-wafer-per-month fab experiences a 24 percent cost penalty compared to a 50,000-wafer-per-month fab, even when the two fabs have identical yields, equipment efficiencies, and process technologies (Leachman et al. 1999). Thus there is considerable economic incentive to build and operate large fabs, yet an investment of over $2 billion is impossible for many and perhaps most companies. The outcome of this problem can only be some sort of cost sharing or a reduction of the number of firms in the industry and very few new entrants.

The foundry-fabless partnership offers a market-based collective solution to the imperative of decreasing each individual firm's large capital expenditures for fabrication. The capacity investment risk of a large foundry company can be diversified across the product portfolios of all of its potential customers. The risk and difficulty of assembling sufficient capital can be further defrayed by securing capital investment from potential customers (in return for guaranteed capacity or higher priority). The result for the foundry is that regardless of which fabless firms experience market success, the fab's capacity has a higher probability of being filled, and capacity can be allocated to where it obtains the greatest return. In the face of substantial market risk this pooling of investment risk suggests a greater average return for the fabless-foundry partnerships on investments in manufacturing capacity and development of process technology than for integrated firms independently investing.

The other important economic force is the extraordinary importance of being early to market. Prices for integrated circuit devices generally decline steeply with time, as the devices rapidly become obsolete because of the introduction of superior devices. This results in the prices for semiconductor devices typically declining by 25 to 35 percent per year.

The longer the elapsed times for development and qualification of process technology, fabrication plant construction, ramp-up of yield and wafer volume, and manufacturing cycle, the less the revenue for that particular device. A benchmark comparison by the UC Berkeley CSM Program showed that between manufacturing costs and "delay costs," it was the delay costs that were the most significant. In fact, the importance of delay costs was striking. For example, the difference between lowest manufacturing cost and average manufacturing cost (for a hypothetical, standardized 0.25-micron process technology operated in all the plants), was only $80 per wafer, or about 5 percent of wafer cost. However, the difference between benchmark delay cost and average delay cost was $700 per wafer (Leachman et al. 1999). These results are from a group of seven outstanding factories including fabs operated by the two leading foundry firms in Taiwan, leading DRAM companies in Korea and Japan, and advanced logic firms in the United States and Japan.

The increased importance of speed is striking. Fifteen years ago, in the face of rising Japanese competition, the competitiveness of U.S. semiconductor companies was the focus of U.S. policy-makers. Although U.S. policy-makers attributed Japanese success to unfair government intervention, in fact manufacturing yields at U.S. firms trailed those achieved in Japan. Today, the gap in manufacturing costs between fabs in different regions of the world largely has been narrowed. The chief discriminator of semiconductor firm performance had shifted to speed. Earlier volume sales of advanced products enable a firm to enjoy higher sales prices.

To understand the economic implications of speed-to-market dynamics, consider a semiconductor merchant with an attractive new product that requires an advanced process technology that is not currently in use by the company. The merchant could invest the time and money to develop and qualify the process technology needed to manufacture the product; purchase and install the new process equipment needed to operate the technology; then de-bug the equipment and process to ramp the yield and volume of the process; and finally learn how to reduce the duration of the manufacturing cycle. By the time all this is completed, the value of the device will have dropped considerably.

Then, in addition to the time problem, the capital investment involved is very formidable. The risks thus would be enormous, with the possibility of very low payback.

The contract manufacturer (i.e., a foundry) is already operating a process technology that is nearly suitable for producing the new product. Furthermore, they already have proven good yields and cycle times. It is only necessary to design the new chip to be compatible with the foundry's process technology, though this can lead to a slight performance loss. The cost charged by the contract manufacturer can even be significantly higher—say, 20 to 30 percent higher—than the expected in-house manufacturing cost in a fully loaded economic-scale fab over the life of the process technology. But the time-to-volume can be dramatically lower. If the company anticipates that the average selling price over the life of the product will drop precipitously, then even factoring in the higher cost and the slight performance loss, the foundry option is superior. Moreover, the firm's risk is dramatically lowered.

For many companies, especially start-ups, the foundry alternative is an attractive choice and can be very successful, provided the following three conditions exist:

A willing foundry provides competitive yields, cycle times, and on-time delivery performance.
The new product will be compatible with the foundry's process technology.
The merchant company has the proper electronic data interchange networks for managing their supply chain well, even though their fabrication is subcontracted.

It is widely recognized that the leading Taiwanese foundries satisfy condition (1). TSMC and the UMC Group enjoy excellent reputations for manufacturing service among their North American and European customers and investors. The CSM Program's performance data for these companies confirms this conclusion in terms of manufacturing cycle time, on-time delivery, wafer throughput, and yields for logic devices. These companies are among the industry leaders for logic devices.

Technological innovations including commercial design software and web-based supply chain management systems have allowed conditions (2) and (3) to be met. These innovations enable partnerships of fabless and foundry firms to function nearly as efficiently as integrated firms. One of the key precursors for meeting conditions (2) and (3) was the result of research at UC Berkeley and Stanford undertaken in the early 1980s in the area of computer-aided design of integrated circuits. This led to the development of software now known as electronic design automation (EDA) software. EDA software is a suite of design tools that enable circuit designers not expert in the fabrication process technology to design products that are compatible with that process technology. The parameters of the manufacturing process are supplied to the software, which in turn expresses design rules to the user in terms understandable to a circuit designer. The software analyzes proposed designs supplied by the user to verify that the designs satisfy the design rules.

In practice, a foundry informs its prospective customers of the particular commercial design software for which it will supply process data. The foundry electronically supplies the customer with a data file of its process technology parameters. The user purchases a copy of the design software, also delivered electronically, and proceeds to design semiconductor devices. Typically, each user will maintain an electronic library of designs and partial circuit designs, editing, combining, and adding to them as necessary to complete the new design.

Once the user has verified a design, it contracts with the foundry for its production. The design software outputs specifications to be used for the photomasks. These instructions are sent electronically by the designer to a third-party mask manufacturer. The completed masks are shipped to the foundry, whereupon production may commence. Each step in this process can be undertaken in different countries and companies.

EDA software has proved to be highly effective for digital logic products. Fabless firms generate successful new product designs in rapid succession. Foundry yields for customer-designed logic products have been quite competitive. However, for reasons that will be discussed in the next section, EDA has been somewhat less successful for memory devices and for analog products.

The second important innovation concerns the deployment of software for supply chain management. Semiconductor fabrication is characterized by variability in manufacturing yields and cycle times; it is important to track work-in-progress closely in order to respond to these variations as quickly as possible. The leading foundries offer their customers web-based access to their manufacturing tracking systems. In practice, a foundry user can in real time check the status and progress of each of its manufacturing lots. Process inspection and yield data also are made available electronically, so that the customer may investigate design-process incompatibilities.

Given timely information on the status of work-in-progress and reliable delivery performance from its foundry, the fabless semiconductor merchant can manage its supply chain as well as an integrated company. In fact, given that the availability of manufacturing information is comparable, fabless companies are successfully adopting the very same supply chain management systems used by certain large integrated companies. It is interesting to note that the locations of the three largest concentrations of fabless companies are Silicon Valley; Vancouver, Canada; and Shanghai, China. None of these areas possess advanced foundry fabs, a testimony to the functionality of web-based logistics tools.

## Limitations to Further Transformation of the Industry

As of 2001, there appear to be limits to the continued penetration of the foundry-fabless business model. While the major foundries offer advanced process technology, the foundries still slightly lag the industry leaders. Thus for firms whose business strategy is based on a leadership position in process technology, such as Intel, TI, and IBM, the foundry-fabless model is not attractive for their leading-edge products. Second, commodity memory devices, especially DRAMs and SRAMs, have been difficult for the foundries to manufacture competitively. For such high-volume commodity products, it is essential to strive for the lowest possible manufacturing cost. This requires the development and refinement of a fabrication process technology optimized for the specific product. The number of process steps must be reduced wherever and whenever possible, certain process machines may need to be dedicated and tuned to perform specific process steps, and frequent relatively small modifications of the process technology enabling smaller design rules ("shrinks") likely will be advantageous.

In contrast, the generic process technology typically offered by the foundries is not optimized for fabrication of any particular memory device; instead, the technology must serve to produce a variety of products, and the technology likely will be fixed until replaced by a succeeding generation. According to CSM Program data, DRAM and SRAM yields and manufacturing cycle times achieved by the foundries sometimes have been markedly inferior to those achieved by the integrated DRAM and SRAM companies. The exact cause is difficult to pinpoint, but it could be related to the extreme tightness of the design margins that require considerable process tuning or refinement of the product design based on manufacturing feedback. Likely these kinds of improvements are inhibited by the geographical and corporate separation of product designers and process engineers, as well as the needs of the foundry to service many other customers.

The fabless model also seems to be less prevalent in certain analog and mixed signal products, although there exist several quite successful fabless analog and signal processing companies. Here the problem appears to be the difficulty in achieving design verification. Therefore, there are many more integrated companies in the analog, linear, and mixed signal markets. Here again, these products may require considerable tuning of manufacturing processes on a product-by-product basis, and are thus awkward for foundries to handle. Further, cost pressures are less intense for analog and discrete products that do not require advanced process technology. Many of these devices require process technologies with feature sizes on the order of 1 micron or larger. In these cases, the capital expense for the fabs is an order of magnitude less than for fabrication lines recently built for leading-edge digital products. Typically, secondhand process equipment is used. Given the lower unit costs of process equipment, economies of scale also are less severe. Thus in this sector there are a number of thriving, relatively small, integrated producers of analog, linear, and discrete products.

## The Location of Future Fabrication Facilities[6]

Compared to the number of existing sites, we expect a reduced number of sites worldwide at which new semiconductor fabrication facilities will be constructed. There are two reasons for this. First, as noted in the previous sections of this chapter, there will be fewer firms able to afford new fabrication facilities: a limited number of large foundry firms and a limited number of large integrated device manufacturers (IDMs) or partnerships between large IDMs. Second, the economic scale of fabrication facilities is increasing as the unit cost of process equipment and engineering salaries rise. As a result, fewer fabs are needed, even considering the remarkable growth rate of the industry. To illustrate, the CSM database indicates that approximately 290 fabrication facilities processing 6-inch wafers were built worldwide (beginning in 1984), but only about 180 fabs processing 8-inch wafers have been built (beginning in 1990). We anticipate that, over the next two decades, less than 100 production-volume fabrication facilities processing 12-inch wafers will be built (the first was projected to appear in 2002). Governments in many countries (and states, provinces, and prefectures) will be soliciting the remaining semiconductor manufacturers to locate new fabrication facilities in their homelands. Competition will be keen.

The reasons for locating manufacturing facilities are always quite complicated. The decision about where to locate a new fab is one of the most significant a firm will undertake; for example, the fabrication lines that will process production volumes of 12-inch wafers in advanced process technologies will embody commitments of several billion dollars or more to a particular location. Should that location experience serious difficulties, the potential losses are enormous. To understand the reasoning behind location selection, we queried executives at eighteen major semiconductor firms, and ten responded. In Table 8.7, we indicate the average result for each question on a scale of importance from 1 to 3 (3 = high, 2 = medium, and 1 = low).

TABLE 8.7
*Industry Ranking of Criteria for Locating Fabrication Facilities*

| Advantage | Average score |
| --- | --- |
| Tax advantages | 2.8 |
| Supply of engineering and technical talent | 2.6 |
| Quality of water supply and reliability of utilities | 2.6 |
| Proximity to existing company facilities | 2.6 |
| Environmental permitting process and/or other governmental regulations | 2.5 |
| Opportunity to partner with others in sharing capital expense | 2.4 |
| Cost of living for employees | 2.4 |
| Legal protection of intellectual property | 2.2 |
| Local transportation infrastructure | 2.2 |
| Local college and university programs | 1.8 |
| Manufacturing presence in large foreign markets | 1.6 |

*Source:* Authors' survey.

"Tax advantages" was rated the most important. The reason for the popularity of the tax advantages category is that the fab process equipment is so expensive ($600 million or more in many existing fabs) that sales tax is a very significant cost. For example, California's sales tax of approximately 7 percent would cost $42 million or more. Thus government policies offering tax discounts can be important for attracting new fabs. There is, of course, an important proviso—namely, that sufficient technical talent and appropriate utility services are available. Indeed, during the second half of the 1990s, U.S. states such as Oregon, Washington, and Virginia using such policies attracted considerable investment in advanced fabrication facilities

If taxes were considered most important, only slightly lower marks were received by "supply of engineering and technical talent," "quality of water supply and reliability of utilities," and "proximity to existing company facilities." In fact, the supply of talent category and the utility category can be seen as prerequisites for receiving any consideration at all. The more interesting category was "proximity to existing facilities." Here we believe there was a matrix of considerations. First, an existing site may already possess environmental permits and other approvals needed for the construction of a new fabrication facility on the site, obviating potentially lengthy delays to obtain such permits for a new site—though this explanation may be partially accounted for in the "environmental permitting process" category. Probably the most important consideration in this category is the ability of the firm to leverage its existing investment in staff and infrastructure and avoid the time and cost of creating basic manufacturing knowledge in a newly hired workforce, including line workers, technicians, and especially engineers. When engineering staff can be shared among multiple manufacturing facilities, the savings in staff—and in time to develop that staff—are quite significant. It is also possible to move the experienced technicians and engineers from the existing, though now older and less sophisticated, fabs to the new fab to help ramp it up to full production.

"Cost of living" and the "Opportunity to share capital expense" received medium-high scores on average. Interestingly, the scores were quite disparate for the sharing of capital expense category. The large Taiwanese foundries, the two largest U.S. integrated logic companies, and the largest DRAM producer rated it of low or medium importance, while other integrated American companies and all of the Japanese integrated producers responding to the survey gave it high importance. Receiving only medium importance were the local transportation category and protection of intellectual property category. Receiving relatively low importance scores were the categories for local colleges and universities and the manufacturing presence in large foreign markets.

These results suggest to us that the United States possesses few advantages for attracting new fabrication facilities. It is not considered important by most of the large manufacturers to have a substantial manufacturing presence in the United States—or any other market, for that matter. U.S. strengths in the areas of protection of intellectual property, transportation infrastructure, and local colleges and universities are not considered important from the perspective of manufacturing. Also, firms are concerned about the cost of living, plentiful supply of water and utilities, and a swift environmental permitting process, factors for which the United States may not offer any clear advantage over locales such as Taiwan, South Korea, Japan, and parts of Europe. If firms already have a major manufacturing presence in the United States, the importance of the "proximity" factor suggests that the prospects of keeping manufacturing activity may be good. But for attracting new manufacturing presence, the prospects are not so good. Since tax advantages are the most important category, it is probable that tax relief will be necessary to entice companies to locate new fabs in the United States.

We also asked the firms to mention any other considerations of great importance in selecting locations for fabrication facilities. A major Taiwanese foundry firm indicated that it attached high importance to the fact that the U.S. federal government's Export Administration prohibited the export of semiconductor manufacturing equipment capable of sub-0.25 micron fabrication to certain countries, notably mainland China. In the short run, this effectively blocks China from being able to construct advanced fabrication facilities, though this might also provide a market opportunity for firms that compete with U.S. equipment makers. Evidently China will not be a major locale for leading-edge semiconductor manufacturing until either U.S. export regulations are changed, or else competitive suppliers located in countries willing to export to China come into existence for all major types of fabrication equipment.

## Summary

The semiconductor industry is experiencing a remarkable transformation. Until the early 1990s, the industry consisted almost entirely of integrated firms. Increasingly, the industry now includes fabless firms carrying out the product definition, design, and marketing functions, partnered with foundry firms that develop process technology and provide contract-manufacturing services. Increasing from an 8 percent share at the beginning of the 1990s, pure-play foundry companies commanded more than 25 percent of worldwide capacity in 2001. Almost all of this capacity is located in the Asia Pacific region.

The key economic and technological factors fueling this transformation are as follows: first, the capital cost of economic-scale, advanced fabrication facilities is beyond the financial reach of most firms, yet small start-up firms account for many new, innovative products. The fabless-foundry organization diversifies the risk of large fabrication facilities across the product portfolios of all firms that are potential customers. It reduces barriers to entry and the time-to-market for small and medium-sized design firms, thereby enabling these firms to secure considerably more revenue than if they had to undertake process development and manufacturing on their own. Second, effective software and communications tools have been developed that enable fabless-foundry partnerships to successfully compete with integrated firms. These tools include design automation software and supply chain management systems. Application of design automation software, involving considerable exchange of technical data between fabless and foundry partners, enables product designers unfamiliar with the manufacturing process technology to design devices that achieve competitive yields. Application of supply chain management software, also involving considerable exchange of technical data, enables fabless companies to efficiently manage their work-in-process despite subcontracting its manufacture, and it enables foundry operators to sustain full utilization of their manufacturing facilities. Third, there have been a number of successful start-ups in the Asia Pacific region of pure-play foundry companies, led by TSMC and the UMC Group in Taiwan. Availability of competitive foundry services from these companies has made possible a rapid growth in the United States of fabless company start-ups, as well as an increasing trend among established integrated firms to outsource portions of their fabrication needs to the foundries.

Few integrated firms excel at both design/marketing and manufacturing. Vastly different management skills are needed, and each area thrives in a different kind of business culture. The new industry structure facilitates the success of firms strong in one area but not the other.

Nevertheless, the fabless/foundry reorganization of the industry has limitations. It has proved very successful for digital logic products, and, to a lesser extent, for mixed signal and analog products. But there are two principal digital markets where this business model is not yet applied or has not worked well: (1) microprocessors, digital signal processors, and other sophisticated semiconductors utilizing leading-edge process technology; and (2) commodity memory devices with tight design margins and low-cost requirements, especially DRAMs and SRAMs.

The resulting dynamics lead to a polarized organization of the industry. Where the foundry-fabless business model has proved successful—that is, in logic and certain mixed signal markets—the industry is reorganizing into fabless firms supported by a number of foundry companies in the Asia Pacific region. Those portions of the industry for which the fabless/foundry model is not successful or not applicable are concentrating into a few very large integrated firms or partnerships of large integrated firms able to afford new fabrication facilities. Those portions include commodity memory devices and the most sophisticated logic devices requiring leading-edge process technology. Only the discrete and analog/linear/mixed signal portions of the industry that are able to utilize older process technology continue to feature successful integrated firms with a wide range of sizes, from small to large. When expressed as a percentage of total fabrication capacity, those businesses utilizing older process technologies are relatively small.

The foundry-fabless transformation of the industry has enabled the United States to increase its dominance of the design and marketing of integrated circuits. Nevertheless, the share of worldwide fabrication capacity located in the United States has stagnated since 1985 and seems likely to decline in the future as the fabless/foundry model makes further inroads. Considering that both DRAM production and foundry production have become concentrated in the Asia Pacific region, that region now commands about 40 percent of worldwide fabrication capacity, with more than 85 percent of that amount located in Taiwan and South Korea. It is arresting how rapidly world fabrication capacity is becoming concentrated in a handful of countries, and a testimony to how fast industrial organization can be transformed when strong economic forces and enabling technologies are in place.

Three of the five cross-cutting themes of this book are strongly present in semiconductors. First, Internet connections used for transmission of fabless company designs to the foundries and for transmission of work-in-process status back to fabless companies carrying out their supply-chain management demonstrate how advanced communications have facilitated this evolution of the industry. Second, speed in the sense of time-to-market is arguably the strongest determinant of success in the industry, both for the integrated firms developing and deploying advanced process technology to bring huge volumes of the latest standard microprocessors or standard memory chips to market, as well as for the fabless firms utilizing foundries to gain early market access for their niche products. And third, pricing pressures also have shaped the modern organization of the industry, but in a different way. In particular, prices in the industry are most competitive for standard memory products such as DRAMs and SRAMs, whose cost pressures have hindered fabless/foundry partnerships from making significant inroads on the market shares of integrated firms in this segment of the industry. More broadly, the relentless pace of technological advances and consequent obsolescence drives a rapid decline in the price for virtually every semiconductor product and manufacturing service, bringing us back to the speed theme.

The two themes of clustering and proximity to customers are not very descriptive of the modern semiconductor industry today. While in its early days the semiconductor industry was concentrated in Silicon Valley, nowadays advanced semiconductor fabrication is successfully carried out in many locations across the United States, Japan, Europe, and the Asia Pacific region. While there are concentrated sites of fabrication activity such as Hsin-chu, Taiwan, Kiheung, Korea, or Portland, Oregon, these are more the result of government incentives and individual firm strategy than of any synergies from collocation of firms or of unique concentrations of specialized knowledge. And while Silicon Valley features a large concentration of fabless firms and design centers of integrated firms, nonetheless there are many successful fabless firms and integrated firm design centers spread throughout the four regions.

To return to the question of whether "real men have fabs," we have shown that for deploying certain product and technology strategies, integrated device manufacturers indeed have an edge. But for the design and marketing of a growing number of semiconductor products, fabless companies forging networks of alliances are a great success.

## Notes

This research was performed as part of the Competitive Semiconductor Manufacturing Program at the University of California, Berkeley. The CSM Program is sponsored by the Alfred P. Sloan Foundation, the Semiconductor Industry Research Institute of Japan, the Electronics Industry Association of Japan, SEMATECH, Taiwan Semiconductor Manufacturing Corp., United Microelectronics Corp., Winbond Electronics, Samsung Electronics Corp., Ltd., MiCRUS, Cypress Semiconductor Corp., and ST Microelectronics. The views expressed herein do not necessarily reflect the views of any sponsor.

1. By "Asia Pacific" we mean all Asian countries excluding Japan. The primary countries in the Asia Pacific region for semiconductor fabrication are Taiwan, South Korea, and, to a lesser extent, Singapore.

2. Use of contract P&T manufacturers located in the Asia Pacific region also has been common for many years.

3. Curiously, the merchant hard disk drive firms described in McKendrick's contribution actually learned about the advantages of assembling in Asia from the semiconductor firms (see McKendrick, this volume, and McKendrick et al. 2000).

4. In the case of the Korean firms, capital was readily available at subsidized rates from the Korean government. This facilitated the entry of the Korean firms, because DRAMs are very capital intensive, so low-cost capital is a significant advantage.

5. "Midyear Investment Guide," *Business Week*, June 26, 2000.

6. This section discusses the results of a survey we conducted of executives of eighteen major manufacturers of advanced digital integrated circuits regarding the reasons they had for locating a fab.

# CHAPTER NINE

# The Net World Order's Influence on Global Leadership in the Semiconductor Industry

GREG LINDEN

CLAIR BROWN

MELISSA M. APPLEYARD

The large and diverse market space for semiconductors has both product and geographic dimensions. The product dimension of semiconductor applications spans a vast range of assembled goods, from musical greeting cards to cars to supercomputers. Geographically, there are significant differences among the consumption and trade patterns of the major semiconductor-producing regions, and these patterns impact the ability of semiconductor firms to compete globally. This chapter combines a geographical analysis with an examination of location in market space.

In the electronics industry product space, the gradual but fundamental shift currently underway serves as the focus of this chapter. First and foremost, the PC sector is declining in relative importance as a market for chips as communications applications grow. Although the spectacular boom and bust that began in 1998 has impacted the trend, it has not stopped it, as PC sales remain flat while certain wireless and networking applications continue to grow.

This shift in the electronics industry has been widely heralded as the dawn of the "Post-PC era," in which the central application is the Internet, along with the home, office, and wireless networks connected to it.[1] These networks represent a convergence that is progressively blurring the distinctions between the computer, consumer, and communications industries. The global mass of large and small companies involved in creating, producing, and serving these networks we call the "Net World Order" (NWO).

But even as the electronics industry coalesces around networks, the global semiconductor market remains stubbornly divided by geography. In the decades following its U.S.-based origins in the 1960s, integrated circuit technology diffused to companies located in Europe, Japan, and then the rest of

Asia (Tilton 1971; Braun and Macdonald 1982; Borrus 1988). The industry was one of the first to develop a globalized production system beginning with the 1960s relocation to low-cost countries of final assembly plants serving major markets, which was followed by the gradual relocation of some design and fabrication activities (Henderson 1989). Yet while sales were similarly global in scope, important regional variations in demand persist.

This chapter argues that the emergence of the NWO is shifting the bases for leadership in the semiconductor industry. Leadership is less heavily influenced than before by production capability and competitive pricing and is more dependent upon product development and marketing. This argument is based upon several interrelated global transformations in the semiconductor industry:

- the growing fragmentation of product markets further diversified by regional patterns,
- the increasing commoditization of semiconductor production (discussed in Leachman and Leachman), and
- the presence of the network service provider (or carrier) as a major player in the NWO value chain.

In this era of more differentiated regional and product markets, location in market space (i.e., product choice and regional market positioning) requires focused attention just as much as the locational choices considered in the other industry chapters of this book. Our research indicates that for semiconductor firms, profitable participation in the regional markets of the NWO often requires involvement in setting standards or collaborating with a carrier from a different region than that of the chip company.

This is in sharp contrast to the historical pattern in the industry, in which chip firms participated in locally embedded value chains that subsequently globalized as a product market developed. Successful development of chips for NWO markets requires competency in systems-integration skills, a wide variety of design-related intellectual property, and, increasingly, software competency. This skill set was of much less relevance to chip companies focused on the PC market.

We do not expect the chip industry of the Net World Order to be dominated by one company, as Intel dominated in the PC era. Overall we expect a shift in revenues away from U.S.-based chip firms toward European and Asian competitors, although the size of the shift is unpredictable at this point.

Our findings are based on fieldwork, public information sources, and private data sets. We conducted interviews at over a dozen semiconductor and system firms in the United States and Europe, and we supplemented this, especially to learn about companies not in our sample, with publicly available information in trade journals and company reports. We obtained data to document industry trends from Dataquest.

This chapter begins with an analysis of the evolving product space for semiconductors and the underlying skills required for the primary markets (wireless applications, consumer multimedia, and networking infrastructure) that are converging into the Net World Order. Relationships along the NWO value chain are discussed, with emphasis on the critical position occupied by regional carriers. Since global performance depends increasingly upon the firm's ability to market to diverse regional customers, a chipmaker's regional advantage may depend heavily upon its ability to form strategic partnerships with carriers as well as system companies. In section 2, the geography of product markets is presented, and data related to the impact of regional market differences on semiconductor firm performance are analyzed. The chapter concludes with a summary and outlook.

## The Semiconductor Industry In Product Space

The product space supplied by the semiconductor industry changes with shifts in demand patterns and technology, and it is undergoing a steady evolution from dominance by the PC industry to a proliferation of network-related applications. The computing, communications, and consumer industries are converging around a small set of networking technologies that has induced experimentation with products that cross what used to be solid boundaries. So far this convergence has presented companies with the opportunity to compete in new markets. Most likely, the product markets of the NWO will never be as uniform as the PC market.

We begin with a quantitative overview of the evolving product space faced by chip makers. From there we focus specifically on the four key product markets of the emerging NWO. The four markets are presented and then compared with regard to the relative importance of chip company skills for succeeding in each one.

### Semiconductor Sales by Final Product Market

Figure 9.1 documents the importance of the PC (and data processing equipment more generally) for the semiconductor industry since 1988, and the relative increase in importance of communications equipment since the mid-1990s. During the early 1990s, the share of semiconductor sales to products in the data processing sector climbed steadily to a 1995 peak of more than 50 percent of all semiconductors sold. By 2000, data processing's share,

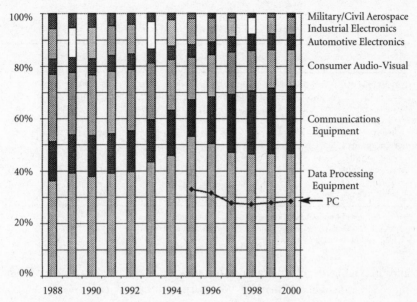

FIG. 9.1. Sales of Semiconductors by Final Product Market, 1988–2000. Source: Dataquest (July 2000).

about three-fifths of which is accounted for by personal computers alone, had fallen to 47 percent, while the share of chip sales to the communications sector (both wireline and wireless) almost doubled to 26 percent.

Figure 9.1 suggests the emergence of the NWO by the relative decline of the PC sector, but also obscures it. It does not, for example, show how many chips went into set-top boxes (classed as consumer electronics) that are now connected to the Internet.

*Four Key Industries of the Semiconductor Industry*

The four key product segments of the emerging NWO are

- fixed computing (PCs, servers, mainframes, LAN equipment);
- wireless applications (digital cell phones and infrastructure);
- consumer multimedia (video game consoles, digital set-top boxes); and
- wired infrastructure (central office equipment, routers).

Although some products in these categories, such as cell phones and game consoles, are not yet universally capable of transmitting data, we assume that they will be in the near future. Of course even without an Internet connection, cell phones and set-top boxes are connected to a network service provider (carrier),

TABLE 9.1
*The Chip Markets of the Net World Order*

|  | Fixed computing | Wireless applications | Consumer multimedia | Wired infrastructure | All electronics |
|---|---|---|---|---|---|
| Largest product category | personal computer | digital cell phones | video game consoles | central office equipment |  |
| Share of chip market revenue in 1999 | 37% | 10% | 3% | 4% | 100% |
| Forecast growth rate[a] to 2004 | 11% | 20% | 23% | 25% | 14% |
| Average ratio of ICs to system wholesale price | 32% | 20% | 51% | 10% | 17% |

*Source:* Calculated from Dataquest reports issued in Spring 2000.
  *Note:* This table uses product categories built from product-level detail.
  [a]Compound annual growth rate.

and this fact is one of the features that separate NWO product markets from the older, nonconnected markets. We return to this point below.

Table 9.1 provides a rough quantitative characterization of these four markets, which amounted to approximately 54 percent of all chip sales in 1999. The computer market for chips is projected to grow at a rate less than the industry average for the next few years, while the opposite is true for chip sales in the other NWO categories. These projections predate the severe downturn in the semiconductor industry during 2001, but they should still be useful for indicating the expected relative sizes of these markets, if not their absolute magnitude, by 2004.

Overall, the combined chip sales in these NWO products are predicted to grow at roughly the same rate as the semiconductor market as a whole and will continue to amount to just over half of all chip sales. Many products whose primary function is far removed from networking, such as cars, appliances, and industrial robots, will also contain networking chips but are excluded from the NWO segments in the table. Network-related chip sales in these product markets will further augment the relative importance of the NWO for the chip industry.

Integrated circuits are at the heart of all Internet-related devices, but their importance relative to the total product value varies widely across (as well as within) these segments, as shown in the last line of the table. PCs are relatively high (32 percent) in the share of wholesale price attributable to chips, as are new consumer products such as the video game consoles and digital set-top boxes, which contain few other parts. At the other extreme, cell phones and telecom infrastructure are relatively low (under 20 percent) in the value of the chips they contain, since software adds a larger share of value in these products.

Fixed computing will remain the most important market of the NWO for the near future, but the faster growth of the other network-related segments (wireless, multimedia, and infrastructure) will produce increasing fragmentation relative to the much more homogeneous computing sector. Even memory chips, one of the most commoditized semiconductor devices of the PC era, are becoming a more fragmented market in which multiple standards (particularly Rambus and Double-Data Rate) are competing for market share. Application-specific variants have also appeared—for example, for fast networking infrastructure equipment. Growth markets for memory chips in mobile consumer products have still different technology requirements, such as low power consumption, which will further fragment the product category.

*Product Market Attributes*

Four attributes of NWO product markets (Table 9.2) affect the ability of semiconductor firms to capture value commensurate with their innovative contributions.

Standards for PCs have been relatively stable (for further discussion of the PC, see Chapter 5). Although the underlying technology for PCs has evolved dramatically, the market's dominance by Intel and Microsoft has kept the development path predictable. Intel's control of a de facto standard has given it tremendous bargaining power with its customers.

Standards for wireless applications and network infrastructure are also fairly stable, but for a very different reason—namely, that they are determined by negotiation within international committees. The underlying intellectual property may still be owned by firms, as in the case of Qualcomm's CDMA, but they must be available for licensing to become de jure standards. A public standard, in sharp contrast to proprietary standards such as Intel's, reduces the bargaining power of chip firms because the public standard reduces or removes intellectual property entry barriers, increasing the likelihood that systems firms will be able to purchase their components from multiple sources.

The equipment comprising the Internet infrastructure must meet strict re-

TABLE 9.2
*Market Attributes in the Net World Order*

|  | Personal computers | Wireless (mobile) applications | Consumer (fixed) multimedia | Networking infrastructure |
|---|---|---|---|---|
| Standards | Stable/Owned | Stable/Shared | Unstable | Stable/Public |
| Market Size | Very large | Large | Potentially large | Small |
| Adoption | Network Effects | Network Effects | Individual | Individual |
| Infrastructure | Independent | Dependent | Dependent | Dependent |

*Source:* Authors' compilation.

quirements for interoperability set by official bodies like the International Telecommunications Union and industry organizations, such as the Internet Engineering Task Force. Reflecting the importance of underlying chip technology in meeting infrastructure standards, Cisco acquired a U.S.-based chip company, AuroraNetics, Inc., in 2001, to own the IP central to a new metropolitan area delivery standard (802.17) that was under development by an IEEE working group.[2] Because of this predictability in technical standards, the primary challenge for chip companies serving the markets of the Internet infrastructure is to be first to market with the newest generation, such as a faster Ethernet chip. This has led some chip producers to launch their designs ahead of the completion of the bureaucratic standard-setting process. This strategy entails risk, however, because the chip may need an expensive redesign to be compatible with the ultimate official standard.

In sharp contrast, standards in the emerging market for Internet-related consumer products are quite fragmented. First, there are a wide variety of machine types that consumers can potentially adopt to access the Internet. In addition to PCs, which are still by far the largest means of access, consumers may also choose from among a box connected to the television set, a cell phone or PDA, and a host of "Internet appliances" such as a dedicated e-mail device. The set-top box could be designed to handle cable, satellite, or broadcast transmission. Each type of application requires mastery of a different type of technology (e.g., radio transmission and power management for cell phones, or video processing in the case of set-top boxes). In each instance, the relevant standards are likely to be some combination of public, proprietary, or even undetermined, as in the case of high-definition television in the United States.

The second attribute, market size, has played a greater role for the PC market than it will likely play for NWO (and most electronics) products. At the other extreme, the market for Internet infrastructure products is relatively small because the total number of routers and switches that can be sold in any one year is necessarily limited by demand for capacity.

Wireless and consumer multimedia applications are an intermediate case. The Net-connected parts of these sectors are in the early stage of product development and acceptance, but Internet-enabled devices have already demonstrated the potential for tremendous growth. NTT DoCoMo's "i-mode" Web-enabled cell phone system expanded its subscriber base from zero at its introduction in February 1999 to more than 5 million by March 2000.[3]

The third attribute, adoption, characterizes a market by whether user choices are made in isolation or are made in the presence of network effects. The IBM-standard (sometimes known as "Wintel") PC is a classic case of network effects because software development and the ability to share files depended upon other people using the same platform—that is, the attractiveness of adoption to one individual increases with the total number of users.

NWO products are unlikely to exhibit network effects at the hardware level, even in cellular telephony, where technological innovation in cell phones allows access across incompatible standards. Chip customers in all markets are very wary of allowing another Intel-style standard to emerge that gives a single supplier undue market power. Cable companies, for example, are promulgating an open standard (DOCSIS) that will ensure the availability of multiple, interchangeable suppliers in the interactive set-top box market.[4] Public standards, such as the W-CDMA wireless data specification, are also designed through protracted negotiation to avoid giving individual companies an inordinate amount of leverage. More fundamentally, the Internet's success is built on the notions of interconnectivity and interoperability at the hardware level, which will likely prevent the cumulative phenomena of the PC era from recurring.

What is true for hardware need not be true for services, however. The tremendous growth of DoCoMo's i-mode service reflects network effects because DoCoMo's strict veto power over which services have access to its proprietary portal can keep some functions out of the hands of its rivals.[5] Issues of access by non-AOL portals to Warner-owned cable systems were also addressed in the antitrust negotiations over the AOL-Time Warner merger. These issues of dominance of a service are also in the forefront of what Microsoft will be allowed to do with the bundling of services in Windows XP.

The fourth market attribute is the importance of infrastructure, which is closely related to adoption in defining the market. All Web access devices, whether fixed or wireless, require an extensive and specific infrastructure (e.g., cable, DSL, satellite) before the device can be used by customers, and some devices (e.g., a DirecTV satellite receiver) are specific to the technology of a single network. Infrastructure dependency deserves special attention because it emphasizes the importance in the NWO value chain of the carrier, who owns or controls the network required to connect the user to the service. The relationship between the chip maker and the carrier can have a major impact on the ability of chip companies to innovate and earn rents, as discussed in more detail below.

Service provider strategies may ultimately lead to fragmentation of the Internet in a way that would make network effects more common. The prolonged coexistence of three multiple, incompatible Instant Messaging programs may be a harbinger. But unless a successful software or service option is tied to a particular hardware platform, which has so far not been the case, the network effects at the software level will be irrelevant for semiconductor suppliers except to the extent it underscores the importance of forming strategic alliances.

*Firm Competencies*

The competencies needed by chip firms, especially in integration skills and design-related IP, in the nascent markets of the NWO differ markedly from those that have been relevant to the PC era (Table 9.3). When we interviewed representatives at semiconductor and systems firms, a competency that was often mentioned as an attribute of successful chip companies was speed, or "time-to-market." This cuts across both the PC era and the NWO because the steady improvement of chip technology leaves products relatively short market windows before something better, faster, or cheaper comes along. Often the chip maker must know from the customer what technologies will be used in the next generation in order to have the chip ready when the customer wants it, and often this knowledge is shared only between strategic partners. The need for speed is not included in the table because it is so pervasive in the electronics industry, but it is worth noting that a reputation for delivering working chips in a timely manner is a basic requirement for chip firms to create and capture value. With that, we turn to the competencies that distinguish, to differing degrees, the PC era from the NWO.

Process skills have played a critical role in differentiating chip producers in the PC era, but fabrication skills are less important to the NWO. In the PC market, Intel created a competitive wedge between itself and its rivals by remaining in the forefront of process technology, and it has maintained its own manufacturing capability for microprocessors rather than using contract manufacturing services (Appleyard et al. 2000). Process skills are also vital to the competitiveness of memory chip manufacturers.

Process skills are relatively less important in the other three NWO markets thanks to the rise of "foundries"—semiconductor manufacturing service providers that design no chips of their own. Foundries have achieved technical levels in manufacturing that rival those of the leading vertically integrated producers, and they have built up formidable capacity (Leachman and Leachman, this volume). The availability of high-quality foundry service permits some chip firms to specialize in design and avoid building costly fabrication facilities ("fabs").

TABLE 9.3
*The Relevance of Competencies in the Net World Order*

|  | Personal computers | Wireless applications | Consumer multimedia | Networking infrastructure |
|---|---|---|---|---|
| Process skills | Yes | No | No | No |
| Integration skills | No | Yes | Yes | No |
| Intellectual property | Yes | Varies by application | | |

*Source:* Authors' compilation.

In wireless, for example, Qualcomm was able to grow rapidly to account for more than 7 percent of the market for digital cellular chips while owning no fab of its own. Qualcomm's strength is the intellectual property that it owns, along with the system-level knowledge needed to successfully design a highly integrated chip set.

Many successful companies in the consumer broadband and network infrastructure markets, such as Broadcom and PMC-Sierra, are also fabless and compete on the strength of their intellectual property and fast time-to-market. Such fabless companies account for about 10 percent of the chip industry's sales.[6]

Integration of multiple functions on a chip, which requires system-level engineering skills, has become a critical skill in the NWO for several reasons (Linden and Somaya 1999). High levels of integration provide the means for chip companies to offer their customers faster time to market by providing a ready-made system. A system-level chip will contain at least the central processor and most of the main memory plus any of a range of additional functions, including protocol converters, signal processors, and various input and output controllers. Of equal importance is the software (operating system and programming interfaces) included in the package, which is often the basis by which the chip customer can differentiate its product in the downstream market.

Integration brings other benefits, including increased reliability, greater speed, lower unit manufacturing cost, lower power consumption, and smaller size. Lower cost is especially attractive for consumer markets, where high price is often the biggest barrier to the adoption of new technologies such as digital set-top boxes and personal digital assistants (PDAs). Small size and low power are clearly important for mobile wireless applications, but also for uses where space and heat dissipation are problematic, such as Web hosting data centers and telecommunications central offices.

For the chip company, a high level of integration on one or a few chips requires that all the necessary technologies must be brought together at one time either through internal efforts, licensing, or acquisition. Horizontally diversified firms that already own a broad range of intellectual property tend to have an advantage in these markets because they do not need to negotiate agreements for outside IP, which may slow product release, or pay royalties to third parties. For example, the firms that had announced system-on-a-chip solutions for digital set-top boxes by 1999 were Motorola, IBM, LSI Logic, STMicroelectronics, and Matsushita Electric Industrial. Each of these firms carries an extensive product portfolio and has sufficient system engineering expertise in-house to design system-level semiconductors.

Even large, diversified chip firms may, however, be missing pieces of the system. This need has given rise to a growing market for the exchange of "intellectual property (IP) blocks," which are partial chip designs that can be integrated in a single system-level design. Intellectual property can also be acquired rather than licensed. An example on a large scale was the $800 million purchase in 1999 by Philips of VLSI Technology for its strong portfolio of communications-related intellectual property that Philips needed to pursue new applications such as home networking.[7]

Integration is also increasingly important in the PC market as it confronts the NWO, although, historically, system-level integration skills were not a required competency of PC-oriented chip companies. Specialized niches in the PC, such as graphics chips, are being absorbed by the ever-larger microprocessor or its closely connected logic chip set. In the case of graphics, Intel chose to acquire the necessary know-how by purchasing a U.S.-based graphics chip supplier called Chips & Technologies in 1997, and incorporated the technology in an integrated chip set beginning in 1999.[8]

The importance of the third competence, design-related (as opposed to process-related) intellectual property, has already been touched on with regards to both the PC and the emergent applications of the NWO. Intel owned, refined, and defended the x86 architecture, which forced rivals to invent around this architecture while complementary component makers had to guarantee compatibility with it. In the NWO, chip firms still develop or acquire unique IP as a means of earning higher rents. Philips, for example, developed the TriMedia processor for consumer multimedia applications including set-top boxes. Ultimately, Philips decided to spin-off the TriMedia business to make it more attractive to outside customers.[9] Chip companies specializing in network infrastructure, such as PMC-Sierra, also boast a large portfolio of patented technologies.[10] As discussed above, Qualcomm provides an example of the importance of intellectual property in wireless applications.

However our interviews also revealed some negative aspects of IP development and ownership. One executive from a large chip maker warned that IP ownership could lead to technological "lock-in" that might prevent the company from pursuing more successful alternatives—a problem exacerbated by the unsettled nature of many NWO standards. Another interviewee pointed out that development of elaborate IP, such as a potential proprietary standard, can be so costly that it is not necessarily more profitable in the long run unless the actual size of the eventual market meets expectations.

## NWO Value Chains

The NWO value chain differs from the PC value chain by the very important addition of the carrier, who controls the infrastructure that connects users to networks. Carriers have a regional focus, since they must operate under regional standards and usually have a regionally situated infrastructure for delivery (satellites being the exception). For these reasons, carriers play the regional gatekeepers to the rest of the NWO value chain. Carriers may interact directly with chip suppliers to develop, sponsor, or test new products and services. The distribution of rents in this more complex value chain differs from one case to the next based on the relative bargaining power of participants, which we examine next.

During most of its existence, the PC was a stand-alone phenomenon, or at most was used within corporate networks. Even with widespread adoption of the Internet, the network specificity of a PC usually ends at its modem or network interface card. All Web access devices, whether fixed or wireless, require an extensive and specific infrastructure (e.g., cable, DSL, satellite) before the device can be used by customers, and many devices (e.g., a DirecTV satellite receiver) are network-specific.

Network dependence tends to increase the bargaining power of the network service provider, particularly since the number of networks is usually limited in any given location for economic or regulatory reasons. However the presence of network service providers in the value chain also presents chip firms with the possibility of developing and marketing new services for a specific network, which will increase the chip company's leverage with system firms.

Table 9.4 presents the ways a chip firm can interact with the rest of the value chain and designates the most likely relationships as primary and secondary pathways. The starting points of the arrows in the table represent the source of control (e.g., who is placing an order), and a double-headed arrow indicates a strategic partnership. The structure of a pathway has implications for the bargaining power of the chip maker.

The PC era has a simple configuration because of the absence of carriers from the value chain. Although PCs are used to access the Internet, they have important stand-alone uses independent of any infrastructure. As shown earlier, Intel has commanded enormous bargaining power with systems (i.e., PC) manufacturers, which translated into high profits.

As we learned in our interviews, carriers, for the most part, do not care what chips are used in the systems they buy, provided the system meets the necessary functional specifications. Chip companies, however, told us that contact with carriers could be beneficial for several reasons. A chip company executive reported that contact with carriers sometimes revealed special needs that could be addressed at the chip level. We also learned of one instance where carriers provided support for a chip-level standard that systems firms had rejected. Finally, a consumer chip firm explained that if they understand the carrier's cost

TABLE 9.4

*Value Chain Configurations of the Net World Order*

| | Personal computers | Wireless applications | Consumer multimedia | Networking infrastructure |
|---|---|---|---|---|
| Primary Pathways | IC → S | IC ← S ← C | IC ← S ↔ C | IC ↔ S ↔ C |
| Secondary Pathway (if any) | | IC S ↔ C | IC ↔ S → C | |

*Source:* Authors' compilation.

*Key:* IC = chip company; S = system company; C = carrier (network operator); ↔ = strategic partnership; → = arm's length supply relationship (arrow's origin indicates source of authority).

structure, they can structure their own costs to match. In contrast, if the chip firm deals exclusively with a systems firm, the systems firm will have already set a price for its deal with a carrier, and will be focused on driving down the chip price to raise its own profit.

These examples point to the possible relationships in the NWO value chain and their impact on the bargaining position of the chip maker. Wireless devices are infrastructure-dependent and must be compatible with an available network. The compatibility can be limited to the interface, as in the case of a hand-held computer with an interchangeable modem, or network features can be tightly integrated, as in upcoming third-generation cell phones that will exploit network-specific features such as music downloading or global positioning services. The common arrangement is for the carrier to work with a system firm to design a new handset, and then to let the system firm decide which chips to use. This primary pathway minimizes the bargaining position of chip suppliers.

In cases where they can enable new network services, chip companies may work directly with carriers (secondary pathway). For example, Qualcomm developed a multimedia software suite known as Wireless Internet Launchpad to run on its CDMA chip set. In order to enable adoption in Japan, Qualcomm had to first work with the local CDMA network providers to run complementary software on their systems before striking deals with individual handset manufacturers.[11]

Qualcomm's entire business was built on working not only with carriers but also with government agencies across regional boundaries.[12] Its CDMA technology faced resistance because of doubts about its technical feasibility. To grow the market, the company sought alliances in any receptive location so that the feasibility could be demonstrated. One of the earliest and most important of these alliances was in Korea, where the government entered a Joint Development Agreement with Qualcomm in 1991. Qualcomm was actively involved during the following years of development and trials by local carriers and man-

ufacturers while the technology and the CDMA chip sets that ran it were refined. Korean CDMA service was rolled out on a large scale in 1996, when the
technology was just beginning to take root in the United States. Korean CDMA
subscribers continued to outnumber those in the United States in 2001.

The strategic relationship between Qualcomm and the carriers greatly increased the chip company's bargaining power vis-à-vis the system (i.e., handset
and base-station) manufacturers. Although the chip company must maintain
good relationships with the system manufacturers to avoid being shut out of
future business opportunities, the chip company will exert more bargaining
power over the system house when it can offer a chip that has been tightly tailored to the specific functionality requirements of a carrier. Another wireless
chip supplier, Motorola, anticipates that carriers will be in even closer contact
with chip suppliers because systems will increasingly be built around programmable platforms (i.e., system-level chips and associated software).[13]

The primary path in the consumer multimedia market is the same as in
wireless—designs derive from interactions between a system firm and a network service provider. Thus a cable company might promulgate a set-top box
specification across several potential suppliers. These system companies, in
turn, work with potential semiconductor suppliers to develop the proposed
product. The carrier then selects one or more system suppliers, only indirectly
selecting the chip suppliers at the same time. America Online, for example,
chose Philips to assemble its initial cable set-top box, and Philips in turn tapped
Boca Research, a communications company, for a reference design that was
based on a processor from National Semiconductor.[14]

Strategic partnerships between chip and systems firms (secondary pathway)
are one coping mechanism for chip makers in the face of the unstable standards
of the consumer market, and one of the major proponents of this approach is
STMicroelectronics, a Franco-Italian joint venture created in 1986. In the words
of Jean-Phillipe Dauvin, the company's chief economist: "System-on-chip
means the silicon must be developed in a very tight linkage to the final users. . . .
The winning companies will be the companies that form strategic alliances
with customers."[15] In the words of a stock analyst that follows the company,
STMicro "works with leading manufacturers in principal sectors on the next-
generation products so they get locked into the design cycle."[16] STMicro's
strategic partners include Nokia, Ericsson, and Alcatel.

In the rare cases where the chip company initiates a product development
pathway, the chip firm can structure its relationships to leave it with maximum
leverage in future price negotiations. In an extreme example of chip maker initiative, National Semiconductor created a coalition around a design for a "Web-
pad" to be based on a specialized processor for which it saw a need to jump-

start the market. National worked with Taiwan's Acer for manufacturing plus two U.S.-based firms—Merinta for software and Internet Appliance Network for marketing and network services.[17] The initial customer was Virgin, a British retail company interested in exploring a new business model. In this scenario, the carrier was probably in the weakest bargaining position.

Finally, the network infrastructure market is characterized by two strategic partnerships centered on systems companies. The system firm works closely with network operators to develop a network architecture and also with chip suppliers to coordinate technology roadmaps. This relationship often takes place across regional boundaries, as evidenced by the market for DSL (digital subscriber line) chips, where the biggest provider in the United States is Alcatel, a French company with a long history in telecommunications.

But, as we will detail in the next section, NWO markets are regionally fragmented. The small but fast-growing Japanese DSL chip market, on the other hand, is dominated by a U.S.-based start-up, Centillium Communications.[18] Centillium successfully worked with the Japanese national carrier, NTT, to develop a DSL chip set that responded to the particular needs of the Japanese market. Japan developed and adopted a DSL variant called "ADSL Annex C" that accommodated the country's large installed base of ISDN (integrated services digital network) lines and the prevalence of paper—rather than plastic—insulation on Japanese phone lines. By participating in the standard-setting process and being first to market with a compliant chip set, Centillium was able to secure a dominant market position.

The bargaining power of the semiconductor companies in the infrastructure market is enhanced relative to the high-volume consumer and wireless markets because the downstream partners understand that small volumes require a higher mark-up to cover the fixed engineering costs of the specialized chips.

Although it seems that vertical integration would make the infrastructure equipment more competitive by limiting the profit margin on the chips, two major producers of telecommunications equipment—Germany's Siemens and U.S.-based Lucent—have spun off their semiconductor operations (as Infineon and Agere, respectively). This reflects the reality that chips are a relatively small share of the total costs for software-intensive infrastructure goods, and suggests that the benefits of tight chip-system coordination are smaller than the need for both parties to be able to work with others outside the relationship.

To summarize, the network-dependent segments of the NWO introduce new players (the carriers) that can either reduce or enhance the profitability of a chip company depending on the strategic pathways the chip company selects. The denser value chains of the NWO add complexity to the standard international business challenge for chip firms in one region to successfully participate in value chains in other parts of the world. We now turn to a more direct consideration of the geographic aspects of the semiconductor market space.

## The Market Geography of the Semiconductor Industry

The product market changes considered above are taking place in a variegated market space made up of large, established consuming regions, such as Japan and Western Europe, and new, fast-growing areas, particularly China. Competitive advantage increasingly resides in marketing to a region which may be different than the one where the chip company is based. As described above, Qualcomm, whose CDMA technology first appeared in the market in 1995, was able to achieve sales of roughly $1 billion by 1998 by building on an initial customer base in Hong Kong and Korea.

Marketing across regions, however, is never simple, especially in NWO-related industries that are affected by local standards and regulations for communications.

In this section, we analyze the global semiconductor market space from two different perspectives. First, how does demand differ across regions? Second, how successful are chip firms in one region at selling to other regions? We consider four "home" territories corresponding to the four primary locations of chip firms: Western Europe, Japan, the United States, and Asia-Pacific (excluding Japan).

The data presented below suggest that while the semiconductor industry is highly globalized in both demand and sales, notable cross-region differences remain.

### Regional Demand Patterns

Global product market patterns take on distinctive shapes by region, as shown in Table 9.5, which gives the breakdown of sales by region for each product market. For data processing chips, the Americas' market is dominant. Europe and the Americas are both important in communications and automotive markets. Japan and Asia-Pacific loom large in consumer electronics.

These patterns reflect the use of chips in products that may ultimately be shipped to users in other regions. To better understand regional differences in final user demand, we next compare per capita levels of key products by country.

The PC era has been U.S.-centric, and while the United States has a high adoption rate of most Internet applications, many parts of the world have been

TABLE 9.5

*Regional Chip Consumption By Product Markets, 2000*

|  | Asia-Pacific (excluding Japan) | Japan | Europe, Middle East, Africa | Americas |
|---|---|---|---|---|
| Data processing (share of $106,504 million total) | 25.9% | 14.4% | 20.6% | 39.1% |
| Communications (share of $59,075 million total) | 21.7% | 13.1% | 33.0% | 32.2% |
| Consumer (share of $31,439 million total) | 37.1% | 34.1% | 10.9% | 17.9% |
| Automotive (share of $13,627 million total) | 8.7% | 26.9% | 32.4% | 32.0% |

*Source:* Authors' calculations based on Dataquest data from January 2001.

*Note:* The Dataquest data include more aggregated product categories than those reported above in Table 9.5. This standard Dataquest product classification scheme is the only level at which regional data were available.

quicker than the United States to adopt wireless technologies like cell phones. Depending upon which devices become the preferred appliances for voice, video, and data exchange, the next phase may be less dominated by U.S. firms.

The World Competitiveness Yearbook provides country-by-country comparisons for a number of products (IMD 2000). In the case of computers per 1,000 population in 1999, the United States (539) ranks much higher than Japan (325) or the large countries of Europe such as the United Kingdom (379), France (319), Germany (317), and Italy (245). In sharp contrast, the United States ranks only twenty-fourth globally for cellular subscribers per 1,000 population, at 315, behind Japan (383), Italy (521), the United Kingdom (409), and France (350).

The world of the Internet is still largely U.S.-centric. For the number of Web host computers per 1,000 population, the United States is again ranked first at 137, far ahead of Japan (17) and the large European countries (28 in the UK, 18 in Germany, 11 in France, 7 in Italy). However as wireless Web appliances become available at attractive prices, the Internet will be embraced in countries with low PC penetration, which will induce a rise in the number of host computers for regional content.

The disproportionate lead of the United States in Internet adoption does not necessarily mean that U.S. firms, including chip suppliers, will have the same advantages that helped them excel in the PC era. The absence of network effects in many NWO applications may prevent the United States from benefiting from its own large market, and de facto standards (should any arise) in the United States will not necessarily displace those in other countries.[19]

The data on cellular penetration, combined with evidence presented below that chip firms still rely disproportionately on home-market sales, suggest that the advent of the NWO may lead to outcomes in the semiconductor industry different from patterns of the 1990s. In many NWO applications, Japan, Europe, and the United States are pursuing somewhat different technology trajectories that reflect a combination of differences in regulation, legacy infrastructure, and consumer preferences.

In Japan, for example, the leading cellular carrier, NTT DoCoMo, adopted a relatively low-tech interactive cellular standard ("i-mode") that became a huge success. Most other providers have waited for more technically advanced systems before rolling out cellular Internet access. This has given DoCoMo a lead in terms of developing services and a business model, which it is now trying to export by investing in cellular companies in Europe and the United States. The Japanese phone and chip companies that are DoCoMo's primary suppliers are hoping to piggyback on their customer's global expansion.[20]

The widespread adoption of cellular telephony by European consumers was stimulated by Europe's uniform adoption of GSM cellular technology and the relatively high cost of wireline telephone service. This high adoption rate has been credited with providing the well-known European handset producers, Ericsson and Nokia, an advantage in world markets, where they command a combined share of more than one-third.

European dominance at the system level has not translated to a similar dominance at the chip level, but market leadership is considerably more balanced than is the case for PC chips. The leading vendors of non-memory chips in the cellular market as of 1999, according to Dataquest, were Motorola (also the second largest handset producer at the time) and Texas Instruments. TI derived its leadership position from its early commitment to digital signal processor technology. But the list of leading vendors includes the three main European chip makers—STMicroelectronics, Infineon, and Philips (through its acquisition of U.S. company VLSI Technology)—as well as three Japanese producers—NEC, Fujitsu, and Hitachi. The share of European firms is noticeably larger in the wireless market (21 percent) than for non-memory chip sales overall (10 percent). The acquisition of U.S.-based VLSI by Philips boosted Europe's share in the wireless semiconductor market, and the fact that this acquisition was essentially a hostile takeover signaled Europe's new readiness to aggressively pursue market share.

To summarize, strong local markets for cell phones in the early days of the NWO may have helped European and, to a lesser extent, Japanese chip firms compete globally. The reverse proposition, however, does not appear to hold— that is, U.S. chip firms were not hindered by a relatively slow domestic adoption rate of cellular technology, since U.S. chip makers have been able to remain competitive in the European markets, either through partnerships or acquisitions. Time will tell if continued differences across regional markets will undermine the global dominance of the U.S. chip industry established during the PC era.

### Revenues by Producer Region

We now turn to data for sales of all chips by producer (headquarters) region as a prelude to analyzing inter-regional sales. Although large chip companies have globalized their production, sales, and design to varying degrees, the location of a company's headquarters is potentially important for two reasons. First, headquarters location determines where the company's strategic decisions are made and where the high-value home office jobs are located. Second, headquarters location—and the corresponding institutional environment—influence the company's performance in its home or regional market and in markets outside its region.

Figure 9.2 shows the breakdown of chip sales over a twenty-year period for the Top-40 suppliers, grouped according to whether their headquarters are located in the United States, Japan, Europe (France, Germany, Italy, and the Netherlands), or Asia-Pacific (South Korea and Taiwan). The well-known rise and subsequent decline of the Japanese share is shown as U.S. firms responded to Japan's challenge with both improved manufacturing capabilities and more sophisticated designs (Macher, Mowery, and Hodges 1998). The growing distance between the U.S. share and the "U.S. ex-Intel" share shows the enormous role Intel has played in the U.S. "comeback." Without Intel, the U.S. share has been almost flat since 1988, during which time the share of Japanese companies declined. Intel's share dropped over the 1999–2000 period, and this accounted for almost the entire drop in U.S. share over that period. At the end of the 1990s, U.S. firms held almost one-half of the market, while Japanese firms had about 30 percent and Europe and Asia-Pacific each had about a tenth.

One possible interpretation of the relative growth of the U.S. semiconductor industry in the 1990s is that Japan and Europe were slower to embrace both the personal computing revolution and the subsequent networking phenomenon. U.S.-based chip firms reaped a considerable advantage because of the rapid adoption of PCs in the United States by both businesses and households. However the underlying forces are not clear. The empirical relationship between domestic adoption and company performance presents us with a chicken-and-egg problem, as well as the accompanying task of identifying important institutional forces that may be driving both adoption and performance. For example, did rapid adoption of computers by the business community give a competitive advantage to U.S. chip firms, or did rapid adoption occur because the U.S. IT

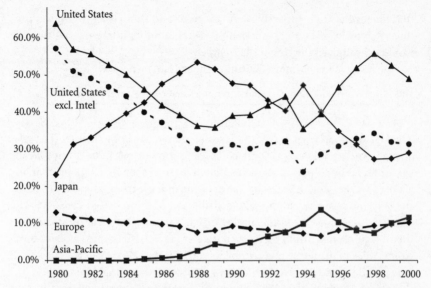

FIG. 9.2. Share of Worldwide Sales by Top 40 Semiconductor Firms, Grouped by Region, 1980–2000. Source: Calculated from Dataquest data, based on location of company headquarters.

firms were instrumental in convincing the business community—by example and advertising—of the value of using computers? In addition, we must ask what was the role of the U.S. university system in the adoption process, both in terms of creating educated users, semiconductor engineers, and the technology itself? How did the federal government (especially the Defense Advanced Research Projects Agency and National Science Foundation) interact (directly, or indirectly through universities) with private industry in fostering the development and wide acceptance of the Internet and the World Wide Web? The answers to these important questions, which we do not address in this paper, would contribute to an understanding of the relationship between the regional markets and the fortunes of local companies that we describe.

*Inter-regional Sales Patterns*

With these long-term trends in mind, we now turn to an analysis of inter-region sales by focusing on the ability of firms to sell to customers outside their home region. Because our data cover nine years (1992 to 2000), we created a summary statistic rather than presenting a 4 x 4 region-to-region matrix for each year.

In every year, each regional grouping had its biggest share of sales in its home (i.e., headquarters) region. We standardize for the size of home market so that the results are comparable across regions and show whether a given producer region realizes a greater share of revenue in its home market than we would expect given the size of that market.

The result is the Home Substitution Index (HSI) where:

$$HSI = \frac{[(\% \text{ of sales in "home" region}) - (\text{"home" market as } \% \text{ of world market})]}{\text{foreign markets as } \% \text{ of world market}} \times 100$$

The HSI shows to what extent the "excess" sales to the home market (i.e., sales above home's market size) "replace" sales to foreign markets. Given that the share of sales by chip firms in each region was larger than that regional market's share of world sales, the relevant range of the index is from 0 to 100. The lower the HSI, the more global the sales distribution of home-based firms. At zero, the share of sales to the home market matches the market's relative size. If true for all regions, this would represent a state of perfect, frictionless globalization. At 100, sales to the home market replace 100% of the sales to foreign markets. If true for all regions, the world is broken into isolated regional blocs.

Table 9.6 reports the HSI for semiconductor firms headquartered in four major regions (the Americas; Japan; Europe, the Middle East, and Africa; and Asia excluding Japan). For example, in 1992, U.S. companies replaced 30 percent of the foreign sales that would have been predicted if the industry were perfectly globalized with sales in the Americas. In other words, in 1992, U.S. companies' sales to foreign markets were 70 percent of what would be expected based upon the relative size of the four markets.

Companies in all regions except Japan show a decline in reliance on home market sales during the 1990s. European, Korean, and Taiwanese firms rapidly became more global in sales as their HSI converged toward the low U.S. value of 20 in 2000.

To look at product markets in more detail, we break out memory chips because such chips are interchangeable (within a given specification) regardless of producer. Sales for chips of this type presumably face low barriers to overseas sales because of the limited need for sales support. Non-memory chips, on the other hand, are more design intensive and likely to be linked to specific applications and even specific customers (Linden 2000). As this distinction would suggest, the HSI for memory chips is lower than that for non-memory semiconductors within each region. U.S. companies decreased their reliance on their home market for non-memory chip sales during this period, and Asia-Pacific companies posted a similar decline, although to a much higher end point. The declining HSI of European firms for non-memory chips found them at the level of home substitution (31) at which U.S. firms began the period.

Perhaps the most interesting entries are those of Japan, which, at the end of

TABLE 9.6

*Home Substitution Index For Global Semiconductor Sales, 1992-2000*

| | 1992 | 1993 | 1994 | 1995 | 1996 | 1997 | 1998 | 1999 | 2000 |
|---|---|---|---|---|---|---|---|---|---|
| | | | | *All Semiconductors* | | | | | |
| U.S. firms | 30 | 27 | 26 | 24 | 22 | 22 | 21 | 19 | 20 |
| Japan firms | 46 | 41 | 37 | 34 | 40 | 42 | 44 | 44 | 46 |
| Euro firms | 53 | 47 | 43 | 45 | 40 | 40 | 40 | 34 | 27 |
| A/P firms | 42 | 38 | 27 | 25 | 26 | 30 | 32 | 24 | 23 |
| | | | | *Memory* | | | | | |
| U.S. firms | 24 | 18 | 20 | 18 | 24 | 24 | 26 | 22 | 19 |
| Japan firms | 21 | 19 | 15 | 14 | 18 | 22 | 25 | 24 | 32 |
| Euro firms | 49 | 44 | 41 | 43 | 44 | 34 | 35 | 19 | 13 |
| A/P firms | 27 | 24 | 14 | 16 | 15 | 14 | 16 | 13 | 11 |
| | | | | *Non-memory* | | | | | |
| U.S. firms | 31 | 30 | 28 | 27 | 23 | 22 | 21 | 20 | 21 |
| Japan firms | 57 | 53 | 51 | 50 | 51 | 49 | 50 | 50 | 51 |
| Euro firms | 54 | 47 | 44 | 45 | 39 | 40 | 41 | 37 | 31 |
| A/P firms | 80 | 83 | 79 | 80 | 76 | 79 | 80 | 69 | 70 |

*Source:* Authors' calculations from Dataquest data.

the period, has the highest HSI across all semiconductors. Japan's HSI for memory chips declined through 1995 then rose sharply to finish higher than it started, which reflects a relative loss of competitiveness to lower-cost producers headquartered outside of Japan. Meanwhile, Japan's HSI for non-memory semiconductors stagnated at about 50 for most of the period.

In absolute terms (not shown), the home country share for Japanese firms' sales in each of the three categories ranks first or second highest of the four regions. Furthermore, the size of the Japanese market relative to the world market for semiconductors, declined from 31 percent in 1992 to 23 percent in 2000. Japanese firms as a group therefore are relying heavily on a market whose global importance has declined. This apparent loss of competitiveness in overseas markets is a major force driving the retreating global market of Japanese chip firms.

In a similar analysis (not shown), we looked at the same data from the perspective of markets and found that the Japanese market is also the least penetrated by foreign chip vendors. Europe, by contrast, is as open to foreign vendors as the United States—in contradiction of claims that Europe is a protected market. Japan is clearly an exceptional case in the global semiconductor industry. Or as one chip executive put it: "Japan is Japan."

To summarize, these data show that the demand and revenues of the semiconductor industry market space display distinctive regional patterns. Just as the PC era contributed to a realignment of global market shares toward U.S.

chip producers and away from their Japanese counterparts, the NWO may re-
align global regional markets away from U.S. chip makers toward Asian and, especially, European, rivals.

The ongoing impact of globalization on the semiconductor industry will be
determined in large part by the ability of firms to navigate the diversity of demand structures in regions other than their own. For small firms serving niche
markets, this may be no more than a matter of shouldering the transaction
costs of selling a given product in an overseas market. But for the leading semiconductor firms that sell a broad line of chips, a successful transition to the
NWO will require a solid grasp of product market attributes, of relevant firm
competencies, and of building alliances in the NWO value chain structure.

## Conclusions

The shift toward communications and networking applications leading to a
NWO of ubiquitous computing will likely leave its stamp on the global chip
market during the next twenty years much as the emergence of the PC industry
has done since 1980.

The medium-term implications for the market space occupied by the semiconductor industry are clear. In the product dimension, the comforting predictability of the PC-centric electronics industry is giving way to greater fragmentation as numerous products compete for overlapping roles, such as the
current struggle between personal digital assistants that incorporate cell phone
modules and cellular phones that add organizer functions.

Although the geographic market dimension of the semiconductor industry
as a whole presents a trend toward uniformity (in terms of the propensity of
firms to export), the growing importance of communications-dependent products, where local standards are still important, will tend to maintain regional
differences.

The "five dynamics" discussed in Chapter 1 apply as much to the semiconductor market space as to geographical space. In the case of improvements in
transportation and communication, advances in communication chips are an
essential enabler of these enabling industries. At the same time, advanced communications networks permit even relatively small, fabless chip firms to have a
global reach. The second dynamic, speed, is every bit as essential in the market
space as in the spatial dimension, since the generation life of technology is so
short. However the massive downturn that the telecommunications sector is
now traversing has slowed the shift toward computing-communications hybrid
applications. This slowdown has brought the fourth dynamic, cost pressure,
into play with a vengeance, because the high fixed costs of semiconductor design and production require high volumes to be economically feasible. The fail-

ure of those volumes to materialize is causing massive losses and an industry shake-out. The third dynamic, locally embedded knowledge, is driven in part by the regional fragmentation we described above. In telecommunications, for example, local standards sometimes make it necessary for chip firms to have on-site staff in order to effectively serve a market. Where regional specializations exist, such as wireless communications in Europe, foreign chip firms license or acquire know-how and engineers to tap into the local skill base. The fifth dynamic of proximity to customers is exactly what we are arguing will become increasingly important in NWO markets.

Global competitiveness requires understanding how product markets and the value chain have changed so that firms can position themselves in order to leverage their value-added into value capture. Our research documented geographic product market patterns and presented an analysis of how strategic partnerships in the NWO value chain, which includes carriers as a powerful new player, become an important determinant of a chip company's ability to successfully develop and market products destined for specific regions.

The chip market at the height of the PC era was predominantly U.S.-based because of Intel's sustained market dominance. The greater regional and product market diversification of the emerging NWO may permit firms from other regions to excel for reasons including access to markets and strategic alliances. However the proven ability of U.S. chip firms to adjust (at least collectively) to new competitive landscapes means they will continue to play a central role.

One of the conclusions that emerges forcefully from our analysis is the low probability that the chip industry will ever be dominated by a single company in the way that Intel has done for nearly a decade. Intel itself is under great pressure to change as competitors gain a foothold in the PC space and the PC market itself assumes a flatter growth path. System firms and network operators are wary of permitting any supplier to own a comparable standard in the NWO.

Company performance in the NWO depends upon speed, integration skills, and design-related intellectual property. Process skills, which were so central to the DRAM and microprocessor competitions that defined the PC era, are much less relevant in the current round of competition, not just because the product focus is changing but also because production can be outsourced much more readily than a decade ago. Still, the requirement for greater on-chip integration and system-level engineering favors the existing set of large, diversified firms, which seem to be learning how to perform well in regional markets.

Since the transformation of the semiconductor market space that we are studying is ongoing, we present our findings with the realization that the world may be a very different place by the end of the decade. That said, U.S. chip producers are likely to face greater global competition in the NWO from European and Asian producers that have learned from earlier rounds of competition, are better placed than ever before in the U.S. market, and stand ready to capitalize on any home market advantages available to them.

## Notes

The authors would like to thank the Alfred P. Sloan Foundation, the Batten Institute, and the Darden Foundation for funding. We are also grateful to Sara Beckman, Neil Berglund, David Hodges, Jeff Macher, David Mowery, Tim Sturgeon, and reviewers for helpful comments. The authors are responsible for all errors.

1. In a telling example, albeit one that was perhaps driven in part by the dot-com bubble, Ziff-Davis changed the name of its venerable *PC Week* magazine to *eWeek* in May 2000.

2. Craig Matsumoto, "Rivals Vie to Reshape Net Topology," *EE Times*, September 7, 2001.

3. "NTT DoCoMo's i-mode Subscribers Exceed 5 Million," *Asia Biz Tech*, March 21, 2000.

4. For predigital equipment, most U.S. cable companies are locked in to proprietary end-to-end deals with either General Instrument (now part of Motorola) or Scientific-Atlanta.

5. "NTT DoCoMo-Style Business Model Includes a Few Pitfalls," *Asia Biz Tech*, December 11, 2000.

6. Based on data from the Fabless Semiconductor Association reported in "Order Up?" *Electronic Business,* November 1999. Chip firms that own fabs are increasingly turning to the foundries for part of their output.

7. "Philips' Bulging Portfolio Poses Integration Problem," *Electronic Buyers' News*, November 1, 1999.

8. "Intel Quits Discrete Graphics-IC Market for Integrated Approach," *Electronic Buyers' News*, August 19, 1999.

9. "Philips Spins Off TriMedia Processor Technology as Separate Company," *Semiconductor Business News*, March 29, 2000.

10. "CEO of the Year: PMC-Sierra's Bob Bailey," *Electronic Business*, December 2000.

11. "Qualcomm CDMA Technologies Announces Widespread Adoption of Compact Media Extension Software in the Japanese CDMA Market," Qualcomm Press Release, July 17, 2000.

12. The following description is based on publicly available sources.

13. "Moto Exec Sees Future of Comms in Programmable Platforms," *Electronic Engineering Times*, October 2, 2001.

14. "Boca Research's Design Chosen for Philips' Co-Branded AOL TV Set-Top Box," Boca Research Press Release, May 11, 1999.

15. "ST Micro Execs See Chip Market Driven by 'e-society,'" *Electronic Buyers' News*, December 12, 2000.

16. "It's Europe's Turn," *Electronic Business Asia*, March 1999.

17. "Virgin Territory," *Electronic Business*, September 2000.

18. The following description is based on publicly available sources.

19. This situation can be compared with the existence of incompatible television standards that have long coexisted in the United States (NTSC) and Europe (PAL/SE-CAM). See Katz and Shapiro (1994) for a discussion of network effects.

20. "Panasonic Looks to Expand Its International Cell Phone Reach," *Electronic News*, November 6, 2000.

# PART THREE

# Conclusion

# CHAPTER TEN

# From Regions and Firms to Multinational Highways

*Knowledge and Its Diffusion as a Factor*
*in the Globalization of Industries*

BRUCE KOGUT

The chapters in this book are studies in the complex dynamics among firms, country resources, and institutions. They pursue a common question in understanding how firm strategies not only responded to shifting comparative advantage but also in fact contributed to the development of new regional economies and institutions. It is this latter theme that deserves our attention, because it directs us to understand how governments and firms act to shape the global competitive landscape.

The element that looms large in the historical accounts of these chapters is the growing importance of firms from diverse national origins operating in third country locations and markets. The classic economic studies on direct investment have sought to understand how competitive advantages located in one country can be brought to bear upon competition in a second country within a common governance structure called the multinational corporation. During the past decade, there was increasing interest in direct investment in terms of the comparison of the relative strengths of two countries, often summarized by measures of relative technological advantage.

Because these studies looked at investment patterns measured bilaterally, they miss an important observation about global competition. A few industries, and a few hundred firms in them, are the dominant investors across many countries. There has been, in other words, an emergence of global firms that are powerful actors in world competition. These are the protagonists for the dynamics analyzed in many of the preceding chapters.

This comes as no surprise to many, especially to those who recall the writings of Hobson and Lenin on international finance capitalism at the start of the previous century. There is, however, another aspect to this competition that is intriguing: these global firms never escape the pull of geography. In the first approximation, as Kenney notes in the introduction, geography is a major factor in the trade-off of time and cost that looms as a major factor in many of these chapters. The threat that certain production activities will shift to nations having lower cost factor inputs, especially labor, forces firms wishing to continue to produce in developed countries to move to higher value-added production, and also to speed innovation and production to address evolving customer demands, most of which continue to be located in developed countries (DCs).

In 1985, I suggested a way to understand these structural changes on the world economy by a simple figure that mapped comparative and competitive value-added chains (Kogut 1985). Unlike the emphasis on trade in products that had been the focus of trade models, as Figure 10.1 illustrates it is more useful to think of location economics in terms of the location of processes. The straight line is a budget constraint called an isocost line. This illustrates the idea that in developed countries, it is possible to purchase relatively larger amounts of capital than labor, whereas in less developed countries (LDCs) labor is comparatively less expensive.[1] The curved lines are isoquants. They represent the (physical and human) capital and unskilled labor requirements to undertake a particular process in a value-added chain. Because of competition, the isocost lines are tangent to the isoquants; this represents the point where marginal cost and benefits are equated.

The emergence of newly industrializing countries (NICs) perturbed these relationships by absorbing more of the capital-intensive production processes, forcing DCs to specialize more in technology and knowledge-intensive activities. The chapter by Leachman and Leachman reflects this pattern: as the Taiwanese-owned semiconductor foundries developed global-class fabrication skills, Taiwan evolved into the fastest growing location for semiconductor production in the world. The increasing strength of Taiwanese firms in fabrication was accompanied by the establishment of a vibrant community of application-specific integrated circuit (ASIC) fabless semiconductor firms in developed countries, and especially Silicon Valley. The operations of firms in DCs that experience competition from either NICs or LDCs migrated to more innovative products, as well as relying upon customization and marketing, as Dell Computers has so effectively done. The long ensuing debate in the 1980s and 1990s on the relative effects of trade and technology on job loss and structural change missed the overall endogeneity, or interdependence, of these effects. Structural change in the world economy increased the incentives to invest in activities rich in human capital.

Purchasing inputs or services from NIC or LDC firms was one option, but

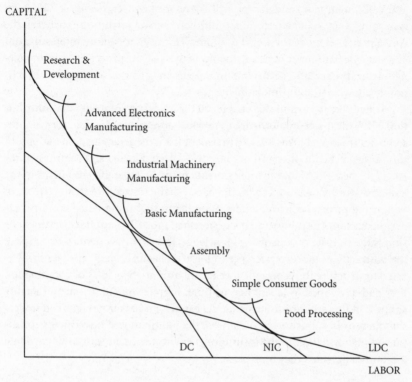

FIG. 10.1. Comparative Advantage and the Location of Economic Activities. Source: Kogut (1985).

of course, there was another possibility (besides appealing to the government for protection)—namely, DC firms can invest in production in foreign locations. The past two decades witnessed an explosion of direct investment, and concomitant trade growth, in Asia, much of it stimulated by multinational corporations. The studies in this book trace the histories of this internationalization at the level of firms and industries. The loss of *industrial* advantage prompted a finer grain, though temporally dependent, matching of activity to location. The value chains became internationally dispersed and, sometimes, globally coordinated by multinational corporations. The chapters in this book offer a number of fine examples of this. For example, as the chapter by David McKendrick shows, in hard disk drives (HDDs), U.S. firms continue to be the world leaders. However, by 2001 more than 90 percent of the world's production was located in Asia, substantially all of it owned and operated by DC firms.

The impact of these changes was the dramatic expansion and deepening of international commodity chains, a term first proposed by Wallerstein (Hopkins and Wallerstein 1994) and substantially developed by Gereffi (1994). This term is in some ways a characterization of the commercial relationship between the core and periphery of the world economy. However, it is more interesting not as a static description, but as a dynamic analysis of the process by which internationalization creates new economic spaces and regions by transferring economic knowledge and stimulating its growth.

I would like to turn in this chapter to the evidence regarding the contribution of the diffusion of knowledge to regional development and, in turn, to how some multinational firms learned to benefit from these new agglomerations. In this sense, I echo an observation made by Richard Florida and Martin Kenney (1991) in their work, that the investments made by Japanese auto firms in the United States created new economic spaces, characterized by a distinctive set of organizing principles within and among firms, that represented a radical experimentation. These investments represented more than capital investment or simply the transfer of organizing knowledge. Rather, investments—or, to speak less abstractly or more in reference to the actual actors, these Japanese firms—acted to structure the economic investment around principles of coordination they had developed in Japan: just-in-time, supplier qualification, and quality control. In this sense of influencing the explicit and taken-for-granted understandings of how business is organized, the multinational investments constitute a transformation in the institutional environment, at least in the regional economies in which they took place.

## Of Institutions and Organizations

The internationalization of industries is a fairly recent phenomenon in world history. The great histories of Braudel (1982) discuss the role of trade, fairs, and merchants. The control of production in one country by an owner located elsewhere surely existed, but it was largely the backdrop to the larger panorama of arbitrage that propelled ships along the trade routes and caravans along the silk route. The dominance of the Dutch empire was built upon the import of raw materials for higher value-added processing in Holland.[2] There was trade, but few examples of spatially dispersed production organized and controlled by multinational corporations. There were, however, international organizational forms and institutions that governed trade in the world economy.

This economy was local in terms of the occupations of everyday life, but surprisingly global in terms of the wealth generated by international commerce. Such trade was hazardous and required private and public mechanisms to ameliorate risk. Private solutions emerged gradually through the evolution of agreements such as the *comenda,* to more sophisticated joint-stock companies that sprang up in the 1600s but took off only with the growth of limited liability, the loosening of royal charters in the nineteenth century, and the emergence of shipping insurance schemes such as those of Lloyds of London, founded at the beginning of the eighteenth century. These organizational solutions required as well the evolution of information and control technologies, such as dual entry accounting, that has its origins in northern Italy but gradually spread throughout Europe. By and large, at that time cost accounting was far less developed. After all, trade did not require production, and production, being within the purview of an owner and relatively modest in capital investment and complexity, was managed and monitored by metering the sweat on the brow of workers, craftsmen, and owners laboring together. To illustrate, even the great ore mines of Kopparsberg, Sweden, operated by allocating shares to partners who then oversaw their workers.

Organizing, stabilizing, and making the environment safe for trade required public solutions or institutions, sometimes in the form of military protection and colonial "market interventions," other times in the form of trade treaties and guarantees of legal redress. Such action was not original to Europe. For example, fifteen hundred years earlier, Roman law had already established the liability of the owner for his agent, even in distant lands. But in the absence of a Pax Romana, traders were dependent upon ethnic ties (Greif 1989). It is possible to hypothesize that commitments within these ethnic trading networks were the result of a trust framed by a credible threat of being punished by expulsion from the community. Gradually, as institutions arose, and governments could exercise military and commercial authority over the activities of international traders, ethnic ties gave way proportionally to the embryonic forms such as the quasi-public British East India Company that in time evolved into the multinational corporation.

## Organizing Principles

Although most firms and workshops were small, the ancient and early modern world was capable of creating large organizations for public works such as pyramids, dam construction, and the operation of mines. For example, in France mines employed hundreds of workers. The industrialization of France is heavily marked by the prominent role played by mining firms, shipyards, and water works. Armies were large in many countries, and their management required knowledge of organization and command. These armies were often multinational, requiring sophistication in communication and coordination.

In general, such organizing principles constitute the generative knowledge of firms that guide their growth and development. The knowledge regarding Tayloristic practices, shop floor organization, and corporate growth are examples of principles that structure the definition of tasks and coordination in the division of labor. These principles are not reducible to individuals—that is, organizations are not simple aggregates of individuals. There is not a "tacit" knowledge inside the heads of employees that represents collectively how work is divided and coordinated. Principles are encoded as learned repertoires that are not reducible to individual knowledge. In fact, no one is likely to know the daily expectations that replicate coordination of work throughout a firm, or among them.[3]

There are considerable anecdotal reports and academic studies which show that these principles vary by country. The comparative studies on the multinational corporation published as a series of doctoral theses at the Harvard Business School in the early 1970s document the historical effects of national origins on firm structure.[4] As an illustration, the large European multinational relied more heavily upon organic structures that represented holding company patterns, a form especially prevalent in Germany. Reporting structures were more informal than American. As the firms internationalized, they grew on the basis of "Mother-Daughter" structures (Franko 1976), a term that reflects, on the one hand, simply the Germanic expression for headquarters and subsidiaries (i.e., *Muttergesellschaft* and *Tochtergesellschaft*), and on the other, the heavier reliance on long-term relationships than on formal accounting methods.

That firms are "imprinted" by their national origins is a thesis that is derived from Stinchcombe's (1965) seminal work on firms and social stratification. The mechanisms by which this occurs are less well understood. Surely, entrepreneurs carry cognitive "templates" of how to organize. An entrepreneur studies other firms, draws upon past experiences, relies upon local experts for advice. DiMaggio and Powell (1983) explained these forces for homogeneity within organizational fields as arising from three "isomorphic" pressures: imitative, coercive (legally mandated), and normative. The recent work of Castilla and his colleagues (2000) shows that these pressures appear to have a strong local character to them, proscribed within regional networks. These results confirm Stinchcombe's thesis of imprinting and stratification, but within the more nuanced analysis of exactly how external commercial and social affiliations act to buttress the internal capabilities of firms.

These observations explain the local diffusion without addressing why we observe these differences among regions and nations. The answer that "history matters" is not entirely satisfactory, even if we grant Marx's observation that man can change the world only on the basis of how he found it. The term *coevolution* provides an analytical window on understanding organizational homogeneity within spatial bounds, though it too is open to abuse. Coevolution posits that firms' tendencies to develop particular traits that compose their capabilities influence, and are influenced by, other firms and larger institutions. Thus, the ability of the United States to rapidly spawn firms to exploit the opportunities that arose from the commercialization of the Internet surely is an expression of the particularities of the extant political economy and financial institutions such as venture capital (Kenney 2002; Zook 2002).

Coevolution has the virtue of imposing a "developmental constraint" on what otherwise would seem to be adaptive behavior. This concept of developmental constraints is critical to understanding the importance of time and place in economic history. There are two observations that can be drawn from the new biology of complexity deserving scrutiny. The first is that constraints matter. As we move from static theories of isomorphism to historical explanation, it is important to understand how interdependence acts to constrain the firm's choice. It is not simply that law acts coercively to create particular organizational features insofar that it acts to rule out (and rule in) particular avenues of explorative growth. Similarly "cultural" expectations are more than normative statements on good or bad, but represent shared and evolving preferences for "what goes with what" (venture capital with equity) that inform the decisions of economic actors.

The second observation follows from the first: there is a value in understanding evolutionary logics. Studies on the Silicon Valley generally note that firms have flat hierarchies and organize by projects (Baron et al. 1996). Labor markets tend to be fluid, with people having the option to change positions without cultural or economic sanctions (Gilson 1999; Hyde 1996). (I stress "option," as many firms in the Silicon Valley have low turnover rates, presumably because they are attractive places to work.) Fluid labor markets for skilled engineers permit capabilities, routines, and knowledge to migrate across firms. Paul Almeida and I (1997, 1999) tracked the movement of people holding key patents and made two findings: regions within the United States differed in their labor market dynamics; and in the Silicon Valley, migrating engineers re-established their research programs at their new firms—that is, hiring key people changed the research direction of the firm.

The importance of coevolution is to ask if flat hierarchies and fluid labor markets are dynamically coupled. A hypothesis is that it is obvious that extensive firm hierarchies would appear "out of sync" with fluid labor markets; few would wait a decade to be promoted and move up the ladder. Management by project provides a solution (probably among many), whereby the employment contract is implicitly renewed or terminated by the mutual interest in subsequent projects. In this way, the fluid labor market and the flat hierarchy are coevolved and are emergent characteristics of the Silicon Valley. However, I flag the caution that functional reasoning needs to be disciplined by attention to historical conditions. History is required to understand the embryonic seeds of these complementary traits—including the lack of other models to guide the choices of the Hewletts and Packards who opened shop without any nearby large firms to imitate. And history is also required to understand how these dynamics were displaced, or perturbed, by wars, changed legal environments, the arrival of new actors, such as corporate subsidiaries that are large relative to the existing firms. Assumptions of initial conditions or of functional analysis run the hazard of ignoring the power of exogenous events and context to alter local and individual histories.

There are important implications from the claim that organizing principles diffuse within regions and spatial boundaries. I have argued before that this implies a radical hypothesis: organizing principles diffuse more quickly among firms within a region than between regions and countries (Kogut 1991; 1992; 1993). Modern economic history shows strong patterns in national leadership that can be traced to particular kinds of organizing innovations: factories and machinery in the UK, mass production in the United States, or quality mass production in Japan. These principles were not unique to those countries, but they succeeded in initiating powerful developmental trajectories that created organizational capabilities common to firms, small and large, located within national borders. Regional economies are often characterized by the shared properties among firms relating to how they organize themselves and their relations with each other.

## Multinational Corporations

But how do these principles diffuse across borders? Was the itinerant Gothic cathedral builder/architect able to transfer organizational patterns as well as technical solutions? Were the iron puddlers of England who moved as a group able to reconstitute their knowledge overseas (Fremdling 1991)? The great difference between individual knowledge and organizing principles is that the latter consist of learned repertoires among people, of which no one has mastery of the full array of skills and practices. In such cases, the best way to transfer such knowledge is the movement of groups of people, it would seem. But not only does this pose a coordination problem; it may not incorporate the practices that organize groups, such as accounting principles, hierarchy, or style of leadership.

In short, organizing knowledge often requires an organizational medium for diffusion. This suggests a radically different definition of the multinational corporation than the standard one of control held over an entity by another located in a different country, or as the resolution of contracting problems between two firms by joint ownership. The multinational corporation is the medium by which organizing principles are transferred (Kogut 1993).

The focus on regional and national economies obscures the observation that their growth never took place in isolation from a world economy. There is an important implication in the above description of organizing principles and their spatial properties. When a multinational firm goes overseas, it brings its organizing principles from one country to another; these countries vary in their institutions and their reception of these principles. The histories of multinational corporations are filled with complaints of local managers regarding the controls of home country firms. (See the study by Surie [1997] on the fragile interplay of foreign firm technologies and host country learning.) Foreign environments may well be characterized by a set of market and institutional characteristics that are not consistent with home country principles. Eleanor Westney (1993) described these tensions as caught between the global isomorphic pressure imposed by the other corporate units on any given subsidiary.

The history of American investments overseas shows a similar pattern. U.S. investments were coupled with the transfer of such practices as managerial accounting, divisionalization, management by objectives, and human resource policies. These practices consisted of a new language expressed in standards, measurements, and terminology, much of which was incorporated in foreign languages without translation. Thus, for example, Japanese terms such as "kaizen" crept into the vocabulary of U.S. auto manufacturers, and terms such as "venture capital" have become global. It has long been observed, however, that these practices are never transferred without modification. Westney's (1987) splendid study on the importation of Western institutions into Japan notes correctly that Japan did not imitate, but rather "emulated," what they thought to be best practices in foreign countries. This emulation occurred initially without multinational corporations, though the Japanese did send out missions and engineers to observe and to work overseas. Thus foreign practices are rendered into discrete ingredients, some of which are adopted, some rejected, and yet others adapted, depending upon the host environment. This observation seems to be chronically forgotten in studies that assume there is a core body of knowledge that cannot be tampered with. Rather, the multiple ingredients that constitute a practice (think of how many activities constitute a just-in-time inventory process) need not have a core to be effective: adopting four out of five ingredients might work for Thailand, adopting a different four out of five will work for Malaysia, though it is also true that the outcome may not be exactly the same in each case.

In other words, multinational investments serve as experimental designs and as agents of cultural change. In the heady debate that reigned once over the topic of "appropriate technologies," there was a charge that multinationals deliberately failed to adjust their capital and labor ratios to developing countries to hire more people. But a more prosaic explanation is advanced by Howard Davies (1977): multinationals did not know how to run operations with less capital intensity. In fact, for many of the industries discussed in this book, it may no longer be possible to operate with significantly less capital or smaller factories. For example, as Leachman and Leachman indicate in semiconductors, the cost penalty for operating a significantly smaller fab is so great as to make it uneconomic. Similarly, Sturgeon and Florida show that it is not viable to build an operational assembly plant that produces fewer than 100,000 units per year. For auto plants, low-capacity levels result in economics that favor knock-down kit assembly. Ultimately, the advantage of the multinational corporations (MNCs) was embedded in the know-how they transferred in terms of practices, plant design, and supplier and customer relations. Changing the recipe would dramatically *raise* costs of production, despite the capital savings.

It is often overlooked that foreign subsidiaries fail quite often. In Table 10.1, I summarize the data (provided to me by Myles Shaver) on failures of subsidiaries. Failure is frequent. For example, Kenney shows that nearly all the Japanese television plants in the United States have closed—that is, they failed. It is important to note that the production was not returned to Japan but rather was relocated to Mexico. These failure rates are not high compared with a population of new firms, but it should be remembered that these are subsidiaries of established companies with established and proven advantages.

Failure itself does not signal, obviously, that subsidiaries are established as experiments. But it is possible to consider each investment as an experiment from which learning can occur, especially if their adaptation to local environments can fruitfully serve the rest of the corporation. (I note that, for the most part, though firms do not conduct business experiments in the scientific meaning of the term, they learn from their activities—and some far more than others.) The Institute of International Business at the Stockholm School of Economics has been exploring the thesis that subsidiaries do more than transfer and adapt to local environments. They become agents of change in the local economy *and* for the multinational corporation. Gunnar Hedlund (1986) called the emergent multinational corporation a "heterarchy" to capture that its exposure to high environmental variety breaks down hierarchy into cooperative and competing divisions that vie for global command over resources and responsibilities. This heterarchic form represents a cybernetic adaptation to environmental complexity. Divisions act out independent experiments, and the feedback from multiple experiments is transferred and reintegrated through transnational teams.

TABLE 10.1

*Estimated Failure Rates of Foreign Subsidiaries*

| Source | Parent location | Investment location | Industry | Years observed | Failure rate |
|---|---|---|---|---|---|
| Mitchell, Shaver and Yeung (1997) | Canada | U.S. | Medical equipment | 1968–89 (assessed until mid-1991) | 32% |
| Mitchell, Shaver and Yeung (1997) | | U.S. | Manufacturing | 1987–92 | 24% (Greenfield and acquisition— acquisition with higher rate of failure) |
| Shaver (1998) | | U.S. | Manufacturing | 1987–92 | 18% (same data as above but conditioned on the foreign parent being publicly traded) |
| Shaver and Flyer (2000) | Japan, France, U.K., Germany, Netherlands, Canada | U.S. | Manufacturing | within 8 years of foreign greenfield investment | 21% |
| Barkema, Bell, and Pennings (1996) | Netherlands | | | 1966–88 | 49% |
| Li (1995) | | U.S. | Computers; Pharmaceuticals | 1974–88 | 7% |
| Delios and Beamish (2001) | Japan | | | 1986–97 | 21% |
| Pan and Chi (1999) | | China | | 1992–93 | 14.2% |
| McCloughan and Stone (1998) | | UK | Manufacturing | 1970–93 | 26% |
| Zaheer and Mosakowski (1997) | | | Financial Services | 1974–93 | 42% |

*Source:* Author's compilation.

This line of thinking points to the emergent properties of the multinational corporation. Multinational corporations develop in their home environments, and they carry the imprint of their home environment as organizational luggage transported to new locations (Kogut 1993). Yet, through their foreign investments, they are also subjected to local pressures to adapt and to global pressures to coordinate their activities. These countervailing pressures are never fully resolved, but their tensions are the source of creative solutions, as practices are transferred back from subsidiaries and as new ways to organize are found.

Such learning is often a by-product of investments made for other reasons, such as market entry or cost savings. This learning can be seen in the discussion by Sturgeon and Florida of how U.S. and European automakers use their new assembly plants in emerging economies to experiment with innovative forms of work and supply chain organization. For example, the new German factories in Alabama and Brazil use far more parts outsourcing than do comparable factories in Germany. GM has been even more aggressive. In the Eisenach plant in the former East Germany, it integrated its learning from its NUMMI joint venture with Toyota in Fremont, California, and its CAMI joint venture with Suzuki in Ingersoll, Canada, to implement a lean system. The learning from the Eisenach joint venture was then used in the assembly plants it opened in Thailand, China, and Brazil.

The multinational corporation is not a passive channel of technology transfer. The evidence that it evolves and learns is transparent in each chapter. However, beneath these broad claims lies a more subtle set of issues regarding the process by which multinational corporations are transformed. In a rare examination of this transformation, Thomas Malnight (2001) traces the evolution of two pharmaceutical companies from national to global firms as a series of functional switches: certain functions globalize before others, others remain focused on countries. The process by which this evolution occurs is marked by a firm's developmental constraints, which reflect its history and the imprint of its origins, and by the challenges of foreign environments. Firms thus evolve a high degree of internal complexity in order to address proactively their highly differentiated environments. His study is a reminder that globalization is not a linear process and is highly contingent on form and strategy. And it is a process that requires time for the capabilities to evolve and mature.

That this is a contingent process can be seen in the chapter by McKendrick showing that Japanese firms did not internationalize their production rapidly to Asia and hence lost the market for HDDs. Although Japanese firms are not homogeneous (see Fruin 1992), there are national patterns in the rates of overseas expansion. One explanation might be that Japanese firms had extraordinarily little experience operating foreign plants, at least in the immediate postwar period. Another explanation is cognitive: American firms watch other American firms, Japanese firms watch each other. They expand in herdlike waves. This thesis has a degree of support (Vernon 1966; Knickerbocker 1973; Mascarenhas 1982; Yu and Ito 1988). There is ample empirical evidence for this in both the automobile and television chapters, though this may be an unsatisfying theoretical explanation. A third answer, providing a more nuanced explanation, rests upon the degree to which multinational corporations are able to reassemble their competencies in overseas markets. Here "reassembling" is important, because this implies a process, which is exactly what occurred in the industries studied in this book, whether it be autos, garments, or television production. We turn to this explanation further below, in discussing regions.

## Regional to Global R&D

The extensive studies on foreign direct investment and the multinational corporation document the importance of knowledge to overseas expansion. While the idea that "how to do marketing" may, to some, appear to be more an example of an asset called a brand label as opposed to knowledge, the research and development activity clearly represents the economic pursuit to create innovations and new knowledge. As we saw before, innovations historically have been transferred by individuals. The multinational corporation is a recent phenomenon that represents the increasing importance of organization as an input into economic production.

By 1942, Schumpeter was already noting that "technological progress is increasingly becoming the business of teams of trained specialists who turn out what is required and make it work in predictable ways" (Schumpeter 1942: 132). The growth of central R&D laboratories was a common trend for major industrial countries.[5]

The routinization of innovation in the form of industrial laboratories is evident in the patent statistics. In his famous study, Schmookler (1966: 26) noted the decline of patents given to individuals in the United States. In 1901, 81.4 percent of patents were issued to individuals, 18.6 percent to firms; by 1960, individuals received 36.4 percent of the patents issued, firms 63.6 percent (though about a third of these were bought from the outside).

The distribution of patents has clear spatial dimensions. Jaffe et al. (1993) found that citations to patents are influenced by proximity. Belonging to the same region increases the chances that a patent will be cited. This means that new technology tends to build upon technical advances within close spatial proximity. We can couple this observation with the recent work which shows that venture capital is drawn to technology. Not only does venture capital remain largely regional but, in addition, technology—even in an age of advanced communication and transportation—tends to be spatially clustered (Florida and Kenney 1988; Sorenson and Stuart 2001; Zook 2002).

These findings suggest a quandary. If technological expertise is still spatially bounded, what are the implications for the claims by many chapters in this book that knowledge diffuses? Of course, the most obvious one is that trade patterns will reflect the technological comparative advantages of countries, a claim that has some support. A more important claim by John Cantwell (1989) is that multinational firms are drawn to regions to source their technological advantage. This claim is radically different from the traditional explanations regarding direct investment for market access or for cost effective sourcing. This is very evident in the chapter on flat panel displays by Murtha, Lenway, and Hart. In this case, prior investments by Corning, IBM, and Applied Materials evolved into a situation in which the U.S. multinationals became part of a cluster in formation and thus sustained and advanced their technological competence.

Ivo Zander investigated the micro foundations of this claim by looking at the patenting history of the largest Swedish multinationals over time and by tracing their decisions to operate R&D domestically or globally. In two studies, Zander (1998, 1999) found, despite heterogeneity across firms and industries, an overall trend toward global R&D. Some firms remain home-centered (steel, pulp and paper, telecommunications, automotive), while others are highly dispersed in terms of both centers of excellence and overlap within individual technologies (firms carrying out explicit acquisition strategies).

It is hard to know if these industry-specific trends have shifted. As the chapters in this book indicate the explanations are likely to be highly specific to the particular industries. Biotechnology is surely an industry where science and scientists are key to research productivity. Individuals are clearly important to semiconductors, since, as discussed earlier, the movement of key patent holders from one firm to the next leaves a trace in the patent activity of the hiring firm. Paul Almeida and I (1997) made the discovery, in the true sense of the word, in reanalyzing patent data. In the study that was to be published two years later and discussed above, we found no substantial effects between small and large firms. However, we had created the sample by looking at major patents measured by citations. We decided to change our sampling strategy and look at a sample of highly cited patents stratified by small and large firms. We found that inter-regional effects of mobility of major innovators was far more pronounced for smaller firms. Mobility was higher, and so was the effect of mobility on subsequent patenting in that technological area of the innovator who switched employment.

Again, we have the finding that people matter, but the effects vary by region (labor market dynamics differ across regions), by technology (for example, semiconductor manufacturing patents did not show a spatial effect), and by type of firm (spatial patterns of citations were more pronounced for small firms). There is nothing inherent in technology that determines these patterns. The importance of space is contingent upon other social and economic factors.

A powerful expression of how the character of space changes is the finding by Irwin and Klenow (1994), who estimated experience curves for semiconductor production. They found that learning rates averaged 20 percent. Firms learned three times more from an additional unit of their production than from others. Learning spills over as much between firms internationally as domestically. These are incredible findings: one-fourth of the experience effects depend upon the production of competitors, no matter where they are located globally. Of course, the spillover effect might itself reflect a kind of Solow residual of general technological progress and, in this sense, may not be a spillover. Instead, it might represent the knowledge embedded in the semiconductor equipment, such as Nikon and Canon steppers and Applied Materials wafer etchers, all of which are available globally. So even if it is technological progress, it is an amazing statement that all are able to dip into this technical reservoir regardless of their location.

Almeida (1996) provides a clue into how general knowledge might be captured globally by analyzing whether foreign subsidiaries behave like local ones or simply as listening posts. He finds that their patent citation behavior is biased toward the local market, but that they also serve as a bridge to the technological developments of the parent company. Frost (2001) similarly finds that multinational corporations build upon findings of subsidiaries. In one of the more detailed studies of this question, Song et al. (2001) found that mobility of engineers had the same effect on the hiring firm's patents, whether or not the transfer was to a domestic or a foreign location. The majority of the transfers show a strong ethnic pattern—that is, engineers of Korean, Taiwan, and Japanese lineage were hired by firms from those respective countries. Thus, the micro patterns of the global high-technology economy reveal oddly the long hand of ethnicity. Even in high technology, international migration plays its continuing historical role.

## Internationalizing Regions

There are two conflicting visions of the global economy: its regional character and its global linkages. First, the internationalization of production introduces an expansion of the regional economies. Herbert Simon (1969) noted that from the position of space, the world economy looks as if there is intense economic activity within the firm, with weaker activities between them in the form of market transactions. As intriguing as this view is, it misses the second corollary observation: a great deal of modern production is done by multinational corporations, but with local sourcing. In a study on alliances in semiconductors and biotechnology, we found that these alliances are global ties among large firms, with intense regional ties among small firms. This image indeed is the reflection of the earlier study I described, in which citation patterns are far more regional among small firms than large ones (Almeida and Kogut 1997).

There is, in fact, a puzzle. If part of the capabilities of the firm is its location and consists of ties among firms, then how can a region internationalize? In this regard, it is probably useful to distinguish between different kinds of regions, or districts, and then look at the evidence regarding internationalization. Herrigel

(1996) and Locke (1995) describe the German and Italian economies, respectively, as consisting of variegated regions with distinctive industrial and socio-economic structures. They individually propose that these districts can be characterized into centralized and decentralized structures. The former consists of dominant large firms that contract to smaller and medium-size ones; the other consists of many small to medium-size firms, engaged in intensive cooperative and competitive relationships. In a detailed ethnographic and statistical study, Brookfield (1999) observes a similar pattern by which the Taichung region in Taiwan reveals greater specialization than other more centralized regions.

The internationalization of these two kinds of districts confronts very different kinds of problems. The centralized region poses a prisoner's dilemma in which the large firm, facing a decline in the local competitiveness of the domestic region, can defect to overseas production. The decentralized region has more of a collective action problem. Since the value of the operations of any individual firm rests in the quality of their relations with each other, there is an incentive to move to a cooperative solution. We can expect to see firms jointly trying to improve their productivity, investments in training and infrastructure, and export promotion efforts. If these efforts fail, the response to the loss of comparative advantage might be an effort to bolster regional productivity by a collective, perhaps even coordinated, migration of some activities offshore. Government policies, such as free trade agreements and duty free zones, are critical to fostering or impeding these efforts.

We do not know enough about these relationships between regional economies and direct investment to conclude whether these speculations are correct. I suspect, given the high degree of coordination required, that collective action might be better orchestrated by large firms. An intriguing example of this was in the Weil et al. chapter. They discuss the Hong Kong apparel supply chain management firm, Li & Fung, which now coordinates a network of manufacturers based not only in Asia but also in the Mediterranean, Eastern Europe, and Central Europe. Many of these are branch plants of Asian manufacturers, though apparently some plants are also operated by nationals in the various host nations. In effect, Li & Fung's contribution is coordination for its customers. This role should not be underestimated, for it is based on a specialized knowledge of who can do what and how fast.

There are also cases in which regional dynamics may cause investment in anticipation of, or in consequence of, the investment of a dominant firm. Research on direct investment by Japanese firms in the United States shows that Japanese auto suppliers invested in large numbers ahead of the massive investments by assemblers in the mid- to late-1980s (Kogut and Chang 1991). A somewhat different pattern can be seen in the chapter by Kenney on the Japanese and Korean television manufacturers in Mexico, where the parts and component suppliers came in distinct waves. The first wave of Japanese firms consisted of suppliers with bulky inputs for which transportation costs were prohibitive; many of these relocated because of encouragement and even pressure from the assemblers. Later waves of suppliers were attracted because of the increasing number of assemblers. Many of these received few guarantees, but it was easy to see that there was ample business opportunity, because of the large number of potential customers. This wave of relocations culminated in the relocation of the capital-intensive television tube manufacturers to the region, completing the creation of an integrated manufacturing complex.

Of course, these polar cases might well explain some of the differences between the fate of regions in the United States and the European experience. Other factors intervene, such as fiscal policy, federal government structures, and tariff policies. The significance of the U.S. tariff code provisions termed 806/807 (9802 under the Harmonized System) that permitted the export for further processing and then reimport of those goods paying tariffs only on the foreign value-added clearly influenced the internationalization of a number of U.S. firms, especially those in electronics and textiles (Feenstra et al. 2000).

Location economics also vary by technology. Software, because it is so inexpensive to transport, is far more open to global sourcing, as witnessed in the stunning growth of Indian software exports in the past decade, though it is interesting to note that India exports very little in the way of packaged software. Here again, the ability to divide and scatter portions of the creation process across locations creates a complex division of labor within firms and between firms.

### Creating Regions

For developing countries, foreign investments have frequently dwarfed the local economy. McKendrick offered one of the more stunning examples of the impact of foreign investment:

Consider that, in 1999, American firms made almost 80 percent of the world's hard disk drives. In that year, they assembled fewer than 1 percent of their drives in the United States and roughly 70 percent in Southeast Asia; in 1985 almost all drives made by U.S. firms were assembled at home. In 1995, 29 percent of the employees who worked for American firms in the HDD value chain worked in the United States; 55 percent worked in Southeast Asia (Gourevitch et al. 2000). One American disk drive company, Seagate Technology, became the largest employer in Thailand and Malaysia, and the largest private sector employer in Singapore. It was also the largest single exporter from China in 1998, with almost $1 billion in exports.

The large literature on the consequences of investment by multinational corporations for developing countries is split in its judgment whether foreign direct investment is positive or negative. It is, in fact, a subject of current efforts to distill whether on *average* foreign direct investment is good or bad for a country. Of course, even if good on average, it would be wanton neglect to advise countries to attract investment without trying to understand why or, perhaps, more correctly, what types of foreign direct investment may be poor.

One reason is that foreign direct investment can be "footloose." I have made the argument that a source of advantage for the multinational corporation is the option value of utilizing the operating flexibility of its global network. It can move people around, transfer innovation, and switch production if real wages should rise in one country (see Kogut and Kulatilaka [1995] for a formalization), though, at least to some extent, this conceptualizes production factors as undifferentiated in a variety of locations. Jaeyong Song looked at this question a number of years later by studying the establishment of Japanese factories in East Asia (Song 1998, 2002). When the yen began to increase in value from 1985 to 1995, Japanese firms rapidly relocated factories offshore to lower their manufacturing costs. Then he asked a further question: as wages increased in Korea, Taiwan, and Singapore in particular, did these Japanese firms shut down these plants and move the capital equipment to lower cost platforms, such as in China? He proposed that to the extent that the plants were able to upgrade their capabilities and move to more sophisticated production activities, they were less likely to be closed. He found strong support for this, finding further that local suppliers had a positive effect on the choice to upgrade rather than to exit.

In the chapter on the television industry there is a similar logic. As Kenney found:

The Tijuana factories were not static; they would evolve. During this period, often, there was a division of labor between the United States and the Mexican factories known as the "twin plant" arrangement. However, twin plant proved to be a misnomer, because the overwhelming tendency was for the U.S. plants to shrink while the maquiladoras grew. Frequently this resulted in the closure of the U.S. factory in favor of its Mexican counterpart, though this was not always the case. For example, the Sony San Diego factory began by assembling televisions, then gradually transferring its various assembly operations, first to its Tijuana facilities and later also to Mexicali. Sony San Diego graduated to CRT production, R&D, and the assembly of various other Sony products.

It is not well understood, however, whether multinational corporations are *necessary* factors in this process of technological diffusion and upgrading. The case of memory semiconductors did not suggest it, nor has the foundry capacity of Taiwan been documented to be a platform of migration into higher value-added semiconductor design activities. As Leachman and Leachman noted, the fabrication undertaken in Taiwanese fabs operates at the global productivity frontier, and the engineers and operators are among the best paid in the world. Contract fabrication is a capital- and skill-intensive activity that is richly rewarded. Despite the fact that the Taiwan foundries have been careful not to challenge the market of their customers, they have become very profitable ventures.

This theme of trust also rears its head in the study by Anca Metiu on the choice of an American software firm to collocate development in the United States in one case, but to place offshore part of the code writing in India for another project (Metiu 2001). For the Indian project, she found that the U.S. managers worked well with their Indian partners (who belonged to the same firm) if they were brought to the U.S. site and rated highly in their abilities. However, the U.S. managers doubted the capabilities of the Indian site, with the same Indian engineers, apparently unaware of the contradiction. Boundaries do not simply represent transportation and communication costs; they represent contours of bias. Again, we hear the echoes of Greif's and Curtin's cross-cultural brokers.

Global integration may decay the importance of cultural distance as a factor in investment and location. For example, the manufacturing standards promulgated by the International Standards Organization have far greater importance in developing countries than in developed nations. They are an expression of the development of a language by which a set of capabilities to manufacture are, in a sense, declared modularized and then can be used as a signal of competence. It is not surprising that ISO adoption is fiercely advertised by Indian software companies, as it was by Russian companies immediately after the collapse of the Soviet Union (Sabel and Prokop 1996). Standardization is the substance that permits modularity to function both globally and as an industrial Esperanto that liberates perceptions of space from the residues of national and ethnic preferences that have always been a factor in world trade and investment.

## Conclusions

In considering the results of the preceding chapters, it is interesting to assess the degree by which industries have assembled the building blocks of global coordination. A critical measure is the extent to which modularity prevails globally, allowing for dispersed production. A second measure is to evaluate the extent to which production and innovation are also dispersed.

My inference from these chapters points to the incredible degree of modularity in personal computer design and manufacturing, drawing upon the remarkable globalization of the hard disk drive, semiconductors, and assembly. The automobile industry wavers in the middle, a case perhaps of stalled internationalization. For while the pressure of the market is considerable, the product development cycle for autos still has a far longer gestation period than that found in textiles. Much of the innovation comes in the form of customization, rather than product innovation; surely, there is the perception of a convergence in style and performance over the years. Here modularity is critical, as it provides a way to achieve scale economies in modules and customization in assembly. Because the supplier industry is more fragmented than the auto assemblers, a movement of value up the production chain toward suppliers potentially opens the door to a far greater degree of national diversity. Beneath the account of the history of the flat screen technology, one sees in fact how the evolution of the embodied technology—the materials, semiconductors, manufacturing processes—allowed for an impressive uncertainty regarding which region, and which country, will dominate this industry. The answer appears to be none, as the real dynamic is in the componentry rather than in the assembly.

In other words, globalization is less and less about national competition around sectoral dominance but about the location of the value-added *activities* that compose the global commodity chains. From this perspective, firm strategies matter more, since comparative advantage and firm advantage are more delinked today than they have ever been before. The textile industry is a classic example, where we see the same firms outsourcing some products to China, while other products are made in other lower cost enclaves (Mexico, Tunisia, and northern Spain) near the final markets, and still other products are assembled in the final market. The continuing dominance of the Italian textile manufacturers, the resilience of the Sentier district in Paris, and the overlooked but strong German position all point to firm strategies that couple design, advanced supply chain technology, and customer knowledge as features that trade cost against time.[6]

It should be remembered that in some industries, coordination costs overwhelm the savings of global sourcing. The Swiss-located manufacturing of the watch, called the Swatch, entails only a few hundred workers to produce ten million watches. The sourcing of production in Asia adds expensive labor to supply chain management, increases working capital requirements, and slows delivery to markets that are largely European and American. It might also raise costs regarding the protection of intellectual property. The alternative strategy of expending more resources in design and advertising, while maintaining capital-intensive production near the market, is not based so much on comparative advantage, but on the time-cost tradeoff that is so salient in fashion-oriented businesses. This issue of understanding the customer, the costs of global coordination, and the economies of time management is well illustrated by the case of Dell, discussed in this book, and it serves as a critical reminder that static comparisons of manufacturing costs miss the more dynamic elements in global competitive strategies.

The value of these chapters is the vision of the world seen through a detailed analysis of a few industries. The world economy has progressed rapidly over the past hundred years, even if the diffusion of knowledge has ancient roots and distance remains as much cultural as spatial. The speed of diffusion and the element of time are what have changed most remarkably. Britain had more than a century to enjoy its productivity lead, the United States over half a century, and Japan perhaps barely two decades. In this view, the relative decline of Japan is a result of the speed by which its innovation in organizing principles diffused to the rest of the world. Multinational corporations, consulting firms, governments, academics, tourists, and itinerant businesspeople render borders more porous today than before. It is this undulating pulse of innovation and diffusion that has always marked world economic history, but only more quickly today.

## Notes

I would like to thank Rachel Barrett for her assistance, and Sue Helper, Martin Kenney, John Paul MacDuffie, Mari Sako, Myles Shaver, and Ivo Zander for providing me with comments and help. The Reginald H. Jones Center provided financial assistance to support this research program.

1. In measuring human capital, it does not matter if you count master's degrees in engineering or in business; they both are human capital investments, a point remembering to counter the bias that a patent is worth more than a trademark!

2. See, for example, Pirenne's (1937) description of how by the twelfth century Flanders was importing English wool to be woven into cloth and exported as a luxury good to markets as far away as Russia and Rome.

3. See Kogut and Zander 1992, 1996, for a discussion.

4. See Rumelt 1974; Channon 1973; Dyas and Thanheiser 1976; Pavan 1972.

5. See Mowery (1984) for a discussion of the United States and the UK; Dornseifer (1994) gives an overview of Germany.

6. See Schoenberger (1994).

# References

Abernathy, Frederick H., John T. Dunlop, Janice H. Hammond, and David Weil. 1999. *A Stitch in Time: Lean Retailing and the Transformation of Manufacturing—Lessons from the Apparel and Textile Industries.* New York: Oxford University Press.

———. 2000a. "Retailing and Supply Chains in the Information Age." *Technology in Society: An International Journal* 21, no. 1 (winter): 2–27.

———. 2000b. "Control Your Inventory in a World of Lean Retailing." *Harvard Business Review* (Nov./Dec.): 169–76.

Abrahamson, Eric. 1996. "Management Fashion." *Academy of Management Review* 21: 254–85.

Almeida, Paul. 1996. "Knowledge Sourcing by Foreign Multinationals: Patent Citation Analysis in the US Semiconductor Industry." *Strategic Management Journal* 17: 155–65.

Almeida, Paul, and Bruce Kogut. 1997. "The Exploration of Technological Diversity and the Geographic Localization of Innovation." *Small Business Economics* 9, no. 1: 21–31.

———. 1999. "Localization of Knowledge and the Mobility of Engineers in Regional Networks." *Management Science* 45, no. 7: 905–17.

Angel, David. 1990. "New Firm Formation in the Semiconductor Industry: Institutional Infrastructures." *Regional Studies* 24: 211–21.

Appleyard, Melissa M., Nile W. Hatch, David C. Mowery. 2000. "Managing the Development and Transfer of Process Technologies in the Semiconductor Manufacturing Industry." In *The Nature and Dynamics of Organizational Capabilities*, ed. G. Dosi, R. R. Nelson, and S. G. Winter, 183–207. London: Oxford University Press.

Armour, H. O., and D. J. Teece. 1978. "Organizational Structure and Economic Performance: A Test of the M-Form Hypothesis." *Bell Journal of Economics* 9, no. 2: 196–222.

Arrow, Kenneth J. 1971. *Essays on the Theory of Risk Bearing.* Chicago: University of Chicago Press.

Arthur, W. Brian. 1986. "Industry Location and the Importance of History." Center for Economic Policy Research, Paper 84, Stanford University. Reprinted in W. Brian Arthur, *Increasing Returns and Path Dependence in the Economy*, 49–67. Ann Arbor: University of Michigan Press, 1994.

————. 1994. *Increasing Returns and Path Dependence in the Economy.* Ann Arbor: University of Michigan Press.

Asahi Glass Co., Ltd. 1992. *AGC Company.* Tokyo: Asahi Glass Corporation.

Audretsch, David B., and Maryann P. Feldman. 1996. "R&D Spillovers and the Geography of Innovation and Production." *American Economic Review* 86: 630–40.

*Automotive News.* 1996. "Top 100 Automotive Suppliers, 1995." http://www.autonews.com/.

Baldwin, Carliss, and Kim Clark. 1997. "Managing in an Age of Modularity." *Harvard Business Review* (Sept./Oct.): 84–93.

————. 2000. *Design Rules.* Cambridge: MIT Press.

BANCOMEXT. 1999. "Electrical and Electronic Equipment." http://www.businessline.gob.mx/sectorial_i/elec_i.html.

Baranson, Jack. 1980. *Sources of Japan's International Competitiveness in the Consumer Electronics Industry.* Washington, DC: Developing World Industry & Technology, Inc.

Barkema, Harry G., John H. J. Bell, and Johannes M. Pennings. 1996. "Foreign Entry, Cultural Barriers, and Learning." *Strategic Management Journal* 17, no. 2: 151–66.

Barnes, Paul (Abit Corp., Taipei, Taiwan). 1997. Personal interview by and personal correspondence with James Curry, Jan., Mar.

Baron, James, M. Diane Burton, and Michael Hannan. 1996. "The Road Taken: The Origins and Evolution of Employment Systems in High-Tech Firms." *Industrial and Corporate Change* 5, no. 2: 239–75.

Bartlett, Christopher A., and Sumantra Ghoshal. 1989. *Managing across Borders.* Boston: Harvard Business School Press.

Bashe, Charles, Lyle Johnson, John Palmer, and Emerson Pugh. 1986. *IBM's Early Computers.* Cambridge MA: MIT Press.

Bigelow, Lyda S., Glenn R. Carroll, Marc-David Seidel, and Lucia Tsai. 1997. "Legitimation, Geographic Scale, and Organizational Density: Regional Patterns of Foundings of American Automobile Producers, 1885–1981." *Social Science Research* 26: 377–98.

Bilby, Kenneth. 1986. *The General: David Sarnoff and the Rise of the Communications Industry.* New York: Harper and Rowe.

Blake, Linda, and Jim Lande. 2001. *Trends in the International Telecommunications Industry.* Washington, DC: Federal Communications Commission.

*Bloomberg News.* 2000a. "Samsung to Spend $35 Million on India Monitor Plant" (Nov. 8).

————. 2000b. "Canceled IBM Contract Costs Acer $643 Million in Sales" (Sept. 7).

Borrus, Michael. 1988. *Competing for Control: America's Stake in Microelectronics.* Cambridge: Ballinger.

Borrus, Michael, and Jeffrey A. Hart. 1994. "Display's the Thing: The Real Stakes in the Conflict over High Resolution Displays." *Journal of Policy Analysis and Management* 13 (winter): 21–54.

Borrus, Michael, and John Zysman. 1997. "Globalization with Borders: The Rise of Wintelism as the Future of Global Competition." *Industry and Innovation* 4, no. 2: 141–66.

Bradsher, K. 1998a. "GM's Plant in Brazil Raises Fears Closer to Home." *New York Times,* Business/Financial Desk, June 17.

————. 1998b. "Subtext of the G.M. Strike Focuses on Global Strategy." *New York Times,* Business/Financial Desk, June 23.

————. 1998c. "General Motors Plans to Build New, Efficient Assembly Plants." *New York Times,* Business/Financial Desk, Aug. 6.

Braudel, Fernand. 1982. *The Wheels of Commerce*. New York: Harper and Row.

Braun, Ernest, and Stuart Macdonald. 1982. *Revolution in Miniature*. Cambridge: Cambridge University Press.

Bresnahan, Timothy, and John Richards. 1999. "Local and Global Competition in Information Technology." Stanford Institute for Economic Policy Research Policy Paper No. 99–7 (June).

Brinkley, Joel. 1997. *Defining Vision: The Battle for the Future of Television*. New York: Harcourt Brace.

Brooke, James. 2002. "Japan's Export Power Drift across the China Sea." *New York Times*, International Section, Apr. 7.

Brookfield, Jonathan. 1999. "Localization, Outsourcing, and Supplier Networks: A Study of Taiwan's Machine Tool Industry." Ph.D. dissertation, Wharton School, University of Pennsylvania, Philadelphia, PA.

Brown, John Seely, and Paul Duguid. 2000a. *The Social Life of Information*. Boston: Harvard Business School Press.

———. 2000b. "Mysteries of the Region: Knowledge Dynamics in Silicon Valley." In *The Silicon Valley: A Habitat for Innovation and Entrepreneurship*, ed. Chong-Moon Lee, William Miller, Henry Rowen, and Marguerite Hancock, 16–45. Stanford: Stanford University Press.

*Business Times Singapore*. 1993. "Plugging into an Asian Gold Mine" (May 3).

———. 1994. "Asia's Hard Drive for an Even Bigger Role" (Mar. 18).

*Business Week*. 1987. "Seagate Goes East—and Comes Back a Winner" (Mar. 16).

———. 2000. "Midyear Investment Guide" (26 June).

*Business Wire*. 1994. "Seagate Announces Multi-million Dollar Asia-Pacific Expansion Plans" (Sept. 7).

———. 1994. "Seagate's Recording Head Operations Ship 250,000,000th Thin Film Recording Head" (Nov. 1).

———. 1997. "Fujitsu Ranked the Fastest Growing Hard Drive Manufacturer" (June 17).

Cairncross, Frances. 1997. *The Death of Distance: How the Communications Revolution Is Changing Our Lives*. Boston, MA: Harvard Business School Press.

Cantwell, John. 1989. *Technological Innovation and Multinational Corporations*. Oxford: Blackwell.

Castells, Manuel. 1996. *The Rise of the Network Society*. Vol. I of *The Information Age: Economy, Society, and Culture*. Oxford: Blackwell.

Castilla, Emilio, Hokyu Hwang, Ellen Granovetter, and Mark Granovetter. 2000. "Social Networks in Silicon Valley." In *The Silicon Valley Edge: A Habitat for Innovation and Entrepreneurship*, ed. Chong-Moon Lee, William Miller, Marguerite Gong Hancock, and Henry Rowen. Stanford: Stanford University Press.

Chandler, Alfred Dupont. 1962. *Strategy and Structure: Chapters in the History of the Industrial Enterprise*. Cambridge, MA: M.I.T. Press.

———. 1977. *The Visible Hand: The Managerial Revolution in American Business*. Cambridge: Harvard Belknap Press.

———. 1990. *Scale and Scope: The Dynamics of Industrial Capitalism*. Cambridge: Harvard Belknap Press.

———. 2001. *Inventing the Electronic Century*. New York: Free Press.

Channon, Derek F. 1973. "The Strategy and Structure of British Enterprises." Division of Research, Graduate School of Business, Harvard University, Boston, MA.

*Chilton's Electronic News.* 1990. "Market Share Moves Seen Squeezing Disk Drive Margins" (Dec. 24).

Choi, Dae Won, and Martin Kenney. 1997. "The Globalization of Korean Industry: Korean Maquiladoras in Mexico." *Frontera Norte* 9 (Jan.–June): 5–22.

Chposky, James, and Ted Leonsis. 1988. *Blue Magic: The People, Power and Politics Behind the IBM Personal Computer.* New York: Facts on File.

Cohen, Stephen S., J. Bradford Delong, Steven Weber, and John Zysman. 2001. "Tools: The Drivers of E-Commerce." In *Tracking a Transformation: E-Commerce and the Terms of Competition in Industries,* ed. BRIE-IGCC E-conomy Project, 3–26. Washington, DC: Brookings Institution.

Collins, Robert. 1970. Hearings on Trade and Tariff Proposals before the Committee on Ways and Means, House of Representatives, 91st Congress, Second Session.

*COMLINE Daily News Computers.* 1995. "NEC Hard Disk Drive Plant in Luzon Now Operational" (Oct. 9).

*Computergram International.* 1992. "Thailand: Fujitsu Slashed Local Production of Small Hard Drives as Prices Collapse" (Jan. 3).

*Computerworld.* 1985. "Made in Japan Tag Penetrating Components Market; U.S.-Japan Pacts Create Added Equipment Sales" (Dec. 9).

Computex Online. 2001. "Taiwan's Desktop Industry" (Feb. 22) http://www.computex. com.tw/show_Special.asp?id=151.

Courant, Bruno, and Elisabeth Parat. 2000. "A Closer Look at the New Filiere: The Establishment Surveys in Roanne and Cholet." Working Paper, Harvard Center for Textile and Apparel Research (Sept.).

*Crain's Detroit Business.* 2002. "Largest OEM Parts Suppliers; Ranked by 2001 Sales of Original Equipment Manufacturer's Parts." Crain's Lists, (July 8) http://www.crains-detroit.com.

Cringely, Robert X. 1996. *Accidental Empires.* New York: HarperBusiness.

Curry, James, and Martin Kenney. 1999. "Beating the Clock: Corporate Responses to Rapid Change in the PC Industry." *California Management Review* (fall): 8–36.

Curtin, Philip. 1984. *Cross-Cultural Trade in World History.* Cambridge: Cambridge University Press.

Curtis, Philip J. 1994. *The Fall of the U.S. Consumer Electronics Industry: An American Trade Tragedy.* Westport: Quorum.

Custer, Walt. 2001. "Big-Time Slowdown or Extended Inventory Correction." *Circuitree* (Mar.) www.circuitree.com.

Dassbach, Carl. 1989. *Global Enterprises and the World Economy: Ford, General Motors, and IBM, the Emergence of the Transnational Enterprise.* New York: Garland.

D'Aveni, Richard A. 1994. *Hypercompetition: Managing the Dynamics of Strategic Maneuvering.* New York: Free Press.

David, Paul. 1986. "Understanding the Economics of QWERTY: The Necessity of History." In *Economic History and the Modern Economist,* ed. W. Parker, 30–49. New York: Basil Blackwell.

Davies, Howard. 1977. "Technology Transfer through Commercial Transactions." *Journal of Industrial Economics* 26, no. 2: 161–75.

Dedrick, Jason, and Kenneth L. Kraemer. 1998. *Asia's Computer Challenge: Threat or Opportunity for the United States & the World?* New York: Oxford University Press.

Delios, Andrea, and Paul W. Beamish. 2001. "Survival Profitability: The Roles of Experience and Intangible Assets in Foreign Subsidiary Performance." *Academy of Management Journal* 44, no. 5: 1028–38.

Depp, Steven W. 1994. *Flat Panel Display Strategic Forum Proceedings: Creating a U.S. Industry.* Presentation made at the Center for Display Technology and Manufacturing, College of Engineering, University of Michigan, Nov. 15–16.

Developing World Industry and Technology, Inc. 1978. *Sources of Competitiveness in the Japanese Color Television and Video Tape Recorder Industry.* Report prepared for the U.S. Department of Labor, Oct. 16. Washington DC: Developing World Industry and Technology, Inc.

Dicken, Peter. 1998. *Global Shift: Transforming the World Economy,* 3d ed. New York: Guilford.

DiMaggio, Paul, and Walter Powell. 1983. "The Iron Cage Revisited: Institutional Isomorphism and Collective Rationality in Organizational Fields." *American Sociological Review* 48: 147–60.

Disk/Trend. 1981. *Disk/Trend Report: Rigid Disk Drives.* Mountain View, CA: Disk/Trend.

Dornseifer, Bernd. 1994. "Aufstieg der kleinen Multinationale Unternehmen aus Fuenf kleinen Staaten vor 1914," *Business History Review,* 68 (4): 612–13.

Dosi, Giovanni, Richard R. Nelson, and Sidney G. Winter (eds.). 2000. *The Nature and Dynamics of Organizational Capabilities.* Oxford: Oxford University Press.

Dossani, Rafiq, and Martin Kenney. 2003. "Went for Cost, Stayed for Quality?: Moving the Back Office to India." Berkeley Roundtable on the International Economy Working Paper Number 147 (September).

Dunning, John H. 1980. "Toward an Eclectic Theory of International Production: Some Empirical Tests." *Journal of International Business Studies* 11: 9–31.

———. 1993. *Multinational Enterprises and the Global Economy.* Reading: Addison Wesley.

———. (ed.). 1997. *Governments, Globalization, and International Business.* Oxford: Oxford University Press.

———. (ed.). 2000. *Regions, Globalization, and the Knowledge-Based Economy.* Oxford: Oxford University Press.

Dyas, Gareth P., and Heinz Thanheiser. 1976. *The Emerging European Enterprises: Strategy and Structure in French and German Industry.* London: Macmillan.

*Electronic Business.* 1988. "Hard Times for Hard Drives; Seagate Technology's Difficulties Affect Hard Disk Industry" (Nov. 15).

———. 1990. "How Conner Peripherals Races to Market, Boosts Quality; Sells Products First, Designs Them Later" (May 14).

*Electronic Buyer's News.* 1987. "Fujitsu Execs Stress Globalization" (May 18).

*Electronic Engineering Times.* 2001. "Monitor Industry Shakeout Continues" (June 28).

*Electronic News.* 1968. "Semiconductor Family Tree" (July 8: 5).

———. 1984. "Smaller Business Computers Creating Need for Half-Height, Sub-5.25-inch Winchesters" (June 4).

———. 1985. "IBM PC AT Plan: Source Drive on Availability" (Apr. 29).

———. 1986. "U.S. OEM Vendors Fight Japanese with High-Capacity Drives, Bold Pricing" (July 7).

Ellinger, Robert. 1977. "Industrial Location Behavior and Spatial Evolution." *Journal of Industrial Economics* 25, no. 4: 295–312.

Evans, Carolyn L. 2000a. "The Economic Significance of National Border Effects." Working Paper, Federal Reserve Bank of New York.

———. 2000b. "National Border Effects and Heterogeneous Fixed Costs of International Trade." Working Paper, Federal Reserve Bank of New York.

Evans, Carolyn, and James Harrigan. 2001. "Distance, Time, and Specialization." Working Paper, Federal Reserve Bank of New York.

———. 2003. "Distance, Time, and Specialization." Working Paper No. 9729, National Bureau of Economic Research. Cambridge: NBER.

Feenstra, Robert. 1996. "U.S. Imports, 1972–1994: Data and Concordances." Working Paper No. 5515, National Bureau of Economic Research. Cambridge: NBER.

———. 1998. "Integration of Trade and Disintegration of Production in the Global Economy." *Journal of Economic Perspectives* 12, no. 4: 31–50.

Feenstra, Robert, Gordon H. Hanson, and Deborah L. Swenson. 2000. "Offshore Assembly from the United States: Production Characteristics of the 9802 Program." In *The Impact of International Trade on Wages*, ed. R. Feenstra, 85–122. Chicago: NBER and University of Chicago Press.

Feldman, Maryann. 1994. *The Geography of Innovation*. Boston, MA: Kluwer Academic.

Ferguson, Charles H., and Charles R. Morris. 1993. *Computer Wars: The Fall of IBM and the Future of Global Technology*. New York: Times Books.

Fields, Gary. 2003. *Territories of Profit: Communications, Capitalist Development, and the Innovative Enterprises of G. F. Swift and Dell Computer*. Stanford, CA: Stanford University Press.

*Financial Times*. 1986. "Singapore: Electronics Heads the Revival" (Nov. 3).

Fine, Charles H. 1998. *Clockspeed: Winning Industry Control in the Age of Temporary Advantage*. Reading, MA: Perseus.

Florida, Richard. 1995. "Toward the Learning Region." *Futures* 27, no. 5: 527–36.

———. 2002. *The Creative Class*. New York: Basic Books.

Florida, Richard, and Martin Kenney. 1988. "Venture Capital, High Technology and Regional Development." *Regional Studies* 22, no. 1: 33–48.

———. 1991. "Transplanted Organizations: The Transfer of Japanese Industrial Organization to the U.S." *American Sociological Review* 56, no. 3 (June): 381–98.

Franko, Lawrence G. 1976. *The European Multinationals: A Renewed Challenge to American and British Big Business*. Greenwich, CT: Greylock.

Freiberger, Paul, and Michael Swaine. 1984. *Fire in the Valley*. Berkeley: McGraw Hill.

Fremdling, Rainer. 1991. "The Puddler—A Craftsman's Skill and the Spread of a New Technology in Belgium, France and Germany." *Journal of European Economic History* 20: 529–67.

Frost, Tony. 2001. "The Geographic Sources of Foreign Subsidiaries' Innovations." *Strategic Management Journal* 22, no. 2: 101–23.

Fruin, Mark. 1992. *The Japanese Enterprise System: Competitive Strategies and Cooperative Structures*. Oxford: Clarendon.

Gartner, Inc. 2003. "Gartner Says Worldwide PC Shipments Experienced Third Consecutive Quarter of Positive Growth." (Apr. 17) San Jose, CA: Gartner, Inc. http://www4.gartner.com/5_about/press_releases/prapr172003a.jsp.

Gereffi, Gary. 1994. "The Organization of Buyer-driven Global Commodity Chains: How U.S. Retailers Shape Overseas Production Networks." In *Commodity Chains and*

*Global Capitalism*, ed. Gary Gereffi and Miguel Korzeniewicz, 95–122. Westport, CT: Praeger.

———. 1999. "International Trade and Industrial Upgrading in the Apparel Commodity Chain." *Journal of International Economics* 48, no. 1 (June): 37–70.

———. 2001. "Beyond the Producer-driven/Buyer-driven Dichotomy: The Evolution of Global Value Chains in the Internet Era." *IDS Bulletin* 32, no. 3.

Gereffi, Gary, and Miguel Korzeniewicz (eds.). 1994. *Commodity Chains and Global Capitalism*. Westport, CT: Greenwood.

Gerschenkron, Alexander. 1962. *Economic Backwardness in Historical Perspective: A Book of Essays*. Cambridge: Harvard University Belknap Press.

Gertler, Meric S. 2001. "Tacit Knowledge and the Economic Geography of Context, or the Undefinable Tacitness of Being (There)." Paper presented at the 2001 DRUID Summer Conference, Aalborg, Denmark, June 12–15.

Gilder, George. 2000. *Telecosm: How Infinite Bandwidth Will Revolutionize Our World*. New York: The Free Press.

Gilson, Ronald. 1999. "The Legal Infrastructure of High Technology Industrial Districts: Silicon Valley, Route 128, and Covenants Not to Compete." *New York University Law Review* 74, no. 3: 575–629.

Gourevitch, Peter, Roger Bohn, and David McKendrick. 2000. "Globalization of the Production: Insights from the Hard Disk Drive Industry." *World Development* 28, no. 2: 301–17.

Graham, Margaret. 1986. *RCA and the VideoDisc: The Business of Research*. Cambridge: Cambridge University Press.

Granovetter, Mark. 1985. "Economic Action and Social Structure: The Problem of Embeddedness." *American Journal of Sociology* 91: 481–510.

Gregory, Gene. 1985. *Japanese Electronics Technology: Enterprise and Innovation*. Tokyo: Japanese Times, Ltd.

Greif, Avner. 1989. "Reputation and Coalitions in Medieval Trade: Evidence on the Maghribi Traders." *Journal of Economic History* 49: 857–82.

Greve, Henrich R. 1995. "Jumping Ship: The Diffusion of Strategy Abandonment." *Administrative Science Quarterly* 40, no. 3: 444–73.

———. 1996. "Patterns of Competition: The Diffusion of a Market Position in Radio Broadcasting." *Administrative Science Quarterly* 41: 29–60.

———. 1998. "Managerial Cognition and the Mimetic Adoption of Market Positions: What You See Is What You Do." *Strategic Management Journal* 19: 967–88.

Gu, Q. L., et. al. 1999. "The Development of the China Apparel Industry." Working Paper, China Textile University and Harvard Center for Textile and Apparel Research, Nov.

Hamel, Gary, and C. K. Prahalad. 1994. *Competing for the Future*. Boston: Harvard Business School Press.

Hammond, Janice, and Kristin Kohler. 2001. "E-Commerce in the Textile and Apparel Industries." In *Tracking a Transformation,* ed. the BRIE-IGCC E-conomy Project, 310–31. Washington, DC: Brookings Institution Press.

Hancock, David. 1995. *Citizens of the World: London Merchants and the Integration of the British Atlantic Community, 1735–1785*. New York: Cambridge University Press.

Harrison, Bennett, Maryellen R. Kelley, and Jon Gant. 1996. "Innovative Firm Behavior and Local Milieu: Exploring the Intersection of Agglomeration, Firm Effects, and Technological Change." *Economic Geography* 72, no. 3: 233–58.

Harrison, Linden. 1973. "Liquid Crystal Displays." *Electronics Australia* (Feb.): 22–24. Reprinted from *Electron*.

Hart, Jeffrey A. 1993. "The Anti-dumping Petition of the Advanced Display Manufacturers of America: Origins and Consequences." *World Economy* 16 (Jan.): 85–109.

Harvey, David. 1982. *The Limits to Capital*. Oxford: Basil Blackwell.

Hayter, Roger. 1997. *The Dynamics of Industrial Location: The Factory, the Firm, and the Production System*. New York: Wiley.

Head, C. Keith, John C. Ries, and Deborah L. Swenson. 1999. "Attracting Foreign Manufacturing: Investment Promotion and Agglomeration." *Regional Science & Urban Economics* 29, no. 2: 197–218.

Heaver, Trevor. 2001. "Logistics in East Asia." Paper presented at the Conference on East Asia's Future Economy, Development Economics Research Group, The World Bank/Asia-Pacific Policy Program, Harvard University, Cambridge, MA, Oct.

Hedlund, Gunnar. 1986. "The Hypermodern MNC–Heterarchy." *Human Resource Management* 25: 9–35.

Helper, Susan, and John Paul MacDuffie. 2001. "E-volving the Auto Industry: E-Business Effects on Consumer and Suppler Relationships." In *Tracking a Transformation*, ed. the BRIE-IGCC E-conomy Project, 178–213. Washington, DC: Brookings Institution Press.

Henderson, Jeffrey. 1989. *The Globalisation of High Technology Production: Society, Space and Semiconductors in the Restructuring of the Modern World*. New York: Routledge.

Herrigel, Gary. 1996. *Industrial Constructions: The Sources of German Industrial Power*. New York: Cambridge University Press.

Hicks, Diana. 1994. *Beyond Global: Innovation and Adjustment in U.S. Automobile Manufacturing*. Unpublished manuscript.

Hopkins, Terence, and Immanuel Wallerstein. 1986. "Commodity Chains in the World Economy prior to 1800." *Review* 10, no. 1: 157–70.

———. 1994. "Commodity Chains: Construct and Research." In *Commodity Chains and Global Capitalism*, ed. Gary Gereffi and Miguel Korzeniewicz, 17–19. Westport, CT: Praeger.

Howard, Webster E. 1996. "Foreword." In *Color TFT Liquid Crystal Displays*, ed. Teruhiko Yamazaki, Hideaki Kawakami, and Hiroo Hori. Supervising translator, Shunsuke Obinata for O'Mara and Associates. Mountain View, CA: Semiconductor Equipment and Materials International (SEMI).

Hu, Yao-Su. 1995. "The International Transferability of the Firm's Advantages." *California Management Review* 37, no. 4: 73–88.

Hung, Faith. 2001. "Taiwan EMS Firm Lands China Contract." *Electronic Buyer's News* (May 31).

Hyde, Alan. 1996 "How Silicon Valley Has Eliminated Trade Secrets (and Why This Is Efficient)." Mimeo, Rutgers University, New Brunswick, NJ.

IDC Japan Report. 1991. "Fujitsu Will Produce Small Hard Disk Drives in Thailand Starting This Summer" (Feb. 28).

Infineon Technologies. 2000. *Prospectus for a Public Stock Offering*. Munich, Germany: Infineon Technologies.

Information Technology Information Services. 1999. *2000 Taiwan Industrial Outlook— Information Hardware Industry*. Information Technology Information Services, Taipei, Taiwan: Market Intelligence Center, Institute for Information Industries, Government of the Republic of China.

Institute for Management Development. 2000. *The World Competitiveness Yearbook*. Lausanne, Switzerland: IMD.

Intel Corporation. 2002. "Securities and Exchange Commission 10-K Filing." Santa Clara, CA: Intel Corporation.

Irwin, Douglas A., and Peter J. Klenow. 1994. "Learning-by-Doing Spillovers in the Semi-conductor Industry." *Journal of Political Economy* 102, no. 6: 1200–27.

Jaffe, Adam B., Manuel Trajtenberg, and Rebecca Henderson. 1993. "Geographic Local-ization of Knowledge Spillovers as Evidenced by Patent Citations." *Quarterly Journal of Economics* 63: 577–98.

Jameson, Frederick. 1991. *Postmodernism, or the Cultural Logic of Late Capitalism*. Durham, NC: Duke University Press.

Johnstone, Bob. 1999. *We Were Burning: Japanese Entrepreneurs and the Forging of the Electronic Age*. Boulder, CO: Basic Books (Westview).

Juran, J. M. 1978. "The QC Circle Phenomenon," *Industrial Quality Control*, Jan., pp. 329–36.

Kaplan, David. 1999. *The Silicon Boys and Their Valley of Dreams*. New York: William Morrow.

Katz, Michael L., and Carl Shapiro. 1994. "Systems Competition and Network Effects." *Journal of Economic Perspectives* 8, no. 2 (spring): 93–115.

Kenney, Martin. 1999a. "Institutions and Knowledge: The Dilemmas of Success in the Korean Electronics Industry." *Asian Pacific Business Review* 5, no. 1: 1–28.

———. 1999b. "Transplantation?: Comparing Japanese Television Assembly Plants in Japan and the U.S." In *Remade in America*, ed. Paul Adler, W. Mark Fruin, and Jeffrey Liker, 256–93. New York: Oxford University Press.

———. 2001. "The Temporal Dynamics of Knowledge Creation in the Information So-ciety." In *Knowledge Emergence*, ed. Ikujiro Nonaka and Toshihiro Nishiguchi, 93–110. New York: Oxford University Press.

———. 2002. "The Growth and Development of the Internet in the United States." In *The Global Internet Economy*, ed. Bruce Kogut, 69–108. Cambridge: MIT Press.

Kenney, Martin, and James Curry. 1999. "Knowledge Creation and Temporality in the Information Economy." In *Cognition, Knowledge, and Organizations*, ed. Raghu Garud and Joe Porac, 149–70. Greenwich, CT: JAI Press.

———. 2001. "The Internet and the Personal Computer Value Chain." In *Tracking a Transformation: E-commerce and the Terms of Competition in Industries*, 151–177. Washington, DC: The Brookings Institution Press.

Kenney, Martin, and Richard Florida. 1994. "Japanese Maquiladoras: Production Orga-nization and Global Commodity Chains." *World Development* 22, no. 1: 27–44.

Kenney, Martin, and Shoko Tanaka. 2003. "Transferring the Learning Factory to Amer-ica? The Japanese Television Assembly Transplants." In *Multinational Companies and Global Human Resource Strategies*, ed. W. Cooke, 119–46. Westport, CT: Praeger.

Khurana, Anil. 1994. "Quality in the Global Color Picture Tube Industry: Managing Complex Production Processes." Ph.D. dissertation, University of Michigan.

Kim, Linsu. 1997. *Imitation to Innovation: The Dynamics of Korea's Technological Learn-ing*. Boston: Harvard Business School Press.

Knickerbocker, Frederick T. 1973. *Oligopolistic Reaction and the Multinational Enterprise*. Cambridge, MA: Harvard University Press.

Kogut, Bruce. 1985. "Designing Global Strategies: Comparative and Competitive Value-Added Chains." *Sloan Management Review* 26: 15–28.

———. 1991. "Country Capabilities and the Permeability of Borders." *Strategic Management Journal* 12: 33–47.

———. 1992. "National Organizing Principles of Work and the Erstwhile Dominance of the American Multinational Corporation." *Industrial and Corporate Change* 1: 285–326.

———. 1993. *Country Competitiveness: Technology and the Organization of Work.* New York: Oxford University Press.

———. 2000. "The Network as Knowledge: Generative Rules and the Emergence of Structure." *Strategic Management Journal* 21: 405–25.

Kogut, Bruce, and Sea-Jin Chang. 1991. "Technological Capabilities and Japanese Foreign Direct Investment in the United States." *Review of Economics and Statistics* 73: 401–13.

Kogut, Bruce, and Nalin Kulatilaka. 1995. "Operating Flexibility, Global Manufacturing, and the Option Value of a Multinational Network." *Management Science* 40: 123–39.

Kogut, Bruce, Weijian Shan, and Gordon Walker. 1993. "Knowledge in the Network and the Network as Knowledge: The Structure of New Industries." In *The Embedded Firm: On the Socioeconomics of Industrial Networks*, ed. G. Grabher, 67–94. New York: Routledge.

Kogut, Bruce, and Udo Zander. 1992. "Knowledge of the Firm, Combinative Capabilities, and the Replication of Technology." *Organization Science* 3: 383–97.

———. 1993. "Knowledge of the Firm and the Evolutionary Theory of the Multinational Corporation." *Journal of International Business Studies* 24, no. 4: 625–64.

———. 1996. "What Firms Do: Coordination, Identity, and Learning." *Organization Science* 7: 502–18.

Kraul, Chris. 2001. "Economic Downturn Deepens in Mexico." *Los Angeles Times,* July 1.

Krishna, Kala M., and Ling Hui Tan. 1998. *Rags and Riches: Implementing Apparel Quotas under the Multi-Fiber Arrangement.* Ann Arbor, MI: University of Michigan Press.

Krugman, Paul. 1991. *Geography and Trade.* Cambridge, MA: MIT Press.

———. 1993. "The Current Case for Industrial Policy." In *Protectionism and World Welfare*, ed. D. Salvatore, 160–79. Cambridge: Cambridge University Press.

Landers, Peter. 2002. "Japan's Sony, Hitachi Slash Work Forces." *Wall Street Journal,* Mar. 1: A3, A6.

Langlois, Richard N. 1990. "Creating External Capabilities: Innovation and Vertical Disintegration in the Microcomputer Industry." *Business and Economic History* 19: 93–102.

———. 1992. "External Economies and Economic Progress: The Case of the Microcomputer Industry." *Business History Review* (spring): 66.

———. 2002. "The Vanishing Hand: The Modular Revolution in American Business." Unpublished working paper.

Lappin, Todd. 1996. "The Airline of the Internet." *Wired* 4, no. 12: 234–40, 282, 284, 286, 288, 290.

Law, Kam. 2000. "Flat Panel Display Manufacturing Challenges." In *DisplaySearch U.S. FPD 2000 Conference Proceedings*, CDROM, Session 4. Austin, Texas: DisplaySearch, Mar. 21–22.

Leachman, Robert C. 2002. "Competitive Semiconductor Manufacturing: Final Report on Findings from Benchmarking Eight-inch, sub-350nm Wafer Fabrication Lines." Report CSM-52, University of California, Berkeley, CA.

Leachman, Robert C., and Chien H. Leachman. 1999. "Trends in Worldwide Semiconductor Fabrication Capacity." Report CSM-48, Competitive Semiconductor Manufacturing Program, Engineering Systems Research Center, University of California, Berkeley, CA.

Leachman, Robert C., John Plummer, and Nancy Sato-Misawa. 1999. "Understanding Fab Economics." Report CSM-47, Competitive Semiconductor Manufacturing Program, Engineering Systems Research Center, University of California, Berkeley, CA.

Lecuyer, Christophe. 1999. "Making Silicon Valley: Engineering Culture, Innovation, and Industrial Growth." Ph.D. dissertation, Department of History, Stanford University.

Leopold, George, and Rick Merritt. 1999. "Industry Is Feeling Impact of Taiwan Quake." *Semiconductor Business News* (Sept. 24). http://content.techweb.com/wire/story/TWB19990924S0005.

Levin, Richard, Alvin Klevorick, Richard Nelson, and Sidney Winter. 1987. "Appropriating the Returns from Industrial Research and Development." *Brookings Papers on Economic Activity* 3: 783–820.

Levy, Brian, and Wen-Jeng Kuo. 1991. "The Strategic Orientations of Firms and the Performance of Korea and Taiwan in Frontier Industries: Lessons from Comparative Case Studies of Keyboard and Personal Computer Assembly." *World Development* 19, no. 4: 363–74.

Levy, Jonathan. 1981. "Diffusion of Technology and Patterns of International Trade: The Case of Television Receivers." Ph.D. dissertation, Yale University.

Li, Jiatao. 1995. "Foreign Entry and Survival: Effects of Strategic Choices on Performance in International Markets." *Strategic Management Journal* 16, no. 5: 333–51.

Linden, Greg. 2000. "Industrial Policy, Technology, and Performance: Lessons from the East Asian Electronics Industry." Ph.D. dissertation, University of California, Berkeley.

Linden, Greg, and Deepak Somaya. 1999. "System-on-a-Chip Integration in the Semiconductor Industry: Industry Structure and Firm Strategies." Consortium on Competitiveness and Cooperation Working Paper #CCC 99–2, University of California, Berkeley.

Locke, Richard M. 1995. *Remaking the Italian Economy: Local Politics and Industrial Change in Contemporary Italy*. Ithaca: Cornell University Press.

Lomi, Alessandro. 1995. "The Population Ecology of Organizational Founding: Location Dependence and Unobserved Heterogeneity." *Administrative Science Quarterly* 40 (Mar.): 111–44.

*Los Angeles Times*. 1990. "Why American High-tech Firm Recruits in Asian Ricefields," June 25.

*Los Angeles Times*. 1991. "Toshiba Develops Disk Drive of High Capacity," Aug. 6.

Lowe, Nichola, and Martin Kenney. 1999. "Foreign Investment and the Global Geography of Production: Why the Mexican Consumer Electronics Industry Failed." *World Development* 27, no. 8: 1427–43.

Lynch, Teresa. 1998. *Leaving Home: Three Decades of Internationalization by American Auto Firms*. Globalization and Jobs Project Research Note #2, Cambridge: International Motor Vehicle Program, Massachusetts Institute of Technology.

Macher, Jeffrey T., David C. Mowery, and David A. Hodges. 1998. "Reversal of Fortune? The Recovery of the U.S. Semiconductor Industry." *California Management Review* 41, no. 1: 107–36.

Malnight, Thomas W. 2001. "Emerging Structural Patterns within Multinational Corporations: Toward Process-based Structures." *Academy of Management Journal* 44, no. 6: 1187–1210.

Markusen, Ann. 1999. "Sticky Places in Slippery Spaces: A Typology of Industrial Districts." *The New Industrial Geography: Regions, Regulation and Institutions*, ed. T. Barnes and M. Gertler, 98–126. London: Routledge.

Marshall, Alfred. 1890. *Principles of Economics*. London: Macmillan.

Marx, Karl. 1981. *Capital: Volume Two*. New York: Vintage.

Mascarenhas, Briance. 1982. "Coping with Uncertainty in International Business." *Journal of International Business Studies* 13: 87–98.

Mathew, Robert. 1993. "Fifty Years of CRT Bulbs at Corning." *Information Display* 9: 8–11.

Mathews, John A., and Dong-Sung Cho. 2000. *Tiger Technology: The Creation of a Semiconductor Industry in East Asia*. Cambridge: Cambridge University Press.

McCloughan, Patrick, and Ian Stone. 1998. "Life Duration of Foreign Multinational Subsidiaries: Evidence from UK Northern Manufacturing Industry, 1970–93." *International Journal of Industrial Organization* 16, no. 6: 719–47.

McKendrick, David G. 2001. "Global Strategy and Population Level Learning: The Case of Hard Disk Drives." *Strategic Management Journal* 22: 307–34.

McKendrick, David G., Richard Doner, and Stephan Haggard. 2000. *From Silicon Valley to Singapore: Location and Competitive Advantage in the Hard Disk Drive Industry*. Stanford: Stanford University Press.

Metiu, Anca. 2001. "Owning the Code: Engagement and Innovative Work in the Global Software Industry." Ph.D. dissertation, Wharton School, University of Pennsylvania, Philadelphia, PA.

Micron Technology. 2000. SEC 10-K Report. Boise, Idaho: Micron Technology.

Microsoft Corporation. 2000. SEC 10-K Report. Bellevue, Washington: Microsoft Corporation.

MIT Commission on Industrial Productivity. 1989. *Working Paper: The Decline of the US Consumer Electronics Manufacturing: History, Hypotheses and Remedies*. Cambridge: MIT Press.

Mitchell, Will, J. Myles Shaver, and Bernard Yeung. 1994. "Foreign Entrant Survival and Foreign Market Share: Canadian Companies' Experience in United States Medical Sector Markets." *Strategic Management Journal* 15: 555–67.

Miwa, Yoshiro, and J. Mark Ramseyer. 2001. "Apparel Distribution: Inter-Firm Contracting and Intra-Firm Organization in Japan." Discussion Paper 313, John M. Olin Center for Law, Harvard Law School (Feb.).

Morganstern, Abe. 1970. "Hearings on Trade and Tariff Proposals before the Committee on Ways and Means." House of Representatives, 91st Congress, Second Session.

Morita. Akio. 1986. *Made in Japan*. New York: Dutton.

Mowery, David, 1984. "Firm Structure, Government Policy, and the Organization of Industrial Research: Great Britain and the United States, 1900–1950," *Business History Review* 58: 504–31.

Moxon, Richard. 1973. Offshore Production in the Less-Developed Countries by American Electronics Companies. D.B.A. dissertation, Harvard University.

Murtha, Thomas P., Stefanie Ann Lenway, and Jeffrey A. Hart. 2001. *Managing New Industry Creation: Global Knowledge Formation and Entrepreneurship in High Technology*. Stanford: Stanford University Press.

Nath, Deepika, and Thomas S. Gruca. 1997. "Convergence across Alternative Methods for Forming Strategic Groups." *Strategic Management Journal* 18, no. 9: 745–60.

Nelson, Richard, and Sydney Winter. 1982. *An Evolutionary Theory of Economic Change.* Cambridge, MA: Harvard University Press.

Nevin, John. 1978. "Can U.S. Business Survive Our Japanese Trade Policy?" *Harvard Business Review* (Sept./Oct.): 165–77.

Newpoff, Laura. 2002. "Techneglas Tunes In: HDTV Defining the Tube Producer's Future." *Columbus Business First* (October 21) http://www.bizjournals.com/columbus/stories/2002/10/21/story3.html.

Nickell, Joe. 1997. "Fade to Black. *Wired* (July): 76.

Nippon Electric Glass Co., Ltd. n.d. "Nippon Electric Glass." Otsu, Japan: NEG.

———. 1995. "Annual Report 1994." Otsu, Japan: NEG.

Nishiguchi, Toshihiro. 1993. *Strategic Industrial Sourcing: The Japanese Advantage.* New York: Oxford University Press.

Nishiguchi, Toshihiro, and Alexandre Beaudet. 1998. "The Toyota Group and the Aisin Fire." *Sloan Management Review* 40, no. 1: 49ff.

North, Douglass C. 1958. "Ocean Freight Rates and Economic Development, 1750–1913." *Journal of Economic History* 18 (Dec.): 537–55.

———. 1968. "Sources of Productivity Change in Ocean Shipping, 1600–1850." *Journal of Political Economy* 76 (Sept./Oct.): 953–70.

Office of Technology Assessment. 1983. *International Competitiveness in Electronics.* Washington, DC: OTA.

Ohgai, Takeyoshi. 1996. "Hollowing Out and the Division of Labor with Asia: The Japanese Television and VCR Industry." *Ryukoku Daigaku Keieigaku-ronshu* 36, no. 4: 1–11.

———. 1997. Personal communication with Martin Kenney, Aug. 14.

O'hUallachain, Breandan. 1989. "Agglomeration of Services in American Metropolitan Areas," *Growth and Change* 20, no. 3: 34–49.

Okada, Aya. 1998. *Does Globalization Improve Employment and the Quality of Jobs in India?* Globalization and Jobs Project Research Note #3. Cambridge: International Motor Vehicle Program, Massachusetts Institute of Technology.

O'Malley, Michael. 1990. *Keeping Watch: A History of American Time.* New York: Viking.

Pan, Yigang, and Peter S. K. Chi. 1999. "Financial Performance and Survival of Multinational Corporations in China." *Strategic Management Journal* 20, no. 4: 359–74.

Paul, Catherine, J. Morrison, and Donald S. Siegel. 1999. "Scale Economies and Industry Agglomeration Externalities: A Dynamic Cost Function Approach." *American Economic Review* 89, no. 1: 272–90.

Pavan, Robert J. 1972. "The Strategy and Structure of Italian Enterprise." Graduate School of Business Administration, Harvard University, Boston, MA.

Peck, Merton, and Robert Wilson. 1991. "Innovation, Imitation and Comparative Advantage: The Performance of Japanese Color Television Set Producers in the U.S. Market." In *Emerging Technologies: Consequences for Economic Growth, Structural Change and Employment*, ed. H. Giersch, 195–218. Tübingen, Germany: J.C.B.

Penrose, Edith T. 1959. *The Theory of the Growth of the Firm.* Oxford: Oxford University Press.

Piore, Michael, and Charles Sabel. 1984. *The Second Industrial Divide.* New York: Basic Books.

Pirenne, Henri. 1937. *The Economic and Social History of Medieval Europe*. New York: Harcourt, Brace.

Porac, Joseph, Howard Thomas, and Charles Baden-Fuller. 1989. "Competitive Groups as Cognitive Communities: The Case of the Scottish Knitwear Manufacturers." *Journal of Management Studies* 26: 397–415.

Porac, Joseph F., Howard Thomas, Fiona Wilson, Douglas Paton, and Alaina Kanfer. 1995. "Rivalry and the Industry Model of Scottish Knitwear Producers." *Administrative Science Quarterly* 40, no. 2: 203–27.

Porter, Michael. 1983. *Cases in Competitive Strategy*. New York: Free Press.

———. 1985. *Competitive Advantage*. New York: Free Press.

———. 1986. "Competition in Global Industries: A Conceptual Framework." In *Competition in Global Industries*, ed. M. Porter, 15–60. Boston: Harvard Business School.

———. 1990. *The Competitive Advantage of Nations*. New York: Free Press.

———. 1998a. "Clusters and the Economics of Competition." *Harvard Business Review* (Nov.–Dec.): 77–90.

———. 1998b. "The Adam Smith Address: Location, Clusters, and the 'New' Microeconomics of Competition." *Business Economics* 33, no. 1: 7–13.

Powell W. W., and P. Brantley. 1992. "Competitive Cooperation in Biotechnology: Learning through Networks?" In *Networks and Organizations: Structure, Form and Action*, ed. N. Nohria and R. Eccles, 366–94. Boston: Harvard Business School Press.

Pred, Allan. 1965. "Industrialization, Initial Advantage and American Growth." *Geographic Review* 55: 158–85.

Prestowitz, Clyde. 1988. *Trading Places: How We Allowed Japan to Take the Lead*. New York: Basic Books.

*Reality Research and Consulting*. 2000. "White Box 2000 Research Updated by Reality Research" (Oct. 10) http://cis.channelweb.com/researchrep_WhiteBox2000-wv2.asp.

Reuters. 2001. "Hitachi to Cease Making CRT Monitors" (July 26).

Reynolds, Bruce. 1986. "The East Asian 'Textile Cluster' Trade, 1868–1973: A Comparative-Advantage Interpretation." In *America's China Trade in Historical Perspective: The Chinese and American Performance*, ed. Earnest May and John Fairbank, 129–50. Cambridge: Harvard University.

Robert R. Nathan Associates. 1989. *Television Manufacturing in the U.S.: Economic Contributions—Past, Present and Future*. Washington, DC: Robert R. Nathan Associates.

Rowe, Herbert. 1970. "Hearings on Trade and Tariff Proposals before the Committee on Ways and Means," House of Representatives, 91st Congress, 2d Session.

Rubenstein, James. 1992. *The Changing US Auto Industry: A Geographical Analysis*. New York: Routledge.

Rumelt, Richard P. 1974. *Strategy, Structure and Economic Performance*. Boston, MA: Harvard Business School Press.

Ruottu, Annina. 1998. "Governance within the European Television and Mobile Communications Industries: PALplus and GSM—A Case Study of Nokia." PhD. dissertation, Science Policy Research Unit, University of Sussex, Sussex, U.K.

Sabel, Charles F., and Jane E. Prokop. 1996. "Stabilization through Reorganization? Some Preliminary Implications of Russia's Entry into World Markets in the Age of Discursive Quality Standards." In *Corporate Governance in Central Europe and Russia. Volume 2: Insiders and the State*, ed. Roman Frydman, Cheryl W. Gray, and Andrzej Rapaczynski, 151–91. New York and Budapest: Central European University Press.

Sako, Mari. 1992. *Prices, Quality, and Trust: Inter-firm Relations in Britain and Japan.* Cambridge: Cambridge University Press.

Salmon, Michael (manager, Technoglas, Inc.). 1996. Telephone interview, June 27.

Saxenian, AnnaLee. 1994. *Regional Advantage: Culture and Competition in Silicon Valley and Route 128.* Cambridge, MA: Harvard University Press.

Sayer, Andrew, and Richard Walker. 1993. *The New Social Economy.* New York: Basil Blackwell.

Schiffer, Michael. 1991. *The Portable Radio in American Life.* Tucson: University of Arizona Press.

Schmookler, Jacob. 1966. *Invention and Economic Growth.* Cambridge, MA: Harvard University Press.

Schoenberger, Erica. 1994. "Competition, Time, and Space in Industrial Change." In *Commodity Chains and Global Capitalism,* ed. Gary Gereffi and Miguel Korzeniewicz, 51–66. Westport, CT: Praeger.

———. 1997. *The Cultural Crisis of the Firm.* Cambridge, MA: Blackwell.

Schumpeter, Joseph A. 1942. *Capitalism, Socialism and Democracy.* New York: Harper and Brothers.

Scott, Allen J. 1988. *Metropolis.* Berkeley: University of California Press.

Scott, Allen, and David Angel. 1988. "The Global Assembly Operations of U.S. Semiconductor Firms: A Geographical Analysis." *Environment and Planning* 20: 1047–67.

Semiconductor Equipment and Materials International. 1998. *International Fabs on Disk.* Mountain View, CA: SEMI.

Sharp Corporation. 1995. "Production Volume of Color Television Tubes, 1995." Mimeo provided to Martin Kenney, Dec. 11.

Shaver, J. Myles. 1998. "Accounting for Endogeneity When Assessing Strategy Performance: Does Entry Mode Choice Affect FDI Survival?" *Management Science* 44, no. 4: 571–85.

Shaver, J. Myles, and Fredrick Flyer. 2000. "Agglomeration Economies, Firm Heterogeneity, and Foreign Direct Investment in the United States." *Strategic Management Journal* 21, no. 12: 1175–93.

Shaver, J. Myles, Will Mitchell, and Bernard Yeung. 1997. "The Effect of Own-Firm and Other-Firm Experience on Foreign Direct Investment Survival in the United States, 1987–1992." *Strategic Management Journal* 18: 811–24.

Shih, Stan. 1996. *Me-too Is Not My Style.* Taipei: Acer Foundation.

Sideri, Sandro. 1970. *Trade and Power: Informal Colonialism in Anglo-Portuguese Relations.* Rotterdam: Rotterdam University Press.

Silva Lopes, Teresa da. 2002. "The Growth of Multinationals in the Alcoholic Beverages Industry." PhD. dissertation, Department of Economics, University of Reading, U.K.

Simon, Herbert. 1969. *The Sciences of the Artificial.* Cambridge: MIT Press.

Sklair, Leslie. 1993. *Assembling for Development: The Maquila Industry in Mexico and the U.S.* San Diego: Center for U.S.-Mexican Studies, University of California, San Diego.

Solectron Corporation. 2000. "Solectron Completes Acquisition of IBM's Manufacturing Operations in Brazil" (July 3). Milpitas, CA: Solectron Corporation.

Song, Jaeyong. 1998. "Firm Capabilities, Technology Ladders, and Evolution of Japanese Production Networks in East Asia." Ph.D. dissertation, Wharton School, University of Pennsylvania, Philadelphia, PA.

———. 2002. "Firm Capabilities and Technology Ladders: Sequential Foreign Direct Investments of Japanese Electronics Firms in East Asia." *Strategic Management Journal* 23, no. 3: 191–210.

Song, Jaeyong, Paul Almeida, and Geraldine Wu. 2001. "Mobility of Engineers and Cross Border Knowledge Building." In *Comparative Studies of Technological Evolution*, vol. 7 in *Research on Technological Innovation, Management and Policy*, ed. Henry Chesbrough and Robert Burgelman. New York: Elsevier Science.

Sorenson, Olav, and Toby Stuart. 2001. "Syndication Networks and the Spatial Distribution of Venture Capital Investment." *American Journal of Sociology* 106: 1546–88.

Spooner, John G. 2001. "AMD Responds to Intel with Price Cuts" (Aug. 27) http://news.cnet.com/news/0–1003–200–6982283.html.

Stanwyck, Edmund. 1970. "Hearings on Trade and Tariff Proposals before the Committee on Ways and Means," House of Representatives, 91st Congress, 2d Session.

Steffens, John. 1994. *Newgames: Strategic Competition in the PC Revolution*. Oxford: Pergamon.

Stiglitz, Joseph. 2000. "Addressing Developing Country Priorities and Needs in the Millennium Round." In *Seattle, the WTO, and the Future of the Multilateral Trading System*, ed. Roger Porter and Pierre Sauve, 31–60. Cambridge: Center for Business and Government, John F. Kennedy School of Government, Harvard University.

Stinchcombe, Arthur. 1965. "Social Structure and Organizations." In *Handbook of Organizations*, ed. James G. March, 142–93. Chicago: Rand McNally.

Stokes, John. 1982. *70 Years of Radio Tubes and Valves*. Vestal, NY: Vestal.

Storper, Michael. 1992. "The Limits to Globalization: Technology Districts and International Trade." *Economic Geography* 68: 60–93.

———. 1993. "Regional 'Worlds' of Production: Learning and Innovation in the Technology Districts of France, Italy and the USA." *Regional Studies* 25, no. 5: 433–55.

Storper, Michael, and Robert Salais. 1997. *Worlds of Production: Frameworks of Action in the Economy*. Cambridge: Harvard University Press.

Storper, Michael, and Richard Walker. 1989. *The Capitalist Imperative*. London: Blackwell.

Sturgeon, Timothy J. 2002. "Modular Production Networks: A New American Model of Industrial Organization." *Industrial and Corporate Change* 11, no. 3: 451–96.

Sturgeon, Timothy J., and Richard Florida. 1999. *Globalization and Jobs in the Automotive Industry*. Final Report to the Alfred P. Sloan Foundation. Cambridge: Center for Technology, Policy, and Industrial Development, Massachusetts Institute of Technology.

Surie, Gita. 1997. "The Creation of Organizational Capabilities through International Transfers of Technology." Ph.D. dissertation, Wharton School, University of Pennsylvania, Philadelphia, PA.

Taggart, Stewart. 1999. "The 20-Ton Packet." *Wired* 7, no. 10: 246–55.

Taiwan Technology. 2001. "Motherboard Makers in Taiwan Enjoy Rising Market Share, but Face Downturn" (Feb.). http://www.taiwan-technology.com.tw/edit/p/news/pc/02_02_p3.htm.

Takahashi, Yuzo. 1993. "Progress in the Electronic Components Industry in Japan after World War II." In *Technical Competitiveness: Contemporary and Historical Perspectives on the Electrical, Electronics, and Computer Industries*, ed. W. Aspray, 37–52. Atlanta, GA: Institute of Electrical and Electronics Engineers.

Tan, Baris. 2000. "An Overview of the Turkish Textile and Apparel Industry." Working Paper, Harvard Center for Textile and Apparel Research (Dec.).

Tecson, Gwendolyn. 1999. "The Hard Disk Drive Industry in the Philippines." Report 99–01, Information Storage Industry Center, University of California, San Diego.

Teitelman, Robert. 1994. *The Profits of Science.* New York: Basic Books.

Telegeography. 2002. "Submarine Bandwidth 2002." Washington, DC: Telegeography.

*Television Digest.* Various Years.

*Television Factbook.* 1951. vol. 12 (Jan. 15).

Terwiesch, Christian, Kuong S. Chea, and Roger E. Bohn. 1999. "An Exploratory Study of International Product Transfer and Production Ramp-up in the Data Storage Industry." Report 99–02, Information Storage Industry Center, University of California, San Diego.

Thudichum, J. L. W., and August Dupré. 1872. *A Treatise on the Origin, Nature, and Varieties of Wine: Being a Complete Manual of Viticulture and Oenology.* London: Macmillan.

Tilton, John E. 1971. *International Diffusion of Technology: The Case of Semiconductors.* Washington, DC: Brookings Institution.

Trevor, Malcolm. 1988. *Toshiba's New British Company.* London: Policy Studies Institute.

Trollope, Anthony. 1927. *London Tradesmen.* London: Elking Mathews & Marrot.

Turner, Louis. 1982. "Consumer Electronics: The Colour Television Case." In *The Newly Industrializing Countries: Trade and Adjustment,* ed. L. Turner and N. McMullen, 48–68. London: Allen and Unwin.

*Twin Plant News.* 2000. "Acer Opens Plant in Ciudad Juarez" (Mar.).

United Nations. 1993. *World Investment Directory, Volumes 3, 4, and 5.* New York: United Nations.

U.S. International Trade Commission. 1977. *Television Receivers, Color and Monochrome, Assembled or Not Assembled, Finished or Not Finished, and Subassemblies Thereof.* Washington, DC: USITC.

———. 1992. *Industry and Trade Summary: Television Receivers and Video Monitors.* Washington, DC: USITC.

———. 1996. *The Year in Trade: Operation of the Trade Agreements Program during 1995.* 47th Report, Publication 2971, Washington, DC: USITC.

———. 1999. *Assessment of the Economic Effects on the United States of China's Accession to the WTO.* Investigation No. 332–403, Publication 3229. Washington, DC: USITC.

———. 2000. *The Year in Trade: Operation of the Trade Agreements Program during 1999.* 51st Report, Publication 3336. Washington, DC: USITC.

Vernon, Raymond. 1966. "International Investment and International Trade in the Product Cycle." *Quarterly Journal of Economics* 80: 190–207.

———. 1971. *Sovereignty at Bay: The Multinational Spread of US Enterprises.* New York: Basic Books.

Ward's Automotive. 1996. "Wards Decade of Data." http://wardsauto.com.

———. 2001. "2000 Light Vehicle Sales." http://wardsauto.com.

Waugh, Alec. 1957. *Merchants of Wine: Being a Centenary Account of the Fortunes of the House of Gilbey.* London: Cassells.

Webber, Melvin. 1972. *Impact of Uncertainty on Location.* Cambridge, MA: MIT Press.

West, Joel, and Jason Dedrick. 2000. "Innovation and Control in Standards Architectures: The Rise and Fall of Japan's PC98." *Information Systems Research* 11, no. 2: 197–219.

West, Jonathan, and H. Kent Bowen. 1998. *Display Technologies, Inc.* Case 9–699–006. Version (July 28). Boston: Harvard Business School.

Westney, D. Eleanor. 1987. *Imitation and Innovation: The Transfer of Western Organizational Patterns to Meiji Japan.* Cambridge, MA: Harvard University Press.

———. 1993. "Country Patterns in R&D Organization: The United States and Japan." In *Country Competitiveness: Technology and the Organizing of Work*, ed. Bruce Kogut, 36–53. New York: Oxford University Press.

Wilcox, Joe. 2001. "Yet Another Dim Outlook for PC Sales" (Feb. 6) http://news.cnet.com/news/0-1006-200-4730319.html.

Williamson, Jeffrey. 1998. "Globalization, Labor Markets and Policy Backlash in the Past." *Journal of Economic Perspectives* 12, no. 4 (fall): 51–72.

Winter, Sidney. 1987. "Knowledge and Competence as Strategic Assets." In *The Competitive Challenge—Strategies for Industrial Innovation and Renewal*, ed. David Teece, 159–84. Cambridge: Ballinger.

Wolinsky, Howard. 1998. "Negotiators Planning Funeral of Zenith Plant." *Chicago Sun-Times,* Oct. 16.

Womack, James, et al. 1990. *The Machine That Changed the World.* New York: Rawson/Macmillan.

Woolf, Eric. 1982. *Europe and the People Without History.* Berkeley: University of California Press.

Young, Ross. 1994. *Silicon Sumo: U.S.-Japan Competition and Industrial Policy in the Semiconductor Equipment Industry.* Austin: IC² Institute, University of Texas, Austin.

Yu, ChewMing J., and Kiyohiko Ito. 1988. "Oligopolistic Reaction and Foreign Direct Investment: The Case of the U.S. Tire and Textile Industries." *Journal of International Business Studies* 19: 449–60.

Zaheer, Srilata, and Elaine Mosakowski. 1997. "The Dynamics of the Liability of Foreignness: A Global Study of Survival in Financial Services." *Strategic Management Journal* 18, no. 6: 439–63.

Zander, Ivo. 1998. "The Evolution of Technological Capabilities in the Multinational Corporation—Dispersion, Duplication and Potential Advantages from Multinationality." *Research Policy* 27: 17–35.

———. 1999. "Whereto the Multinational? The Evolution of Technological Capabilities in the Multinational Network." *International Business Review* 8: 261–91.

Zenger, J. P. 1977. "Taiwan: Behind the Economic Miracle." In *Free Trade Zones and Industrialization of Asia.* Tokyo: Pacific-Asia Resources Center.

Zenith Electronics Corporation. 1998. *Securities and Exchange Commission Amendment No. 2 to Schedule 13E-3.* Washington, DC: SEC.

Zook, Matthew. 2002. "Grounded Capital: Venture Financing and the Geography of the Internet Industry 1994–2000." *Journal of Economic Geography* 2, no. 2: 151–77.

# Index

In this index an "f" after a number indicates a separate reference on the next page, and an "ff" indicates separate references on the next two pages. A continuous discussion over two or more pages is indicated by a span of page numbers, e.g., "57–59." *Passim* is used for a cluster of references in close but not consecutive sequence.

National Video Corporation, 106
*Natural History* (Pliny), xv
NCR, 151
NEC, 114, 127–33 *passim*, 151; disk drives, 156f, 168, 173n6; in TFT LCD industry, 183–88 *passim*; in semiconductor industry, 214, 249
NEG, *see* Nippon Electric Glass
Netherlands, 195, 250, 264
Network conceptualization, 3
Networks, 243; in electronics industry, 232–33; PC, 238–39; in chip industry, 245–46
Network service providers, 235, 239
Net World Order (NWO), 232f, 242; semiconductor market and, 234–35, 238–39, 246–47, 252, 255–56; key product segments of, 235–37; and firm competencies, 240–41; and value chains, 242–47
New England, 145
New Jersey, 179
Newly industrialized countries (NICs): investment in, 262–63
New Mexico, 132
New York, 105, 108, 152
New York City, 145
New Zealand, xxiii
NICs, *see* Newly industrialized countries
Nike, xx, 47n6
Nikon, 182, 275
Nippon Electric Glass (NEG), 106–7, 108
Nippon Steel, 214
Nissan, 58, 61, 67, 71, 74
Nokia, xx, 84, 245
North Africa, 13, 42
North America, 23, 133; television industry in, 14, 103–4, 107; automobile industry in, 65–66, 71; semiconductor industry in, 208–9, 211, 216, 222. *See also* Canada; Mexico; United States
North American Free Trade Agreement (NAFTA), 33, 43, 47–48nn9, 15, 22, 103; apparel industry and, 40, 50n30; automobile industry and, 60f, 78
North China, 23
Northern Asia, 129

North Sioux City (S.D.), 122
Northwestern Europe, 63
Notebook computers, 12, 140n2, 141n12; IBM, 178, 187; investment in, 188–89
NTT, 246
NTT DoCoMo, 17, 249
NUMMI, 65, 272
NVIDIA, 136
NWO, *see* Net World Order

Obsolescence, 8, 113, 129
OEM, *see* Original equipment manufacturers
Offley, xxi
Offshore production, 28f, 43, 137, 278; of televisions, 92–93, 108; of HDDs, 142–43
Ohio, 100, 105, 108
OI, *see* Owens-Illinois
OIS, *see* Optical Imaging Systems
Oklahoma City, 152
Olivetti, 126
OMA, *see* Orderly Marketing Arrangement
Opel, 71
Operating systems (OS), 116, 130–32, 135, 139, 140n1, 206
Operational clusters, 148, 172
Oporto, xvi, xix, xxvnn10, 13
Optical Imaging Systems (OIS), 189–92 *passim*
Orange County, 152
Ordering: and delivery speed, 44
Orderly Marketing Arrangement (OMA), 94
Oregon, 132, 226, 230
Organizing principles: knowledge and, 265–66, 268–69
Original Equipment Manufacturers (OEM), xiv, 91, 98, 121–22, 124, 138, 152f
OS, *see* Operating systems
Ottawa (Ohio), 100
Outsourcing, 280; in automobile industry, 9, 73, 75; in PC industry, 116, 125, 138; in semiconductor industry, 218–19